YO-DKB-331

J2EE Performance Testing

With BEA WebLogic Server

Peter Zadrozny

Philip Aston

Ted Osborne

Expert Press

J2EE Performance Testing

With BEA WebLogic Server

© 2002 Expert Press

All rights reserved. No part of this book may be reproduced, stored in a retrieval system or transmitted in any form or by any means, without the prior written permission of the publisher, except in the case of brief quotations embodied in critical articles or reviews.

The author and publisher have made every effort in the preparation of this book to ensure the accuracy of the information. However, the information contained in this book is sold without warranty, either express or implied. Neither the authors, Expert Press, nor its dealers or distributors will be held liable for any damages caused or alleged to be caused either directly or indirectly by this book.

EXPERT

Published by Expert Press Ltd,
Arden House, 1102 Warwick Road, Acocks Green,
Birmingham, B27 6BH, UK
Printed in the United States
ISBN 1904284000

Trademark Acknowledgements

Expert Press has endeavored to provide trademark information about all the companies and products mentioned in this book by the appropriate use of capitals. However, Expert Press cannot guarantee the accuracy of this information.

Credits

Author
Peter Zadrozny

Contributing Authors
Philip Aston
Ted Osborne

Review Board
Joakim Dahlsedt
Bjarki Hólm
Staffan Larsen
Daniel O'Connor
Mika Rinne
Andrew Sliwkowski

Technical Editors
Tony Davis
Pete 'Southpaw' Morgan

Managing Editor
Sonia Mullineux

Production Coordinators
Rachel Taylor
Pip Wonson

Index
Adrian Axinte
Bill Johncocks

Illustrations
Rachel Taylor
Pip Wonson

Proof Reader
Agnes Wiggers

Cover
Dawn Chellingworth

About the Authors

Peter Zadrozny

Peter Zadrozny has been in the computer industry since 1976 when he started working with the Unix operating system (Research Version 6). Since then he has been involved in a wide variety of assignments worldwide, developing and integrating applications using leading edge technologies. Currently he is the Chief Technologist of BEA Systems for Europe, Middle East, and Africa.

Peter is the co-author of "Professional J2EE Programming with BEA WebLogic Server" (Wrox Press) and Founding Editor of the *WebLogic Developer's Journal* magazine. He holds a degree in Computer Engineering from Universidad Simón Bolivar in Caracas, Venezuela.

Philip Aston

Philip Aston is a senior consultant for BEA Professional Services, specializing in WebLogic Server. In this capacity, Phil assists BEA customers with the detailed architecture design, proofs of concept, and implementation of applications using J2EE technology. He also writes for the *WebLogic Developer's Journal*. In his spare time Phil has taken the role of lead developer responsible for The Grinder, the Java load-testing tool used in this book. He hopes one day to have saved enough pennies to give up software and sail the World.

For the crews, old and new, at Parallax and BEA.

Ted Osborne

Ted Osborne (www.tedosborne.com) is an independent software consultant, developer, and author, focusing on performance measurement for applications built on the J2EE platform. He has been a frequent speaker at key industry conferences, and was also a contributing author for Professional EJB (Wrox Press). While at Empirix (then Teradyne's Softbridge division), Ted was one of the founding team members that invented www.TestMyBeans.com (now Empirix's Bean-test), the World's first automated load testing tool for Enterprise JavaBeans middleware. Since that time, Ted has met with hundreds of J2EE developers, project managers, QA staff, and other industry experts around the world, learning about their EJB and J2EE application performance issues. Ted holds a degree in Jazz Composition from Berklee College of Music.

I would like to thank Tony Davis and Peter Zadrozny for the opportunity to contribute, Dan O'Connor for his expert insights, George Friedman for all his generous mentoring, and my wife, Colette, for her love, patience, and support.

The Review Board

Joakim Dahlstedt

Joakim Dahlstedt is the CTO of the Java Runtime Products Group at BEA Systems Inc, where he is responsible for the future development directions of the JVM. He was founder and one of the chief architects of JRockit, the JVM that BEA acquired in Q1 2002. He has been working with Java and dynamic runtime optimizations since 1996.

Bjarki Hólm

Bjarki Hólm is a software engineer at deCODE Genetics, a population-based genomics company in Reykjavík, Iceland. His main areas of interest in the field of computing are Java and Oracle, the two of which he frequently combines in his work. At Wrox, Bjarki has co-authored four books and helped review a few others. When he is not working or writing professionally, he likes to pursue his hobbies, which include hiking and the building of amateur robots.

Staffan Larsen

Staffan Larsen is one of the architects/designers of the JRockit Java Virtual Machine as well as being one of the founders of that company. He has worked for several years analyzing Java performance problems, doing benchmarking on a wide variety of Java applications. He currently works on the JRockit Java Virtual Machine project for BEA Systems.

Daniel O'Connor

Daniel O'Connor is the President/CEO of MVCSoft Inc. He is the author of the MVCSoft Persistence Engine, which provides pluggable EJB 2.0 container-managed persistence for J2EE application servers.

Andrew Sliwkowski

Andrew Sliwkowski works on scalability testing for WebLogic Server Clusters, and also supports customers with mission-critical applications.

Acknowledgments

Thanks to Steve Allen, Senior Vice President of BEA Systems for Europe, Middle East and Africa. He set up the performance lab and supported all the research that ultimately generated the contents of this book. Thank you very much!

Special thanks go to Ted Osborne for taking the challenge of writing the EJB chapter and the JazzCat application at very short notice.

Thanks to Phil Aston for producing the second generation of The Grinder and writing the chapter about it. Also for writing the Grinder plug-ins used in the JMS chapters, the test programs for the servlet chapter, and his general contributions throughout the book.

I have to thank Tony Davis who very patiently edited, assembled and glued together the final version of this book from all the pieces that came from the contributors, reviewers and myself through the various editing cycles. Thanks also to the reviewing team for their great contributions and that "other point of view".

I also have to thank Bjarki Hólm and Gareth Chapman for their help with the HTTP session object and stateful EJB comparisons, Paul Crerand for his contribution on the JMS chapters, Andrew Sliwkowski for the ECperf material in Appendix C, Staffan Larsen for his useful insights into the workings of a JVM, Thomas Kyte for lending a little Oracle expertise, and Gopalan Suresh Raj for additional JMS material. Finally, I would like to thank Richard Wallace and Jay Backory in the BEA support group for all their help.

Peter Zadrozny

Cover Photos

The front cover photo was taken by Samtiago Cogolludo and is used with his kind permission, along with that of the owner and driver of the car, Steve Allen. The car is a Williams FW07B - 08 and can be seen at www.tgp-F1.com (car number 28).

The back cover photo is reproduced with kind permission of Palmersport (www.palmersport.com).

Dedicated to

my children Gracie, Johannes and Kathelijne

my wife Graciela for her infinite patience and incredible support

Peter

Table of Contents

Table of Contents

Table of Contents

Table of Contents

Table of Contents

Introduction

Every J2EE application is truly unique. This makes it extremely difficult, if not impossible, to extrapolate performance measurements from one application to another, no matter how functionally similar they might look. In order to understand the performance of your own application you must test it yourself, according to your own definition of performance.

Some of the common questions that we get asked with regard to performance are along the lines of:

- ❏ How fast will our application go?
- ❏ How well will it scale?
- ❏ What is the performance of your application server?

As our opening paragraph indicates, there are no clear-cut answers, and neither can we provide a silver bullet that will solve all performance-related problems. However, what we felt we could do was to provide a **toolkit** and a performance testing **methodology** that would allow J2EE developers to obtain reliable and meaningful performance data for their own applications. Both are described in this book, along with the results of the research and the performance studies that we have undertaken. These results have only served to underline the veracity of that opening paragraph.

Our testing methodology provides a clear framework that describes how to define your performance metrics and goals, the tests that you will need to undertake, the methods by which you can collect the data, and ultimately the ways in which you can actually perform the tests. The methodology is extremely simple, flexible, and adaptable, to the point that it can be used with applications written in any language.

We have chosen to showcase the methodology using a load generating/data collection tool called The Grinder (along with related software). The Grinder is a Java-based tool that is available in the public domain. Although there are various load generation tools available commercially and in the public domain, the author has been directly involved in the development of The Grinder, and therefore it was a logical choice. This does not, however, mean that you are limited to using this software. On the contrary, the testing methodology is not attached to any particular tool, so feel free to use the one with which you feel most comfortable.

Although the performance tests in this book were carried out using the BEA WebLogic Server, the techniques presented are generally applicable to any J2EE application and to any J2EE-compliant application server. Some components of the code provided for download (such as configuration files), are specific to WebLogic Server, but it should be a relatively simple task to adapt the code and run the tests in your own environment. In addition, some of the environment optimizations that we perform will use proprietary features of this server, but other application servers may well provide for similar optimizations.

In the remainder of this introduction, we will attempt to define exactly what you can expect to get out of our methodology and toolkit, and to position them in relation to other available tools and techniques. We will also provide a clear roadmap for the rest of the book.

J2EE Performance Testing

Our methodology and toolkit is useful in two basic situations:

❑ Performance testing a complete application.

❑ Designing for performance – examining the performance cost of various aspects of the J2EE API and how certain design decisions will impact overall performance.

In the first scenario, we are treating the application like a black box. We can use the methodology and The Grinder to test the performance of the application under various loads. We can investigate the performance of every request made by the application (a simple JSP request, a session bean calling an entity bean, an entity bean interacting with the database to update a record, and so on). We can analyze the data, find the limiting requests, and identify opportunities for improving performance.

While the above is useful, our advice is to performance test as early in the development cycle as possible. In this way, you can use the methodology, and the data you obtain from it, to help you **design for performance**, rather than performance testing "after the fact". Every little sub system that makes up an application will have a direct impact on the overall behavior. By testing early, you will be able to use programming best practices in your design and answer some fundamental questions as they apply to your unique application, such as "Which J2EE API should I use?", "Should I avoid use of stateful session beans?", "Are entity beans are too slow?", "Which J2EE design patterns are appropriate in my case?", and so on.

In this book we devote one chapter to performance testing a black box application and five chapters to exploring common issues and design choices surrounding the use of the popular J2EE APIs (Servlets, EJBs, and JMS). We show you how to evaluate the alternatives and, with the performance results we present, we set a general level of expectation with regard to relative performance. The ultimate conclusion, however, is that you cannot necessarily assume that our results will hold for your environment; you must obtain your own performance data.

What is Performance?

In order to understand the performance of your own application you must test it yourself, **according to your own definition of performance**. This is a very important point. One of the most popular questions that we get asked is: "What will be the performance of my application on your server (meaning, in our case, WebLogic Server)"? There is often an expectation that we will provide a magical number that will give a complete picture of performance. In fact, our response is that it depends on the application and it depends on what exactly they mean by performance.

J2EE is a broad set of APIs and even a relatively simple J2EE application can be written in many different ways. For example, let's consider a simple database access application. Starting at the front end, you can have a set of JSPs and servlets that handle the communication with the end users or clients. This front end can directly communicate with the database by using JDBC. However, the developer can choose to have the front end call a stateless session bean. This stateless session bean can then communicate with the database by using the JDBC API, or delegate the access to an entity bean. The entity bean can use Container-Managed Persistence (CMP) or Bean-Managed Persistence (BMP), and so on (and on).

Even when using the same set of APIs, one developer can use them in a radically different fashion from another, and as we know the quality of code can vary substantially from one developer to the next. Even if the code were identical, the input data would most likely be different. Inevitably this would create a different usage pattern that would produce different performance results. As we stated at the start, every J2EE application is unique and the only way to obtain clear and honest answers about its performance is to test it yourself, in your specific environment.

This takes us back to the actual definition of performance. In some situations, good performance will mean the ability to support a huge number of users, in others the user load might be small and good performance will simply be to run as fast as possible. In order to examine this more closely, we can split the types of application that are developed into two basic categories:

- ❑ Interactive, when an end user is synchronously interacting with an application.
- ❑ Batch or back-end application, when there is no direct interaction with an end user.

Interactive Applications

With interactive applications, performance will commonly be defined by sizing and capacity planning issues, such as the number of simultaneous users the application can handle or, more specifically, the ability to support a specified number of users while satisfying certain key parameters. These "required parameters" might include specific deployment hardware and perhaps a maximum **response time** (the time taken for the application to complete any given request from the end user).

From the point of view of an end user, the key performance attribute is the response time. It has been our experience that users tend to measure the quality of an application by the perceived speed of the responses. Interestingly enough, we have found that the actual functionality or ease-of-use tends to be less influential than response time in determining a user's perception of application quality. We regard response time as a key basic statistic necessary to express application performance.

The response time is directly affected by the number of users interacting with the application at that moment, so you have to consider the number of simultaneous users when working with the response time. From the point of view of the operations people, they need to have information that will help them size the application for capacity planning purposes. They basically want to know how many users can be handled by the application before the hardware being used runs out of steam. As you increase the user load, your tests should indicate the components of your hardware system that are working the hardest, and this in turn can inform decisions about how best to split the hardware budget across application servers, database servers, and the network. In addition, this information can help determine the optimal deployment configuration. The front end (servlets and JSPs) could be run on one instance of the application server and the business logic (EJBs, JMS queues, and so on) on another. These instances could be running on the same computer or separate ones, all using the same or different operating systems. A popular question asked in this category regards the number of instances of the application server that should be used on a multiple processor computer.

Based on this discussion, we can easily conclude that we need a measurement that reflects these two important metrics: number of simultaneous users and response time. In fact, when we first started developing our methodology, we tried to invent a new statistic that would present this information in a simple way, but it proved to be an exercise in futility.

Instead, our methodology proposes the use of short, concise performance statements that allow easy communication of the abilities and limits of the application. For example, if our maximum response time is 1000 milliseconds, then we may arrive at statements such as:

> *The application can handle 750 simultaneous active users with a maximum response time of 1000 milliseconds, and peak to 800 users with 7% degradation in the response time.*

4

We feel strongly that simple statements such as this convey accurately a complete picture of the behavior and the boundaries of the application being tested, while minimizing the possibility of misinterpretation and confusion. The statement also describes the behavior observed when the response time limit has been exceeded. This is a valuable piece of information when doing capacity planning.

Back-end Applications

A performance statement based around response times and the number of users is meaningful when the application's primary interface is user-oriented. However, such metrics may be less applicable when the application has an interface to another system, for example a JMS queue of messages that need to be processed.

As we researched in more detail the requirements of batch or back-end applications, we found that the most useful and common performance statistic used was **throughput**. One of the most popular ways of expressing throughput performance is in **Transactions Per Second** (**TPS**). However, this metric can cause problems if you do not fully understand exactly what it means and what it is that you are measuring.

A common misunderstanding is in what the "T" in TPS actually stands for. What is a transaction? Very often, people fail to understand what a transaction is in their context; everybody assumes they are talking about the same thing, when in practice they are not. We have encountered a case where two groups of developers working on the same project were using different definitions of "transaction". One group defined it as a single query, while the other group defined it as a specific set of queries. Occasionally, the operations group would define it in a different way altogether! This, of course, can lead to complete confusion, with the potential that the application will meet performance requirements according to one team's definitions but not another.

We use the throughput metric extensively in the book when analyzing the J2EE APIs. We feel that it provides a useful comparative measure of system throughput, provided that the context is clearly defined. When investigating servlets, we define a transaction to be a **request** – so the throughput is the number of identical requests executed by a servlet in a set period of time (one second). When examining JMS, it is a **message**, and so on. Where a clear concept of a transaction exists, and test conditions are constant, TPS can provide useful guidance regarding whether a certain code change has improved or degraded the relative performance of a module of an application.

However, we must sound a few notes of caution with regard to this metric. Throughput is not a measure of speed as much as it is a measure of **capacity** – a common misconception. It is also not a clean, clear-cut metric in the way that response time is. Small changes in test conditions can have a massive impact on the value you obtain for throughput – and it does not necessarily mean that your application is performing any worse or better.

Throughput does not always provide a complete picture of the performance of an application. An application might perform 10000 TPS, but what is the response time for the end user? Does the user have to wait 20 minutes to get a response or just 300 milliseconds? Thus, throughput must often be used in conjunction with other measurements in order to provide a complete picture of performance, especially when testing interactive applications.

Finally, this metric does not in itself convey a sense of load on the computer. That is, it does not tell us if the computer is at 100% of its capacity or just 20%. We feel that such measurements should be taken alongside those of throughput.

The Testing Methodology in Context

The title of this book, *J2EE Performance Testing*, sounds straightforward enough, but it was actually very carefully chosen to best reflect the true focus and intent of its content. In order to understand this statement, you only need consider the plethora of expressions that are commonly used in relation to the performance of a software application: **testing**, **benchmarking**, **profiling**, and **tuning**, to name but a few. Each of these terms has an explicit meaning, although they often seem to be used interchangeably. Up to a certain point it is easy to understand why this is so, since everyone has their own ideas about which aspect of performance is most relevant to their work at any given moment.

In this book performance testing means to use a defined methodology in order to collect performance statistics for your own application. However, it is useful to understand what these other terms encapsulate and to discuss how the methodology can be useful in these areas:

- ❑ **Benchmarking** – generally speaking, benchmarking is the process of recording the performance of an application in various environments and under various workloads.

- ❑ **Profiling** – this involves investigating exactly where an application is spending most of its compute cycles and how efficiently it uses system resources.

- ❑ **Tuning** – testing, benchmarking, and profiling all feed the process of tuning, which is the optimization of your application and its environment for maximum performance.

Benchmarking

Our toolset and methodology can be used to benchmark an application. As described previously, as you are developing your application, you may test it in one configuration, then swap one component for another and re-test, or make an environmental adjustment (such as increasing the heap space of the JVM) and then test again. This is the basic process of benchmarking. In fact, we did consider calling the book *J2EE Performance Benchmarking*. However, we ultimately decided to reject the term in order to avoid confusion between what this book sets out to achieve in contrast to **industry benchmarks** such as ECperf (http://java.sun.com/j2ee/ecperf/) and TPC-W (http://www.tpc.org/).

The problem with industry benchmarks is that they are very specific applications that attempt to measure general features of a product or infrastructure such as J2EE, and we insist that you cannot extrapolate performance results from one application to another, no matter how similar they might be.

For example, ECperf is the official J2EE benchmark. It is a complex EJB application that is designed to measure the performance and scalability of a J2EE application server. It is mainly geared for the J2EE application server vendors (such BEA Systems, IBM, and iPlanet) so they can use it to showcase the performance of their products.

> **For the interested reader, we provide a more thorough comparison of ECperf and our toolkit and methodology in Appendix C.**

Other benchmark suites, such as TPC-W (Transaction processing Performance Council – Web e-Commerce) measure performance-related to web server throughput. This can be useful for the engineers developing application servers and perhaps it will be used in marketing the servers, rather like the database companies use the TPC transaction processing benchmark. Ultimately it can aid in the purchasing decision process, but in general will not provide a reasonable idea of the behavior of J2EE.

Again, we insist that you should not use the results of any generic benchmark to try to guess at the performance behavior of your application. Every sub-system that makes up an application will have direct impact on its behavior and you have to test your own application to really understand its performance.

Profiling

As described above, profiling is essentially an in-depth examination of the work that your application is doing, and how it is using system resources. The main goal is to highlight potential performance **bottlenecks** in your system. Our testing methodology will allow you to identify specific areas of the application that are limiting performance. You can then use a complimentary profiling tool to examine these areas in detail. In this book, in addition to The Grinder, we use various tools to investigate each component part of our system:

- ❑ **Database** – in the Oracle database, we use the profiling tools SQL_TRACE and TKPROF, both of which are provided as standard and output the SQL that the application executed and how that SQL performed.

- ❑ **WebLogic Server** – we use the WebLogic console to look in detail at the internals of WLS.

- ❑ **J2EE Application** – we use a tool called Introscope from Wily Technology (http://www.wilytech.com) that is designed to help you accurately pinpoint component-level bottlenecks in your application. Another popular profiling tool for J2EE applications is JProbe (http://www.sitraka.com/software/jprobe/).

7

Tuning

A typical J2EE application will be based on an application server, but this is not the only sub system that makes up an application. There are also databases, Java Virtual Machines (JVMs), operating systems, TCP/IP stacks, web servers, networks, routers, and the actual computer hardware. All of these sub systems have knobs or parameters that can be adjusted to maximize the performance of an application. In this book, we use the results of preliminary tests, carried out using our methodology, to tune various aspects of our environment, such as the JVM and the WebLogic Server itself. This gives us the optimum environment in which to run the formal performance tests.

While we make suggestions for performance improvements at the application level, based on our test measurements and associated profiling, we do not undertake any actual tuning because this is not the focus of this book.

How to Use this Book

The basic, underlying principles of this book are that your own particular J2EE application is unique, that you must test it for yourself, and that we will provide the toolset and methodology by which you can do so – and that it will only cost you the price of this book!

While we will present raw performance data, we will actually focus on comparative performance – the reason being that raw performance numbers are highly dependent on the application server, JVM, and on the underlying operating system and hardware. We want to provide developers, system administrators, and application architects with the comparative cost of using the various features that are available in each of the J2EE APIs. Based on our methodology and the data you obtain from it, you will be able to make informed business decisions, or perhaps help potential customers to make those decisions. You will be able to realistically assess whether or not the relative cost of using a particular feature is worth the price, given the alternatives. You will be able to understand the performance of your own application.

The code used for all the tests in this book is available on the Expert Press web site (http://www.expert-press.com) so that you can use it to run performance tests in your own environment. Always remember that it is not the intention of this book that you extrapolate from the raw performance data to make assumptions about the raw performance of your own application. All we can do is set a general level of expectation – the idea is that you obtain this data for your own unique application.

The Book Organization

The following list provides a roadmap to the rest of the book:

- ❑ Chapter 1 describes in detail the testing methodology we propose.
- ❑ Chapter 2 is a user manual for The Grinder, the load generation tool that we use in this book.
- ❑ Chapter 3 is a detailed case study on how to obtain performance statistics for an interactive application.
- ❑ Chapter 4 delves into various aspects of use of the HTTP protocol and of the Servlet API, investigating the different alternatives available and exploring the costs of using them.
- ❑ Chapter 5 looks at the performance of various EJB design patterns and explores their relevance and cost as applied to a sample *JazzCat* application.
- ❑ Chapter 6 analyzes the JMS Point-to-Point model, touching on the effect of message size, use of message acknowledgement, and the effect of using message persistence.
- ❑ Chapter 7 explores the JMS Publish and Subscribe model, using examples based on the most common use of topics.
- ❑ Appendix A contains a list of parameters for The Grinder.
- ❑ Appendix B contains a description of the computers, operating systems, and software used for the tests performed in this book.
- ❑ Appendix C is a comparison of the testing methodology and toolset provided here with the ECperf benchmark application.

Apart from some cross-referencing for set-up instructions, in order to avoid unnecessary repetition, the chapters detailing our performance investigations (Chapter 3 onwards) are designed to stand alone and can be read in any order. However, in order to fully understand the testing methodology and toolset, and what they can and can't do, it is vital that you read this Introduction, Chapter 1, and Chapter 2, in order.

Customer Support

If you wish to directly query a problem in the book then please e-mail support@expert-press.com with the title of the book and the last four numbers of the ISBN in the subject field of the e-mail.

The Testing Methodology

In the *Introduction* to this book, we discussed in general terms the issues surrounding J2EE performance testing and the performance statistics (response time, number of users, and throughput) that were relevant, depending on the type of application that was being developed and tested (interactive or back-end). An abiding theme was the fact that every J2EE application is unique, and that in order to understand the performance of your own application you must test it yourself, according to your own definition of performance. So, while we knew that we could not provide a silver bullet that will solve all performance-related problems; we did set out to provide the following:

❑ A **methodology** by which to performance test your own J2EE applications. It defines the tests to be performed, and the manner in which the performance statistics will be collected, so that consistent and reliable data is obtained.

❑ **The Grinder** – a freely available load-generating and data collection tool with which to carry out the tests. However, the methodology is not tied to The Grinder. It is equally applicable to any load-generating tool of your choice.

This chapter lays out the testing methodology that we developed and which we apply throughout the book. Chapter 2 provides a user manual for The Grinder. In order to fully understand the testing methodology and toolset, we highly recommend that you read the Introduction, this chapter, and Chapter 2 in order.

An important point to note is that in developing our methodology, we did not simply set out to define a theoretical, mathematical approach to collecting performance statistics. Our approach was more pragmatic. We found that early versions of the methodology were restricted in applicability to certain specific cases. There were other cases that we could not handle without modifying something in the methodology. Based on this experience, we adapted and pared down the methodology so that it was much more flexible and could handle many different cases. It is now flexible to the point where it can be used with any kind of application, not only J2EE-based applications. What we will describe in this chapter is the skeleton of the methodology; its bare bones if you will. There are many things that can be modified in the methodology; things that you might consider make it more rigorous or more statistically accurate. The idea is that you take the core of the methodology and add to it or modify it according to your needs and preferences.

Methodology Overview

The following list gives a high-level overview of the steps that are involved in our methodology. We present and describe them in the logical order in which they will be carried out when performing each test:

❑ **Define the performance criteria** – we must define the relevant performance metric for the specific application in question, and then set a realistic target for that metric (for example, a maximum acceptable response time).

❑ **Accurately simulate the application usage**– the key aspect of this is the definition of **test scripts**. These are configuration files that contain all the information required to run a particular set of requests and define the manner in which each request will be executed.

❑ **Define the sampling method and associated metrics** – by this we mean the type of test to undertake, the sampling size, the duration of the test and so on.

❑ **Perform the tests**.

As you can see, there is some work to be done before we can start the actual tests. Let's look at each step in turn.

Establishing Performance Criteria

Having defined the performance criteria that are relevant to the application, we then need to define a minimum acceptable performance requirement for the application. In this book, our performance criteria depends on the type of application being tested:

❑ For synchronous interactive applications we define a maximum acceptable response time. This is the maximum amount of time we are willing to wait before we get a response from the application.

❑ For a batch or back-end application, we define the minimum acceptable throughput in Transactions Per Second, based on a solid understanding of exactly how a transaction will be defined in our system (see the *Introduction* for more details).

Each of these metrics is inextricably linked to a defined user load. For example, we may define a maximum response time of three seconds, for a load of 400 users.

Our advice is to define your performance metrics clearly and unambiguously, and to test to well-defined requirements. Never performance test with the goal of "making it go as fast as possible". This is an open invitation to test and tune endlessly.

Simulating Application Usage

The objective of this phase of the methodology is to ensure that we are collecting our performance data in test conditions that mimic reality as closely as possible. The key step in this phase is to define realistic test scripts.

Defining Test Scripts

Let's look again at our definition of a test script: a configuration file that contains all the information required to run a particular set of requests against the application, and defines the basic test conditions (the number of users, the size of a message, and so on), and the manner in which each request will be executed. Note that our load-generating tool in this book, The Grinder, refers to a test script as a `grinder.properties` file, so that is the terminology that we will use here. Please bear in mind, though, that the methodology is not in any way tied to The Grinder.

We have to be careful with our terminology here. The basic scenario is as follows: each **performance test** has many **test runs**, each using one or more **test scripts** (which mimic real-life usage of the application). A test script is composed of **requests**.

Each performance test must have clearly defined test conditions. For example: we might run a test to investigate the throughput performance (in requests per second) of our servlet application, when the servlet is generating a response of size 8KB. The response size will be defined in the `grinder.properties` file.

Each test run for the defined test will be performed for a specific user load, say 100 users. This will also be defined in the `grinder.properties` file by setting the number of threads that The Grinder will use:

```
grinder.threads=100
```

13

This is an important point of the methodology: we use a **fixed number of users per test run**, usually increasing the user load with each subsequent test run. In our experience, some people are interested in ramping up the number of users during a single test run. We believe that this introduces a new variable that can have a big effect on the results, and is statistically incorrect for the purpose of finding the maximum user load. Therefore, this is not a part of our methodology and The Grinder is not capable of increasing the user load during a single a test run.

The Grinder must be installed on any client machine that will be making requests of the application. The `grinder.properties` file must be saved in the directory from which The Grinder is being run. The Grinder and the methodology have been designed to be able to handle many types of client, including browser clients (HTTP, WAP, XML, and so on), and Java clients (fat clients, JMS consumers or producers). Each Grinder instance will execute a set of **requests**, as defined in the `grinder.properties` file for that particular instance.

The Grinder uses a specific plug-in component to execute the requests defined in a test script. A request might be a URL, a Java method, a C++ function, a Fortran subroutine, or anything else that is relevant to the application. For example, the HTTP plug-in, a standard and commonly used plug-in for The Grinder, is designed to execute requests using the HTTP protocol. For example a simple request for a web page or a servlet, using the HTTP plug-in, would be of the form:

```
grinder.test0.parameter.url=http://www.expert-press.com
```

Whatever these requests may be, as a whole they must represent a realistic **usage profile** for the application.

Usage Profiles

This is probably the most important step in the whole methodology. Our objective when defining our test scripts is to simulate as closely as possible the requests that will be executed and the way in which they will be executed in reality. The test script(s) reflect the typical usage of the application or a typical user visit to the web site, and so on.

In some cases, we will be able to simulate a usage profile using a single test script and a single request. For example, in our servlet example, a request in the `grinder.properties` file may be as follows:

```
grinder.test1.parameter.url=http://sun1:7001/servlet/generateRandom?leng
th=32768
```

Here we simply call the appropriate servlet and set the response size to 32KB. Notice that The Grinder calls a request a **test**. However, we use the request terminology in the text to avoid confusion in meaning between an individual test in a test script, a test run, and a performance test.

In most cases, however (particularly for interactive applications) a test script is likely to contain numerous different requests, each simulating a real action in the application. For example, if we were testing an e-commerce application, at some stage we would create a new customer by calling the application's `CustomerMaintenance` servlet:

```
grinder.test5.parameter.url=http://sun1:7001/c05/CustomerMaintenanceS
```

Later, we might want to commit an order that the customer has made to the database by calling the `OrderMaintenance` servlet:

```
grinder.test13.parameter.url=http://wls02:7001/c05/OrderMaintenanceS
```

Furthermore, we often need multiple test scripts in order to simulate each appropriate usage profile. Take, for example, a stock trading web site. We could have three profiles of typical users:

❑   Occasional trader, defined as somebody that trades once a month but visits the site on a regular basis to check the status of their portfolio and read related news items.

❑   Heavy trader: somebody that trades at least once a week.

❑   Day trader: somebody that trades at least twice a day.

All three have different behaviors that can be clearly defined. We simulate each one using a separate `grinder.properties` file and use a separate instance of The Grinder to simulate each type of user. In the above case, we can either run three separate Grinder client machines or start three instances on the same client (from different directories).

When using multiple test scripts you should run all of them simultaneously, with appropriate weighting. In this example, the occasional traders might represent 85% of the total visitors to the web site, whereas the heavy traders might represent 12% of the total visitors, and the day traders represent 3% of the total. We would model each user profile in separate test scripts, each containing a fixed sequence of requests. Then, if we were performing a test run with a load of 100 users, 85 users would run the test script for the occasional trader, 12 would run the heavy trader script and 3 would run the day trader script.

It is very important to mention that a test script will not necessarily exercise **all** the code of the application. The test scripts replicate the typical usage of the application. It is possible that the test scripts will use just a small percentage of the total code. Bear in mind also, that sometimes we will be testing a fully functional application and at other times we will be investigating various design issues and will use more abstract test scripts that explore performance in a more general way.

A good understanding of how the application will be used is critical for a successful performance test. Generally speaking this knowledge is found in the business side of the house, not in the development team. Make sure that you meet with the appropriate people and understand how they expect the application will be used. Have them define the profiles of users and the typical behaviors for every profile. As your application matures and adapts to the new needs and trends imposed by the users, you should change the test scripts to reflect this.

Test Data

When we execute a request using The Grinder and a test script, we need to supply realistic test data (for example, customer information). Sometimes, we can just use fixed data. For example, if the address of a customer is not used for anything other than to print it on the invoice and shipping labels, then we can always use the same address for the purposes of the performance test.

However, to best model reality, key user-supplied data must be generated dynamically. For example, if we use a telephone number to identify a user and this number is a primary key of the application, then we must use a different phone number for every simulated user. If we were to use the same number every time, not only do we move away from the reality, but this would also lead to caching of the user record somewhere in the system and would produce faster response times that would not accurately reflect those obtained in normal usage.

In this book, we generate this sort of test data using Grinder string beans, which are simple Java classes that define a number of methods that return strings (see Chapter 2 for full details). When using HTTP POST operations, The Grinder uses a file that contains the arguments for the POST operation. We can also call the Grinder string bean from these post files. Ultimately, the choice of which data to generate dynamically can only be made with knowledge of what the application does with it.

Another example is an e-commerce application that performs searches in a catalog. We do not want to always search for the same item as this would be unrealistic and would again lead to unwanted caching and better response times. We also want to have the system preloaded with realistic data. To test performance of a catalog search, a catalog of reasonable size must exist.

In addition to this, we may also want to select items in a random fashion, or according to some rules that represent a typical **usage pattern** for your users (this would be defined in the plug-in, not the test script).

Realistic Usage Patterns

Consider the actions performed by a user visiting an e-commerce site:

❑   Search the catalog for product X

❑   Obtain detailed information of product X

❑   Search the catalog for product Y

- ❏ Place product Y in the shopping cart
- ❏ Follow recommendation for product Z
- ❏ Check out as user ABC
- ❏ Commit the purchase

In our tests, in addition to making sure that products X, Y, and Z are not always the same, we might want to select them randomly, or be a little sophisticated and try to replicate a common search pattern found in the real world. For example, if product X is the subject of an intensive advertising campaign, or simply a best seller, it would be searched most often. However, this must be balanced against the fact that the more sophisticated the search pattern, the more complex will be the Grinder plug-in code that must simulate this search pattern. You have to decide how much of an impact a particular search pattern might have on your performance results before deciding how realistically you need to implement it.

Another aspect of the realistic modeling of usage patterns is the timing of the execution of each request in a test script. It is easiest to simply execute each request one after the other with no time in between, but this does not accurately reflect typical usage. The choice of the time interval before executing each request in a script, the **think time**, is crucial and will have a dramatic effect on the observed response times and throughput for a given user load.

Think Time

Think time, also known as sleep time, is the amount of time that will elapse between the executions of each individual request in a test script. Think time can be highly variable. It can be as little as a few seconds to click on a button that will takes us to the next page or as much as 5 or 10 minutes, the time it takes us to examine the transactions we have made in our bank account over the past month.

In developing our methodology we spent some time investigating how to model think time. We started by using a fixed think time for every individual test in all the test scripts, using values such as 2, 3, or 5 seconds. The problem with this is that it does not reflect reality. If you consider our e-commerce site example, it might take only a second to add an item to a shopping cart, but much longer to find a credit card and type in the number. We will obtain performance data that seems to be accurate, but by using an unrealistic think time we will end up simulating something very far from reality.

The way a system handles a regular load with the arrival of requests distributed evenly over a period of a minute will be different from how it reacts to more erratic traffic, where requests arrive in groups. Furthermore, if 100 users are all sequentially executing every request in a script with no think time between executions, then the server is clearly going to be much more stressed than for same user load but with significant think times between each request. This will have a big effect on the throughput and response time performance for a given load.

The only true solution is to use realistic think times. This is the only way that we will gain an accurate picture of how the application will perform in the real world. However, there are two factors that counterbalance this. First, if we are exploring the performance of a J2EE API, rather than performance testing a working application, we will not necessarily know what the real think time between requests should be. Second, we have the time factor. The shorter the think time the shorter the test runs, and generally we do not want every test run to take several hours. Consider, for example, testing a JMS application. Say that we want to perform four performances tests, each one investigating performance using a different message acknowledgment mode over five different user loads. That is a total of 20 test runs. If each run takes two hours, that is a total of 40 hours testing time, and of course this is just for one message size. We will need to repeat these 20 runs for each different message size. This is time that many developers will not have.

In response to these factors, we adopted two basic strategies:

- Use the real think time – when performance testing a complete, working application, we would find out what the real think times were, if possible, and use them.

- Use zero think time – when performing more general investigative measurements then we used zero think time. The consequence of this is that we were not testing under realistic usage conditions. However, we could perform accurate comparative measurements and once we had chosen the best scenario from these results, we could then perform a test with more realistic think times, using that scenario.

Using the Real Think Time

When testing a complete J2EE application, such as in Chapter 3, we used the TCPSniffer tool of The Grinder to generate our test script, and this also provides us with real think times (see Chapter 2 for details of TCPSniffer).

For example, consider a request in a test script that simulates a search for a customer based on their phone number.

```
grinder.test3.sleepTime=6953
grinder.test3.parameter.url=http://wls02:7001/c05/CustomerSearchS
```

The end-user must type in and submit a phone number and the real think time for this is almost 7 seconds. The Grinder calls think time sleepTime and it is measured in milliseconds. If the customer exists, the user information is displayed:

```
grinder.test4.sleepTime=62
grinder.test4.parameter.url=http://wls02:7001/c05/CustomerForm.jsp
```

The think time for this operation is much lower.

Before we move on, we would like to note that, tempting as it may be to use a fraction of the think time in order to reduce the length of a test, it is not recommended. We have often observed this tendency when people are using commercial load generators, one of the problems with which is that their licenses restrict the number of simulated users. Often people attempt to simulate more users by decreasing the think time, with the assumption that they can then extrapolate this data to obtain the performance at the real think time. This assumption is incorrect. Applications do not scale linearly over different time scales. The sub-systems of an application such as the application server, the web server, the database, and the operating system do not interact the same way across different user loads. You cannot state that 100 users executing a test script with a fixed think time of 5 seconds for every URL is roughly equivalent to 200 users executing the same test script with a fixed think time of 10 seconds.

Think Time Variation

To more closely model reality we vary the actual think time between each request according to a Normal distribution (a bell-shaped curve). Typically we might set the variation of the distribution such that 99.75% of the times lie within 20% of the specified think time for that request. For example, if the think time is specified as one second, then 99.75% of the actual sleep times will be between 0.8 seconds and 1.2 seconds. We specify a think time variation in the test script, as follows:

```
grinder.thread.sleepTimeVariation=0.20
```

As well as being more realistic, we find that varying the think time typically improves system efficiency. This is because the generated load quickly tends towards a varied workload mix that applications and their underlying subsystems can handle better. There is less contention on individual resources, and the test load does not repeat a set of cheap read-only transactions (such as browsing a catalog) followed by a set of expensive write transactions (submit order) in a stop-start manner.

Another way of looking at this is that when we have no think time variation, the execution of each request in a test script happens pretty much simultaneously, in the form of a very high wave. When using a think time variation the size of the wave decreases over time.

Having said all this, there are some occasions when we use 0% variation. We call the test runs that use 0% variation **precision** test runs. We use them when we are comparing the results of two test runs in which we change some environmental condition (such as the size of the JVM heap space) in order to understand the effect it has on the response time or throughput performance. In these cases we want to minimize the margin of error. Even though adding a variation to the think time will get us closer to reality it will increase the margin of error, making the test runs more difficult to repeat.

Using an Initial Spread

Most other load-generation tools handle the concept of ramping up the user load. Some allow for the tester to define this as "users per minute", while others ramp up over a set period of time. For example, all simulated users will start executing requests over a period of three minutes, rather than everyone starting at the same time. The Grinder does not support this concept directly. However, we do use the concept of an "initial spread", which we set in the test script as follows:

```
grinder.parameter.initialSleepTime = 5000
```

This will cause each user to wait a random length of time between zero and five seconds before beginning execution of the test script.

Other tools also use a ramp down period. We do not use this concept at all.

Using Zero Think Time

As described earlier, if we are performing general investigative tests and do not know the real think time anyway, we adopt the approach of using zero think time. However, it is vital to understand that this can have a massive apparent impact on performance. As an illustration, consider again our earlier servlet request:

```
grinder.test1.parameter.url=http://sun1:7001/servlet/generateRandom?length=32768
```

In Chapter 4, when we execute this test with a think time of two seconds we see an aggregate average response time (see later) of 219 milliseconds for 500 users. With no think time, we see AARTs that are almost twice as long (400 milliseconds) for one fifth of the user load (100 users). Clearly, the server is under a much higher stress in the latter case. This does not mean that it is performing any worse – it just means that we are testing under different and more highly stressed conditions.

As long as this is understood, zero think time tests allow us to perform quick, accurate comparative measurements that could be regarded as giving "worst-case scenario" performance data. Such tests are also useful when the objective is to try to understand which components of the system will break first under highly unusual stress conditions.

Sampling Methods

A fundamental step in this methodology is the selection of the sampling method. This defines how we actually collect the performance data, and which measurements will contribute to the final results that we will analyze. We have devised two sampling methods that are directly related to The Grinder. We call them **fixed number of cycles** (the cycle method) and **fixed time** (the snapshot method) and they are explained in detail below. The method that you choose will depend on the objective of your performance test. When testing existing applications (for capacity planning, architectural configuration, or system tuning) we tend to prefer the cycle method, as The Grinder produces a more complete set of data. When exploring programming best practices we favor the snapshot method.

The load generation tool of your choice may use a different sampling method. Feel free to use that method or any other that you feel comfortable with.

The Cycle Method

We define a cycle as the complete execution of a test script by a simulated user. In one complete cycle, each simulated user will sequentially execute every request in the script once. The raw performance data (say, response time) for each user (for each request and for each cycle) is saved in a Grinder data file.

If we state that a performance test will have 100 cycles, it means that every simulated user will execute the test script 100 times. We stop data collection after the slowest test script has finished executing its 100th cycle and in the analysis we ignore cycles above 100 for all test scripts. In a similar fashion, when there is only one test script we let it run for a few more cycles than we really need. Some simulated users will finish the execution cycles before others so, on the final couple of cycles, we will effectively be running under a reduced load. The response times will improve for those users that are still running and this will skew the average results.

Obviously, the bigger the number of cycles, the more statistically significant will be the data that we obtain. If the average time for the execution of a cycle is one minute, then a 100-cycle test run will last about one hour and 40 minutes. Usually we don't have the time and patience for lengthy test runs, so we tend to reduce the number of cycles. In general, when we use this method, we try to define a number of cycles that will correspond to test runs that last approximately one hour. However, this is not always possible. Sometimes a single cycle can take five minutes or more, if think times are high. This would provide us with only 12 cycles of data over a period of one hour, which is statistically speaking a rather small sample. In this case, we have to increase the cycles to a number that represents a decent statistical sample (perhaps 30 cycles).

The Snapshot Method

Whereas a cycle is based on the concept of completed executions of test scripts, this method represents a time-based view of data. What we do here is collect data for a specified period of time, regardless of how many cycles have been completed. When we use the fixed time method we use the data generated by the Grinder console. The Grinder processes send real-time data to the console every 500 milliseconds. If we set a sample size of five seconds, then every five seconds the Grinder console will calculate the average values for throughput and / or response time over however many times each request has been executed in that period and over however many users. After another five seconds, it calculates these metrics again, so we get an accumulative average over the number of samples that we specify. If we specify 36 samples then the test will last for three minutes.

Again, we need to select the sample size and the number of samples carefully. It can be very easy to make a test run so short that it compromises the statistical significance of the data. You will have to go through the exercise of choosing values that make sense for your application and that provide a good statistical sample.

Exclusion of Data

When we first start to execute requests, the initial response times can be very high. A URL that might typically take 200-300 milliseconds to execute can take as much as five seconds on its first execution. The reason for this is that all the sub systems that make up the application take a little while to get up to speed. For example, the optimizer of a JVM like HotSpot will need a few minutes before its effects are visible. The same goes for the cache of a database, which will take a little time before it is useful. JSP compilation can also have an effect.

An application typically stabilizes within the first few minutes. In order to determine exactly when the application has stabilized, we can perform a preliminary test run and plot a chart of the response times over each cycle:

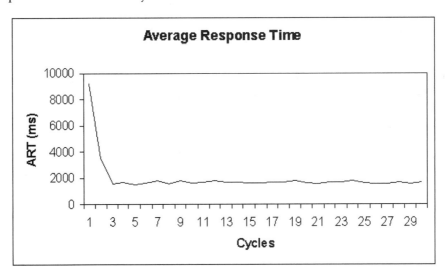

As you can see, for this application the response time stabilizes at the third cycle and thus we would exclude the data from the first three cycles from our analysis. Of course, in some instances the data from the first few cycles might be precisely the data that you're looking for. The time taken to stabilize will vary depending on the application, test scripts, and other factors and must be investigated on a case-by-case basis.

Performance Statistics

Independent of the sampling method we decide to use, we will be collecting data during the performance test runs. We need to have a clear understanding of the basic statistics, so let's examine them in more detail.

Response Time

When dealing with synchronous interactive applications, the concept of response time forms the basis for the performance statements we aim to produce. For the purposes of this book we define response time as follows:

> **The length of time that a client has to wait from the moment it sends a request to the moment that the last byte of the response from the application has been received by the client.**

You should note that other load generation tools might measure up to the moment of the arrival of the first byte of the response.

So, what value should be used for the maximum acceptable response time? There have been various studies conducted to find this number. Jakob Nielsen, in his book *Usability Engineering* (Morgan Kaufman, 1994, ISBN 0-12-518406-9) mentions that 10 seconds is about the limit for keeping the user's attention focused on the dialog with the application. Back in 1997 Peter Bickford in an article entitled *Worth the wait?* (Netscape/View Source Magazine, October 1997) established the rule of thumb that "customers click away after waiting 8 seconds".

Some large corporations define specific response times for all their applications, usually as part of a service-level agreement between the IT group and the rest of the company. In other cases, no such formal agreement exists.

Some e-commerce applications (typically those having a catalog and a shopping cart) use two different acceptable response times. The first is for the majority of the operations and is very small (2 or 3 seconds), while the second is much longer (up to 15 seconds) for the checkout operation. The reasoning behind this is that while people want fast responses for searches in the catalog and general interactions with the system, they are willing to spend more time waiting for a secure operation (such as credit card authorization) as they are predisposed to this by real life.

Let's analyze the components that make up a real-world response time. We can break it down into the following component parts:

- **Processing time**, which we define as the length of time it takes from when the request arrives to the server side, to the time the response is ready to be sent back to the client.

- **Transmission time**, defined as the sum of two parts: the elapsed time between the request leaving the client and arriving at the server plus the time taken for the response to make the return journey. Transmission time is a major factor in Internet applications, where users may be connected via a low-bandwidth modem link.

- **Rendering time**, defined as the length of time the client takes to display or process the response before presenting the result to the end user. For example, the time it takes a web browser to lay out and display an HTML page. It can include processing such as decompression that requires significant CPU and memory resources.

Our performance tests were performed on a clean, high-speed Ethernet environment. The only traffic present on the network was traffic generated by the tests themselves. In order to accurately simulate an intranet environment, we would need to generate extra traffic on the network. If the test application were to run over the Internet, then ideally we would find some way to model that environment (with the longer transmission times) in our performance tests. Practically, though, this is very difficult to achieve.

Recent research has shown just how hard it is to model Internet traffic mathematically (see *Wide-Area Traffic: The Failure of Poisson Modeling*, Vern Paxson and Sally Floyd, University of California, Berkeley, July 18, 1995). Unfortunately, there is little hope of simulating the behavior of the Internet in our test environment. We have sometimes found it useful to configure network interface cards to run at 10Mb/s, but this is the crudest of approximations to a real-world network. Some tools are available that allow simulation of "bad" networks (see, for example, http://www.shunra.com/) but we have not used these.

Rendering time is highly dependent on the type of hardware upon which the client is running. It could be a very powerful computer or a WAP-enabled mobile telephone. It can be considered an easy task to measure the rendering time, but the logistics of doing so on a great variety of client devices make it impractical.

We took a pragmatic approach on how to deal the modeling of "real" transmission and rendering times: we accepted that there was little that could be done and, instead, we compensated by reducing the actual maximum acceptable response time used for the performance tests.

Adopting this approach, if the maximum acceptable response time for your Internet application is 7 seconds, then you might want to use one second as the maximum response time for the actual performance tests. In this case, the assumption is that the six-second difference is a suitable allowance for the transmission and rendering times. On an intranet, you could just subtract a few hundred milliseconds.

Having this background information we can now move on to the details of the performance statistics.

Average Response Time (ART)

The sets of data that we collect from a performance test run consist of the individual response times of every request that makes up the test script. Each request in a test script is executed, one after the other, by each simulated user for a fixed number of cycles (cycle method) or for a certain period of time (snapshot method).

If we use the cycle method, we analyze the data sent to the Grinder data file, which shows us the response times for each request on a cycle-by-cycle basis. If we use the snapshot method, we use the data generated by the Grinder console, in which case the measurement is an accumulative average for each request, over the length of the test.

Our base measurement of analysis is the arithmetic mean of the response times for all users for a particular request (the ART). The fact that we use an average is one of the reasons that performance testing is not an exact science. In the following figure we present a chart with the actual response times of a simulated user for a specific URL during a test run:

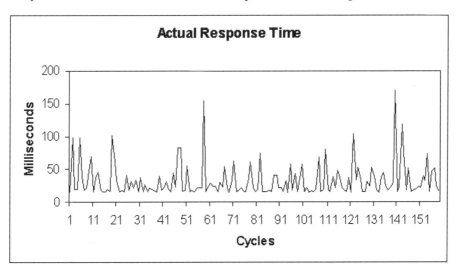

As you can see, the response times vary quite a lot – from as fast as 20 milliseconds in the lowest valley to as slow as 170 milliseconds at highest peak. Please keep this in mind. The fact that the ART might meet performance requirements does not mean that in some cases we will not exceed the limit. When we make a performance statement along the lines that an application can handle X number of users with a maximum acceptable response time of, say, three seconds, we must accept that sometimes the response time will be as much as five or six seconds. By the same token, sometimes the response time will be around one or two seconds.

We have received feedback suggesting that we use a median or geometric mean instead of the arithmetic mean. The median is the number in the middle of a set of numbers; that is, half the numbers have values that are greater than the median, and half have values that are less. We feel more comfortable using the arithmetic mean value, but you could use any other statistical function that you desire, as long as you use it consistently throughout the performance tests.

25

Aggregate Average Response Time

This is another measurement that we use extensively when analyzing performance data. We define it as follows:

> **AART: the addition of the average response times of every individual test in a test script divided by the number of requests in that test script.**

This metric does not include the think times. Admittedly, AART has no real meaning in terms of how the application is performing but it does provide an excellent indicator of how loaded the whole system is. As such, we also refer to this measurement as the **Load Factor**. It is an aggregate number, so this metric can also be used to perform comparisons across different test scripts.

While running a performance test, we suggest that you plot a progressive curve of aggregate ART against increasing user load. Once you have used this chart for a few performance tests, you will be able to predict relatively easily when you are reaching the performance limits of your application.

Maximum Average Response Time

The maximum average response time is the highest value of all the individual average response times in a test script. For example, the following table displays the results for a test run. In this case there is only one test script, and it consists of ten requests:

Test	ART
REQUEST 0	19.38
REQUEST 1	12.67
REQUEST 2	47.13
REQUEST 3	83.68
REQUEST 4	71.70
REQUEST 5	72.75
REQUEST 6	75.19
REQUEST 7	71.64
REQUEST 8	802.31
REQUEST 9	14.31
Aggregate ART	**127.08**
Max ART	**802.31**

The individual ART value for each of the ten requests represents the average response time recorded over all simulated users, for that request. In this example, request 8 shows the maximum average response time and therefore is the most expensive request in the test script. For a given test script, you will often find that the same request is the most expensive in each of your performance tests. Quite often you will find, as in the above case, that it is **substantially** more expensive than any other request in the script. In this manner, the testing methodology will highlight specific areas of the application that are limiting performance. You can then focus your tuning efforts in that area and use a profiling tool to examine them in more detail. Ultimately, if you are able to significantly increase the performance of the most expensive request, then you will achieve an even bigger gain in the overall performance of the application.

Throughput

As described in the *Introduction*, throughput is not a clear-cut metric in the same way as response time. The standard way of expressing throughput is in Transactions Per Second, and it is vital to understand what a transaction represents in the application being tested. It might be a single query, or a specific group of queries. In a messaging system it might be a single message, or in a servlet application it might be a request. In other words, the way in which throughput is expressed in dependent on the application. Even when there is consensus as to exactly what is being measured, the values obtained for throughput can often be misinterpreted. The reason for this is that many people regard the metric in much the same way as they regard "miles per hour": as a measurement of speed. In fact, throughput is a measure of **capacity**. In order to illustrate this point clearly right from the start, we can refer to two results obtained in this book (the details will come in the chapters, for now we just want to concentrate on the high-level concept):

❑   In Chapter 4, we show the results of performance tests using a simple servlet. When the user load was doubled from 20 to 40, the throughput increased from 190 requests per second to 240. When the user load was increased to 60 and then 80, the throughput remained constant at 240 RPS.

❑   In Chapter 7, we detail our investigation of Publish/Subscribe messaging. With zero think time the throughput for the message publisher (producer) was around 200 messages per second, where the throughput of the message subscribers (consumer) was the limiting factor. The messages were being sent faster than they could be processed. With the addition of a 2 millisecond think time for the publisher, the publisher throughput dropped to 50 MPS, and became the limiting factor in the system (the consumers were now working below capacity).

The latter example proves very clearly the importance of using realistic think times, if at all possible. Tests run with no think time (perhaps in order to shorten the length of the test) would lead you to one conclusion, but the addition of a realistic think time (if, indeed, 2 milliseconds was a realistic think time for your system) could lead you to a different conclusion. Also, it does not mean that the publisher is now performing "worse" than before, just that we are measuring under different conditions.

We can attempt to explain how throughput works in terms of a supermarket analogy. Imagine that a supermarket runs a promotion whereby ten shoppers will get for free everything they can put in their shopping trolley in 15 minutes. The supermarket is the application, the shoppers are analogous to requests (or messages) and the supermarket staff that are restocking the shelves are analogous to the components of your system that are working to cope with the demand.

With 10 shoppers, even if every shopper reaches capacity (by completely filling the trolley in 15 minutes), this does not meant that everything in the shopping trolleys at the end of that time was all there was available in the supermarket. However, as we increase the number of shoppers we will reach a point where there are enough shoppers to empty the supermarket in that time. At that point we have reached the throughput capacity of the supermarket. As we increase the number of shoppers beyond that point, we reach a point where crowding in the aisles causes reduced shopper mobility (longer "response times") and, ultimately, an actual drop in throughput.

Assessing the Accuracy of Test Results

The phrase "margin of error" has a precise meaning. We can only determine the exact margin on our performance measurements if we know exactly what the result will be in the first place. Since we do not, we can only really establish a "degree of confidence" in the results.

Our experience from general performance investigations of the J2EE API is that if we repeat exactly the same test under the same conditions, we can reproduce the result to within 5%. Therefore, if we see a change that is greater than 5%, we regard it as significant and allow it to influence the performance analysis and the decisions that are based on it.

However, when performance testing complete applications, we often found that the reproducibility was lower. Consecutive tests could show results varying from 10-20%, or even as high as 50% on some occasions. However, we often found that this difference could be explained by some instability in the conditions and so we developed a separate **quality** measurement when testing complete applications.

Quality of a Sample

In order to obtain an idea of the reliability of the sample data, when testing complete applications, we devised a simple measurement that we feel gives us a pretty good idea of the quality of the sample:

Quality = standard deviation / arithmetic mean

The closer this number is to zero the higher the quality of the sample data. In our experience of performing a vast number of test runs, acceptable quality numbers lie in the range 0.06 to 0.2. When the quality number exceeds 0.25, we immediately suspect the reproducibility of the result and so we study the chart of AART with successive cycles in order to understand the possible reasons that could have caused this bad quality number.

Often, the reason is that the application took more cycles to stabilize than we had excluded from our data analysis (see the earlier *Exclusion of Data* section). For example, based on the results of previous runs, we may be excluding from our analysis data from the first five cycles, but when we analyze the AART curve for the poor quality sample, we may find that it didn't stabilize until cycle 9:

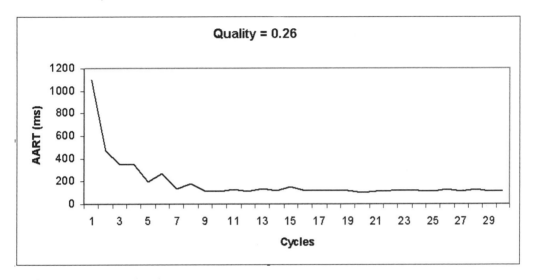

In this case, we would repeat the test run and would usually obtain a better quality number. On other occasions however, the root of the poor quality problem might lie in more unexpected behavior of the application. Consider the following chart, which corresponds to a very bad quality indicator:

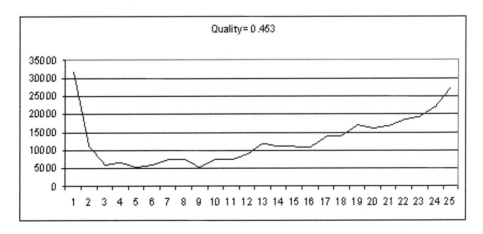

Of course, we would repeat the test run in this case, to verify that the behavior is consistent, but ultimately the fact that the AART is increasing over time may be an indicator of some problem or bottleneck in the system.

The Performance Tests

We can place our performance tests into two basic categories:

- ❑ **Preliminary tests** – initial, exploratory tests that allow us to get a feel for the behavior of the application and to optimize the test environment.

- ❑ **Formal tests** – these are the formal performance measurements upon which we base our analysis. We can sub-categorize these formal tests according to type:

    - ❑ Single instance stress tests
    - ❑ Endurance tests
    - ❑ Architectural tests

Once we have set our environment and test parameters (test scripts, think times, sampling method, and so on) according to the results of our preliminary tests, these factors must remain fixed for any given performance test. If we change any parameter within a given performance test, we invalidate the comparability of the results and will have to perform the test again.

Preliminary tests

When we first start performance testing an application, we find that it is very useful (and ultimately time saving) to perform a few initial test runs that allow us to get familiar with its behavior under various conditions. These tests allow us to determine appropriate test parameters and sampling methods. Also, by performing some quick tests at various loads, we will get an idea of the performance limit of the application (the maximum workload that our application can withstand while still satisfying the established performance criteria). In this way, we can define a strategy for increasing the load during the formal performance tests.

We also run preliminary tests at the special **baseline case**.

The Baseline Case

The baseline case basically provides our main point of comparison for subsequent test runs. For the baseline case we describe the initial conditions of the performance test. We specify the computers and network hardware, the operating systems, databases, and other software and hardware involved. We also describe the conditions under which they are running and what fine tuning, if any, has been done to them.

We aim for the baseline case to approximate the minimum user load we expect the application to be handling when in production. We do this because we want to fully understand the behavior of the application – not only when it is under stress, but also under more ideal conditions. This is important, as typically the application will spend most of its time under these low load conditions. Peak hours of operation will usually happen infrequently.

Test Environment Optimizations

As part of our preliminary tests, we attempt to optimize the environment for our application. This generally involves the following:

- ❑ Choosing the best JVM for the application – this can potentially have a big impact on the performance of your application, as we prove in Chapter 3 when we test the Java Pet Store using various JVMs

- ❑ Optimizing the JVM

- ❑ Tuning various WebLogic Server parameters, such as the number of execute threads

When running your own performance tests, this list, and the impact of each element in the list, varies according to the exact nature of your application.

Single Instance Stress Tests

As the name suggests, these tests are carried out with the application running on a single instance of the application server. We gradually increase the workload over successive test runs (making smaller increments as we approach the limit case, as roughly defined in our preliminary tests) until we exceed our performance criteria (maximum acceptable response time or minimum acceptable throughput).

A stress test is usually of relatively short duration – approximately one hour if we are using real think times, down to around 15 minutes with zero think time, and so our data is based on the performance of the application over such time periods.

Endurance Tests

In order to obtain a more complete picture of the behavior of the application over long time periods, we perform **endurance tests**. These are carried out under exactly the same conditions as the stress tests but last a minimum of 12 hours. Usually this entails leaving the application running overnight or over a weekend. Typically we use the baseline case for an endurance test.

When an application is database bound, the endurance test is extremely useful for the database administrator (DBA). It is a great opportunity to observe the actual functioning of the application and the way it interacts with the database and it provides useful data for fine-tuning.

Architectural Tests

Sometimes the objective of the performance test is to try out different architectural configurations for the application. For example, we may wish to find out how many instances of the application server should run on a multiple CPU computer. In this particular case, we start out testing with a single instance for the baseline and limit cases. We then test with two instances, also using the baseline and limit cases. We continue in this manner until we reach the number of instances that we wish to explore.

Alternatively, it may be that a single instance of the application server cannot handle the minimum required load. In this case, one solution is to deploy the application using a cluster of application servers. We start with a cluster of two members (instances of the application server) and increase the workload over successive tests until we reach the limit case. If the limit case is lower than the minimum required load then we add further members to the cluster until we can handle the required load.

Summary

In this chapter we have presented a methodology to benchmark J2EE applications and discussed the steps to be followed in its implementation. We discussed the following:

- ❑ Test scripts and think time.
- ❑ Sampling methods, sample size, and data exclusion.
- ❑ Performance statistics (AART and throughput)
- ❑ Measuring the accuracy of the results obtained.
- ❑ Obtaining consistent results
- ❑ Different types of performance tests

To illustrate the use of this methodology we present a detailed case study of performance testing a complete J2EE application in Chapter 3.

Since the performance test is based on the simulation of users working with the application, one of the most important tools required for a successful performance test is a load generator and timer. In the following chapter we will describe The Grinder, a very powerful load-generation tool that we use to obtain the measurements and statistics in this book.

The Grinder

The Grinder is the primary performance measurement tool we used to run the tests in this book. During the development of this book, we added many new features to The Grinder to make it suitable for the task. While our testing methodology can be used with commercially available tools, such as Mercury Interactive's LoadRunner, we are not aware of any tool that rivals The Grinder's ease of use and adaptability to a wide range of J2EE performance problems. The Grinder is also difficult to beat on price – it's freely available under a BSD-style license.

If you are developing a J2EE application it will probably fit your requirements for a load-testing tool. We encourage individual developers to use it early in the application development life cycle, since performance problems are exponentially cheaper to resolve the earlier they are identified.

Paco Gómez developed the original version of The Grinder for the book *Professional Java 2 Enterprise Edition with BEA WebLogic Server* (published by Wrox Press, ISBN 1-861002-99-8). Philip Aston took ownership of the source code at the end of 2000 and began The Grinder 2 stream of development. Along with occasional contributions from The Grinder community, Philip continues to actively extend and enhance The Grinder. If you used the version from the Wrox Press book, you may struggle to recognize it. We've included a summary of the key changes at the end of this chapter.

The Grinder is distributed with limited user documentation. This chapter is a full user's guide to The Grinder and will show you how to install The Grinder and run your first test script. Appendix A contains further reference information on The Grinder.

Where To Obtain The Grinder

The Grinder's home page is http://grinder.sourceforge.net. From here you should click the link for the Sourceforge summary page in order to download The Grinder distribution. All of the tests in this book were run using The Grinder 2.8.1.

There are also some mailing lists on the Sourceforge site that you can join in order to participate in The Grinder community:

- ❑ grinder-announce – low volume notifications of new releases
- ❑ grinder-use – the place to ask for help
- ❑ grinder-development – for those interested in developing The Grinder

> *We wish to express our gratitude to VA Software for the Sourceforge site (http://sourceforge.net/). Sourceforge is without doubt a great resource for the open source community and is responsible for the continued success of many open source projects.*

An Overview of The Grinder

So what is The Grinder? As we answer this question, we'll examine the role of the three processes that make up The Grinder:

- ❑ **Agent processes,** a single agent process runs on each test client machine and is responsible for managing worker processes on that machine
- ❑ **Worker processes**, which are created by Grinder agent processes and are responsible for performing the individual tests
- ❑ The **console**, which coordinates the other processes and collates statistics

Each of these processes is a Java Virtual Machine (JVM), and can be run on any computer with a suitable version of Java installed.

We'll also introduce two additional concepts:

- ❑ **Plug-ins,** Java components that define what a test means and contain the code to execute the tests. For example, an HTTP plug-in is provided; so each request performed by the HTTP plug-in corresponds to an HTTP request to a URL.

❑ The **grinder.properties** file, a text file that is read by the agent, worker processes, and the plug-in and contains the entire configuration for a particular test run. For most plug-ins, this file is used to specify the number of tests to run and details for each of the individual test – it can be thought of as the "test script". For example, when using the HTTP plug-in the `grinder.properties` file contains the URL for each test.

There are four distinct aspects of The Grinder: load generation, request definition, statistics recording, and the console. We'll look at each in turn.

Load Generation

The Grinder is a load generation tool. Typically you will have begged, bought, or borrowed a number of test client machines with which to test applications running on one or more servers. The Grinder is a pure Java application so you have a wide choice of platforms to use for your client machines.

You might wonder why you need to use separate test client machines at all: couldn't the performance tests be run on the same machine as your application server? The Grinder lets you do this but we'll continue to focus on distributed testing, using separate client test machines, as this provides better simulation of J2EE production deployments for the following reasons:

1. Most J2EE systems are designed with distributed client processes, such as web browsers or applications acting as EJB clients. For realistic performance testing you have to run the test client (The Grinder) on a discrete machine connected via a network.

2. Most J2EE applications support large numbers of users, each running a client process on a commodity PC. If your application fits this scenario, the more test machines you have the closer you can model reality.

You can use The Grinder console to control many processes, each running many threads of control, across your test client machines. To run a given set of tests an agent process is started on each test client machine. The agent process is responsible for creating a number of worker processes. Each worker process loads a plug-in component that determines the type of tests to run and then starts a number of worker threads. Each of the worker threads uses the plug-in to execute the individual tests that make up the `grinder.properties` file. For example, one of these individual tests may be as follows:

```
grinder.test0.parameter.url=http://localhost:7001/index.html
```

You will notice that The Grinder refers to these individual tests as *testX* (`test0`, `test1`, `test2`, and so on). However, in the text, this can lead to confusion as to the exact meaning of the word "test", since we have the following situation:

1) A Performance test (has a number of)
   1.1) Test runs (each of which has one or more)
      1.1.1) Test scripts (which are composed of one or more)
         1.1.1.1) Tests

In the remainder of this book each of these individual tests consists of the execution of a URL (which may invoke a Java method) and can accurately be referred to as **requests**. This is the terminology that is used in these chapters: "A *performance test* has one or more *test runs*, each using one or more test scripts (which mimic real-life user profiles). A *test script* is composed of several *requests*". In this chapter, however, we stick to the more generic term, test, to indicate the possible broader use of The Grinder.

The `grinder.properties` configuration file contains all the information necessary to run a particular set of test runs, such as the number of worker processes, the number of worker threads, the plug-in to use, and the details of the tests to run. The agent process and the worker processes read their configuration from `grinder.properties` when they are started. We normally put the `grinder.properties` file on a shared network drive so we don't have to copy it to each of the test client machines.

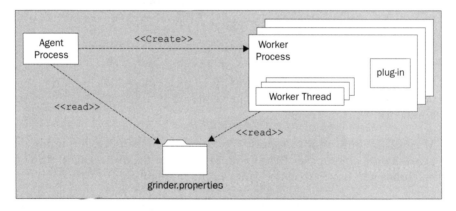

The net effect of this scheme is to allow the easy configuration of many separate client contexts, each of which will run the same set of tests against your server or servers. Each context simulates an active user session. The number of contexts is given by the following formula:

(Number of agent processes) × (Number of worker processes) × (Number of worker threads)

Test Definition

The standard Java properties file format is used for the `grinder.properties` file. Here's a simple example:

```
# An example grinder.properties file

grinder.processes=3
grinder.threads=5
grinder.cycles=10

grinder.plugin=net.grinder.plugin.http.HttpPlugin
grinder.plugin.parameter.useCookies=true

grinder.test0.parameter.url=http://localhost:7001/index.html
grinder.test1.parameter.url=http://localhost:7001/logo.jpg
```

Do not try to use this file just yet. It requires that The Grinder console is started and that the HTTP server to test is listening on port 7001. If you're itching to start The Grinder, look ahead to the *Getting Started* section. The first few lines set the number of worker processes and worker threads to use. The number of test *cycles* is also configured; this is the number of times that each worker process will execute the test set defined by the plug-in.

> *You may be asking "On a given test machine, is it better to use 1 process of 10 threads, 10 processes of 1 thread, or some other combination?" The answer may depend on the plug-in; for example, some client libraries use server connections from a process-wide shared pool, irrespective of the thread that makes the request. A previous implementation of the HTTP plug-in that was based on the standard* `java.net.HttpURLConnection` *class does precisely this. However, this is rare, and in general we recommend that you use threads rather than processes (so the answer is "1 process with 10 threads"). Beware when using large numbers of threads, say more than 100. Typical Java Virtual Machine/operating system combinations do not run well under these conditions and you may find that you make better use of your test client machines by splitting these across a number of processes. It may also be worthwhile using more processes if you have the luxury of multi-CPU test client machines.*

The next two lines specify that the HTTP plug-in be used, and set a property that the HTTP plug-in understands. The plug-in is configured using the full package name of the Java class that contains its implementation. The sourcecode for the HTTP plug-in is provided with The Grinder distribution. Finally, two tests are defined. The HTTP plug-in interprets these lines as URLs to request using HTTP.

Other plug-ins have a different concept of what an individual test is and might also require that their tests be specified by some other mechanism. For example, the JUnit plug-in uses Java introspection to examine a JUnit test case for tests to run. Later on we use a plug-in that calls an EJB to show you how to write your own plug-ins.

Each worker process that is started using this example properties file will have five worker threads. Each of the five threads will repeat the following sequence ten times:

❏ Make an HTTP request to the URL http://localhost:7001/index.html

❏   Make an HTTP request to the URL http://localhost:7001/logo.jpg

Each test invocation is referred to as a *transaction*. A key performance metric in our methodology is throughput, which is measured in Transactions per second (TPS). When using The Grinder, the plug-in is used to determine the answer to the question "What is a transaction?"

Statistics Recording

The worker process measures the elapsed time taken for each transaction that is performed (the "response time"). The results for each transaction are recorded in a data file and there is a separate data file for each worker process.

The worker process also records whether the transaction was successful or caused an error to occur. The meaning of "success" is defined by the plug-in. In addition the plug-in can add its own statistics values.

When the worker process finishes, it writes out a summary table:

	Transactions	Errors	Average Response Time (ms)
Test 0	100	0	14.81
Test 1	100	0	244.58
Totals	200	0	129.70

The average response time is the sum of all the elapsed times recorded for each test divided by the number of times the test was executed.

Individual data file and summary tables are written out for each worker process, so they are less useful when there is more than one worker process, and in particular when there are multiple test client machines. What is needed is a way of collating information from many worker processes – it's time to introduce the console.

The Console

The Grinder console is used to coordinate the actions of the worker processes by sending them start, reset, and stop commands. IP multicast is used to broadcast the commands simultaneously to processes running on many machines. You can learn more about IP multicast at http://java.sun.com/docs/books/tutorial/networking/datagrams/index.html.

The worker processes send statistics reports to the console. The console combines these reports to produce graphs and tables showing test activity. The results of a particular test run can be saved for further analysis.

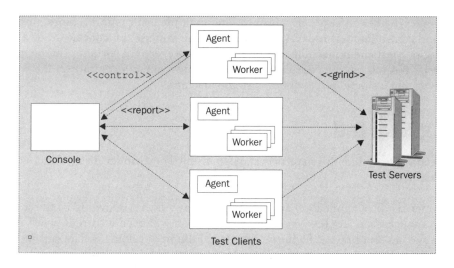

The console also calculates and displays derived statistics. A key derived statistic that the console can calculate, but the individual worker processes cannot, is a combined Transactions Per Second (TPS) figure for all the worker processes. This is because a rate, such as TPS, can't be calculated without a shared notion of the beginning and the end of the timing period. The console performs the required timekeeping function.

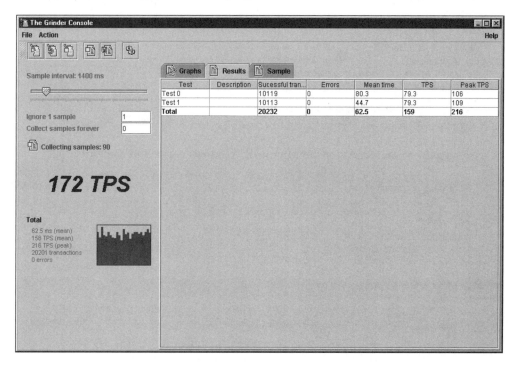

The console provides an easy way of controlling multiple test client machines, displaying test results, and controlling test runs. We recommend that you use the console, even if you are only using one test client machine and one agent. However, The Grinder can be used without the console. We will put the console to one side for now and concentrate on the steps necessary to run a simple test script on a single machine.

Getting Started

In this section we outline the steps necessary to install The Grinder distribution, and run a simple test script.

The Grinder is a Java application and is distributed as a Java Archive (JAR) file so that it can be easily unpacked on any Java-enabled platform. You will need a current Java Virtual Machine such as Sun's Java 2 Platform, Standard Edition, version 1.3. The current Sun Microsystems JVM is Java 2 Platform, Standard Edition v 1.4, available from http://java.sun.com/j2se/1.4/. The Grinder will not run on JVM versions earlier than 1.3. Ensure that the correct Java `bin` directory is in your `PATH` before continuing.

You should create a directory to hold distributions of The Grinder, change to that directory, and expand the distribution using the Java `jar` command. This will create a directory hierarchy containing the full source code, documentation, examples and pre-built programs. Under UNIX this can be achieved with the following commands:

```
$ mkdir /grinder
$ cd /grinder
$ jar xf mydownloads/grinder-2.8.1.jar
$ cd grinder-2.8.1
$ ls
AUTHORS   COPYING    README   build.xml  etc/        lib/  tests-src/
CHANGES   ChangeLog  TODO     doc/       examples/   src/  webapps/
```

The corresponding commands for the Microsoft Windows command shell are:

```
C:\> mkdir c:\grinder
C:\> cd c:\grinder
C:\grinder> jar xf mydownloads\grinder-2.8.1.jar
C:\grinder> cd grinder-2.8.1
C:\grinder\grinder-2.8.1> dir /w
 Volume in drive C is system
 Volume Serial Number is 18C4-E5DB

 Directory of C:\grinder\grinder-2.8.1

[.]          [..]         [doc]       [etc]       [examples]  [lib]
[src]        [tests-src]  [webapps]   AUTHORS     build.xml   ChangeLog
CHANGES      COPYING      README      TODO
               7 File(s)        172,936 bytes
               9 Dir(s)   6,104,801,280 bytes free
```

The Grinder

As you can see, the UNIX and Windows commands are very similar. We'll use UNIX commands for the rest of our examples as they are less verbose, but we'll give the Windows equivalents as we introduce new commands.

The key file of interest is lib/grinder.jar. The Grinder is shipped pre-built and this file contains all of the compiled code. Documentation is provided in text files both in the top-level directory (in particular, you should scan through the README file) and in the *doc* directory. The examples directory contains some example grinder.properties files. If you are not interested in the sourcecode of The Grinder you can safely ignore the remaining etc, src, tests-src, and webapps directories.

You have now installed The Grinder. Change directory out of The Grinder hierarchy and create a new directory to hold your test script and test output. Also, set the Java CLASSPATH environment variable to include the grinder.jar file.

```
$ mkdir /grinder-tests/myFirstTest
$ cd /grinder-tests/myFirstTest
$ CLASSPATH=/grinder/grinder-2.8.1/lib/grinder.jar; export CLASSPATH
```

The Microsoft Windows equivalent command to set the CLASSPATH is:
set CLASSPATH=c:\grinder\grinder-2.8.1\lib\grinder.jar

Here's the grinder.properties test script we will use. Use a text editor to create this file in your test directory:

```
# My first grinder.properties file

grinder.processes=1
grinder.threads=1
grinder.cycles=1

grinder.receiveConsoleSignals=false
grinder.reportToConsole=false

grinder.plugin=net.grinder.plugin.http.HttpPlugin
grinder.plugin.parameter.useCookies=true

grinder.test0.parameter.url=http://www.wrox.com
grinder.test1.parameter.url=\
     http://www.wrox.com/Includes/images/newwroxlogo.gif
```

This is similar to the test script we encountered earlier, but we have added two lines to disable the use of the console and used URLs from Wrox Press's public Internet site. The above URL should be fairly static but bear in mind that it may change.

If you're connected to the Internet you can now try the script. Here's the magic command:

```
$ java net.grinder.Grinder
The Grinder version 2.8.1 started
Grinder Process (paston-0) started with command line: java -classpath /g
rinder/grinder-.8.1/lib/grinder.jar net.grinder.engine.process.GrinderPr
ocess paston-0
03/11/01 12:16:07: Grinder Process (paston-0) starting threads
03/11/01 12:16:13: Grinder Process (paston-0) finished
The Grinder version 2.8.1 finished
```

This command starts an agent process, which reads the grinder.properties file from the local directory. It is normal to have a separate directory per test script. Alternatively, if you want to store many test scripts in the same directory, you can pass the name of the test script as a command line argument to the net.grinder.Grinder class, for example:

```
$ java net.grinder.Grinder my-other-test-script.properties
```

Examining the terminal output we see that the agent process spawned a worker process called paston-0 (paston being the machine's hostname). The worker process started its threads and finished about six seconds later. To find out more we have to look at the output file:

```
$ ls
data_paston-0.log  grinder.properties  out_paston-0.log
$ cat out_paston-0.log
03/11/01 12:16:07: Grinder Process (paston-0) Sun Microsystems Inc. Java
 HotSpot(TM) Client VM 1.3.0-C
03/11/01 12:16:07: Grinder Process (paston-0) Windows NT x86 4.0
03/11/01 12:16:07: Grinder Process (paston-0) starting threads
03/11/01 12:16:07: (thread 0) Initialized net.grinder.plugin.http.HttpPl
ugin$HTTPPluginThreadCallbacks
03/11/01 12:16:07: (thread 0) About to run 1 cycles
03/11/01 12:16:13: (thread 0 cycle 0 test 0) http://www.wrox.com OK
03/11/01 12:16:13: (thread 0 cycle 0 test 1) http://www.wrox.com/Include
s/images/newwroxlogo.gif OK
03/11/01 12:16:13: (thread 0) Finished 1 cycles
03/11/01 12:16:13: Grinder Process (paston-0) Final statistics for this
process:
                   Transactions  Errors        Average
                                               Response
                                               Time (ms)

Test 0             1             0             5698.00
Test 1             1             0             691.00

Totals             2             0             3194.50
```

The Microsoft Windows equivalent to the ls command is dir. The equivalent of cat out_paston-0.log is type out_paston-0.log.

If an error occurred during one of the tests, such as not being able to connect to the Wrox site, an additional file error_paston-0 containing the error details will have been created.

The data file contains statistical information about the individual tests in a form that can easily be imported into a spreadsheet application:

```
$ cat data_paston-0.log
Thread, Cycle, Test, Transaction time, Errors
0, 0, 0, 5698, 0
0, 0, 1, 691, 0
```

In this particular set of tests the large transaction time is due to the Internet connection being via a slow dial-up line.

Before we go on to examine the console, we suggest that you edit the grinder.properties file to try other URLs. Also try varying the number of processes, threads, and cycles. If you are using public Internet sites, please accord them due respect and do not use large numbers of processes and threads.

Using The Grinder Console

The Grinder Console is a useful interface to the workings and reporting facilities of The Grinder. Let's take a closer look.

Communication Settings

The worker processes report statistics to the console using a TCP connection. The console listens for connections on a TCP port. Any free TCP port can be used. TCP ports have numbers in the range 0 to 65535 but we recommend using a port above 1024 since, under UNIX, ports with numbers less than 1024 are treated as reserved and require the console to be started with root permission.

IP multicast is used for communication of broadcast commands from the console to the worker processes. To use the console you need a valid multicast address and port. Multicast addresses are IP addresses in the range 224.0.0.1 to 239.255.255.255; ports have numbers in the range 0 to 65535. You should ensure that the address and port you choose does not clash with other applications running on your LAN.

For most modern TCP stacks multicast works straight out of the box – there is no set-up to do. Under Linux, you may need to set up the routing table for multicast. If you have root permission you can do this with a command like:

```
$ route add -net 224.0.0.0 netmask 240.0.0.0 dev eth0
```

This command declares that all IP multicast packets should be routed via the network device eth0.

Under Windows NT, you might find that you can't use multicast in conjunction with dial-up networking. We've spent many an hour trying to configure Windows NT routing tables to bind a multicast address to a particular local interface, but to no avail.

Under Windows 2000, multicast will not work unless your machine is connected to a network. Unfortunately the Windows 2000 software loopback connector does not handle multicast packets correctly, and the operating system disables the network card if no network carrier signal is found. The easiest way to make multicast work with a standalone Windows 2000 machine is to buy a cheap hub. We sometimes use an even cheaper solution, which is to use a physical loopback connector created out of a spare piece of network cable.

If you have trouble with multicast while running the examples in this section you should contact your local system administrator or network guru.

In our examples, we will run the console on the machine paston and set it to listen on port 12345. The worker processes will listen for commands on the multicast address 234.1.1.1, port 10000. The worker processes read communication settings from grinder.properties. Our modified test script is:

```
# An example grinder.properties file for use with the console

grinder.processes=2
grinder.threads=5
grinder.cycles=0

grinder.consoleAddress=paston
grinder.consolePort=12345
grinder.grinderAddress=234.1.1.1
grinder.grinderPort=10000

grinder.plugin=net.grinder.plugin.http.HttpPlugin
grinder.plugin.parameter.useCookies=true

grinder.test0.parameter.url=http://www.wrox.com
grinder.test1.parameter.url=\
    http://www.wrox.com/Includes/images/newwroxlogo.gif
```

As well as specifying the communication details, we have increased the number of processes and threads and set the number of cycles to 0. Setting grinder.cycles to 0 causes the worker processes to continue running tests until the console interrupts them.

Starting the Console

The Java code for the console is also stored in the grinder.jar file. Set up your Java CLASSPATH as discussed earlier and type:

```
$ java net.grinder.Console
```

The main console window should appear:

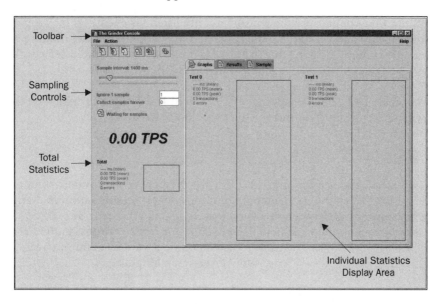

The console does not read `grinder.properties`, so the multicast address and ports need to be separately configured. To do this, select **Options...** from the **File** menu. This will bring up an options dialog where the multicast details can be set:

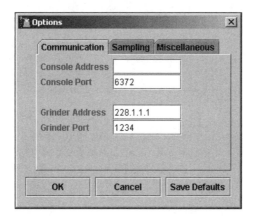

To match the settings we used in the worker processes' `grinder.properties` files, fill in 12345 for the **Console Port**, 234.1.1.1 for the **Grinder Address** and 10000 for the **Grinder Port**.

Leave the **Console Address** field blank. If your machine is multi-homed, you can use this field to set a specific hostname or IP address belonging to the console machine. Don't use "localhost", as this would cause the console to only listen for events on the loopback adapter, which would mean that it could only be contacted by worker processes running on the same machine as the console. Leaving this field blank causes the console to listen on all network interfaces belonging to the local machine – this is usually what you want.

If you press **Save Defaults**, the settings will be stored in a file in your home directory and the console will automatically load this file the next time it is started.

A First Run

We will now start The Grinder processes. It is worth opening a separate terminal window to do this, in order to keep the terminal output of the console separate from the terminal output of the worker processes. Create a new directory containing the `grinder.properties` file given earlier, remembering to change the `grinder.Console` address in the file to the name of your computer. Set the Java CLASSPATH environment variable, and run `java net.grinder.Grinder`. This time you will see something like:

```
$ java net.grinder.Grinder
The Grinder version 2.8.1 started
Grinder Process (paston-0) started with command line: java  -classpath
d:\src\grinder\lib\grinder.jar net.grinder.engine.process.GrinderProcess
paston-0
Grinder Process (paston-1) started with command line: java  -classpath
d:\src\grinder\lib\grinder.jar net.grinder.engine.process.GrinderProcess
paston-1
04/11/01 13:39:19: Grinder Process (paston-0) waiting for console signal
04/11/01 13:39:19: Grinder Process (paston-1) waiting for console signal
```

Two worker processes have been started and are waiting for a console signal before they proceed.

When the worker processes start they report details of their test sets to the console. If you look at the console you should see that it now is aware of the two tests:

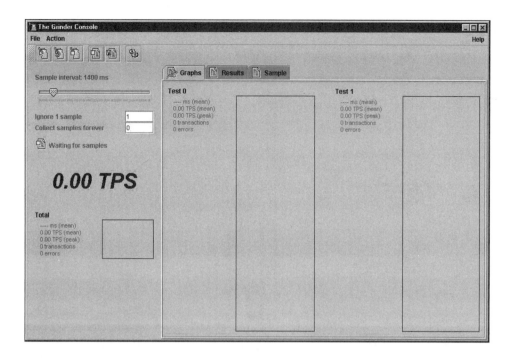

If the console is not running, start it as described in the previous section and choose 'Reset processes' *from the* Action *menu. The processes will restart and the console display will be updated.*

To instruct the worker processes to start the test run, select **Start processes** from the **Action** menu. Look at the agent process terminal window. The two worker processes have reported that they have started:

```
04/11/01 14:53:11: Grinder Process (paston-1) starting threads
04/11/01 14:53:11: Grinder Process (paston-0) starting threads
```

After a short delay, the console display will show graphs of the incoming reports:

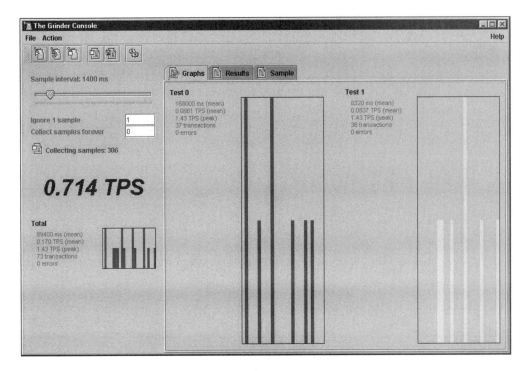

There are individual graphs showing the transactions per second for each test, and a graph showing the total transactions per second. Alongside each graph, the mean transaction time ("Average Response Time" in our terminology), mean transactions per second, peak transactions per second, number of transactions, and number of errors recorded for each test are shown. The colors of the individual test graphs vary from yellow to red to indicate the tests that have the longest mean transaction times. The more red a test graph, the longer the transactions for that test are taking.

Try selecting the Results tab to see the results in a tabular form. You can also select the Sample tab to show the sum of all reports received during the current console sample interval. Before continuing, select Stop processes from the Action menu. This will stop the worker processes:

```
04/11/01 15:30:42: Grinder Process (paston-1) waiting for threads to
terminate
04/11/01 15:30:42: Grinder Process (paston-0) waiting for threads to
terminate
The Grinder version 2.8.1 finished
```

The Console Recording Model

The console aggregates reports coming from the worker processes and updates its display at regular sample intervals. The collection of reports received within a sample interval is referred to as a *sample*. The size of the sample interval can be changed with the **Sample interval** control. A small sample interval results in a more interactive display, but makes the console more CPU-intensive and reduces the accuracy of the mean TPS and peak TPS statistics.

The console starts collecting statistics when reports are received from the worker processes. The sample that contains these first reports is discarded, as it may not contain a full complement of reports. An optional additional number of samples can be discarded – this is commonly done to allow the test system to "warm up", ignoring start-up effects due to TCP slow start, Java HotSpot compilation, and so on.

Collection of statistics continues until either the specified number of samples has been collected or **Stop collection** is selected from the **Action** menu. (Collecting data on running tests only affects the statistics recording; the worker processes will happily continue to perform tests and report results until they are stopped using the **Stop processes** control).

> *Full documentation for the console controls and a table of all the properties that can be used in* `grinder.properties` *can be found in Appendix A.*

Using the HTTP Plug-in

The HTTP plug-in is designed to test web servers using the HTTP protocol. It is the most commonly used and the most sophisticated standard plug-in. We have covered its basic usage in the examples above and, in this section, we will now go on to look at the plug-in's other features, which are controlled through plug-in properties.

> *A summary of all the HTTP plug-in properties can be found in Appendix A.*

Defining HTTP Requests

We have seen the basic format of an HTTP plug-in test:

```
grinder.test0.parameter.url=http://www.wrox.com
```

The `url` parameter specifies the URL to call. By default, the HTTP `GET` method is used. Web browsers use this method to request pages typed into their URL fields. Browsers use another HTTP method, `POST`, to send form content; this typically occurs when you click a submit button. Other HTTP methods exist, but they are rarely used in practice and the HTTP plug-in does not support them. If you wish to use the `POST` method, specify the `post` parameter in addition to the `url` parameter:

```
grinder.test0.parameter.url=http://www.wrox.com
grinder.test0.parameter.post=MyPostData.txt
```

The value of the `post` parameter is the name of a file that contains the data you wish to post to the URL. The file must exist and be readable by the worker processes. Here's an example file that contains two name/value pairs, specifying a username and password, such as would be suitable to submit as part of a J2EE Servlet form-based authentication.

```
j_username=admin&j_password=yorba
```

You can specify arbitrary headers to be sent with the request using `header` parameters. These take the form `grinder.test0.parameter.header.NAME=VALUE` where `NAME` and `VALUE` can be arbitrary strings. For example:

```
grinder.test2.parameter.header.If-Modified-Since=Sat, 06 Jan 2001
13:36:49 GMT
```

This property will result in the following header being added to the HTTP request for `test2`:

```
If-Modified-Since: Sat, 06 Jan 2001 13:36:49 GMT
```

The HTTP plug-in supports HTTP basic authentication, the authentication credential details being specified using three parameters: `basicAuthenticationRealm`, `basicAuthenticationUser` and `basicAuthenticationPassword`:

```
grinder.test0.parameter.basicAuthenticationRealm=myrealm
grinder.test0.parameter.basicAuthenticationUser=phil
grinder.test0.parameter.basicAuthenticationPassword=mypass
```

If you specify one of these values, then you must specify all three. The plug-in sends an appropriate `Authorization` header if challenged by the server, just as a browser would. The string specified with `basicAuthenticationRealm` must match the realm required by the `WWW-Authenticate` header in the challenge.

Does setting all of these properties sound like a lot of work? Later we'll see how all of these properties can be recorded automatically.

Checking the Response

By default, the HTTP plug-in only records IO exceptions and HTTP protocol problems as errors.

The HTTP plug-in also provides a simple way to assert that the body of a response contains a certain string. The expected string is specified using the `ok` parameter, for example:

```
grinder.test0.parameter.ok=Success
```

This property will cause an error to be logged if the result body of a `test0` test does not contain the string `Success`. Additionally, a file will be created in the log directory containing the response body that was received.

We recommend that you specify `ok` strings for key tests in your test script, in order to check that the server is behaving as expected.

Modeling a Web Browser Session

The HTTP plug-in simulates many client browsers. Each cycle executed by a specific thread models a single browser session. Each thread uses a single connection at a time to contact the server. If HTTP 1.0 Keep-Alive or HTTP 1.1 persistent connections are used, the connection is established at the start of a cycle and closed at the end of a cycle. In Chapter 7 we use The Grinder to investigate the cost of different connection models.

Some of the subtleties that this model does not take into account are as follows:

❑ Browsers can use more than one connection to retrieve resources from servers. (The HTTP 1.1 specification allows two connections to be used per server.)

❑ Browsers can pipeline requests. This involves not having to wait for the response to a request before sending a request for another.

The Grinder does not support these features. However, we believe that the HTTP plug-in model is an adequate tradeoff between simplicity and adequacy.

Cookies and Sessions

Why are cookies interesting from a testing perspective? Well, HTTP is a stateless protocol, so it does not have a notion of a connection between each client and the server, and there is no HTTP mechanism for identifying which client is making a request. Cookies are designed to complement HTTP and provide these features. The most common reason J2EE applications use cookies is to identify server sessions. A server session contains information that pertains to a single user, such as navigation information about where they are in the web interface, references to their account details, security information, and so on. Servers hand out unique cookies to client browsers, which return them in each request they make to the server.

The `useCookies` parameter controls the manner in which the HTTP plug-in uses cookies. You may recall that we specified this parameter in the earlier test scripts. Setting `useCookies` to `true` causes the plug-in to parse `Set-Cookie` headers in the responses returned by the web server and extract appropriate cookies. Each thread builds up a set of cookies that will set cookie headers in subsequent requests to the web server. When a thread reaches the end of a cycle its set of cookies is discarded, corresponding with our model of one cycle per web browser session.

String Beans

Suppose that you want to vary the data a test uses when making a request to the server. For example, your test may call a URL that returns customer account information and to realistically test your server you may wish to pass a different account number in each request. A simple way to achieve this is to use a feature of the HTTP plug-in called **string beans**.

String beans are simple Java classes that define a number of methods that return strings. Here's an example:

```
package net.grinder.plugin.http.example;

/**
 * Example String Bean.
 *
 * @author Philip Aston
 * @version $Revision: 1.3 $
 */
public class ExampleStringBean {
    private int m_count = 0;

    public String getCount() {
        return Integer.toString(m_count++);
    }

    public String getTime() {
        return Long.toString(System.currentTimeMillis());
    }
}
```

Note that some of the examples used in this section are available in The Grinder distribution in the `src/net/grinder/plugin/http/example` *directory.*

This class defines two methods, getCount and getTime, both of which take no arguments and return a String. The first method, getCount, returns the number of times that it has previously been called. The second method, getTime, returns a String representation of the number of milliseconds between the current time and midnight, January 1, 1970 UTC.

If you compile this class, add it to the CLASSPATH that you use to start the agent process, and declare the class in your grinder.properties file, you can then invoke these methods from your test script. The line you need to add to your grinder.properties file is:

```
grinder.plugin.parameter.stringBean=net.grinder.plugin.http.example.Exam
pleStringBean
```

With this line included, when each worker thread starts it will instantiate an
`ExampleStringBean` instance. Java introspection is used to identify all `public` methods
that begin with `get`, return a `String` and take no arguments. These methods are then
available to be invoked from your test script using a special template syntax, namely enclosing
the name of the method with the symbols < and >. For example:

```
grinder.test1.parameter.url=http://localhost:7001/index.jsp?time=<getTim
e>,count=<getCount>
```

*Unfortunately this means that you will not be able to pass XML elements as parameters,
but this will be possible with The Grinder 3.*

Whenever a particular thread invokes this test, `<getTime>` and `<getCount>` are replaced
with the results of invoking the corresponding method on the thread's `ExampleStringBean`
instance. The `<beanMethodName>` syntax can be used in any URL string, `POST` data file,
header, authentication parameter, and in `ok` strings.

Here's another example. The following string bean allocates a unique login identifier to each
worker thread:

```
/**
 * String Bean to generate login ids.
 */
public class StringBean {
    private final static String[] s_loginIDs = {
      "PhilA",
      "PhilB",
      "PhilD",
      "DavidG",
    };

    private static int s_nextID = 0;

    private final String m_loginID;

    public StringBean() {
      synchronized(StringBean.class) {
        m_loginID = s_loginIDs[s_nextID++];
      }
    }

    public String getLoginID() {
      return m_loginID;
    }
}
```

This particular string bean only supports four worker threads and will fail with an
`ArrayIndexOutOfBounds` exception if a fifth thread tries to create an instance. We leave
making this string bean more robust as an exercise for the reader.

Wouldn't it be nice for a string bean to be able to access context information such as the worker process identity, and in addition receive callbacks when key events happen, such as the beginning and the end of cycles? Advanced string beans can do this by implementing the `net.grinder.plugin.http.StringBean` interface.

Before we leave string beans, a word of warning is in order. They are a simple, cheap, and effective way of implementing dynamic data and we encourage you to use them, but we are not planning to enhance this feature in the next major release of The Grinder. Instead, The Grinder 3 will support the use of scripting languages such as Jython, JavaScript, and Visual Basic.

Advanced String Beans

Here are a few things that are difficult to achieve using the simple string beans described above:

❑ Log messages to the output and error files.

❑ Include the worker process identity in generated strings, or vary generated strings using the process identity.

❑ Reset your string bean at the beginning of each test cycle.

Advanced string beans can achieve all of these by implementing the `net.grinder.plugin.http.StringBean` interface. This interface defines four methods, which are described in the following table:

Method	Description
`void beginCycle()`	This method is called at the beginning of every cycle.
`boolean doTest(` `Test testDefinition)`	This method is called before each test. From the `Test` argument the string bean can obtain the test number, description, and parameters.
`void endCycle()`	This method is called at the end of every cycle.

`void initialize(`
`PluginThreadContext`
`context)`
	This method is called when the plug-in is initialized. The `PluginThreadContext` argument is described below.

The `PluginThreadContext` argument passed to initialize supports a large number of methods that allow a string bean to:

❑ Obtain the worker process identity, test cycle number, the calling thread's number

❑ Query plug-in parameters, including custom parameters that you have declared yourself

❑ Log messages and errors to the log files

`PluginThreadContext` also contains some methods that are designed for use by plug-in implementations and are not frequently used in string bean implementations. These methods allow:

❑   Registering new statistics with the console

❑   Controlling the timing of tests

❑   Aborting the current test or test cycle

Please refer to the Javadoc documentation provided with The Grinder distribution for full details on `PluginThreadContext`.

Here's an example string bean that implements `net.grinder.plugin.http.StringBean`:

```
package net.grinder.plugin.http.example;

import net.grinder.common.Test;
import net.grinder.plugininterface.PluginException;
import net.grinder.plugininterface.PluginThreadContext;
import net.grinder.plugin.http.StringBean;


/**
 * Example String Bean that implements StringBean.
 *
 * @author Philip Aston
 * @version $Revision: 1.3 $
 */
public class ExampleStringBean2 implements StringBean {
    private PluginThreadContext m_pluginThreadContext;
    private int m_count = 0;

    public void initialize(PluginThreadContext pluginThreadContext)
        throws PluginException {
      m_pluginThreadContext = pluginThreadContext;
      m_pluginThreadContext.logMessage("StringBean: initialize");
    }

    public void beginCycle() {
      m_pluginThreadContext.logMessage("StringBean: beginCycle");
      m_count = 0;
    }

    public boolean doTest(Test test) {
      m_pluginThreadContext.logMessage("StringBean: doTest");
      return false;
    }

    public void endCycle() {
      m_pluginThreadContext.logMessage("StringBean: endCycle");
```

```
    }

    public String getCount() {
      return Integer.toString(m_count++);
    }

    public String getTime() {
      return Long.toString(System.currentTimeMillis());
    }

    public String getCycle() {
      return Integer.toString(m_pluginThreadContext.getCurrentCycleID());
    }
  }
}
```

ExampleStringBean2 defines three string bean methods. The first method, getCount, returns the number of times it has previously been invoked *this cycle* (whereas ExampleStringBean.getCount, as used previously, returns the number of times it had previously been invoked *ever*). The second method, getTime, is the same as ExampleStringBean.getTime. The third method, getCycle, returns the number of the current cycle number.

Miscellaneous HTTP Plug-in Properties

By default, the HTTP plug-in simply logs HTTP redirection responses returned by the server (namely 301 *moved permanently*, 303 *see other*, 307 *temporary redirect*). In order to accurately simulate browser behavior, you would typically define two tests: one that calls the URL that returns the redirect and the other that calls the final URL itself. Alternatively you can set the followRedirectsproperty to instruct the HTTP plug-in to follow redirects automatically:

```
grinder.plugin.parameter.followRedirects=true
```

When debugging server interaction, it is sometimes useful to see the response bodies. Typically these contain HTML pages. You can instruct the HTTP plug-in to write all received response bodies to individual files in the log directory using the property:

```
grinder.plugin.parameter.logHTML=true
```

HTTPClient

The library used to implement the HTTP plug-in is Ronald Tschalär's excellent HTTPClient library. HTTPClient has many more features than HttpURLConnection from the standard Java library (see http://www.innovation.ch/java/HTTPClient/urlcon_vs_httpclient.html for a comparison).

We hope to lever features such as proxy support, connection timeouts, and persistent cookies into future versions of The Grinder. You can access many HTTPClient features by setting system properties (see http://www.innovation.ch/java/HTTPClient/advanced_info.html for a list of available properties). For example, the following property will force the use of HTTP 1.0 instead of HTTP 1.1:

```
grinder.jvm.arguments=-DHTTPClient.forceHTTP_1.0=true
```

One of the key advantages of HTTPClient is that it allows explicit control of connection management, whereas HttpURLConnection uses connection pooling "under the covers". Because HTTPClient uses extra connections it may appear slower (reporting longer response times) – particularly if the client and server are co-hosted. However, it's a closer model of reality (see *Modeling a Web Browser Session* earlier).

In our experience, HTTPClient is **much** more standards-compliant and less bug-ridden than HttpURLConnection. However, an alternative implementation of the HTTP plug-in, HttpURLConnection, is available. To use it, specify the following property:

```
grinder.plugin.parameter.useHTTPClient=false
```

The HttpURLConnection implementation does have two features that the HTTPClient implementation doesn't:

❑ It has an additional parameter, useCookiesVersionString. Setting this parameter to false removes the $Version string from cookies (it defaults to true). This is to work around cookie parsing problems experienced with a JRun 2.3.3 server. The HTTPClient cookie support is much better than the homegrown support used for the HttpURLConnection implementation, and probably does not require this feature.

❑ It allows the reporting of the "mean time to first byte" statistic, in addition to the normal total transaction time statistic. This feature will be supported by the HTTPClient implementation in a future release.

HTTPS

The Grinder supports HTTPS (HTTP over SSL). There are patches available that allow HTTPClient to work with several SSL implementations. See http://www.innovation.ch/java/HTTPClient/https.html for details. The instructions that follow assume you are using the Sun Microsystems reference implementation, JSSE 1.0.2.

1. Install JSSE1.0.2. Follow the instructions in http://java.sun.com/products/jsse/INSTALL.html. We recommend installing the JSSE as an installed extension.

2. Download the HTTPClient JSSE patch from
   http://www.innovation.ch/java/HTTPClient/JSSE.zip. Extract the class files
   contained within the .zip into a directory called HTTPClient, then create a
   .jar containing that directory:

```
$ mkdir HTTPClient; cd HTTPClient
$ jar xf /download/JSSE.zip
$ cd ..
$ jar cf HTTPClient-JSSE.jar HTTPClient
```

   Add this .jar to the **start** of your CLASSPATH before running The Grinder. It's
   worth reading the file README in JSSE.zip.

3. In your grinder.properties file, you can now use URLs that start with https:

You may well need to create a trust store containing CA certificates that sign the server
certificate. I would direct you to the JSSE documentation for full details, but here's a quick hint:

```
$ keytool -import -v -keystore ./mycastore -file d:/wls5/myserver/ca.pem
```

You should then add -Djavax.net.ssl.trustStore=mycastore to
grinder.jvm.arguments in your grinder.properties. Refer to the JSSE
documentation for other useful properties. In particular, Djavax.net.debug=ssl might
come in useful.

HTTPClient checks that the host name in each request URL matches the subject DN field in
the certificate. If this isn't the case, you might need to add an entry to /etc/hosts,
c:\WINNT40\system32\drivers\etc\, DNS or whatever, and then use that host name in the
request URLs.

The JSSE SSL implementation isn't quick. This should be taken into account when comparing
round trip times, as a compiled browser version is likely to be a lot faster. When using SSL,
you will also find that you can support fewer worker threads on a given test client machine
due to the intensive CPU requirements of cryptography.

Writing a Grinder Plug-in

The HTTP plug-in is by far the most refined of the three plug-ins that are shipped with The
Grinder. However, not all J2EE applications have an HTTP interface, and sometimes you find
that it's appropriate to write a custom plug-in.

In this section we show you how to write your own plug-in, and walk through an example
implementation. The example used is the JMS queue sender plug-in from Chapter 6.

Designing Your Plug-in

The first thing you need to decide is what constitutes a test. For the HTTP plug-in it is a call to a URL; for our JMS example it is sending a message to a JMS queue; for your example it might be making an RMI call to an EJB. Whatever the test is, you need to be able to perform it using Java code. This may require that you add extra client libraries to your `CLASSPATH`.

Next, you need to decide how the tests should vary. For example, would you allow the target JMS queue to be varied on a test-by-test basis? What about the JMS message contents? You need to find a convenient way for the user to configure this information for each test by providing a set of per-test parameters. The conventional way to do this is to use per-test entries in the `grinder.properties` file (`grinder.test0.parameter.myparameter`). Property settings are a simple way to define test sets, but do not fit all cases. For example, the JUnit plug-in discovers its tests by using Java reflection on a JUnit test case class.

Some things are easier to parameterize than others. It would be difficult to write a generic EJB plug-in that could call any EJB. Each test would need to pass Java language-level information about the individual method to call and the types and values of each parameter. This is one of the factors that are motivating the move to a full scripting language in The Grinder 3. However, it is still perfectly reasonable to write a plug-in that exercises a specific EJB.

Consider what should happen at the start and end of the test cycle. At the start of each cycle, the HTTP plug-in discards the old HTTP connection and any cookies from the previous cycle. Our JMS example allows the use of the start and end cycle events to start and end a JMS `QueueSession`.

Finally, design the plug-in level parameters that will affect all the tests in a test run and the per-test parameters for the HTTP plug-in (see Appendix A).

We made the following choices for our JMS plug-in:

❑   A test will involve sending a JMS `BytesMessage` to a JMS queue.

❑   Each test will specify the JMS queue to use and the size of the message. The message contents will be randomly generated.

❑   By default, a single JMS `QueueSession` will be used for each thread. The user will be able to override this behavior so that a `QueueSession` will be used for each cycle for each thread.

❑   A single JMS `QueueConnection` will be used.

The following tables show how we've mapped these choices into parameters that can be set in `grinder.properties`:

JMS Plug-in Properties

The following table defines the general plug-in parameters that we will be able to set:

Property	Description
connectionFactory	The class name of a JNDI initial context factory to use to look up the JMS connection factory. The default value is `weblogic.jndi.WLInitialContextFactory`.
connectionFactoryJNDI Name	The JNDI name of the JMS connection factory to use. The default value is `jms.connectionFactory`.
serverURL	The URL of the JMS server to use. The default value is `t3://localhost:7001`.
sessionPerCycle	Set to `true` to specify that a new JMS `QueueSession` should be used for each test cycle. The default value is `false`.

JMS Plug-in Per-test Properties

The following table defines the parameters that we can vary on a test-to-test basis:

Property	Description
messageSize	The size of the message in bytes. This is a mandatory property; there is no default value.
queueJNDIName	The JNDI name of the queue to post the message to. This is a mandatory property; there is no default value.

Here's a sample test script that uses these properties:

```
#
# Sender test script
#

grinder.processes=1
grinder.threads=1
grinder.cycles=0

grinder.receiveConsoleSignals=true
grinder.grinderAddress=228.1.1.1
grinder.grinderPort=1234

grinder.reportToConsole=true
grinder.consolePort=6372
```

```
grinder.thread.sleepTime=1000

grinder.plugin=com.wrox.paston.jms.queue.grinder.SenderPlugin
grinder.plugin.parameter.serverURL=t3://localhost:8001
grinder.plugin.parameter.connectionFactoryJNDIName=jms.myConnectionFacto
ry
grinder.plugin.parameter.sessionPerCycle=false

grinder.test0.parameter.queueJNDIName=jms.queue.PASTON-0.0
grinder.test0.parameter.messageSize=1

grinder.test1.parameter.queueJNDIName=jms.queue.PASTON-0.0
grinder.test1.parameter.messageSize=10

grinder.test2.parameter.queueJNDIName=jms.queue.PASTON-0.0
grinder.test2.parameter.messageSize=1000
```

The Grinder Plug-in SPI

The Grinder plug-in service provider interface (SPI) exists in three Java packages. As a plug-in writer you will use at least two of these packages:

❑   `net.grinder.plugininterface`, which contains the interfaces that you must implement.

❑   `net.grinder.common`, which contains commonly used classes and interfaces.

If you want to report additional statistics you will also use:

❑   `net.grinder.statistics`, which allows new statistics types to be created. Our JMS plug-in does not report any additional statistics, so we have deferred discussion of this package until later.

The Two Key Interfaces

To implement a plug-in you must implement the `GrinderPlugin` and `ThreadCallbacks` interfaces. The `GrinderPlugin` implementation is the class that you specify in the `grinder.properties` file.

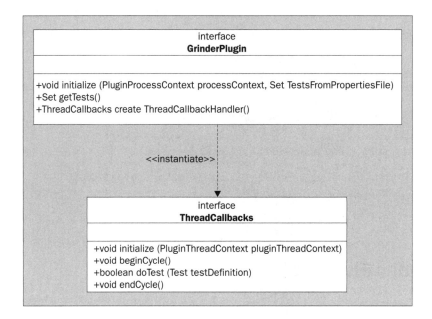

The `GrinderPlugin` interface defines three methods. The first method, `initialize`, is called when the worker process loads the plug-in. It is passed a `Context` object and a set of tests, as defined in the `grinder.properties` file. It allows the plug-in to perform one-time initialization. Your implementation of the second method, `getTests`, should either return the set of tests passed to `initialize` or, if your plug-in doesn't use `grinder.properties` to define tests, a different set of tests. The third method that `GrinderPlugin` declares, `createThreadCallbacks`, is called once for each thread when the worker process starts. Your implementation should create and return an object that implements the `ThreadCallbacks` interface.

When various events occur, the `ThreadCallbacks` interface is invoked by its associated worker thread. It has four methods:

❑   The `initialize` method is called at start-up and is passed a `Context` object specific to the worker thread.

❑   The `beginCycle` and `endCycle` methods are called at the beginning and end of every test cycle respectively; your implementation can use these to add per-cycle behavior.

❑   The `doTest` method is called for each test. It is passed a `Test` object (described later), and your implementation should perform the test and return `true` if the test succeeded or `false` if the test should be counted as an error. The `doTest` method can also throw an exception, in which case the test will be counted as an error and the current test cycle will be aborted.

The Context Objects

The object passed to
GrinderPlugin.initialize supports
the PluginProcessContext interface
and allows the plug-in to obtain
information about its configuration and to
log messages to The Grinder log files. A
similar object, which implements
PluginThreadContext (see the
advanced string beans section), is passed
to ThreadCallbacks.initialize, and
supports the same methods as
PluginProcessContext together with
methods to access information about the
worker thread, to abort the current test
cycle, and to control the timing of the
current test.

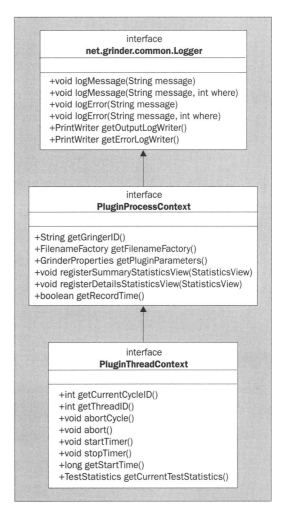

The Test Interface

The net.grinder.common.Test interface is used to represent the configuration of an
individual test. The plug-in is responsible for returning a set of objects that support this in its
implementation of GrinderPlugin.getTests. One of these objects is passed whenever the
ThreadCallbacks.doTest method is called so that the plug-in knows which test to
perform. The Test interface provides methods to get the test number and description, and
also to get the test properties.

The net.grinder.common package contains a simple implementation of the Test interface
which you might find useful when implementing plug-ins that do not simply return the test set
they were passed in GrinderPlugin.initialize.

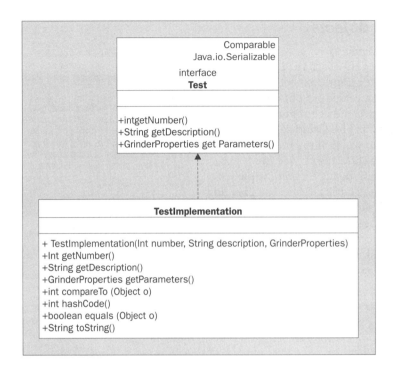

The JMS Queue Sender Plug-in

In this section we present the source code to the JMS queue sender plug-in. The full sourcecode can be downloaded from the Expert-Press Internet site.

First the plug-in declares its package and imports the classes that it uses from other packages:

```
package com.wrox.paston.jms.queue.grinder;

import java.util.Iterator;
import java.util.HashMap;
import java.util.Map;
import java.util.Random;
import java.util.Set;
import javax.jms.BytesMessage;
import javax.jms.JMSException;
import javax.jms.Message;
import javax.jms.Queue;
import javax.jms.QueueSender;
import javax.jms.QueueSession;
import javax.jms.Session;
import javax.naming.NamingException;

import net.grinder.common.GrinderException;
import net.grinder.common.GrinderProperties;
```

```
import net.grinder.common.Test;
import net.grinder.plugininterface.GrinderPlugin;
import net.grinder.plugininterface.PluginProcessContext;
import net.grinder.plugininterface.PluginThreadContext;
import net.grinder.plugininterface.PluginException;
import net.grinder.plugininterface.ThreadCallbacks;
```

It creates an implementation of `GrinderPlugin` and declares various member fields:

```
/**
 * @author Philip Aston
 */
public class SenderPlugin implements GrinderPlugin {
    private static Random s_random = new Random();
    private QueueInitialisation m_queueInitialisation;
```

The `Random` is used to randomly generate message data. `QueueInitialisation` deals with the initialisation of the `QueueConnection`:

```
    private Set m_tests;
    private Map m_testData;
    private boolean m_sessionPerCycle;
```

The `m_tests` Set will hold the test objects passed to `initialise`. `m_testData` will hold a HashMap which associates a custom `TestData` object with each `Test`. The `m_sessionPerCycle` Boolean is used to define whether a new `QueueSession` should be used for each cycle.

The `initialize` method sets up all of the member fields. The `TestData` class constructs a new message for each test. This requires a `QueueSession`, so we create a temporary one which is used just for initialisation:

```
    public void initialize(PluginProcessContext processContext,
                           Set testsFromPropertiesFile)
    throws PluginException {
    m_tests = testsFromPropertiesFile;
    m_testData = new HashMap(m_tests.size());

    final GrinderProperties parameters =
        processContext.getPluginParameters();

    m_sessionPerCycle = parameters.getBoolean("sessionPerCycle",
false);

    try {
        m_queueInitialisation = new QueueInitialisation(parameters);

        // Temporary session for the creation of messages.
```

```
            final QueueSession queueSession =
              m_queueInitialisation.getQueueConnection().
              createQueueSession(false, Session.AUTO_ACKNOWLEDGE);

            final Iterator iterator = m_tests.iterator();

            while (iterator.hasNext()) {
        final Test test = (Test)iterator.next();
              m_testData.put(test, new TestData(queueSession, test));
            }

            queueSession.close();
        }
        catch (Exception e) {
            throw new PluginException(
              "Failed to perform JMS initialisation", e);
        }
    }
```

The `TestData` class is used to store additional plug-in information about each test, namely a `BytesMessage` and a `Queue`. We implemented `TestData` as an inner class so it can directly access information in its outer class such as the queue initialisation object. Note how the test specific parameters are obtained from the passed `Test` object.

```
    private class TestData {
      private final BytesMessage m_message;
      private final Queue m_queue;

      TestData(QueueSession queueSession, Test test)
          throws GrinderException, JMSException, NamingException {
          final GrinderProperties parameters = test.getParameters();

          // Create a bytes message containing random bytes.
          m_message = queueSession.createBytesMessage();

          final byte[] bytes =
            new byte[parameters.getMandatoryInt("messageSize")];

          s_random.nextBytes(bytes);
          m_message.writeBytes(bytes);

          // Look up the test's Queue.
          final String queueName =
            parameters.getMandatoryProperty("queueJNDIName");

          m_queue = m_queueInitialisation.getQueue(queueName);
      }

      public final Message getMessage() {
          return m_message;
      }
```

```
    public final Queue getQueue() {
        return m_queue;
    }
}
```

The implementations of `getTests` and `createThreadCallbackHandler` are straightforward.

```
    public Set getTests() throws PluginException {
      return m_tests;
    }

    public ThreadCallbacks createThreadCallbackHandler()
      throws PluginException {
      return new ThreadCallbacksImplementation();
    }
```

We now come to the guts of the plug-in, the `ThreadCallbacks` implementation. This is also an inner class. Remember that there will be one instance of this class for each worker thread. Its `initialize` implementation simply stores the context object for later use.

```
    private class ThreadCallbacksImplementation implements
  ThreadCallbacks {
        private PluginThreadContext m_pluginThreadContext;
        private QueueSession m_queueSession;

        public void initialize(PluginThreadContext pluginThreadContext)
            throws PluginException {
          m_pluginThreadContext = pluginThreadContext;
        }
```

In begin cycle, we create a new `QueueSession` for the thread unless we have one already.

```
    public void beginCycle() throws PluginException {
        if (m_queueSession == null) {
          m_pluginThreadContext.logMessage("Creating queue session");

          try {
              m_queueSession =
                m_queueInitialisation.getQueueConnection().
                createQueueSession(false, Session.AUTO_ACKNOWLEDGE);
          }
          catch (JMSException e) {
              throw new PluginException(
                "Failed to create queue session", e);
          }
        }
    }
```

The `doTest` method sends a JMS message to the queue. Note the `startTimer` call just before the message is sent. The Grinder starts the timer before `doTest` is called so restarting it is not necessary; we do it so as not to include the cost of creating the `QueueSender` in the test time.

```
public boolean doTest(Test test) throws PluginException {
    final TestData testData = (TestData)m_testData.get(test);

    final Queue queue = testData.getQueue();
    final QueueSender queueSender;

    try {
        queueSender = m_queueSession.createSender(queue);
    }
    catch (JMSException e) {
        throw new PluginException(
            "Failed to create queue sender", e);
    }

    m_pluginThreadContext.logMessage("Sending message");

    m_pluginThreadContext.startTimer();

    try {
        queueSender.send(testData.getMessage());
    }
    catch (JMSException e) {
        throw new PluginException("Failed to send message", e);
    }

    return true;
}
```

Finally in `endCycle`, if `m_sessionPerCycle` is set we discard the current `QueueSession`.

```
public void endCycle() throws PluginException {
    if (m_sessionPerCycle) {
        m_pluginThreadContext.logMessage("Closing queue session");

        try {
            m_queueSession.close();
        }
        catch (JMSException e) {
            throw new PluginException("Failed to close queue
session");
        }

        m_queueSession = null;
    }
}
```

Additional Statistics

It is possible for a plug-in to define custom statistics that the plug-in can report against. These are presented in the console, the data files, and the log files. The implementation is quite complex, and the best way to understand how to use this feature is to look at an example.

We shall use the JMS queue receiver plug-in from Chapter 6 which adds an extra "delivery time" statistic. The classes that we use in this section come from the net.grinder.statistics package.

The statistics used by The Grinder are contained in a set of "raw statistics". Each raw statistic has a well-known name, has either a long or a double value, and appears once in the set. Every value you see in the log files, the data file, or the console is a value calculated from one or more of the raw statistics in the set. There are a number of predefined raw statistics as shown in the following table.

Statistic name	Type	Description
Errors	long	The number of errors.
timedTransactions	long	The number of timed transactions.
untimedTransactions	long	The number of transactions that weren't timed. These are successful tests that should contribute to the overall transaction count but shouldn't be used in ART calculations.
timedTransactionTime	long	The total transaction time in milliseconds for timed transactions. Dividing this value by timedTrasactions gives the ART in milliseconds.
Period	long	The period in milliseconds over which the other statistics in the set were recorded. Used to calculate TPS.
PeakTPS	double	Used by the console to store peak TPS figures.

A plug-in can define additional raw statistics values, but it must use one of the names userLong0 to userLong4 (for long values) or userDouble0 to userDouble4 (for double values). The JMS queue receiver plug-in gets a handle to such a statistic value as follows:

```
private StatisticsIndexMap.LongIndex m_deliveryTimeIndex;

//...
m_deliveryTimeIndex =
    StatisticsIndexMap.getInstance().getIndexForLong("userLong0");
```

71

It then uses this handle to store the cumulative delivery time:

```
m_pluginThreadContext.getCurrentTestStatistics().addValue(
        m_deliveryTimeIndex, deliveryTime);
```

That deals nicely with informing the statistics engine about the new statistic, but we also need to tell The Grinder how to display it – which we do by creating new `StatisticsView` objects.

`StatisticsView`'s are composed of a number of `ExpressionViews`. Each `ExpressionView` has a name, a key that the console can use to internationalize the name, and an expression. Here's a simple example of a `StatisticsView` from the JMS queue receiver plug-in.

```
final StatisticsView detailView = new StatisticsView();
detailView.add(new ExpressionView("Delivery time", "", "userLong0"));
processContext.registerDetailStatisticsView(detailView);
```

This particular `StatisticsView` just displays the raw value of our delivery time statistic and gives it a name. It is registered as a "detail view", which means it will appear in the data files and "Sample" tab in the console, but not in the log file summary table or the "Results" tab in the console.

The JMS receiver plug-in goes on to register a more complex `StatisticsView` as a "summary view". This means it will appear in the log file summary table and the "Results" tab in the console.

```
final StatisticsView summaryView = new StatisticsView();

summaryView.add(new ExpressionView(
                "Mean delivery time",
                "statistic.deliveryTime",
                "(/ userLong0 (+ timedTransactions
untimedTransactions))"));

processContext.registerSummaryStatisticsView(summaryView);
```

The expression is composed using a simple post-fix format and is equivalent to `userLong0/(timedTransactions + untimedTransactions)`. We record our delivery time for every transaction, timed or not, so we need to sum `timedTransactions` and `untimedTransactions` to get the total number of transactions for the raw statistics set.

Timing

So far we have not seen how to control the timing of tests. Let's take some time to go into this in detail.

Properties That Control Timing

The Grinder allows you to control timing using the `grinder.thread.sleepTime` property, which specifies how long each thread should sleep before running a test. This can be used to simulate user think time, as described in Chapter 1.

The following example shows how to set the sleep time between tests to 5000 ms (5 seconds):

```
grinder.thread.sleepTime=5000
```

This can be overridden on a test-by-test basis. For example, to set the sleep time immediately before test 5 to be 2 seconds:

```
grinder.test5.sleepTime=2000
```

The actual sleep time used is randomly varied according to a normal distribution. The normal distribution has the classic bell-shaped curve as shown in the following figure:

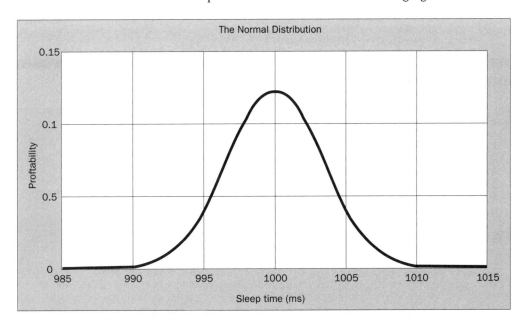

The width of the normal distribution is controlled by the `grinder.thread.sleepTimeVariation` property. This property specifies a fractional range within which nearly all (99.75%) of the times will lie. For example, if the sleep time is specified as 1000 and the `sleepTimeVariation` is set to 0.1, then 99.75% of the actual sleep times will be between 9900 and 11000 milliseconds. The default value of `sleepTimeVariation` is 0.2.

The other sleep time that you can control is the initial sleep time. This is the maximum time in milliseconds that each worker thread waits before starting. Unlike the before-test sleep times, this is varied according to a flat random distribution. The actual sleep time will be a random value between 0 and the specified value. The default value is 0 milliseconds. The purpose of the initial sleep time is not intended to be used to model user interaction, rather it should be used to ensure that the individual worker threads are spread evenly throughout the test script. Consequently, we recommend that you set the initial sleep time to be quite high relative to your before-test sleep times, and use the console "ignore samples" feature to be sure that all the threads are active before statistics recording begins. The following example shows how to set the initial sleep time to 10 seconds:

```
grinder.thread.initialSleepTime=10000
```

Finally, during the creation and debugging of test scripts, it is sometimes useful to be able to run everything faster. This can be done using the `grinder.thread.sleepTimeFactor`, which is a fraction that applies to all of the sleep times (including the initial sleep time) that you have specified. For example, setting the following property will cause the worker processes to run your test script ten times as fast:

```
grinder.thread.sleepTimeFactor=0.1
```

Timing Issues

The Grinder records transaction times for each successful test. This is done by a section of code that looks like the following:

```
m_context.startTimer();      // Critical section starts

try {
    // do test
}
finally {
    m_context.stopTimer();   // Critical section ends
}
```

This is repeated for each test. If any of the following are true:

- There are many threads within The Grinder process (and the sleep time is small)
- The test takes a long time
- The test performs a lot of I/O
- The host machine on which you are running The Grinder is also running other active processes (such as other Grinder processes)

...it is **highly likely** that the VM will swap the thread out in the critical section. Similarly, if the host machine on which you are running The Grinder is also running other active processes (such as other Grinder processes), it is **highly likely** that the JVM will swap the process out in the critical section. If The Grinder is co-hosted with the target server, and the plug-in uses a synchronous protocol, (like the HTTP plug-in), such swapping is a certainty. Both of these situations will cause an erroneously large transaction time to be reported.

As the number of worker threads rises, the contention on the critical section rises non-linearly and in a way that is difficult to quantify. The recorded time becomes more a measure of how the OS and JVM can swap between multiple threads and less a measure of server performance. *This is a generic problem with all test harnesses that measure timing and is not limited to The Grinder or Java.* Within the scope of a single machine there is little that can be done about this while realistically using multiple threads and processes. The recorded response time should always be considered an upper bound on the actual response time.

One solution to this problem is to dedicate a single machine to the measuring of response times. We call this the **Timer Client** model. The following property setting will cause the worker processes that use that grinder.properties file not to report transaction times to the console:

```
grinder.recordTime=false
```

To use the Timer Client model, you should run all but one of your grinder processes with this property set to false. These are the "load clients". You should copy the grinder.properties file to a dedicated "timer client" machine, change grinder.recordTime to true, and set grinder.processes=1 and grinder.threads=1. A single worker process will run on the timer client, recording all timing information and reporting it to the console. The fewer other processes you run on the timer client, the better. The disadvantage of this method is that the statistical sample of the transaction times is much smaller because only one worker thread is reporting the information.

Our testing has shown that the difference the Timer Client model makes is only measurable when those clients are co-hosted with the server. When you have separate server and client machines, it's better not to use the Timer Client model because it decreases the sample size of transaction times. We recommend trying both models. If you discover something interesting, please report it to: grinder-use@lists.sourceforge.net.

Using the TCPSniffer to Create Test Scripts

It is quite feasible to have HTTP plug-in grinder.properties test scripts containing hundreds or thousands of individual tests. Writing such test scripts by hand quickly becomes impractical. The Grinder is shipped with a tool called the TCPSniffer, which can help by automatically capturing test script entries corresponding to the HTTP requests a user makes using a browser, and generating corresponding test script entries.

75

The TCPSniffer is configured to sit between the user's browser and the target server and captures all the requests the browser makes before proxying the requests on to the server. The responses the TCPSniffer receives from the server are returned to the browser.

Running the TCPSniffer

To use the TCPSniffer to generate HTTP plug-in scripts, you need the Jakarta Regexp package, which can be obtained from http://jakarta.apache.org/.

To run the TCPSniffer, you should add both the Jakarta Regexp JAR file and The Grinder JAR file to your CLASSPATH:

```
export CLASSPATH=/opt/grinder/lib/grinder.jar:/opt/jakarta-regexp-
1.2/jakarta-regexp-1.2.jar
```

The TCPSniffer can then be started with the command:

```
java net.grinder.TCPSniffer
```

Use the following command to list the available options:

```
java net.grinder.TCPSniffer -?
```

Full details of the TCPSniffer command line options can be found in Appendix A.

The Sniffer in Action

The TCPSniffer is arguably misnamed. It should really have been called TCP Proxy since it is interposed in TCP streams rather than "sniffing" established TCP streams. The TCPSniffer listens on one TCP port, and proxies requests on to another TCP host and port.

Suppose your target server is listening on the machine olive and port 7001. Use -remoteHost and –remotePort to start the TCPSniffer:

```
$ java net.grinder.TCPSniffer -remoteHost olive -remotePort 7001
Initialising standard sniffer engine with the parameters:
   Request filter:  net.grinder.tools.tcpsniffer.EchoFilter
   Response filter: net.grinder.tools.tcpsniffer.EchoFilter
   Local host:      localhost
   Local port:      8001
   Remote host:     olive
   Remote port:     7001
Engine initialised, listening on port 8001
Starting engine
```

By default, the TCPSniffer listens on port 8001 on the local machine and installs an echo filter in both the request stream and the response stream. The echo filter simply copies all data to the standard output stream. This is very useful for debugging HTTP interactions. You should now direct your browser at http://localhost:8001/ instead of http://olive:7001/. Apart from the URL in the address bar, the browser display should appear as if you were connected directly to the target server. Use your browser as normal to navigate around the site as normal. All data sent to and from the server will appear in the terminal that you used to start the TCPSniffer.

The following diagram illustrates how the browser, TCPSniffer and HTTP server are connected.

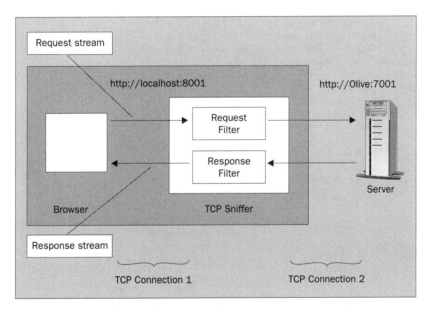

Here's a typical session using the TCPSniffer to talk to WebLogic Server 6.1. The WebLogic Server instance is listening on port 9001.

```
$ java net.grinder.TCPSniffer -remotePort 9001
Initialising standard sniffer engine with the parameters:
    Request filter:   net.grinder.tools.tcpsniffer.EchoFilter
    Response filter:  net.grinder.tools.tcpsniffer.EchoFilter
    Local host:       localhost
    Local port:       8001
    Remote host:      localhost
    Remote port:      9001
Engine initialised, listening on port 8001
Starting engine
--- localhost:1850->localhost:9001 opened --
--- localhost:9001->localhost:1850 opened --
------ localhost:1850->localhost:9001 ------
```

```
GET /console HTTP/1.1
Host: localhost:8001
User-Agent: Mozilla/5.0 (Windows; U; WinNT4.0; en-US; rv:0.9.5+)
Gecko/20011116
Accept: text/xml, application/xml, application/xhtml+xml,
text/html;q=0.9, imag/png, image/jpeg, image/gif;q=0.2,
text/plain;q=0.8, text/css, */*;q=0.1
Accept-Language: en-gb, en-us;q=0.50
Accept-Encoding: gzip, deflate, compress;q=0.9
Accept-Charset: utf-8, *
Keep-Alive: 300
Connection: keep-alive


------ localhost:9001->localhost:1850 ------
HTTP/1.1 401 Unauthorized xxx
Date: Sun, 02 Dec 2001 15:02:52 GMT
Server: WebLogic WebLogic Server 6.1  07/23/2001 22:31:20 #129251
WWW-Authenticate: Basic realm="weblogic"
Content-Type: text/html
Transfer-Encoding: Chunked
Connection: Close


------ localhost:9001->localhost:1850 ------
0659
<!DOCTYPE HTML PUBLIC "-//W3C//DTD HTML 4.0 Draft//EN">
<HTML>
<HEAD>
<TITLE>Error 401--Unauthorized xxx</TITLE>
<META NAME="GENERATOR" CONTENT="WebLogic htmlKona WebLogic Server 6.1
07/23/201 22:31:20 #129251 ">
</HEAD>
<BODY bgcolor="white" alink="#397F70" link="#640078" vlink="#DE7E00">

[Body ommitted.]

</BODY>
</HTML>


------ localhost:9001->localhost:1850 ------
0000
```

Here we can see that the URL, http://localhost:8001/console, has been requested using the browser. You can see all of the HTTP headers that the browser sends. The TCPSniffer passes the request on to the WebLogic Server instance, which returns an HTTP 401 "Unauthorized" response. The 401 response causes the browser to display a password dialog box. The "0659" and "0000" strings in the response are length delimiters which are part of the HTTP 1.1 chunked transfer protocol.

78

To format the output in a manner suitable for use in `grinder.properties` files, use the `-httpPluginFilter` option. This is a shortcut to specifying `-requestFilter HTTP_PLUGIN -responseFilter NONE`, and places the HTTP plug-in filter in the request stream and a `null` filter in the response stream. Here's what the TCPSniffer outputs if we rerun the example above using this option:

```
$ java net.grinder.TCPSniffer -remotePort 9001 -httpPluginFilter
Initialising standard sniffer engine with the parameters:
    Request filter:  net.grinder.plugin.http.HttpPluginSnifferFilter
    Response filter: net.grinder.tools.tcpsniffer.NullFilter
    Local host:      localhost
    Local port:      8001
    Remote host:     localhost
    Remote port:     9001
Engine initialised, listening on port 8001
Starting engine
grinder.test0.sleepTime=5789
grinder.test0.parameter.url=http://localhost:9001/console
grinder.test0.description=console
```

As you can see, the TCPSniffer output can be copied and pasted directly into a `grinder.properties` script. The actual time between starting the TCPSniffer and making the request via the browser is written out as a `sleepTime` property and a `description` property based on the requested URL has also been output.

The properties format information is sent to the standard output stream whereas the other information the TCPSniffer produces is directed to the standard error stream, so the two can easily be separated using the shell redirection operator (>).

We'll repeat the example using this technique. This time we'll also type a valid username and password into the browser dialog.

```
$ java net.grinder.TCPSniffer -remotePort 9001 -httpPluginFilter
> sniffer.log
Initialising standard sniffer engine with the parameters:
    Request filter:  net.grinder.plugin.http.HttpPluginSnifferFilter
    Response filter: net.grinder.tools.tcpsniffer.NullFilter
    Local host:      localhost
    Local port:      8001
    Remote host:     localhost
    Remote port:     9001
Engine initialised, listening on port 8001
Starting engine

[Type control-C to interrupt the sniffer.]
$ cat sniffer.log
grinder.test0.sleepTime=7180
grinder.test0.parameter.url=http://localhost:9001/console
```

```
grinder.test0.description=console
grinder.test1.sleepTime=3685
grinder.test1.parameter.url=http://localhost:9001/console
grinder.test1.description=console
grinder.test2.sleepTime=301
grinder.test2.parameter.url=http://localhost:9001/console/images/home.gi
f
grinder.test2.parameter.header.If-Modified-Since=Mon, 23 Jul 2001
22:00:14 GMT
grinder.test2.description=home.gif
grinder.test3.sleepTime=10
grinder.test3.parameter.url=http://localhost:9001/console/images/help.gi
f
grinder.test3.parameter.header.If-Modified-Since=Mon, 23 Jul 2001
22:00:14 GMT
grinder.test3.description=help.gif
grinder.test4.sleepTime=10
grinder.test4.parameter.url=http://localhost:9001/console/images/bea_logo
_right.gif
grinder.test4.parameter.header.If-Modified-Since=Mon, 23 Jul 2001
22:00:14 GMT
grinder.test4.description=bea_logo_right.gif
grinder.test5.sleepTime=10
grinder.test5.parameter.url=http://localhost:9001/console/images/transpa
rent.gif
grinder.test5.parameter.header.If-Modified-Since=Mon, 23 Jul 2001
22:00:14 GMT
grinder.test5.description=transparent.gif
grinder.test6.sleepTime=10
grinder.test6.parameter.url=http://localhost:9001/console/images/popup.g
if
grinder.test6.parameter.header.If-Modified-Since=Mon, 23 Jul 2001
22:00:14 GMT
grinder.test6.description=popup.gif
```

The contents of the file sniffer.out can be copied directly into a grinder.properties file.

test1 is the result of the browser re-requesting the URL http://localhost:8001 and including the authorization details provided in the dialog. It looks the same as test0. This is because the HTTP plug-in filter does not capture the HTTP Authorization header. To correctly reproduce the authorization information, add the following entries to your grinder.properties script:

```
grinder.test1.parameter.basicAuthenticationRealm=weblogic
grinder.test1.parameter.basicAuthenticationUser=system
grinder.test1.parameter.basicAuthenticationPassword=password
```

As a result of test1, the WebLogic Server application returns an HTML page to the browser. This HTML page contains a number of references to images, which the browser proceeds to request in order to render the page. This explains the next four tests that the TCPSniffer wrote out. They are all similar, so let's consider test3:

```
grinder.test3.sleepTime=10
grinder.test3.parameter.url=http://localhost:9001/console/images/help.gi
f
grinder.test3.parameter.header.If-Modified-Since=Mon, 23 Jul 2001
22:00:14 GMT
grinder.test3.description=help.gif
```

Notice the `If-Modified-Since` header. The TCPSniffer captures this header directly from the browser request. The browser includes the header because in the browser cache there is a copy of `help.gif` with a `Last Modified` date of 23rd July. If `help.gif` has not been modified since then, the server will respond with a `304 Not Modified` response, thus removing the need to transfer the image over the network again. Otherwise, the server will return the new copy of `help.gif`. Recording the `If-Modified-Since` headers allows the TCPSniffer to create a test script that directly models browser cache behavior. When recording test scripts, decide whether you want to simulate a brand new user session or a session using a browser that has already been used to visit your server. To simulate a brand new browser session, clear out your browser cache before using the TCPSniffer to record the test script.

We hope you can see that even though you need to tweak the output of the TCPSniffer a little, it allows you to very quickly build up a `grinder.properties` test script for use with the HTTP plug-in.

The TCPSniffer as a Debugging Tool

As mentioned above, the TCPSniffer can be an effective debugging tool. We often use the TCPSniffer to trace the interaction between The Grinder HTTP plug-in and a server. Typically this involves altering `grinder.properties` to set the number of worker processes and worker threads to 1 and to alter the test URLs to use the TCPSniffer host name and port. The TCPSniffer itself is started using echo filters in both the request and response streams, with the output directed to a file for later analysis.

Installing the TCPSniffer as a Browser Proxy

One problem with using the TCPSniffer occurs if the target server returns HTML pages or other responses to the browser that contain absolute URLs. An absolute URL is one that contains the host name and port. For example http://olive:7001/console/help.gif rather than help.gif (a relative URL) or /console/help.gif (a root-relative URL). Absolute URLs have a valid use to direct the browser to different servers but unfortunately are often used inadvisably to refer to local server resources where a relative or root-relative URL would suffice. Using absolute URLs causes problems for proxy and firewall schemes, which often alter the host and port that a user browser connects to, as well as for the TCPSniffer.

The problem occurs where the server returns a page containing an absolute URL. The TCPSniffer will pass the page back to the browser. If the user selects the URL, the browser will connect directly to the server and port specified in the URL, bypassing the TCPSniffer. The TCPSniffer has a special option that can be used to avoid this problem, -proxy. This mode also allows the TCPSniffer to record test scripts that use more that one HTTP server. To use the -proxy mode, start the TCPSniffer as follows:

```
$ java net.grinder.TCPSniffer -httpPluginFilter -proxy
Initialising standard sniffer engine with the parameters:
    Request filter:   net.grinder.plugin.http.HttpPluginSnifferFilter
    Response filter: net.grinder.tools.tcpsniffer.NullFilter
    Local host:       localhost
    Local port:       8001
    Proxying requests
Engine initialised, listening on port 8001
Starting engine
```

Alter your browser proxy settings to specify the TCPSniffer as the HTTP proxy. In our example, the host is localhost and the port is 8001. The following dialog shows appropriate settings for Microsoft Internet Explorer 5.

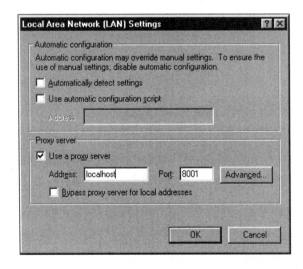

Use your browser as normal, specifying URLs using the target server host and port instead of the TCPSniffer host and port. The browser will direct all requests via the TCPSniffer.

Please note that, currently, the –proxy mode only works with the HTTP plug-in filter.

Hints and Tips

This section contains miscellaneous tips for using The Grinder.

Use a Shared Disk for grinder.properties

When you have many test client machines it is tedious to have to make the same changes to each `grinder.properties` script. We recommend storing your test script file on a disk shared by all of the test client machines. You can then simply edit the file and press the console Reset processes button to update all of the worker processes.

More Than One Test Case

What if you have more than one sequence of tests that you want to simultaneously run against your test servers? One approach to this is to run two sets of worker processes. You can vary the relative loading of each test case by varying the number of worker processes and worker threads in each set.

If you give each test case a unique set of test numbers you can easily distinguish between the two in the console. Alternatively, you might want to give the same number to a request that exists in both test cases but represents the same action; the console will collate the results for that request for both test cases.

Reducing Network Usage

The console may continue to receive and display report data after the worker processes have been stopped. This is an indication that the console could not process the incoming network packets fast enough and typically occurs only when using a lot of worker threads.

To alleviate this problem you can reduce the frequency at which the worker processes send reports to the console by increasing the time between reports:

```
grinder.reportToConsole=1000
```

The default setting is 500 milliseconds. Setting this property to a higher value means that fewer reports will be sent from the worker processes to the console, but each report will contain more information. Increasing the value will not result in the loss of test data; the console display will just be updated less frequently.

The History and Future of The Grinder

The Grinder has come a long way during the development of this book. Highlights of The Grinder 2 development include:

- ❑ New plug-in interface, communications layer, new statistics engine
- ❑ New Console
- ❑ HTTP plug-in re-implemented using the HTTPClient library
- ❑ HTTP plug-in support for arbitrary headers, cookies, HTTP authentication, HTTPS, dynamically generated requests
- ❑ TCPSniffer, allowing test scripts to be automatically recorded
- ❑ JUnit plug-in
- ❑ Raw socket plug-in
- ❑ Ant build environment, JUnit unit tests
- ❑ Distribution moved to Sourceforge

The Grinder 3

As we write, development has begun on The Grinder 3. This is a major piece of engineering that will address the following deficiencies in The Grinder 2.

Fixed Test Schedule

The Grinder is quite limited in that each worker process executes the tests in the test script sequentially, in a fixed order.

The Grinder 3 will address this by allowing tests to be specified using scripting languages. IBM's Bean Scripting Framework will be used to allow a variety of languages to be used including Visual Basic, Jython, and JavaScript. Plug-ins will be provided for the TCPSniffer, which will generate simple test scripts. These can then be modified to introduce arbitrary branching and looping, perhaps using the scripting languages support for random variables.

Dynamic Data

Currently the HTTP plug-in's string bean feature provides simple support for requests that contain dynamic data. The Grinder 3 will provide interfaces that allow the scripting language to create dynamic requests of arbitrary complexity.

Checking Responses

There is very limited support in some of the The Grinder 2 plug-ins for checking the results of tests. The Grinder 3 will make these results directly available to the test script. This will allow various test paths to be taken based on the responses returned by the server.

Test Script Distribution

From the Grinder 3 console you will be able to edit test scripts and then distribute them to the worker processes. It will no longer be necessary to copy `grinder.properties` files around or to use a shared disk.

Summary

In this chapter we have introduced The Grinder. We have seen how to

- ❏   Create simple test scripts.
- ❏   Use the console to control the actions of many test worker processes.
- ❏   Write Grinder plug-ins.
- ❏   Use the TCPSniffer to create test scripts.

The Grinder is easy for developers to use. We recommend that you use it as early as possible in your J2EE project. We will continue to use The Grinder throughout the rest of the book. In the next chapter we use it to test a full J2EE application.

Application Case Studies

In this chapter we will illustrate the use of the methodology described in Chapter 1 along with The Grinder, the load generation tool described in the previous chapter. The objective of this chapter is to show how the methodology can be used to find the boundaries of an application within a defined environment. The idea is that if you were to test the same application under more or less the same conditions, you should obtain more or less the same results. However, it is **not** meant as a study of the performance of the application server, thus the results presented here are not a guarantee of performance. The focus is not so much on the actual performance statistics as the fact that, using the methodology and The Grinder, you can understand the performance of your own, unique application.

We present the results of two case studies. The first one investigates the potential impact of your choice of Java Virtual Machine (JVM) on the performance of an application. We used the Java Pet Store and investigated its behavior with the following JVMs: Sun JDK 1.3.0, Sun JDK 1.2.2, IBM JDK 1.3, and JRockit 3.1.

The main focus of the chapter is on the second case study, a detailed performance test based on an e-Pizza application, first featured in the book *Java 2 Enterprise Edition Using the BEA WebLogic Server* (Wrox Press, ISBN 1-861002-99-8). This application was developed largely for didactic purposes and can be considered to be a first build. We find the limits of the application in its current state and then, based on our results and analysis, make recommendations for improvement. The e-Pizza application, and all the associated files used in this performance test, can be obtained as part of the code download for this book, from the Expert Press web site (http://www.expert-press.com).

Choosing a JVM for the Java Pet Store

To clearly illustrate the behavior of a JVM, and the way in which it interacts with an application, we present a pathological case. It is important to note that we have observed the same behavior with various combinations of single and multiple test scripts. We will not go through the setup and code files in detail because we want to focus only on the results – which prove that even something you take for granted, such as a JVM, can have a profound impact on your application.

> **Although not presented here, the Grinder string bean and the test script (`grinder.properties` file) used in these tests can be found in the `PetStore.zip` file of the code download.**

We ran our tests on version 1.0.1 of the Java Pet Store – a showcase of J2EE technologies and design patterns that is available for download from http://java.sun.com/j2ee/download.html.

We used WebLogic Server version 5.1, Service Pack 10, running on Windows NT. The reason that we chose to use version 5.1 was that we had a reasonable range of supported JVMs to choose from with this version. At the time when these tests were performed the only JVM that was certified for use with version 6.1 was Sun's JDK 1.3.1.

> *For useful information regarding platform support for JVMs, for all versions of WebLogic, please refer to the following page:*
> http://edocs.bea.com/wls/platforms/index.html#win2000AS

In our tests, WebLogic was used as the HTTP server, Servlet engine, and EJB container. The database was Oracle 8.1.7, with no optimizations, accessed with the WebLogic Type 2 JDBC driver (which is the easiest to set up for this version of WLS).

The original catalog included with the Pet Store only contains 22 pets. As we did not consider this to be large enough to do a serious performance test, we modified the catalog so that it contained 1000 pets equally distributed over 10 pet categories. The new pets use the following naming convention:

```
cXXpYYY
```

where XX is the number of the category to which the pet belongs and YYY is the actual pet number within that category. For this performance test we used categories 00 through 09 and pet numbers 000 through 099. In order to generate these pet names, we created a Grinder string bean, `PetStoreStringBean`, which contains the following methods:

Method	Description
getNewPet	Randomly creates a pet name that follows the naming convention explained above.
getLastPet	Returns the name of the pet generated the last time the getNewPet method was called.
getItem	Returns the name of the pet generated the last time the getNewPet method was called, preceded by I-. This is done to maintain the naming convention used to access the inventory table of the Pet Store.
getRegisteredUser	Generates the name of a known user of the application with the following naming convention: userGJJTTT, where G is the host ID of the Grinder, JJ is the JVM number within the Grinder process and TTT is the number of the thread within the Grinder simulating a user.
getNewUser	Generates the name of an unknown user of the application. It uses the same naming convention as getRegisteredUser, but adds three characters at the end that represent the cycle. This is done to guarantee a new user for every cycle of the test run.

For this test run we used a single test script with 33 requests. This test script assumes that all the users are registered, so we did not use the getNewUser method of the string bean. The test script performs the following requests:

- ❑ Search for a random pet
- ❑ Get details of the pet
- ❑ Search for another random pet
- ❑ Get details of the pet
- ❑ Place in the shopping cart
- ❑ Search for another random pet
- ❑ Search for a non-existent random pet
- ❑ Search for a random pet
- ❑ Get details of the pet
- ❑ Place in the shopping cart
- ❑ Check out as a random existing user
- ❑ Log out

For example, the following excerpt from the script shows the requests to search for a pet, get details of the pet and place the pet in the shopping cart:

```
grinder.test30.description=First Search
grinder.test30.sleepTime=7766
grinder.test30.parameter.url=http://wls06:7001/estore/control/search?sea
rch_text=<getNewPet>

grinder.test57.description=Product details
grinder.test57.sleepTime=1485
grinder.test57.parameter.url=http://wls06:7001/estore/control/product?pr
oduct_id=<getLastPet>

grinder.test134.description=Place in shopping cart
grinder.test134.sleepTime=2171
grinder.test134.parameter.url=http://wls06:7001/estore/control/cart?acti
on=purchaseItem&itemId=<getItem>
```

The test script was generated using the Grinder Sniffer Proxy (see Chapter 2) and then we erased all the calls for images. We did this because it is easier to deal with 33 URLs than 500, and because we can easily assume that the images are in the cache of the browser.

We set numerous other important parameters in the test script. We set 20 simultaneous users from one JVM:

```
grinder.processes=1
grinder.threads=20
grinder.cycles=0
```

We specified that the single test script will be executed with no think time variation (each request has its own think time, as you can see from the code for the individual requests. No think time variation means that The Grinder will always wait exactly that length of time before executing the request and all the simulated users will execute the request at about the same moment):

```
grinder.thread.sleepTimeVariation=0
```

Following is the line in the test script that allows us to create and use an instance of our grinder string bean:

```
grinder.plugin.parameter.stringBean=com.wrox.paston.petstore.PetStoreStr
ingBean
```

We performed tests on the following six JVMs:

- ❏ Sun JDK 1.3.0-C using the HotSpot Server, HotSpot Client, and Classic options
- ❏ Sun JDK 1.2.2
- ❏ IBM JDK 1.3
- ❏ JRockit 3.1

As indicated above, the Sun JDK 1.3.0 JVM has three high-level options that could affect the performance of the application:

❑ HotSpot Server. This option is designed to cater for the needs of applications running on the server side, having been tuned for maximum peak operating speed.

❑ HotSpot Client. This option is designed for applications running on the client side, with reduced application start-up times and a small memory footprint.

❑ Classic. This option disables HotSpot and reverts to the old JIT compiler, which Sun licensed from Symantec, and the old memory management system. This option, as such, is only available on Windows. The more platform-independent way to refer to it is "Sun JDK 1.3.0 with the -Xint option".

Our expectations were that we would obtain best performance on the Sun JDK 1.3 HotSpot Server, Sun JDK 1.3 HotSpot Client, JRockit 3.1, and the IBM JDK 1.3 JVMs – it would be a close run thing between these four. We expected the Sun JDK 1.2.2 to be a distant fifth, being a somewhat older model, and the Sun JDK 1.3 Classic, which has HotSpot disabled, to be a remote sixth.

Each JVM has available many parameters that can be modified to improve the performance, and we discuss this further at the end of this section. However, for the sake of simplicity, we decided to use them out of the box, only specifying a heap space of 128MB.

The statistics were collected using the **cycle** method and the results presented are based on 30 cycles, with the first 5 cycles excluded. We started with Sun JDK 1.3 Hotspot Server and the results were rather disappointing:

REQUEST	Approximate ART (seconds)
Commit Order	31
Place item in shopping basket (2nd time)	16
Place item in shopping basket (1st time)	9

As you can see, the most expensive request is that to commit the order, and it averaged about 31 seconds. This is very high, especially when we only have 20 simultaneous users.

At a value of 0.237, the quality indicator is close to our acceptable limit of 0.25 (see the section, *Quality of a Sample*, in Chapter 1). The network utilization averaged at about 1.5% and the CPU usage of the computer running Oracle was rather low at 5%. In the following chart you can see the CPU usage of the computer running the WebLogic Server:

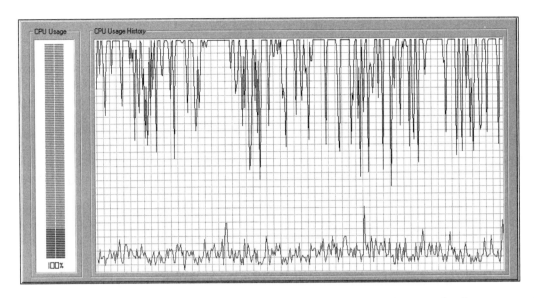

The top line represents the total utilization of the CPU and bottom is the Kernel utilization out of the total. As we can see, the CPU usage is at 100% for long periods during the execution.

We repeated these tests, exactly as above, for each JVM. The results defied many of our expectations, based on perceived JVM efficiency:

JVM	Maximum ART (ms)	Aggregate ART (ms)	Quality
JDK 1.3.0 HotSpot Server	30,991	2,267	0.237
JDK 1.3.0 HotSpot Client	10,995	926	0.139
JDK 1.3.0 Classic	6,339	537	0.220
JDK 1.2.2	2,571	186	0.142
IBM 1.3	2,062	138	0.135
JRockit 3.1	2,079	137	0.248

We were very surprised, to say the least, that disabling HotSpot produces better performance, and that using the JDK 1.2.2 could lead to better performance than with JDK 1.3. To make the point graphically, the following figure presents a screenshot of the CPU usage of the computer running the WebLogic Server with the JRockit JVM:

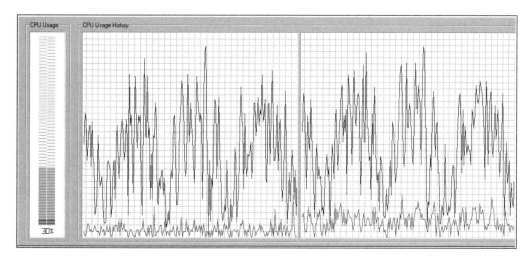

Contrast this figure with the earlier screenshot of Sun JDK 1.3 server. The trace is very spiky but you can see a hint of six execution peaks (representing six requests) with valleys in between for the think times. We are generally well below 100% usage.

> *The trace characteristics are a result of the use of no think time variation – when you don't use a think time variation all the simulated users execute the request at about the same moment. This is seen graphically as very high curves of execution with well-defined valleys (no execution) during the think time. When using a think time variation, the curves would be smoother.*

The IBM and JRockit JVMs presented similar behaviors, whereby the network usage increased to an average of 4% and the CPU usage of the computer running Oracle remained pretty much the same at an average of 5%. The only difference was on the quality indicator, where JRockit presented a much higher number because the AART curve did not stabilize until cycle 10.

At the current time we are not able to speculate on the reasons for these differences, but it is amazing that they are so dramatic. As we mentioned earlier, this is a pathological case, which we use to illustrate that even something you take for granted, such as the choice of JVM, can have a profound impact on the performance of your application. This also shows that the runtime behavior of your J2EE system can depend on its subsystems in unique and subtle ways.

Here, then, is another reason why you cannot generalize performance results, and much less extrapolate results from another application, to guess at the behavior of your own – no matter how much they look alike.

JVM Tuning

In this book, we did not wish to delve deeply into issues surrounding JVM tuning but, of course, deciding which JVM to use is not quite as simple as running your application on different JVMs and measuring which one is the fastest, although even this is something that many people do not do. Different JVMs have different options that you can set during start-up which may have an effect on the performance of your Java applications. At a high level, the most common features that can impact performance are those that relate to the configuration of the Garbage Collection (GC) and to thread management.

The most common GC options configure what GC mechanism to use, the size of the heap, and the size of the youngest generation of the heap (also known as the nursery). When you analyze the heap options try the `-verbose:gc` (Sun/IBM) or the `-Xverbose:memory` (JRockit) option when running the GC: they will give you printouts that indicate how often the JVM GCs and how long the pauses are. Naturally, you want to have as few and as short GCs as possible. Most JVMs stop the world while doing the garbage collection. If you notice that your application occasionally becomes unresponsive, this might be the case and you should consider using a concurrent garbage collector. (Sun has plans to add a concurrent garbage collector to HotSpot, and JRockit has two different concurrent GCs `-Xgc:gencon` and `-Xgc:singlecon` that you can try out.)

The thread system options usually define how Java threads are mapped to operating system threads. For example, JRockit has an option called `-Xthinthreads`, which enables an m-to-n mapping of Java threads to operating system threads on Linux and Windows. This option makes it possible for these operating systems to handle a huge number of threads.

You can find more information about the different JVMs on their respective web sites, for example http://java.sun.com/docs/hotspot/VMOptions.html and http://www.jrockit.com/download/userguide31.html.

The e-Pizza Application

The e-Pizza application models the activity of a call center for a fictitious pizza delivery company called Pizza2Go. The general idea is that customers can phone a central call center to order home delivery pizzas. So, an operator at the call center (these operators are the end users of our e-Pizza application) receives a call from a customer. The customer's phone number is entered. If the number does not exist in the database, the operator requests and enters a few details before proceeding to take the order. When the order details are committed, a fax is automatically sent to the Pizza2Go outlet that will prepare and deliver the order.

The application was originally developed to show the progression from a simple JSP and stored procedure architecture to a full J2EE architecture, introducing most of the popular J2EE APIs along the way, specifically:

❑ Simple servlets and JSPs, some of which directly access the database via JDBC.

❑ Stateless session beans, which offer services related to creating and handling the pizza order. Again, some of these beans will access the database using JDBC.

❑ A stateful session bean to keep the state of the order while it is being handled.

❑ Entity beans:

  ❑ Using Container Managed Persistence (CMP) to access some of the database tables.

  ❑ Using Bean Managed Persistence (BMP) to perform an outer join of three database tables.

Application Architecture

This diagram shows the application architecture:

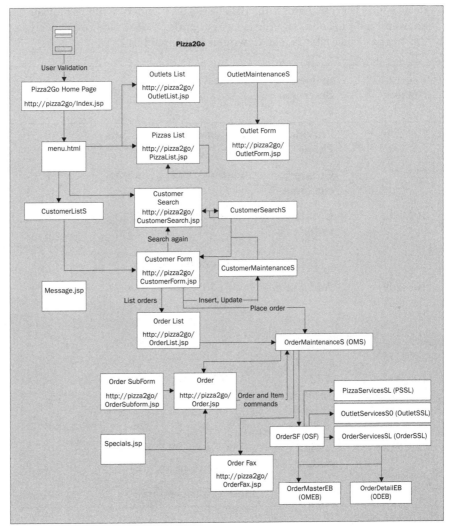

In common with most e-commerce applications, e-Pizza makes heavy use of a database. The e-Pizza database contains:

❑ Catalog data about the available pizzas, ingredients, prices, and Pizza2Go outlets in PIZZA, INGREDIENT, DOUGH, UNITS, OFFER, CONVERSION, and OUTLET tables. This information is fairly static and is only read during normal operations.

❑ Customer, order, and stock level data in the CUSTOMER, ORDER_MASTER, ORDER_DETAIL, and EXISTENCE tables. This information is both read and written.

Through analysis of the source code and JDBC logs we created the following table of the requests (these requests form part of the test scripts that we use in this chapter, which are explained in detail a little later) that access the database. The R and W symbols indicate whether the database access is read (select) or write (insert, update, delete) respectively; an asterisk indicates that the particular table is read or written to many times.

Request Number	Request Description	Request Process	R/W	Database Table
103/203	**Provide Phone**	CustomerSearchS -->	R	CUSTOMER
205	**Create customer**	CustomerMaintenanceS -->	W	CUSTOMER
105/207	**Create order**	OMS-OSF-OutletSSL -->	R	CUSTOMER
		-->	R*	OUTLET
		OSF controls commit		
107/209	**Add pizza**	OMS-OSF-PSSL -->	R*	PIZZA
		-->	R	OFFER
		-->	R	CONVERSION
		OSF controls commit		
109/211	**Add another pizza**	As 107 / 209	R*	PIZZA
			R	OFFER
			R	CONVERSION
111/213	**Assign outlet**	OMS-OSF-OMEB -->	W	ORDER_MASTER
		OMS-OSF-ODEB -->	W*	ORDER_DETAIL
		OSF controls commit		

Request Number	Request Description	Request Process	R/W	Database Table
113/215	**Commit order**	`OMS-OSF-OrderSSL-OMEB -->`	R	`ORDER_MASTER`
		`-ODEB -->`	R*	`ORDER_DETAIL`
		`-OrderSSL -->`	R*	`UNITS`
		`-->`	W*	`EXISTENCE`
		`-->`	R*	`DOUGH`
		`-OMEB -->`	W	`ORDER_MASTER`
		`OMS -->`	R	`OUTLET`
		OSF controls commit, except for read from `OUTLET`		
114/216	**Order fax**	`OrderFax.jsp-ODEB-->`	R*	`ORDER_DETAIL`
		`ODEB` controls commit		

The Request Process column describes how the database interaction occurs. For example, during request 107/209 the `OrderMaintenanceS` servlet calls the `OrderSFBean` stateful session bean, which calls the `PizzaServicesSL` stateless bean, which reads the `PIZZA`, `OFFER`, and `CONVERSION` tables.

The previous book, *Java 2 Enterprise Edition Using the BEA WebLogic Server*, uses the journey through the addition of each of these J2EE features to provide an introduction to building J2EE applications on WebLogic Server. Developers who have read that book should be equipped to write their own fully-fledged J2EE applications with robust and coherent architectures. However, the e-Pizza application, in the state provided, is essentially a "first build". While the architecture is sound, more work is required before it could be considered production-ready. Since we will define concrete performance metrics and our philosophy is to test early, this application makes an ideal target for a performance testing exercise!

Applying the Methodology

We are now ready to see how we can use our methodology, along with our load-generating tool (The Grinder) to understand the behavior of this application. As you will recall from Chapter 1, the steps we follow are as follows:

❑ **Define the performance metrics** – this should be the first thing that you do. Never performance test an application with the objective of "making it go as fast as possible". You must have concrete and realistic goals in mind and develop to those goals.

❏ **Define the test scripts** – you must understand **how** the application will be used, via detailed usage profiles. This must then be accurately reflected in the test scripts (the `grinder.properties` files) so that our test conditions reflect the live environment as closely as possible.

❏ **Define the sampling method and associated metrics** – the logistics of how you will actually collect your performance data.

❏ **Perform the tests** – you will generally perform a series of preliminary tests that will allow you to get a feel for the behavior of the application under various conditions and to optimize the environment for that particular application. From this foundation, you can then set out and execute a structured series of detailed tests, to enable you to collect all of the data you need to produce an accurate performance statement for the application.

We started by defining the performance metrics for the e-Pizza application.

Defining Performance Metrics

In the case of e-Pizza, our performance metric takes the form of a **maximum acceptable response time** – the maximum length of time for the results of a request to be returned to the end user (the call-center operator who takes the pizza order). Based on an informal survey of call centers, we chose to use **three seconds** as the maximum acceptable response time for the performance test. Generally we would make allowance for slow connections (over the Internet) and traffic other than that generated by the use of the application, and consequently set the maximum ART in our tests somewhat below the required three seconds. However, since this application ran on a private intranet, the assumption was that there would be very little traffic other than that generated by running the application, so we stuck to the value of three seconds.

We estimated a reasonable user load under production conditions to be 100 operators. However, one of the objectives of the performance test was to find out how many simultaneous operators the application could handle before we reach our performance limit.

Usage Profiles

As discussed in Chapter 1, this (and the subsequent definition of a test script) is one of the most important steps of the methodology. The way the application works is as follows. A customer telephones a call center operator to place an order. The operator requests the customer's telephone number and enters it into the system (the phone number format follows the North American convention whereby the area code is always three digits and the phone number is always 7 digits). The telephone number of the caller is the "access key" of the system. If the number already exists in the system, this means that the customer is already registered and the order can proceed directly. If the number is unknown, the system must register the new customer, which requires that the customer provide certain details in order to ensure successful delivery and payment.

Thus, we determined two usage profiles, which together represent the majority of the end user (operator) interactions with the application:

- **Registered customer** – when the customer placing the order is already known to the application, in which case it is not necessary to request any user-related information (such as the address). This profile accounts for approximately 70% of typical application usage.

- **New customer** – when the customer placing the order is not known to the system, and therefore we need to gather the relevant customer information. This profile accounts for approximately 30% of typical application usage.

Once the customer is registered, the order can be placed and the sequence of events is the same for both profiles. First, a new order is created. When that order is submitted, the application assigns it to the outlet closest to the customer. Before the order is finalized the application verifies that the assigned outlet has sufficient stock to fulfill the order. If so, then the order is closed and a fax detailing the order is sent to the outlet.

Once you have a good appreciation of how your application will be used, then you must decide how to translate that to the tests. You want the test to accurately reflect real-world conditions but without overcomplicating them by trying to cover every conceivable scenario. For example, in converting our profiles to test scripts we made two simplifications:

- The size of the order is always two pizzas – although it would have been interesting to investigate a wide range of order sizes at some stage, it would have greatly complicated matters, so in our tests a caller always requested two pizzas, which represents a typical order size for Pizza2Go.

- We did not generate different pizzas for each order – since this will have a negligible impact on the actual functioning of the application.

However, we want to accurately simulate the usage profile established above for registered and new customers. In order to do this, we need a way of generating unique phone numbers, both known and unknown to the system, for which we use a Grinder **string bean**.

The Grinder String Bean

In order to simulate both new and registered customers, we need a way to generate unique phone numbers, each of which can be compared to a set of numbers we have already entered into the database. If a match is found, we are simulating a registered customer. Otherwise, the customer is new.

As discussed in Chapter 2, a simple way to achieve this is to take advantage of a feature of the Grinder HTTP plug-in, called **string beans**. In order to simulate our two usage profiles, our e-Pizza string bean has three key methods:

- `getPhone` – generates a number that is guaranteed to already exist in the database.

- `getNewPhone` – generates a number that is guaranteed **not** to exist in the database.

❑   getLastPhone – returns the last phone number generated by the getNewPhone method. Our New Customer test script can then generate customer details associated with this number.

With inclusion of the appropriate line in our test script (grinder.properties) files we can then call instances of our string bean and invoke these methods. Let's take a look at the full source code for the string bean, EPizzaStringBean, and then we'll discuss the getPhone and getNewPhone methods in more detail (we'll see how getLastPhone is used when we describe the New Customer test script a little later):

```
package com.wrox.paston.epizza;

import java.text.DecimalFormat;
import java.text.NumberFormat;
import java.util.Random;

import net.grinder.common.Test;
import net.grinder.plugininterface.PluginException;
import net.grinder.plugininterface.PluginThreadContext;
import net.grinder.plugin.http.StringBean;


public class EPizzaStringBean implements StringBean
{
    private static NumberFormat s_twoDP = new DecimalFormat("00");
    private static NumberFormat s_threeDP = new DecimalFormat("000");

    private PluginThreadContext m_pluginThreadContext;
    private String m_lastPhone = "3214567";
    private String m_hostIDString;
    private String m_processIDString;

    public void initialize (PluginThreadContext pluginThreadContext)
     throws PluginException
    {
     m_pluginThreadContext = pluginThreadContext;
     final String grinderIDString = m_pluginThreadContext.getGrinderID();
     final int split = grinderIDString.lastIndexOf('-');

     if (split > 0)
     {
        // Restrict hostID to a single character - hopefully its
numeric!
        m_hostIDString = grinderIDString.substring(split-1, split);
     }
     else
     {
        m_hostIDString = "";
     }

     if (split >= 0)
```

```
        {
          m_processIDString = grinderIDString.substring(split + 1);

          // Restrict processID to single digit
          m_processIDString.substring(m_processIDString.length()-1);
        }
        else
        {
          m_processIDString = "";
        }
    }

    public void beginCycle () {}

    public boolean doTest(Test test) { return false; }

    public void endCycle () {}

    /**
     * Phone format HPTTCCC
     **/
    public String getNewPhone()
    {
    m_lastPhone =
        m_hostIDString + m_processIDString +
        s_twoDP.format(m_pluginThreadContext.getThreadID()) +
        s_threeDP.format(m_pluginThreadContext.getCurrentCycleID());

    return m_lastPhone;
    }

    public String getLastPhone()
    {
    return m_lastPhone;
    }

    /**
     * Phone format 555HPTT
     **/
    public String getPhone()
    {
    return "555" +
        m_hostIDString + m_processIDString +
        s_twoDP.format(m_pluginThreadContext.getThreadID());
    }
}
```

Please refer to Chapter 2 for details on what the `initialize`, `beginCycle`, `endCycle` and `doTest` methods do and when they are called.

The getPhone Method

As discussed, this method generated a phone number that is guaranteed to find a match in the database. It is created according to the following format:

```
555GHTT
```

Where G stands for the last character of the Grinder host ID, H stands for the last digit of the Grinder process ID, and TT stands for the thread ID number. This information is available in the Grinder properties file. So, if we have a Grinder machine with ID number 3, running 2 JVMs each with 25 threads (in other words, 50 simulated users), then the sequence of telephone numbers generated will be 5553000 through to 5553024 for the first JVM and 5553100 to 5553124 for the second.

Using these rules, we know exactly which phone numbers we need to create in the corresponding database tables, for every test run.

This method has some limitations. Since we want to ensure that we have one user per telephone number, the Grinder should not run with more than ten JVMs. JVM 10 and JVM 0 will give rise to the same value of H (namely, 0) and duplicate numbers will be generated. Secondly, and for the same reason, the Grinder should not run with more than 100 threads (users) per JVM.

The getNewPhone Method

It would be simple to generate numbers guaranteed **not** to be in the database using the same scheme as above – say, 444GHTT. However, the numbers generated would only not exist in the database for the first cycle (complete execution of the test script). For example, a simulated customer generated by grinder 3, JVM ID number 0, and thread 17 will be identified by a phone number of 4443016. The NC script will generate customer details for this number and they will be entered into the database. On the second cycle the same number will be generated and it will now already exist in the database. Thus, we modified the rules so that numbers generated by this method had the following format:

```
GHTTCCC
```

Where G, H, and TT are defined as in the getPhone method, and CCC is the **cycle number**. In this manner, we can guarantee that a unique phone number is generated for every cycle. For our Grinder ID number of 3, the JVM number of 0, and thread 17: on the first cycle it will generate the number 3016000. On the second cycle it will generate 3016001, and so on. This method has the same limitations as the previous one, plus the limitation that it cannot be executed more than 1,000 times, otherwise it will wrap around.

Test Scripts

Let's now move on to look at the actual test scripts that execute the series of requests that simulate typical end user interaction with the application. According to our usage profile we need two test scripts: one Registered Customer (RC) script and one New Customer (NC) script. The ratio of the number of registered users to new users should be 70:30.

The series of requests for the test scripts in this chapter were generated using the sniffer proxy utility of The Grinder (see Chapter 2, *Using the TCP Sniffer to Create Test Scripts*, for details). However, at the start of every test script, we must ourselves define several key properties.

We uniquely identify a Grinder instance:

```
# E-Pizza test script
grinder.hostID=1
```

We run the JVM in interpreted mode only (on NT it can also be invoked by using the -classic option):

```
grinder.jvm.arguments=-Xint
```

We use interpreted mode only to make absolutely sure that The Grinder generates the load in a consistent fashion. When using HotSpot, it is possible that by the end of the test runs the generation would be a little faster than at the beginning.

We specify 70 simultaneous users from one JVM and run forever:

```
grinder.processes=1
grinder.threads=70
grinder.cycles=0
```

We identify addresses and ports for the Grinder instance and the Grinder console (in the code below, control is the name of the computer where The Grinder console is running). We also specify that we will start and stop each Grinder from the console and that we report real-time data to the console:

```
grinder.receiveConsoleSignals=true
grinder.grinderAddress=228.1.1.1
grinder.grinderPort=1234

grinder.reportToConsole=true
grinder.consoleAddress=control
grinder.consolePort=6372
```

We store our performance data in a directory called log:

```
grinder.logDirectory=log
grinder.appendLog=false
grinder.logProcessStreams=false
```

Each run generates two files: data_2-0.log and out_2-0.log. The data file contains the actual response time for every simulated user (thread) for every request for every cycle.

The out file contains a summary of the results. If we set logProcessStreams=true it will also contain full details of what every thread has done while executing the test script (rather lengthy and used only for debugging).

Every time an individual request fails, an HTML page is generated in the log directory, named in such a fashion that we can identify not only the request that failed, but also the exact thread and cycle that failed. For example, the following indicates a failure of the Customer Search request (202), executed by thread 20 (30 threads in total, numbered 0 to 29) on the first cycle:

```
page_2-0_20_0_202_Customer search
```

In order that the simulated clients don't all start at the same time, we have staggered the execution start time for each thread over a period of five seconds. We call this the initial spread or spread time. We define it as follows:

```
grinder.thread.initialSleepTime=5000
```

The effect of this is that each thread will wait a random length of time, between 0 and 5000 milliseconds, before executing the first cycle.

The Grinder allows us to vary the length of time to wait between the executions of successive URLs in the script (the think time). For example:

```
grinder.thread.sleepTimeVariation=0.20
```

Here, we set a 20% variation on the think time. The Grinder will select a value for the think time that is somewhere between 20% below or 20% above the specified value, according to a normal distribution. We feel that this makes for a more realistic simulation.

We set a host of other parameters, most of which are self-explanatory:

```
# User the HTTP Plugin with HTTP Client model
grinder.plugin=net.grinder.plugin.http.HttpPlugin
grinder.plugin.parameter.useHTTPClient=true

# Use cookies, no HTML debugging
grinder.plugin.parameter.useCookies=true
grinder.plugin.parameter.logHTML=false
```

Finally, the following line of code allows us to call an instance of our string bean:

```
grinder.plugin.parameter.stringBean=com.wrox.paston.epizza.EPizzaStringBean
```

With these parameters defined, we can then specify each individual request that the script should execute.

The Registered Customer Test Script

As described above, we must specify the appropriate parameters for this script. Here, we specify:

```
grinder.hostID=1
```

and:

```
grinder.threads=70
```

All other parameters are as described in the previous section. Let's walk through each request in the RC test script. We start with the first request:

```
grinder.test101.description=Home Page
grinder.test101.sleepTime=1000
grinder.test101.parameter.url=http://wls02:7001/c05/index.jsp
```

The think time for this first request is 1000 milliseconds. Thus, the worker thread will wait this length of time (plus or minus 20%) before executing the request. The second line defines the URL to be requested. In this case it will request index.jsp, which is the home page of the application. This presents a menu with the actions the Pizza2Go operator can perform. The first line simply adds a description so that it is easy to understand what this test does when looking at the console of The Grinder.

You will also notice that we chose to number this request 101, rather than just 1. Each request in the RC script is numbered sequentially starting at 101, and the request numbering in the NC script starts at 201. This makes it easy to monitor the execution process on the console of The Grinder and, furthermore, if we had used an identical numbering system in each script, then The Grinder console would have presented compound results for each pair of identically-numbered URLs and we would have been unable to distinguish the results of one test script from the other.

From the home page, the operator clicks on the **Customer Search** button, which requests the following JSP:

```
grinder.test102.description=Customer search
grinder.test102.sleepTime=2032
grinder.test102.parameter.url=http://wls02:7001/c05/CustomerSearch.jsp
```

The sniffer proxy generates the individual think time (sleepTime) for each request. Bear in mind that the total sleep time for a test script will obviously have a bearing on how long the test script takes to execute.

The next request asks the operator to input the telephone number of the caller. This is an HTTP POST operation and the arguments are in the file defined on the last line of the following request:

```
grinder.test103.description=Provide phone
grinder.test103.sleepTime=6953
grinder.test103.parameter.url=http://wls02:7001/c05/CustomerSearchS
grinder.test103.parameter.header.Content-Type=application/x-www-form-
urlencoded
grinder.test103.parameter.post=old-post-phone.dat
```

The content of the `old-post-phone.dat` file is as follows:

```
c_country_code=1&c_area_code=305&c_phone=<getPhone>&Submit=Search
```

As you can see, here is where we call the `getPhone` method of the Grinder string bean. The line:

```
grinder.test103.parameter.header.Content-Type=application/x-www-form-
urlencoded
```

is generated by the browser for every POST operation (recall that we generated the script using the sniffer proxy) and is omitted from the code listing from here onwards.

The next URL is used to produce the response of the operation:

```
grinder.test104.description=Existing customer
grinder.test104.sleepTime=62
grinder.test104.parameter.url=http://wls02:7001/c05/CustomerForm.jsp
```

Since the phone number belongs to an existing customer, the response will always present the information for that customer. Once the operator has the customer details, a new order can be created (by clicking the corresponding button):

```
grinder.test105.description=Add order
grinder.test105.sleepTime=3438
grinder.test105.parameter.url=http://wls02:7001/c05/OrderMaintenanceS
grinder.test105.parameter.post=old-post-addorder.dat
```

This calls the `OrderMaintenanceS` servlet, which in turn creates a stateful session bean called `OrderSF`, which will maintain the state of the order as it is filled. The content of the `old-post-addorder.dat` file is simply:

```
command=Add+Order
```

The response of this servlet is given by a JSP, as follows:

```
grinder.test106.description=Order created
grinder.test106.sleepTime=156
grinder.test106.parameter.url=http://wls02:7001/c05/OrderForm.jsp
```

Now we are ready to add pizzas to the order:

```
grinder.test107.description=Add a pizza
grinder.test107.sleepTime=3891
grinder.test107.parameter.url=http://wls02:7001/c05/OrderMaintenanceS
grinder.test107.parameter.post=old-post-pizza1.dat

grinder.test108.description=Pizza OK
grinder.test108.sleepTime=47
grinder.test108.parameter.url=http://wls02:7001/c05/OrderForm.jsp

grinder.test109.description=Add another pizza
grinder.test109.sleepTime=9656
grinder.test109.parameter.url=http://wls02:7001/c05/OrderMaintenanceS
grinder.test109.parameter.post=old-post-pizza2.dat

grinder.test110.description=Pizza OK
grinder.test110.sleepTime=297
grinder.test110.parameter.url=http://wls02:7001/c05/OrderForm.jsp
```

As described previously, in our simulation every order is for two pizzas (and the same two pizzas in every case). Thus, the `old-post-pizza1.dat` file contains the following:

```
Pizza=Calabrese&Size=Medium&Dough=Classic&Quantity=1&command=Add
```

and the corresponding `-pizza2.dat` file contains:

```
od_number=0&Pizza=Romana&Size=Large&Dough=Thin+Crust&Quantity=1&command=Add
```

In the next step the operator clicks on the **Update Order** button, which assigns the order to the customer's closest outlet and specifies whether the order is for delivery or pick-up. The corresponding requests are:

```
grinder.test111.description=Assign outlet
grinder.test111.sleepTime=3906
grinder.test111.parameter.url=http://wls02:7001/c05/OrderMaintenanceS
grinder.test111.parameter.post=old-post-update.dat

grinder.test112.sleepTime=47
grinder.test112.parameter.url=http://wls02:7001/c05/OrderForm.jsp
grinder.test112.description=Outlet OK
```

The contents of `old-post-update` are as follows:

```
od_number=0&Delivery=Address&Remarks=&command=Update+Order&or_o_outlet_code=0
```

Next, we simulate the action that occurs when the operator clicks on the **Deliver Order** button. The application verifies that there is enough inventory in the selected outlet to fulfill the order, closes the order, and sends a fax to the outlet with the details of the order:

```
grinder.test113.description=Commit order
grinder.test113.sleepTime=1656
grinder.test113.parameter.url=http://wls02:7001/c05/OrderMaintenanceS
grinder.test113.parameter.post=old-post-deliver.dat

grinder.test114.description=Send fax
grinder.test114.sleepTime=219
grinder.test114.parameter.url=http://wls02:7001/c05/OrderFax.jsp
```

The contents of `old-post-deliver` are as follows:

```
od_number=0&Delivery=Address&Remarks=&or_o_outlet_code=0&command=Deliver
```

Finally, the operator goes back to the main menu and cancels the session with this user by performing what is (slightly misleadingly!) called a logout. The logout operation invalidates the session and destroys all of the session state:

```
grinder.test115.description=Go back
grinder.test115.sleepTime=2437
grinder.test115.parameter.url=
                http://wls02:7001/c05/OrderMaintenanceS?command=Current

grinder.test116.description=Show menu
grinder.test116.sleepTime=16
grinder.test116.parameter.url=http://wls02:7001/c05/OrderForm.jsp

grinder.test117.description=Logout
grinder.test117.sleepTime=3078
grinder.test117.parameter.url=http://wls02:7001/c05/Logout.jsp
```

The New Customer Test Script

Again, we must specify the appropriate parameters for this script. Here, we specify:

```
grinder.hostID=2
```

and:

```
grinder.threads=30
```

All other parameters are as described in the *Test Scripts* section. The NC test script differs from that for a registered customer only in that the telephone number provided when the customer search is performed does not exist in the database, so the information for the customer must be inserted. This is the section that differs from the RC script (Content-Type lines that are generated by the browser for the POST operations are omitted):

```
grinder.test203.description=Provide phone
grinder.test203.sleepTime=10125
grinder.test203.parameter.url=http://sun1:7001/c05/CustomerSearchS
grinder.test203.parameter.post=new-post-phone.dat

grinder.test204.description=Non-existent
grinder.test204.sleepTime=47
grinder.test204.parameter.url=http://sun1:7001/c05/CustomerForm.jsp

grinder.test205.description=Add info
grinder.test205.sleepTime=25922
grinder.test205.parameter.url=http://sun1:7001/c05/CustomerMaintenanceS
grinder.test205.parameter.post=new-post-info.dat

grinder.test206.description=Customer created
grinder.test206.sleepTime=94
grinder.test206.parameter.url=http://sun1:7001/c05/CustomerForm.jsp
```

The new-post-phone.dat file contains:

```
c_country_code=1&c_area_code=415&c_phone=<getNewPhone>&Submit=Search
```

As you can see, here we are calling the getNewPhone method instead of the getPhone method. We have a different area code just to be sure that it is a non-existent phone number. The new-post-info.dat file for the POST operation of test 205 contains the information of the new customer:

```
c_country_code=1&c_area_code=415&c_phone=<getLastPhone>&c_first_name=First
\
&c_last_name=Last&c_postal_code=95123&c_address_line_1=123+High+St.\
&c_address_line_2=&c_remarks=&c_city=Leeds&c_major_cr=Maple+St.&c_colonia=
\
&c_state=CA&c_country=USA&command=Insert
```

We need to create the customer record for the same phone number for which the search was done, so we use the getLastPhone method, which just returns the same phone number that was created the last time the getNewPhone method was called. Since changing address details will not have any significant impact on the functioning of the application we can afford the luxury of always repeating the same information.

The remainder of the test script is the same as that for a registered customer, but with different think times, as recorded by the sniffer proxy. The request that handles the commit of the order is now request 215. There are a total of 19 requests in this test script.

The Test Environment

The hardware configuration for the performance tests in this chapter was as follows:

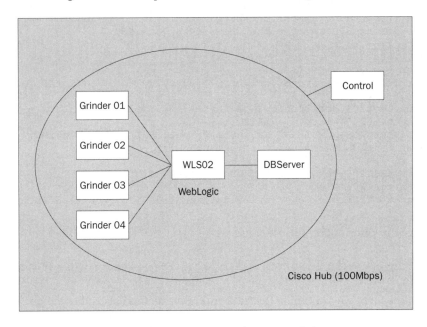

Full descriptions of the machines used in these tests (memory, disk space, operating system, available software, and so on) can be found in Appendix B – simply refer to the name of the machine (Grinder01, WLS02, and so on).

The workload was generated using four client machines, each running The Grinder 2.8.1. Grinder01 and Grinder03 ran the RC test script and the other two ran the NC script. Each Grinder machine used the Sun JDK 1.3.1 with the -Xint option.

Our application server was WebLogic Server version 6.1 with Service Pack 2, running as a managed server on Windows NT. For these tests, WebLogic functioned as the HTTP server, Servlet/JSP engine, and EJB container. For the JSP compilation, we used the Jikes 1.15 compiler (http://oss.software.ibm.com/developerworks/opensource/jikes/), as we have found it to be substantially faster than javac when compiling on the fly. Since this application will run on an intranet we decided not to use the option of logging HTTP access. The heap space for the Java Virtual Machine was defined as -ms64m -mx64m.

For data access we decided to use the Type 4 JDBC driver from Oracle, known as the Thin Driver, rather than the WebLogic Type 2 JDBC driver (jDriver). The application has one connection pool with the following parameters:

❑ Initial capacity 30

❑ Maximum capacity 30

The database we used was Oracle 8.1.7.0.0 in the default state (out-of-the-box). We performed no optimizations on the database server or tables. We are aware that performance can be increased with some standard database tuning but the exact figures will always vary depending on **your** database server configuration, and it is not the objective of this case study to teach database tuning. However, we do analyze the e-Pizza application and its use of the database, and make recommendations for improvements, after we have completed our performance tests.

Basically, we were defining the limits of our application with our particular setup and environment. You will be able to do the same for your setup and gauge for yourself just how big an impact basic application and database tuning has on the performance figures.

Selecting the Sampling Method

The main aim here was to establish a technique that could be used for every detailed performance test that models real-world conditions. As described previously, in order to simulate the variable length of time that elapses between requests, depending on the user, we used a 20% variation on the think time for these tests. When performance testing an application, we prefer to use the *fixed cycle* method of data collection – one cycle being one complete execution of a test script. As described in Chapter 1, we aim for a total test time of one hour. Thus, when we run the first test, we simply record the time it takes for the last request of the slowest script to be executed and this roughly defines the number of cycles to be performed. For example, we found that, for 100 users, the slowest test script (in this case the NC script) took approximately 95 seconds to complete. Therefore, we determined that if we collected our data over 30 cycles, then our test run would last approximately 47 minutes (this rose to 1 hour and 10 minutes for 400 simultaneous users). We felt that 30 cycles represented a reasonable testing period and a reasonable statistical sample

Note, however, that we actually set the number of cycles to be somewhat higher than this. We then wait until 30 cycles have been completed on the slowest test script, at which moment we take all the screenshots we need and stop The Grinder. The reason for doing this is that we want the application to be running under the full workload for every one of the 30 cycles. If we set The Grinder to run for exactly 30 cycles, then inevitably the last few cycles would be carried out under a lesser load as the simulated users start to finish their work.

> *Note that we also have to decide how many of these 30 cycles will be **excluded** from the performance statistics – we will discuss this a little later.*

For certain tests, we are more interested in making accurate comparisons than with simulating the real-world conditions – for example, when assessing the best choice of JVM for the application. In these cases, we use the established cycle method but with **zero variation in think time**. We have many simultaneous users, each user executing requests in the test script at the same time as every other user. This means that the "spread" in the timings is much lower so we can get more accurate results. Of course, for a given user load, such conditions will put the application and the database under considerably greater stress than for the corresponding load using a think time variation (thus we would expect longer response times).

Of course, if we are only running preliminary tests to get a feel for the behavior of the application, then we do not want each test to last an hour. In this case, it is more appropriate to use the *fixed time* (or *snapshot*) method – collecting data for a specified, short time period, regardless of whether or not a particular cycle is completed. We continuously take fixed-sized samples of data. For example we could use five seconds as the sample size and collect 120 samples (ten minutes). These tests would again use a 20% variation on the think time.

Setting Up and Running the Tests

To set up and run the tests we need to follow these steps on the various computers that make up our test environment. The instructions given here specifically detail the cycle method, but the process is basically the same for the fixed time method.

Setting Up the Database Schema

On the *dbserver* computer we must reset the database schema **before the start** of each new test. It is very important that all the test runs happen under the same conditions. Thus for every test run we "initialize" the database – drop all of the tables, create them again, and populate them with the test data. Also, at the end of each test run, we erase all of the log files that have been produced.

To initialize the database, we provide the `pizzaloader.cmd` file, which can be found in the `EPizzaData.zip` file of the code download folder for this chapter. This file contains instructions for an Oracle database to drop the existing tables (which will fail the first time the script is executed), create the tables, and populate the tables with the minimum necessary data (including the required telephone numbers, as described in the *The Grinder String Bean* section):

```
@ECHO OFF

rem this scripts loads the data in Oracle for the E-Pizza application

set SQLLDRSILENT="silent=feedback"

sqlplus pizzaman/password @pizzatables.sql

rem Load data

sqlldr silent=feedback userid=pizzaman/password control=customer.ctl
sqlldr silent=feedback userid=pizzaman/password control=ingredient.ctl
```

```
sqlldr silent=feedback userid=pizzaman/password control=pizza.ctl
sqlldr silent=feedback userid=pizzaman/password control=units.ctl
sqlldr silent=feedback userid=pizzaman/password control=existence.ctl

sqlplus pizzaman/password @inserts.sql
```

Simply open the command file and all of the above executes automatically (of course you will need to modify the file to supply the correct username and password).

As you can see, the tables are dropped then recreated via the `pizzatables.sql` script and then the data is loaded using the SQL*LOADER, or SQLLDR, utility (Oracle's high-speed, bulk data loader). Also contained in the `EPizzaData` file are the control files and data files required by SQLLDR to bulk load the data. Each control (`.ctl`) file references the appropriate data (`.dat`) file using the `INFILE` command. For example, the following is an excerpt from the `customer.ctl` file:

```
load data
infile "customer.dat"
into table customer
  FIELDS TERMINATED BY ',' OPTIONALLY ENCLOSED BY '"'

(
  c_country_code   ,
  c_area_code      ,
  c_phone          ,
....
```

The `customer.dat` file simply contains the rows of data to be loaded, for example:

```
"1","305","5551000","First","Last","33180","123 High
St.","","","Miami","","","FL","USA","5551000","5551000","","","","0","pi
zzaman@pizza2go.com"
```

As you can see, this is where we load the required phone numbers into the database. The remainder of the tables, for which only minimal data is required, are populated from the `inserts.sql` script.

Configuring and Starting WebLogic Server

The next step is to deploy the e-Pizza application, packaged in the `pizza2.ear` file, to your WebLogic Server.

For reference purposes, here we provide the `config.xml` files for our WebLogic Server machines, wls02 and control. These can be tailored to your setup. For example, if you are not using a WLS administrative server in your tests, then the information regarding the control computer can simply be omitted from our file.

The control computer housed the WebLogic Server, which was the administrative server for all the WebLogic Servers used in our performance tests. The `config.xml` file for an administrative server contains all the information for the WebLogic Server that hosts the e-Pizza application (wls02). Our configuration file is as follows:

```xml
<?xml version="1.0" encoding="UTF-8"?>
<Domain Name="uklab">
    <Server Name="control">
        <Log FileName="control.log" Name="control"/>
        <SSL Name="control"/>
        <ServerStart Name="control"/>
        <WebServer LoggingEnabled="false" Name="control"/>
        <KernelDebug Name="control"/>
        <ServerDebug Name="control"/>
        <ExecuteQueue Name="default" ThreadCount="15"/>
    </Server>

    <Log FileName="uklab.log" Name="uklab"/>
    <JTA Name="uklab"/>
    <SNMPAgent Name="uklab"/>
    <PasswordPolicy Name="wl_default_password_policy"/>
    <Machine Name="wls02">
        <NodeManager Name="wls02"/>
    </Machine>
    <ApplicationManager Name="uklab"/>
    <Realm FileRealm="wl_default_file_realm" Name="wl_default_realm"/>
    <Security Name="uklab" PasswordPolicy="wl_default_password_policy"
Realm="wl_default_realm"/>

    <Server AcceptBacklog="600" JavaCompiler="jikes" Machine="wls02"
Name="wls02">
        <Log FileName="wls02.log" Name="wls02"/>
        <SSL Name="wls02"/>
        <ServerStart Name="wls02"/>
        <WebServer LoggingEnabled="false" Name="wls02"/>
        <KernelDebug Name="wls02"/>
        <ExecuteQueue Name="default" ThreadCount="25"/>
        <ServerDebug Name="wls02"/>
    </Server>

    <Application Deployed="true" Name="epizza"
Path=".\config\uklab\applications\epizza.ear">
        <EJBComponent Name="pizzaEJB"
            Targets="control,wls02" URI="pizzaEJB.jar"/>
        <WebAppComponent Name="pizza"
            Targets="wls02" URI="pizza.war"/>
    </Application>

    <JDBCConnectionPool DriverName="oracle.jdbc.driver.OracleDriver"
        InitialCapacity="30" MaxCapacity="30" Name="p2gPool"
        Password="{3DES}A4JSP5HjN51EukSbAfpdDA=="
        Properties="user=pizzaman" Targets="wls02"
URL="jdbc:oracle:thin:@DBSERVER:1521:UKLAB"/>
</Domain>
```

Now we go to the computer named WLS02 and start the WebLogic Server with a slightly modified version of the `startManagedWebLogic.cmd` script that is included with the product. The main difference is in the following lines:

```
REM Use Jikes instead of javac
set PATH=C:\jikes1.15\bin;%PATH%
```

```
%JAVA_HOME%\bin\java -hotspot -ms64m -mx64m -classpath %CLASSPATH% \
-Dweblogic.Domain=chapter3 \
-Dbea.home="C:\bea" \
-Dweblogic.management.password=%WLS_PW% \
-Dweblogic.ProductionModeEnabled=true \
-Dweblogic.Name=wls02 \
-Dweblogic.management.server=http://control:7001 \
-Djava.security.policy==C:\bea\wlserver6.1sp2\lib\weblogic.policy \
weblogic.Server
```

As discussed earlier, we used the Jikes 1.15 compiler as we have found it to be substantially faster than javac when compiling on the fly.

Setting up The Grinder

If you are not familiar with The Grinder, please refer to Chapter 2 for details – in particular we suggest you run through the simple example in the *Getting Started* section of that chapter. In our lab, we ran the Grinder console on the control computer and had four dedicated Grinder machines. The following instructions reflect that setup. For example, we generated a total load of 100 users, split according to the expected 70:30 usage ratio for registered customers:new customers as follows:

❑ Grinder01 and Grinder03, each with one JVM and 35 threads, running the Registered Customer test script (70 users).

❑ Grinder02 and Grinder04, each with one JVM and 15 threads, running the New Customer test script (30 users).

However, it is perfectly feasible to run the tests from a single machine. In this case we suggest that you simply create three separate directories named console, New Customer, and Registered Customer.

On the *control* computer, start the console of The Grinder:

```
C:\>cd c:\grinder\grinder-tests\ch03\console

C:\Grinder\grinder-tests\Ch03\console>grindersetenv

C:\Grinder\grinder-tests\Ch03\console>set JAVA_HOME=C:\jdk1.3

C:\Grinder\grinder-tests\Ch03\console>set PATH=.;C:\jdk1.3\bin;
```

115

```
C:\Grinder\grinder-tests\Ch03\console>set
CLASSPATH=.;C:\jdk1.3;C:\jdk1.3\lib;c:\Grinder\grinder-2.8
.1\lib\grinder.jar;

C:\Grinder\grinder-tests\Ch03\console>java net.grinder.Console
```

The Grinder console will appear. Once the console has started, select File | Options and set the Console Address to the name of the machine hosting The Grinder. Next, make sure that the fields related to the sample metrics are correctly set. Clear the How many samples to ignore field so that The Grinder will only ignore the first one (this is the minimum number that it can ignore) and clear the field that specifies how many samples to collect. With this setting, The Grinder will collect samples forever, until we click on the stop button. Alternatively, we can set a specified number of samples:

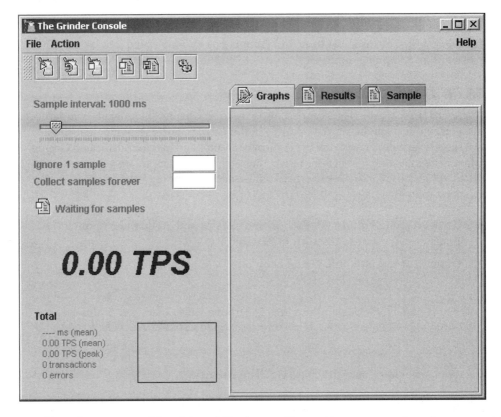

In your New Customer and Registered Customer directories you must place the appropriate test scripts (grinder.properties files). Remember that the grinder.properties file for every Grinder computer is different. Even though the tests scripts are the same for grinder01 and grinder03, and for grinder02 and grinder04, they all have a different value for the grinder.hostID parameter.

> The `grinder.properties` files that we used, along with the `performance-client.jar` file and the required `.dat` files, are supplied in the `test scripts.zip` file of the code download for this chapter.

Then we go to each Grinder computer and start The Grinder process:

```
export CLASSPATH=/home/grinder/shared/grinder-2.8.2/lib/grinder.jar:\
../performance-client.jar
java -Xint net.grinder.Grinder
```

The file `performance-client.jar` contains the Grinder string bean we use for this performance test. Alternatively, when running on Windows, we could execute:

```
C:\>cd c:\grinder\grinder-tests\ch03\Registered Customer

C:\Grinder\grinder-tests\Ch03\Registered Customer>grindersetenv

C:\Grinder\grinder-tests\Ch03\Registered Customer>set JAVA_HOME=C:\jdk1.3

C:\Grinder\grinder-tests\Ch03\Registered Customer>set
PATH=.;C:\jdk1.3\bin;

C:\Grinder\grinder-tests\Ch03\Registered Customer>set
CLASSPATH=.;C:\jdk1.3;C:\jdk1.3\lib;c:\Grinder\grinder-
2.8.1\lib\grinder.jar;

C:\Grinder\grinder-tests\Ch03\Registered Customer> java -Xint
net.grinder.Grinder
```

In the above example, we have performed `jar xf performance-client.jar` directly in the **Registered Customer** directory, which will also house all of the appropriate `.dat` files, such as `old-post-phone.dat`. If successful, the Grinder will start up and the following message will be displayed:

```
24/04/02 15:57:54: Grinder Process (1-0) waiting for console signal
```

If you flick back to the console screen, you will see listed each of the requests defined in the `grinder.properties` file:

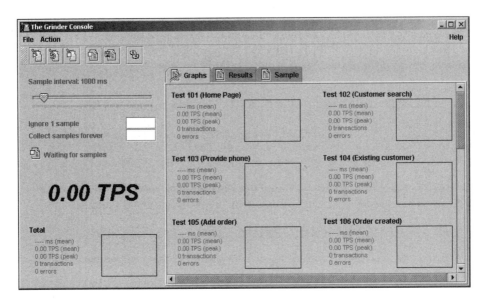

The same procedure should be followed for the New Customers.

Starting the Test

Before we start the actual test run by clicking on the start button of the Grinder console, we verify that all the simulated users required for the test are ready to go. If you are running with version 2.8.2 of The Grinder (or later) you will see that a Processes tab has been added. The following screenshot shows there are 100 simulated users ready to go, 35 of them on host ID 1, JVM 0, and host ID 3, JVM and 15 users on host ID 2, JVM 0, and host ID 4, JVM 0.

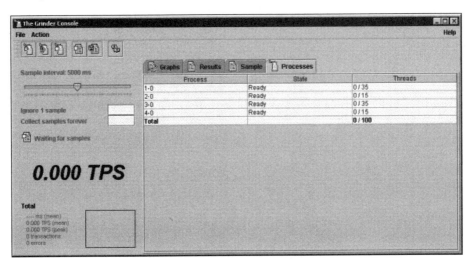

Stopping the Test

To stop the actual test run we wait until the slowest test script has completed 30 cycles. Since we don't know when the slowest test script will complete the 30 cycles, we use the information displayed in the Grinder console to figure this out. In this case the slowest test script is the one for the new customer, so we observe the console for Request 219. When this request reaches a total of 900 transactions (the addition of successful and failed transactions – errors as they are cataloged in the console) we have reached the 30 required cycles. The number of transactions is calculated as 30 users times 30 cycles. The baseline case is 100 users, 30 of which execute the New Customer test script. The following console screenshot was taken while performing a test run:

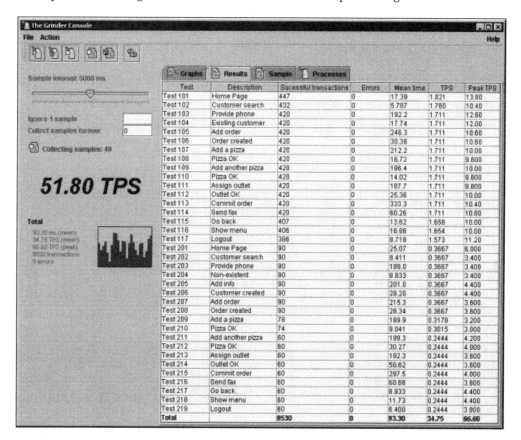

Analyzing the Results

We collect the data files created by The Grinder in the log directories of every Grinder computer and import them into an Excel spreadsheet we use for this set of tests. In the code download for this chapter we have provided a sample spreadsheet, `jdk131_client.xls`. In order to adapt this for your own uses, you will need to be familiar with the use of Excel pivot tables. Good coverage of this topic is given in the book *Excel 2002 VBA Programmer's Reference* (Wrox Press, 1861005709).

The procedure we use is as follows:

- ❏ From within Excel, open the data file and specify that it is delimited by commas.

- ❏ Sort the file by cycle, thread, and request (referred to as *test* by The Grinder). The data file already has the necessary headers.

- ❏ Delete the lines that are for cycles 30 or higher (The Grinder starts counting cycles from 0).

- ❏ When you are done with the four data files, just update the pivot tables in the registered and new sheets. This will automatically update the information and charts on the summary and commit sheets, which contain the desired information.

- ❏ This cycle is repeated for every test run in the performance test. Just modify the `grinder.properties` files appropriately.

Below is a screenshot showing the sample analysis spreadsheet (on the **Summary** tab):

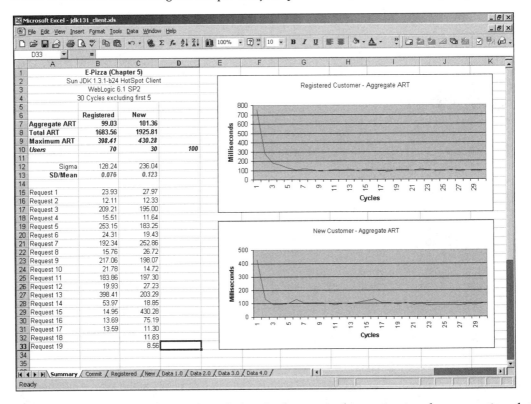

The **Data 1.0 - Data 4.0** tabs on the right-hand side contain the raw imported response time data from the `data_2-0.log` file for each grinder. The **New** and **Registered** tabs contain the pivot tables that we use to calculate our average response time statistics:

	C	D	E	F	G	H	I	J	K
7		Average of Transaction time	Cycle ▼						
8		Test ▼	0	1	2	3	4	5	6
9	27.93067	201	586.6666667	14.53333333	19.46666667	30.13333333	17.13333333	209.2	17.46666667
10	10.68267	202	110.0666667	6.533333333	14.33333333	14.93333333	11.8	15.46666667	9.066666667
11	196.0907	203	675.0666667	249.5333333	173.3333333	186.4	186.6666667	201.2	205.5333333
12	10.62667	204	1222.066667	45.06666667	5.666666667	13.26666667	10.66666667	26.93333333	14.73333333
13	184.856	205	434.2666667	177.4666667	155.8666667	169.2	173.6666667	167.4	170.6
14	18.10667	206	307.6	17.26666667	9.133333333	12.93333333	10.2	16.6	7.6
15	252.9547	207	1421.533333	369.3333333	213.7333333	244.4666667	196.8666667	291.2666667	282.8
16	26.112	208	504.2666667	15.73333333	17.86666667	28.73333333	18.6	22.46666667	25.33333333
17	199.3307	209	384.5333333	223.6	168.2	181.2666667	188.9333333	464.5333333	206.3333333
18	14.624	210	146.5333333	14.2	20.4	16.2	13.33333333	16.4	13.13333333
19	203.6747	211	199.2	208.5333333	180.2666667	175	166.6	202.7333333	192.2
20	28.55467	212	31.06666667	46.73333333	18.6	12.4	13.2	16.93333333	32.26666667
21	201.68	213	275.4	196.8666667	189.9333333	197.8	216.5333333	198.6	193.3333333
22	18.57333	214	74.53333333	43.8	11.53333333	14.46666667	44.93333333	18.6	28.86666667
23	437.224	215	1730.2	880.4	286.8666667	340.8666667	500.0666667	573.6	531.7333333
24	81.032	216	70.33333333	239.3333333	37.6	47.53333333	59	55.93333333	107.7333333
25	11.032	217	7.2	9.066666667	85.33333333	8.666666667	23	13.66666667	10.06666667
26	11.736	218	9.133333333	11.33333333	21.6	6.466666667	11.8	11.13333333	9.266666667
27	7.746667	219	5.066666667	6.066666667	78.26666667	4.266666667	26	5.533333333	5.266666667
28		Grand Total	431.3017544	146.0736842	89.89473684	89.73684211	99.42105263	133.0631579	108.5964912

`Summary` `Commit` `Registered` `New` `Data 1.0` `Data 2.0` `Data 3.0` `Data 4.`

The data in the body of the pivot table above is the average response times for a user for a given cycle (0-29) and for a given request (201-219) in the script. If we have 30 simulated users, in each successive cycle we will have 30 complete executions of the test script and the average time for each request is taken over those 30 executions. Thus we can plot the progression of the average response time with each successive cycle, for any given request.

The C column to the left of the pivot table shows the calculated *overall* ART for cycles 5 to 29 (remember that we exclude the first 5 cycles from the analysis), for each request. This is the core, top-level data presented for each request in the Summary tab of the spreadsheet. If we add together the values in this column for each request and divide by the number of requests in the script, then we arrive at the *overall* Aggregate ART for the test script, which is our **load factor** (see Chapter 1).

The Grand Total row shows the calculated Aggregate ART over all requests in the script, for each cycle. Again, we can plot the progression of the AART with each successive cycle. This is useful when gauging the "stability" of the test times from cycle to cycle (as shown in the graphs on the Summary tab, above).

Preliminary Tests

The first time you set out to performance test an application such as this, it will probably take you about five days. Of course, your timing will vary depending on the objective of the performance test and the complexity of the application, hardware, software, and test scripts. Fortunately, further performance tests of the same application can be automated and can be completed in a matter of hours.

Of those five days the first two will probably be spent setting up the performance test environment, creating the test scripts, and *playing* with the application. By *playing*, we mean running short tests on the application to get familiar with its behavior under various conditions. These initial test runs will allow you to establish reasonable figures for criteria such as:

❑ The **limit case** – you will get a "ballpark figure" for the maximum workload your application can withstand while still satisfying the established performance criteria (in this case, a response time of three seconds).

❑ The optimum number of **WebLogic execute threads** – this is one of the more important knobs that you can tweak in WebLogic Server for fine-tuning performance.

❑ The **optimum heap space** – a key feature of your JVM is, of course, the garbage-collected heap. The size of this heap (and the way in which your particular JVM implements garbage collection) is an important factor in determining performance.

❑ The **baseline case** – the initial point of comparison for our tests. This must at least approximate the minimal load we expect the application to be handling when in production.

At this stage you are only performing quick tests to establish approximate figures. Once you have clearly defined the limit case from our formal tests, you can then tweak parameters such as the number of execute threads and the size of the heap space in an attempt to increase this limit and fine-tune performance.

We performed our preliminary tests using the fixed time (or 'snapshot') method with the console of The Grinder. We set The Grinder to perform an infinite number of cycles and continuously took fixed-sized samples of data. As described previously, we used a 20% variation on the think time. We used five seconds as the sample size and collected 120 samples (ten minutes). In this case, we found that the application stabilized the response times within the first 5 cycles, so to take this stabilization period into account, we ignored the first 36 samples (three minutes). You will have to run a few preliminary tests to find when your application stabilizes since this is really a function of the application and the tests scripts.

For this example, the preliminary tests were performed using the Sun JDK 1.3.1 HotSpot Client JVM, which is the default for WLS running on Windows NT.

A Note on WebLogic Execute Threads

Internally in WebLogic, everything gets broken down into tasks. These tasks are sent to an execute queue, where they might wait for an execute thread to execute the task. When an execute thread is done with the task, it goes and picks up another task from the queue and so on. WLS has a "general purpose" pool of execute threads (which is used by everything except JMS, which has its own dedicated thread pool – see Chapters 6 and 7 for details).

Out-of-the-box, WLS uses 15 execute threads. You may be tempted to take a "more is better" approach to setting the number of threads (as there would be more of them available to tackle the workload), but this is not necessarily correct. As you increase the number of execute threads, you will reach a point when the Java Virtual Machine running the WebLogic Server will start **thrashing** – meaning that it will spend more time administering the thread pool than actually doing useful work. The "thrashing point" is primarily dependent on the operating system and the hardware, but also depends on the JVM, the application and the test scripts.

Another issue that we need to consider carefully is the use of execute threads for database access. WebLogic permits the use of as many simultaneous JDBC connections as the number of execute threads, minus one. The rule here is that fewer execute threads are better than more, in order to minimize the number of simultaneous requests to the database. In general the problem is not actually with the number of simultaneous requests, but with how often they occur. When they occur constantly, one after the other, they tend to overload the database. A database can handle ten simultaneous requests coming in constantly with a better response time than it can handle twenty or more under the same conditions.

For an application like e-Pizza, which uses the database quite extensively, the optimum number of threads will be the minimum number required to handle the workload without affecting the response times too much. In general, as long as we can maintain or improve the response times for the most expensive requests, then we are not too concerned with small increases in the load factor or in the response times for some of the other requests.

Exploring the Limit Case

The way we worked was to set some initial, reasonable values for parameters such as the number of execute threads and the heap space, and then to perform preliminary tests, increasing the client load to get a feel for the limit case.

Out-of-the-box, WLS uses 15 execute threads, so we started with this default value and set the heap space to 64 MB. We were interested to see whether the application could perform adequately with such a small heap space. We found that the limit case was at around 300 users. However, at this point the connection attempts were queuing up at the socket level because there were no threads available to process them, resulting in **connection refused** responses. We found that increasing the numbers of execute threads to 25 solved this problem. Using 25 execute threads, we found that we were reaching the 3 seconds maximum acceptable response time limit at around 360 users. This knowledge helps us to define how we should increment the user load during the formal performance tests. Our strategy during the formal tests is then to decrease the size of the successive increases in user load as we approach the limit case. These tests can take an hour or more to perform so by exploring the limit case here we can minimize the number of full tests that we need to perform and save a substantial amount of time.

A load of 360 users was well in excess of what we estimated to be a reasonable production load, so we saw no reason to increase the number of threads further, with the additional overhead that this incurs. Also, the heap space of 64MB proved to be adequate for an application running under this user load, so we settled on that value. However, a higher heap space, say 128MB, could probably produce slightly better results, as garbage collection would occur less frequently. We leave this as a matter for the reader to investigate further.

The Baseline Case

Finally, we performed some measurements for the baseline case itself. After testing with various numbers of users, we settled on 100 users as the baseline case. As discussed above, this is a reasonable value for the number of operators that will be using the application at any given time in the call center. For both the RC and NC scripts, we observed maximum ARTs (which corresponded to the requests to commit the pizza order in each case) of around **300 milliseconds**. This sets our general level of expectation for subsequent tests.

The following screenshot shows the WebLogic console when running the application with the baseline case. As you can see, the memory heap presents a good measure of the behavior of the garbage collector. You can also see that there are no tasks waiting in queue for execute threads, telling us that we have plenty of execute threads to handle the load presented by the baseline case:

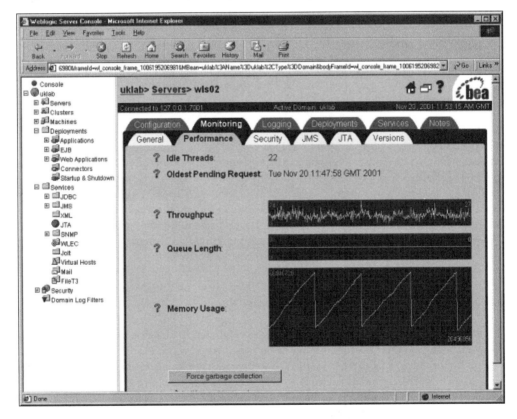

Now that we had done all the preliminary work, we could proceed with the next step of the methodology.

The Test Plan

Bearing in mind the lessons learned from the preliminary tests (and, indeed, from our tests on the Java Pet Store) we set out the following test plan for the application:

- ❑ Perform precision tests at the baseline case to establish the optimum JVM for the application

- ❑ Perform detailed single instance performance tests to establish the limits of our application, given our performance metrics

- ❑ Investigate the behavior of the application when under load for prolonged periods (endurance tests)

- ❑ Fine tune the number of WLS execute threads

- ❑ Investigate the limits of e-Pizza when running a cluster of WebLogic Servers

Selecting a JVM

As we saw in our examination of the Java Pet Store application, investigating the best JVM for your application can be well worth the effort. At the time of writing, BEA had only certified one JVM for use with WebLogic 6.1 and that was Sun's JDK 1.3.1. Thus, we investigated the relative performance of the HotSpot Server, HotSpot Client, and Classic versions of this JVM and expected performance to decrease in that order.

Once again we used the JVMs in their out-of-the-box state – please refer to the earlier *JVM Tuning* section for further information.

To make for accurate comparisons we wanted to minimize the margin of error in the results, so these were precision test runs, using zero variation on the think time. We collected data until the slowest test script had executed 30 cycles.

JDK 1.3.1-b24 HotSpot Client

Using this option on the JVM we obtained the following results for the baseline case (100 users):

	Registered	New
Maximum ART / ms	398.41	430.28
Load factor (AART)	99.03	101.36
Quality	0.076	0.123

As expected when using no think time variation, the system gets more highly stressed quicker and the maximum ARTs – again corresponding to the commit of the pizza order – are around 25% higher than observed for the baseline case when using a 20% variation in think time. The quality measurements for both test scripts are well within our limit of 0.25.

When we analyze the results of a test run, we also look at the ARTs for every request in the test script, so that we get an idea of individual performance. They are presented in the following table:

Request Number	Request Description	Registered Customer	New Customer
101 / 201	Home Page	23.93	27.97
102 / 202	Customer Search	12.11	12.33
103 / 203	Provide phone number	209.21	195.00
204	Customer does not exist	n/a	11.64
104	Customer exists	15.51	n/a
205	Create customer record	n/a	183.25
206	Entry created	n/a	19.43
105 / 207	Create order	253.15	252.86
106 / 208	Order created	24.31	26.72
107 / 209	Add a pizza	192.34	198.07
108 / 210	Pizza added	15.76	14.72
109 / 211	Add another pizza	217.06	197.30
110 / 212	Pizza added	21.78	27.23
111 / 213	Assign outlet	183.86	203.29
112 / 214	Outlet assigned	19.93	18.85
113 / 215	Commit order	398.41	430.28
114 / 216	Send fax	53.97	75.19
115 / 217	Go back to order	14.95	11.30
116 / 218	Main menu	13.69	11.83
117 / 219	Logout	13.59	8.56

It is interesting to note that the response times for business logic (servlet) requests are much more expensive than those for the JSP requests. This is easily explained by the fact that the e-Pizza servlets perform the database and EJB work, while the JSPs do simple page formatting. We can also see that the most expensive URL for both test scripts is the actual commit of the pizza order to the database. Given the rather complex nature of this request, this is perhaps not too surprising. Since these are the requests that will be driving the limit case, let's take a look at the progression of the ART with successive cycles, for these specific requests:

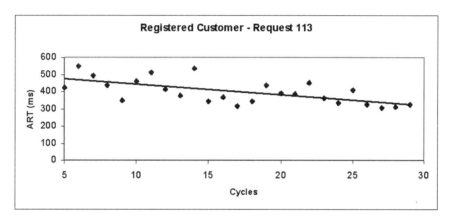

As you can see, there is a reasonably large spread to the data points, but the general trend is that the performance improves with progressive cycles. This trend may well be due to database dynamic optimization and HotSpot optimization. Use of a profiling tool, such as Jprobe, may be able to shed further light on this issue. A similar trend is observed for the equivalent request for the NC script and for request 205 in the New Customer script, which also does a write to the database.

Following is a screenshot of the CPU usage at the end of the test run:

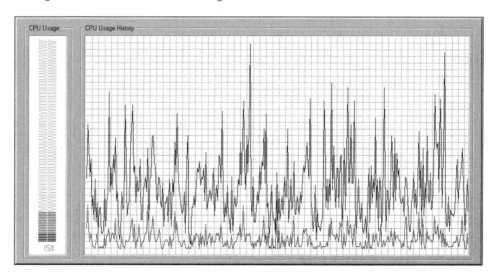

The chart is spiky, as is characteristic of tests with no think time variation, but we are generally well within capacity.

JDK 1.3.1-b24 HotSpot Server

The results obtained using this JVM are summarized in the following table:

	Registered	New
Maximum ART	553.49	449.31
Load factor (AART)	109.88	99.41
Quality	0.272	0.065

As you can see the performance degrades somewhat compared to the HotSpot Client option. In the case of the RC test script, the most expensive request (committing the pizza order) is about 40% slower than that observed previously. However the value for the NC script is very similar. The general load factor (aggregate ART) is also up by about 10% for the RC test script, but about the same for the NC test script.

We also notice that the quality measurement for the sample of the RC test script exceeded our limit of 0.250, so let's have a look at a chart that presents the aggregate ART for this sample:

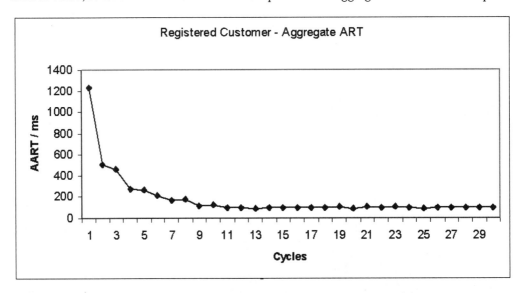

As you can see, it takes a little more than five cycles for the curve to stabilize. The effect of this is that the final average values for aggregate ART and maximum ART might be a little on the high side, but nothing we should be too concerned about.

For comparison purposes let's have a look at the chart for the AART of the NC test script:

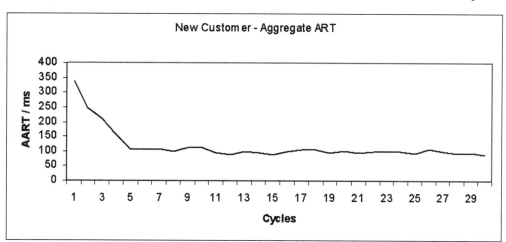

Here we can see that the sample stabilizes right on the fifth cycle, and it holds pretty well from there on. This is reflected in the quality indicator being under 0.100.

In the NC script, the trends observed for the ART versus cycle graphs for the create order (207) and commit order (215) requests were the same as those observed previously – a gradual improvement with successive cycles. The following chart plots the ART for the commit of the pizza order in the Registered Customer test script with successive cycles:

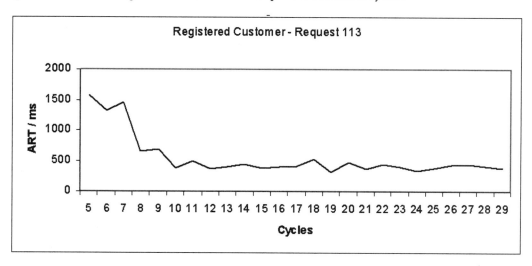

Rather than the gradual decrease from approximately 450 ms to 300 ms, which we saw for the equivalent request using the HotSpot Client option, here we see that the response time improves dramatically up to cycle 10, and then stabilizes at around 400 ms (which is consistent with the behavior observed for the AART for the RC script).

Overall, the HotSpot Server option exhibited poorer performance, and we had good reason to favor the HotSpot Client.

JDK 1.3.1-b24 Classic

As expected, the performance obtained using this option was substantially slower than that seen for the previous runs:

	Registered	New
Maximum ART	1438.37	1326.56
Load factor	473.22	418.34
Quality	0.179	0.190

The maximum ARTs observed here are over three times higher than those observed for the HotSpot Client option. If you need any further convincing, compare the CPU usage to that observed for Client:

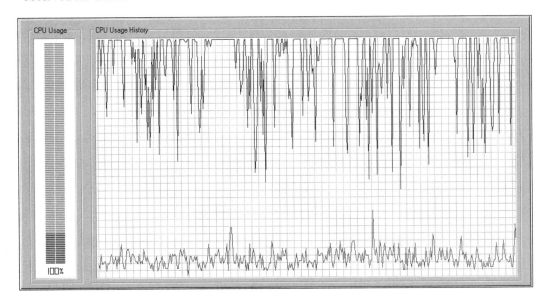

Making the Choice

Analyzing the following chart, it is easy to understand why we selected the HotSpot Client option to run this application:

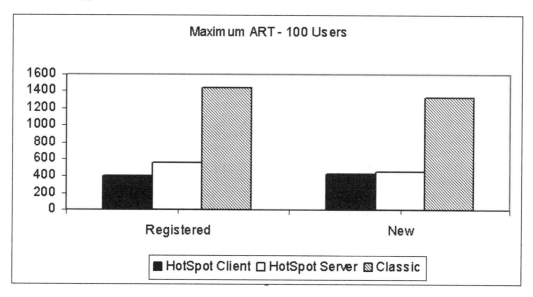

Even though the differences for the New test script are negligible, the differences for the Registered test script are significant enough to select it.

Single Instance Stress Test

Having established our test environment (HotSpot Client JVM, 64 MB heap space, 25 WLS execute threads) we then performed a series of stress tests to determine the number of simultaneous users that the application can handle under our conditions, whilst obeying our performance metric of a 3-second response time.

As discussed earlier, these test runs used a 20% variation on the think time. This spreads the execution of the tests, giving it a closer resemblance to reality.

100 Users (Baseline Case)

The results that we obtained were as follows:

	Registered	New
Maximum ART	296.15	284.32
Load factor	86.64	86.16
Quality	0.056	0.025

For the Registered Customer and New Customer scripts we see 25% and 33% improvements, respectively, over the comparable tests using zero think time variation.

The following histogram shows the ARTs for each individual request in both scripts:

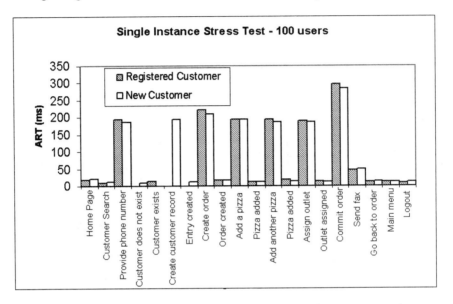

As you can see, the average response times for the JSP requests (less than 20 ms) are much lower than that for the business logic requests, which average around 200 ms and all of which involve reading or writing to the database. Bear in mind that we have tuned neither the application nor the database instance – we will return to this issue later in the chapter. The following chart presents the CPU usage trace for the WebLogic Server:

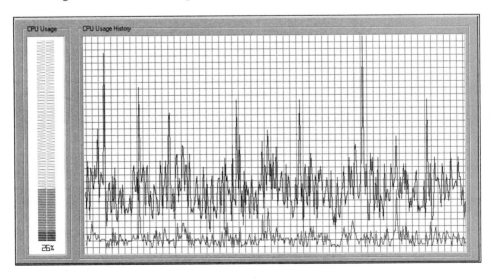

Recall that the traces for 0% think time during the JVM tests presented a very "spiky" profile. As you can see, when using a 20% variation the patterns tend to smooth out. The reason for this smoothness is that when you vary the think time on a test script, you spread the execution of the individual tests in such a way that they don't all occur at the same moment, thus overloading the system at that very moment.

As you can see, this application can easily handle 100 simultaneous active users under the conditions described. The most expensive request is the commit of the pizza order at around 300 milliseconds, which gives us plenty of room to grow before we reach our limit of 3 seconds.

200 Users

The results of our preliminary tests, and the fact that we were so far within our performance limit, gave us the confidence to immediately double the user load. We achieved this by increasing the number of threads in Grinder01 and Grinder03 (running RC test script) from 35 to 70, and the number of threads for Grinder02 and Grinder04 from 15 to 30. The results were as follows:

	Registered	New
Maximum ART	513.12	419.11
Load factor (AART)	126.98	117.17
Quality	0.262	0.041

The first thing to notice is that even though we have doubled the user load, the response time has not doubled and neither has our load factor. This indicates that we are not yet approaching the limits of the system.

Our only concern was that the quality of the RC test script was above our upper limit of 0.250. Again, we found the reason to be that this sample had not stabilized until cycle 9:

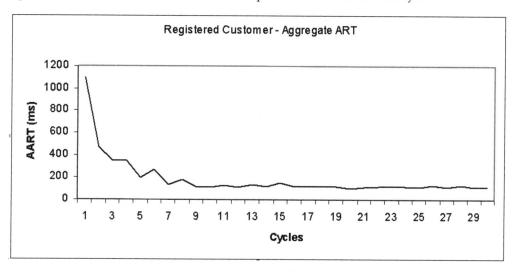

This is not really a problem but it does have the effect that our ART numbers are a little on the high side. However, since we were not close to the test limit of 3 seconds and the sample did stabilize very nicely after cycle 9, we decided not to redo this test run.

Given these results, we decided to be adventurous and increase the user load by 120, to a total of 320 users.

320 Users

To achieve this load, we increased the number of threads in our pairs of Registered Customer and New Customer Grinders to 56 and 24 respectively. The results were as follows:

	Registered	New
Maximum ART	1791.64	1059.40
Load factor	419.23	338.66
Quality	0.287	0.140

This is an interesting run. By increasing the number of users by 120 we have approximately tripled our performance indicators. Even though we are not close to our three-second limit, the application is starting to look pretty loaded. Once again the quality of the RC test script exceeded the limit, but a quick review of the sample chart showed the same pattern as for the 200 users run – the sample stabilized by cycle 9.

The selection of five cycles to exclude was based on the preliminary tests and on the observed behavior during selection of the JVM, but at this point we began to wonder whether we should have excluded ten initial cycles instead of five. We decided that it was not worth recalculating all of the results because we preferred to avoid reducing the sample size from 25 to 20.

As we are starting to see some level of stress, now is a good point to review the ART behavior for the individual requests associated with the database commit tests. First, let us have a look at request 113 of the RC test script, the commit of the pizza order:

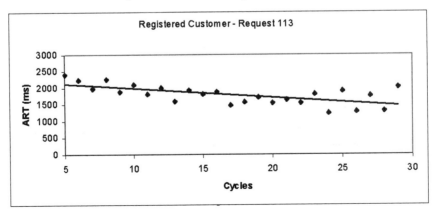

The database is handling the requests very well. The trend line shows a gradual improvement in response time over the test run. The equivalent graph for the order commit request (215) of the NC test script also shows a similar curve. However, the sample for request 205, the commit of the new user information, seems to show a slight increase in the response time over the test run:

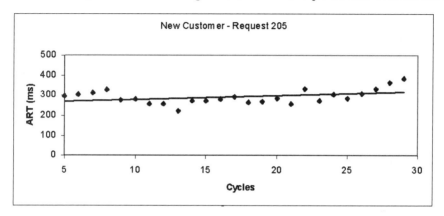

We continued to monitor these particular requests as we increased the load further. As the system was now being stressed, and we knew from our preliminary tests that we were close to the limit, we increased the load by a more conservative 80 users, to a total of 400.

400 Users

To generate this load, we increased the number of threads in our pairs of Registered Customer and New Customer Grinders to 70 and 30 respectively. The results are as follows:

	Registered	New
Maximum ART	3061.49	2040.69
Load factor	1035.81	1035.86
Quality	0.086	0.090

By increasing the user load by 80 we have roughly doubled the values of the indicators and have now reached our 3-second limit (if you are picky you would say that we have slightly exceeded it, but this is not that exact a science). We are happy to call this the limit case and state that we reached the end of the single instance stress test.

We now know the boundaries of the application and can make the performance statement that was the ultimate goal of these tests:

> **Using the hardware, software and database under the conditions described, the e-pizza application can handle approximately 400 simultaneous active users with a maximum response time of 3 seconds.**

We again analyzed the ART behavior for the individual requests associated with the database commit tests and found that the order commit of the RC test script showed a gradual increase in response time over the test run. For the NC test script, the trend line for the order commit was basically constant (perhaps a minimal decrease) and the trend line for creating a new customer record showed a slight increase.

To better understand what has happened we can have a look at the actual values of the response times for every test in the following tables, starting with the results of the registered customer test script:

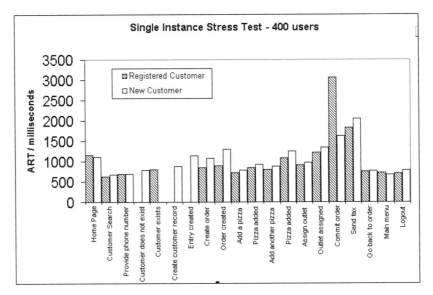

It is interesting to note that there is no longer such a clear disparity in response times between the JSP requests and the requests that involve reading and writing to the database. The Commit Order request is the limiting request, with the Send Fax request (which reads the Order_Detail table) being the next most expensive. However, the rest of the requests all come in around the 750-1000 ms mark. The fact that the JSP requests are now on a par with the servlet requests in terms of response time, tends to suggest that the WebLogic Server is now considerably loaded and stressed. It is also worth noting that the first test, which has to establish the HTTP connection, is now pretty expensive.

The following screenshot shows the CPU usage chart of the WebLogic Server computer running the application:

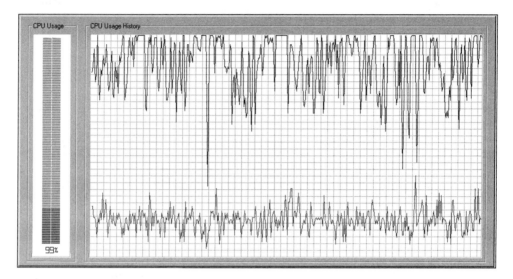

As we expected from the results, it is now very loaded, spending a lot of time at 100%. In contrast, the CPU usage of the machine running the database presents a cyclical pattern directly related to the commit operations performed by the test scripts:

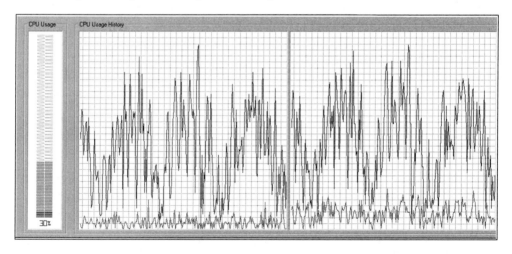

Being aware that the performance test is conducted in a dedicated standalone network, it is interesting to analyze the network traffic for these tests:

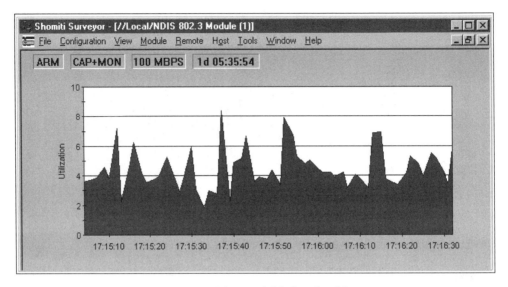

We see an average of 3-4% utilization of the available bandwidth.

It is interesting to think about the performance statement that we produced. It means that 400 operators can simultaneously be handling calls at a pretty quick pace. This is pretty impressive if you consider the fact that the application is running on a single Pentium computer. Now that we understand the limits or boundaries of our application, we decided to do an additional run with a few more users – just to understand what would happen when we exceed the limits. This sort of test run can produce very useful information for capacity planning.

Beyond the Limit – 440 Users

We did not increase the user load by much because we knew that the response time had the potential to degrade exponentially at this point. The results with 440 simultaneous users were as follows:

	Registered	New
Maximum ART	3432.43	2573.41
Load factor	1348.13	1350.30
Quality	0.066	0.095

The performance impact of adding 40 users to the load is significant, but it is interesting that it only increases the maximum ART by about 400 milliseconds. The operations people might decide that 400 milliseconds is not a big enough performance hit to justify having bigger hardware to handle a potential peak in the number of simultaneous operators. We can now add another paragraph to our performance statement:

> **By increasing the load to 440 simultaneous users, the maximum average response time degrades approximately 12% to 3.4 seconds.**

The following chart presents the values of the load factor for the test runs that we have done. It is interesting to see the apparent increases in gradient at 200 and 320 users:

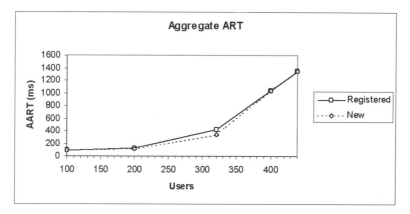

By plotting graphs such as these during the test runs, it is relatively easy to predict when the performance limit will be reached. We see a similar pattern when we plot the maximum response times, as shown in the chart below:

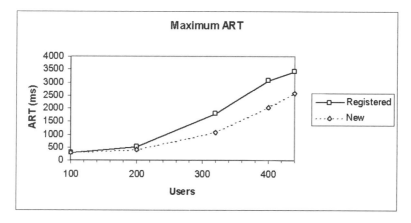

With this set of test runs we were able to find the boundaries of the application running on a single instance of the application server. We already had an idea of the limits from the preliminary test runs performed at the beginning of the performance test efforts, but here we were able to fully consolidate those results.

However, there is one issue to bear in mind. For logistical reasons, the length of the test runs was about one hour, so we still didn't have a complete picture of the behavior of the application over an extended period of time. We decided to take a look at that next.

Endurance Test

In order to complete our understanding of the behavior of our application we decided to conduct an endurance test whereby we would leave the application running for an extended period, typically overnight, at the baseline case.

The following table shows the results for the baseline case (100 users), with a 20% variation on the think time, which was left running for approximately 15 hours (600 cycles):

	Registered	New
Maximum ART	357.03	510.09
Load Factor	93.87	112.59
Quality	0.068	0.195

If we compare these results with those for our baseline case, we see an increase in the maximum ART for the RC test script of about 20%. We see a more dramatic increase of about 79% for the NC test script. So, now the tables have been turned – for the first time we see the ART for the New Customer commit substantially exceeds that for the Registered Customer. The exact reasons for this are not clear but it may be related to the cyclical nature of such user simulation. It is possible that we simply get into a cycle whereby Registered Customer requests are executing just ahead of New Customer requests.

Given that we have generally observed a gradual improvement in the ARTs for database commits over the course of the shorter, 30-cycle test runs, these results were not necessarily what we were expecting. Let us have a look at the individual response times for the endurance test:

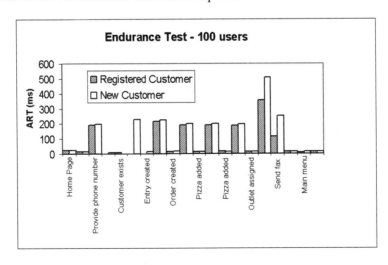

Over the course of the endurance test the average response times for the JSP operations remain low. The ARTs for the servlet requests (create order, add a pizza, and so on) are around 200 ms, which is a similar time to that observed for the equivalent 1-hour stress test. However, we see very noticeable performance degradation for the requests that perform the commit of the pizza order to the database. As such, let's take a look at the ART variation as the test run progressed, first for the RC script:

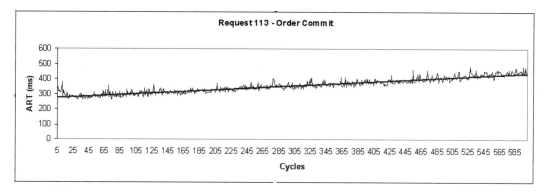

After the initial decrease in the observed ARTs over the first 30 or so cycles, we see a gradual increase with subsequent successive cycles. Now, let us have a look at the chart for the New Customer test script:

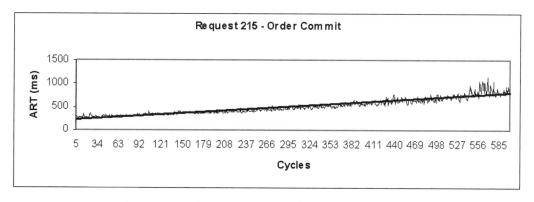

In this case the increase is much more aggressive – the ART almost tripling over the course of the run.

This endurance test created a minimum of 100,000 new orders, each with 2 pizzas. This translates to 100,000 entries in the Order table and 200,000 entries in the Item table.

*We state a **minimum** of 100,000 new orders because the Registered Customer test script executes about two times faster than the New Customer test script. If we add the think times and the actual response times for the baseline case, the results are RC=40,364 ms and NC=87,082ms, so the NC script is more than double in total time of execution (including think times). This does not necessarily mean that they coincide every 2 cycles.*

Additionally, we have created 18,000 new entries in the `Customer` table. It is tempting to state that the more records in the database tables, the slower it becomes, thus the database is the bottleneck. However, we have no proof of this and, indeed, these are not really considered to be large numbers of records for an Oracle database – not one that is correctly set up and tuned to handle such loads and traffic at any rate (as discussed previously, we did not tune our database prior to these tests).

All we can say at this stage is that the request that commits the order to the database is the limiting factor for our application. This not only includes the database, but also the EJB container, the JDBC drivers and the actual connections to the database being handled by the JVM. Before moving on to investigate this issue in more detail, and to look at possible ways of improving the performance of the e-Pizza application, it is important to compare the behavior observed here with that obtained when running the application on the HotSpot Server JVM.

Using JDK 1.3.1-b24 HotSpot Server

Earlier in the chapter we presented the results of 1-hour duration stress tests that assessed which was the optimum JVM for the application (we chose HotSpot Client). We were interested to see if this choice held good when running the application over long periods, since according to the Sun documentation (http://java.sun.com/j2se/1.3/docs/guide/performance/hotspot.html#server):

> [HotSpot Server]... " is intended for running long-running server applications, for which having the fastest possible operating speed is generally more important than having the fastest possible start-up time. "

The results were as follows:

	Registered	New
Maximum ART	408.09	575.33
Total ART	100.04	119.20
Quality	0.074	0.185

Comparing the results with the endurance test using HotSpot Clients we see approximately a 14% degradation in performance for the Registered Customer script and approximately a 13% degradation in performance for the New Customer test script. This is consistent with the results observed for the shorter stress tests and we can conclude that the HotSpot Client option is still the better choice when running the e-Pizza application for longer periods of time.

Optimizing the Number of Execute Threads

As we discussed earlier in the chapter, when testing the limit case, WebLogic defaults to a value of 15 execute threads. This number is suitable for most applications but, as you will recall, for the e-Pizza application it was insufficient to prevent us from getting connection refused messages from the HTTP server functionality of WebLogic, for loads of 300 to 400 users. We chose to increase to 25 execute threads in order to get around the problem, but at the time we did no further tests to discover whether or not this was the optimum value.

In order to investigate this further, we performed single instance stress tests on our e-Pizza application using 20 and 30 execute threads. We performed precision (0% variation in think time) stress tests at the limit case (400 users). Following are the results for both the New Customer and Registered Customer test scripts:

	20 Threads		25 Threads		30 Threads	
	New	**Reg**	**New**	**Reg**	**New**	**Reg**
Max ART	2517.56	2815.35	2483.30	3092.72	2653.40	3464.98
Load factor (AART)	1271.03	1292.60	1233.06	1189.01	1177.73	1162.30
Quality	0.103	0.109	0.097	0.086	0.130	0.095

We see no significant change in ART for the New Customer script (the changes are within our 5% error margin), therefore the results for this script can play no part in determining the optimum number of threads. The results for the Registered Customer script are more interesting – and our previous tests showed the maximum ART in this case to be about 25% more expensive than the equivalent request in the New Customer script, so this is where we'd really like to see a saving. With 20 execute threads we see an improvement in the maximum ART of about 9%. The saving in maximum ART is accompanied by an 8% increase in the load factor, due to an increase in the response times for other requests. This behavior is somewhat expected as we reduce the number of threads. It is possible that we could improve the maximum ART further by reducing the number of threads to 15, but then we would not be able to handle a large user load.

Thus, although there are clearly trade-offs, we are happy to make another performance statement:

> **Under the conditions described above, the ideal number of execute threads for the e-Pizza application running on a single instance of WebLogic is 20.**

The next step would be to repeat the single instance stress tests with 20 execute threads, but we leave this as an exercise for the reader.

143

Improving the Performance of E-Pizza

This section contains the results of our analysis of E-Pizza. The analysis was performed through review of the source code, with the help of the database access table, and using SQL tracing tools in the Oracle database. Many of the recommendations involve moderate coding effort to implement. With The Grinder and our baseline figures it would be straightforward to rerun the tests and generate quantitative data about the performance benefits of the tuning exercise.

From our ART measurements at the baseline case (100 users) we noted that the servlet requests that involved database access gave response times of around 200 ms (approximately ten times that seen for the JSP requests):

Request number	Request description	Database Table	R/W	Registered Customer	New Customer
103/203	**Provide Phone**	CUSTOMER	R	209.21	195.00
205	**Create customer**	CUSTOMER	W	n/a	183.25
105/207	**Create order**	CUSTOMER	R	253.15	252.86
		OUTLET	R*		
107/209	**Add pizza**	PIZZA	R*	192.34	198.07
		OFFER	R		
		CONVERSION	R		
109/211	**Add another pizza**	PIZZA	R*	217.06	197.30
		OFFER	R		
		CONVERSION	R		
111/213	**Assign outlet**	ORDER_MASTER	W	183.86	203.29
		ORDER_DETAIL	W*		
113/215	**Commit order**	ORDER_MASTER	R	398.41	430.28
		ORDER_DETAIL	R*		
		UNITS	R*		
		EXISTENCE	W*		
		DOUGH	R*		
		ORDER_MASTER	W		
		OUTLET	R		
114/216	**Order fax**	ORDER_DETAIL	R*	53.97	75.19

Furthermore, we have explicitly identified requests 113/215 as the limiting requests in the performance of our application. Clearly, our focus needs to be on optimizing database access.

However, before we get started it's worth remembering that what we are basically doing here is *tuning after the fact*. Our application has been built and now we want to see how we can make it run faster, and scale better. Of course, in reality we would want to tune *as* we develop. System tuning is a design-time activity, something you build into the entire system, in order to try and avoid performance problems when your application finally goes live. In this book we provide a simple and versatile means of obtaining performance data for your application. We suggest that you use The Grinder and our methodology from as early in the development process as possible. There are also a number of tuning facilities that are provided for free with your Oracle database and, for an application such as this, it makes sense to use them to find out exactly how your code interacts with the database.

SQL Tuning

There are several tools available in the Oracle database that you can use on a day-to-day basis, in order to be able to identify potential performance issues as you develop:

- ❑ EXPLAIN PLAN – a SQL command that will tell you how Oracle would process a given query, and show you the plan Oracle would use

- ❑ AUTOTRACE – a SQL*Plus facility to show you either how Oracle performed the query, or how it will perform the query, along with statistics regarding the processing of the query

- ❑ SQL_TRACE, TIMED_STATISTICS and TKPROF – two parameters and a command-line tool that will tell you what SQL your application executed and how that SQL performed

Here we will concentrate on SQL_TRACE, TIMED_STATISTICS, and TKPROF. What we present here is very far from being a full tuning analysis – that is beyond the scope of this book. The objective is merely to demonstrate the sort of information we can get about the queries our application is executing in the database and to make some recommendations for improvements in performance. For an excellent discussion on the use of all of the above tools, we highly recommend the book, *Expert One-on-One Oracle*, by Tom Kyte (Wrox Press 2001, ISBN 1-861004-82-6)

SQL_TRACE is a parameter that enables the logging of all the SQL your application performs, performance statistics regarding the execution of that SQL, and the query plans your SQL actually used. TIMED_STATISTICS is a parameter that enables the server to tell us how long each step takes. Finally, TKPROF is a simple program used to format the raw trace file into something more readable.

TIMED_STATISTICS

This feature enables us to collect timing information for various activities in the database. It may be 'globally' set in the initialization file for the database. If you open your init.ora file for your instance and add the following line then the next time you restart the database, it will be enabled:

```
timed_statistics=true
```

It is generally safe to do this since the performance overhead for this is not measurable and the effect of not having this information is that you cannot monitor performance at all (beware, however, that there is an issue in Oracle 8.1.5 whereby shared SQL might be defeated if TIMED_STATISTICS is set to TRUE).

```
tkyte@TKYTE816> alter session set timed_statistics=true;
Session altered.
```

And to turn this on for the entire system:

```
tkyte@TKYTE816> alter system set timed_statistics=true;
System altered.
```

As discussed, this is so useful to have that we suggest you just leave it on all of the time by setting it to true in your init.ora parameter file.

Using SQL_TRACE and TKPROF with e-Pizza

SQL_TRACE may also be enabled for your database instance by adding the following line to the init.ora file:

```
sql_trace=true
```

However, it generates so much output and has such a performance impact that you will rarely want to do this. It is better to enable it on a session-by-session basis:

```
alter session set sql_trace=true;
```

This is most useful in an interactive environment such as SQL*PLUS or embedded in an application so that the application may turn SQL_TRACE on and off at will. It is a nice feature in all applications, as it would allow you to turn SQL_TRACE on and off for the application via a command-line switch or menu selection parameter. Ideally, the e-Pizza application would be instrumented such that this facility can be enabled for selected users. However, since this is not currently possible, the performance statistics here were actually obtained by setting the sql_trace parameter at the database level. Just bear in mind that this is not generally the recommended way to do it.

When set to TRUE, it will generate trace files to the directory specified by the init.ora parameter USER_DUMP_DEST when using dedicated servers to connect to Oracle and BACKGROUND_DUMP_DEST when using a multi-threaded server connection (MTS). It is recommended not to use SQL_TRACE with MTS however, as the output from your sessions queries will be written to many various trace files as your session migrates from shared server to shared server.

So, with sql_trace set to true, we ran a single instance stress test with X hundred users and a 20% variation on the think time. The run generated numerous trace files in the udump directory (we have numerous concurrent sessions active in the database).

We then used the `tkprof` command line utility to format the raw trace files into something easily readable. For example:

```
C:\>cd c:oracle\admin\pizzaman\udump

C:\oracle\admin\nineaye\udump>tkprof ORA01616.TRC report01616.txt

TKPROF: Release 9.0.1.1.1 - Production on Fri Apr 26 14:54:56 2002

(c) Copyright 2001 Oracle Corporation.  All rights reserved.

C:\oracle\admin\pizzaman\udump>
```

This generates a report in the **udump** directory called `report01616.txt`. Following are our major findings from an analysis of these reports. We stress again that this analysis is far from complete. We have concentrated on what we deemed to be the major issues that arose from this analysis.

Use of Bind Variables

A bind variable is simply a placeholder in a query. Bind variables are very important in Oracle because one of the design features of the database is to reuse optimizer plans whenever possible. When you submit any SQL or PL/SQL to the database, Oracle will first search the shared pool to see if it already exists. For example, in the case of a SQL query, Oracle will look to see if that query has already been parsed and optimized. If it finds the query and it can be reused, you are ready to go. If it cannot find it, Oracle must go through the arduous process of parsing the query fully, optimizing the plan, performing the security checks, and so on. This not only consumes a lot of CPU power (typically many more times the CPU processing time than is used in executing the query itself), it tends to lock portions of the library cache for relatively long periods. The more people you have parsing queries, the longer the wait for the latch on the library cache and the system slowly grinds to a halt.

In our report we see the following:

```
select *
from
 customer where (c_country_code = 1 AND c_area_code = 305 AND c_phone =
   5551017)

call     count      cpu    elapsed       disk      query    current  rows
------   -----    -----   --------   --------   --------   --------  ----
Parse        1     0.00       0.00          0          0          0     0
Execute      1     0.00       0.00          0          0          0     0
Fetch        1     0.00       0.00          0          3          0     1
------   -----    -----   --------   --------   --------   --------  ----
total        3     0.00       0.00          0          3          0     1
```

The e-Pizza application executes such statements over and over again, with only the phone number changing, and because the value of c_phone is hard-coded each one is a brand new statement to Oracle and must be hard parsed (this is the process of compiling the SQL and storing it in the library cache), optimized and so on every time.

We would need to consider altering the application so that it used JDBC PreparedStatements (rather than straight Statements) and bind variables, and then supply the actual value for this variable at execution time:

```
select * from customer where
    (c_country_code = 1 AND c_area_code = 305 AND c_phone = :bv)
```

Thus, Oracle will compile the query once and store the query plan in the shared pool (the library cache) from where it will subsequently be retrieved and reused for all of these statements. Indeed, many other statement issued by e-Pizza do make use of PreparedStatements and bind variables – that practice should certainly be extended here.

Parsing and Executing Statements

It is not only unnecessary hard parsing that we wish to avoid – it is also unnecessary soft parsing. Soft parsing is the process of taking a statement, verifying that the user that issues it has permission to access the objects it references, calculating the internal hash value for the statement, and finally looking for a similar compiled statement in the shared library cache. If the statement is not found compiled in the library cache, a hard parse occurs. When building scalable applications with Oracle, the goal is to parse a statement once and use it as many times as necessary.

In the trace reports for the e-Pizza application, we see that we achieve this ideal for certain statements:

```
select o_outlet_code
from
  outlet where o_postal_code = :1
```

call	count	cpu	elapsed	disk	query	current	rows
Parse	1	000	0.00	0	0	0	0
Execute	37	0.00	0.00	0	0	0	0
Fetch	37	0.02	0.01	0	37	148	37
total	75	0.02	0.01	0	37	148	37

However, for other statements the parse count is always equal to the execute count:

```
select d_units
from
  dough where d_name = :1 and d_p_size = :2

call      count      cpu    elapsed       disk      query    current    rows
------    -----    -----    -------   --------   --------   --------    ----
Parse        24     0.01       0.43          0          0          0       0
Execute      24     0.00       0.00          0          0          0       0
Fetch        24     0.00       0.00          0         48          0      24
------    -----    -----    -------   --------   --------   --------    ----
total        72     0.01       0.43          0         48          0      24
```

Notice that in this case we spend a significant amount of time parsing the statement. A general good coding practice to avoid unnecessary parsing is to share statements at the session level (rather than declaring them locally for each method and then closing and releasing them as soon as possible). If we declare them at the session level, we can constrain the classes to a single instance using the Singleton design pattern to make sure that the statement does eventually get closed.

WLS does address statement reuse with prepared statement caching. If you prepare a statement, WLS caches the result against the connection using the statement SQL as a key. When you prepare the same statement again with that connection, WLS will retrieve it from the cache. The default size of the cache is small (10 statements) – you can alter this in the WLS connection. You have to use PreparedStatements in the first place (which e-Pizza doesn't for the phone search code). The fact that certain statements are reused and others are not, suggests that it may be necessary to increase the size of this cache.

Non-use of bind variables and over-parsing leads to a busy shared pool, which in turn can cause you further problems whereby queries end up waiting for the shared pool to become available.

The Commit of the Pizza Order

During our performance tests of e-Pizza, we saw that the request to commit the pizza order to the database was our slowest, and thus limiting, request. The database table access information can be rearranged into a matrix showing how each request accesses each table:

Request description	conversion	customer	dough	existence	offer	outlet	order_detail	order_master	pizza	units
Customer search		R								
Create customer		W								
Create order		R				R*				
Add pizza	R			R					R*	
Add another pizza	R			R					R*	
Assign outlet							W*	W		
Commit order			R*	W*		R	R*	R/W		R*
Order fax							R*			

Notice that during the request to commit the pizza order (113 / 215), we write frequently to the existence table. Consider the following from our trace report:

```
update existence set e_u_units = e_u_units - :1
where
  ((e_o_outlet_code = :2) and (e_i_name = :3))

call      count      cpu    elapsed      disk      query    current   rows
------    -----    -----   --------   --------   --------   --------   ----
Parse       135     0.23      0.73          0          0          0      0
Execute     135     0.06      6.44          0        169        227    135
Fetch         0     0.00      0.00          0          0          0      0
------    -----    -----   --------   --------   --------   --------   ----
total       270     0.29      7.17          0        169        227    135
```

Once again we are not reusing statements – we parse 135 times and we execute 135 times – and this leads to Oracle spending significant time (0.73 s) parsing statements. However, even more interesting is the Execute line. Notice that Oracle spends 0.06 s of CPU time to execute the statement 135 times, but the actual clock time that has elapsed is 6.44 s. The problem is **not** that the database is taking too long to execute this update, as you might have been tempted to assume. In fact, this is a clear indication that we have blocking transactions, concurrency problems with this query – and that is almost certainly an application issue.

This query is waiting on some event in the database, but the `tkprof` report does not tell us what this event is. Fortunately, we can get this information if we perform tracing with **wait events** enabled. In place of the line, `sql_trace=true`, in your `init.ora` file, use the following:

```
set events '10046 trace name context forever, level 12'
```

Now when we run our tests, not only do we get information as above, but when we look in the raw trace files we will get information that will allow us to track down the root cause of this problem.

In the raw trace file, we see the following, pertaining to the existence update:

```
BINDS #11:
 bind 0: dty=2 mxl=22(22) mal=00 scl=00 pre=00 oacflg=01 oacfl2=0
size=48 offset=0
    bfp=093263e0 bln=22 avl=02 flg=05
    value=.5
 bind 1: dty=2 mxl=22(22) mal=00 scl=00 pre=00 oacflg=01 oacfl2=0 size=0
offset=24
    bfp=093263f8 bln=22 avl=01 flg=01
    value=0
 bind 2: dty=1 mxl=4000(4000) mal=00 scl=00 pre=00 oacflg=01 oacfl2=0
size=4000 offset=0
    bfp=0932d370 bln=4000 avl=06 flg=05
    value="Capers"
```

This basically tells us that the exact query we're executing in this case is:

```
update existence set e_u_units = e_u_units - 0.5
    where((e_o_outlet_code = 0) and (e_i_name = "capers"))
```

The information that we are really after comes next: the wait information. In the trace we see a lot of lines like the following:

```
WAIT #11: nam='enqueue' ela= 3071855 p1=1415053318 p2=327688 p3=765
WAIT #11: nam='enqueue' ela= 3072772 p1=1415053318 p2=327688 p3=765
```

Now, we can clearly see why the update took so much clock time to complete even though it took very little CPU time. The trace file shows us we were waiting on a lock (an `enqueue` is one of two locking mechanisms Oracle employs internally to serialize access to shared resources). We were not waiting on I/O, or a log file sync, or waiting for buffers to become free – we were `enqueued` on some resource. If you decoded the `p1` parameter you would find that this actually indicates that we were waiting on an exclusive row-level lock. Basically, this means that another session was holding a lock on the row that this update needed to access.

Now, the question is: why is this lock being held for so long that queues are forming in the database? We know that e-Pizza is either using the JDBC `AutoCommit` feature to perform the commits, or else it is relying on WLS JTA transactions (so the container will do the commit). A missing commit seems unlikely – we would suggest that the commit of the `Existence` update is there but it's not getting through to the database very quickly and hence queues are building up.

What we've done here is highlight how use of a tool that is provided for free in your database can help you accurately pinpoint possible performance issues. In order to solve this problem we would need to find out why this particular JTA transaction was taking so long, and it might well involve code re-architecting, which we will come to shortly.

Other Database-Related Tuning Suggestions

From the table presented previously, we can see that the CUSTOMER, EXISTENCE, ORDER_MASTER, and ORDER_DETAIL tables should be optimized for read/write access, and all other tables should be optimized for read access (although it would be much better if the application cached the read-only information in memory using a read-only cache strategy, discussed below).

In our analysis of the source code, we also noticed there are a number of select operations that do not use the primary key:

- ❏ The **Commit Order** request involves finding the ORDER_DETAIL rows by the ORDER_MASTER order number.

- ❏ The **Create Order** request involves finding rows in the OUTLET table by postcode and by city.

- ❏ The **Add Pizza** requests involve finding rows in the OFFER table by a range of dates. For our test script, the dates always represent `today`.

We recommend that additional indices be added to the database schema to make these select operations more efficient.

Application Code and Architecture Refactoring

Following are various suggestions for improvements in the Java code.

Consistent Use of the Session Façade Pattern

When the e-Pizza application was developed, the Session Façade pattern did not exist. A key advantage of wrapping business logic with session beans is that declarative, container-managed transactions make it very easy to group all of your database access into one transaction. Using many database transactions where one would be enough is a sure way to degrade performance. Unfortunately for application performance, this pattern was not retrofitted to existing code and there are several instances of direct database access from Servlets and JSPs without enclosing transaction demarcation.

Example 1: The servlet that manages the order commit performs an additional database read after the order is committed to obtain details of the outlet that will handle the order. This read is done in an unnecessary separate transaction.

Example 2: The JSP that handles the formatting of the order fax, first finds all the related `OrderDetail` entity beans, then iterates over the list and reads the information for each bean. Each of these operations (the finder call, and each read) occurs in a separate database transaction. If a stateless session EJB had been used as a facade to the entity bean, it would have been simple to set the session bean's transaction attribute to `REQUIRED` which would enclose all of the entity bean access in a single transaction.

> **Direct access to an entity bean without an enclosing transaction is almost always wrong. For this reason we recommend that the transaction attribute of entity beans is always set to `MANDATORY`.**

Use CMP Entity EJBs

E-Pizza only uses entity beans for access to two database tables, `ORDER_MASTER` and `ORDER_DETAIL`. Using container-managed entity beans for access to other tables can improve efficiency, and provide a wealth of tuning options. (Clearly everything that a container can do could also be done with handcrafted JDBC code. However, such code is complex and tedious to write – entity beans make common database access tasks natural and easy).

Example 1: The Create Order request makes an additional database read to the `CUSTOMER` table to retrieve the customer postal code. If an entity bean had been used, the postal code would have been read automatically during the Customer Search request and the additional database operation could be avoided.

Example 2: E-Pizza often selects database rows by their primary key. When an entity EJB was used, the `findByPrimaryKey` call can often access the EJB directly from the cache without having to perform a database read.

Example 3: If the `OrderDetail` entity bean were migrated to an EJB 2.0 CMP entity, EJB instances that result from a finder call would be automatically loaded into the cache when the finder executed (this is controlled by the `finders-load-bean` deployment descriptor option). The Order Fax request could thus be fulfilled with a single `SELECT` statement.

Example 4: The seven tables that are not updated during normal operations could make use of the WebLogic Server read-only entity-caching pattern. Using this pattern, database reads are performed infrequently and the majority of data access occurs directly from the EJB cache. Where the data has to be updated there are various options for invalidating the cache; this is called the "read-mostly" pattern – please refer to the WebLogic Server documentation for the details.

Example 5: The relationship between the OrderMaster and OrderDetail entity beans could be realized with a container-managed relationship. There is a new feature in WebLogic Server 7.0 that would allow the OrderMaster entity and all of its OrderDetail entities to be loaded into the EJB cache using a single database read.

OID Generation

Primary keys for the ORDER_MASTER and ORDER_DETAIL tables are generated using Oracle sequences. Each time a new primary key is required, a database call is necessary. We omitted these calls from the database access table for clarity; they occur as reads during the "Assign Outlet" request.

A more efficient approach would be to reserve primary keys in blocks. Each WebLogic Server would reserve a number of primary keys at a time, say 100, and hand out new primary keys from this pool. This would mean that the Oracle sequence would need to be read far less often, and would greatly reduce the likelihood of a locking conflict on the sequence table.

Performance Tests Using a WebLogic Cluster

One of the most powerful features of WebLogic Server is its ability to work in a cluster. It is very simple to set up a cluster of WebLogic Servers to run your application. It requires very little programming and no special hardware. In the particular case of the e-Pizza application, we are only making use of the clustering capability of WLS from a scalability standpoint – we are only using load balancing, we are not specifying use of replication and failover (so, if a machine in the cluster "goes down" during a test run, all of the sessions on that machine will be lost). In such circumstances, no changes need to be made to e-Pizza in order to take advantage of the clustering functionality of WebLogic. If you do wish to use replication then some changes may need to be made, depending on your application. The servlet developer can code in the same way, regardless of whether the code will be deployed on a single instance or on a cluster. Idempotent stateless session beans require no change, but non-idempotent session beans, entity beans, and so on, will require a little extra work on the part of the developer, in order to use replication.

A cluster of WebLogic servers is typically used when automatic fail-over is required, or when the application does not scale to handle the required load with only a single instance. For example, suppose that our e-Pizza application was required to support 600 simultaneous users, with a maximum response time of three seconds. Our first port of call would be application and database tuning as described previously, but let's say that we've done that and our application, running on a single instance, can only support 400 users given the performance specification. The question then becomes: "How big does the cluster have to be in order to handle 600 simultaneous users with a maximum response time of three seconds (sustained for 1 hour)?"

The conditions were basically the same as for the single instance test runs. The differences were as follows:

❏ Each instance of WebLogic was run with the default value of 15 execute threads. We can do this because now WebLogic will not be used directly as an HTTP server (a WLS cluster requires either a load balancer or a web server that uses a WLS supplied plug-in that acts as a load balancer – we used the latter option), which saves us a few threads.

❏ The cluster was fronted by iPlanet Web Server Enterprise (version 4.1 SP9) running the NSAPI plug-in provided with WebLogic. This web server was running on the same kind of computer as is used to run the WebLogic Server with all the same characteristics (single Pentium III, 512MB, NT 4.0 SP5, etc). The HTTP log remained turned off.

For the purposes of this set of test runs we defined a member of a WebLogic cluster to be a single instance of WebLogic running on a single computer. Every time we added a member to the cluster we were adding a new computer with a single instance of WebLogic, which participated in the cluster. The new hardware configuration is depicted in the following figure:

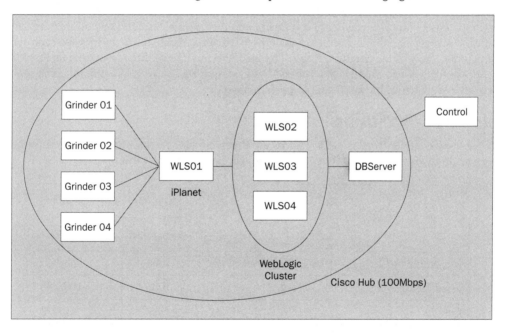

We started the tests with a cluster of two and, in order to get an idea of how the application behaved, we started at the baseline case. The `config.xml` file that we used in these tests (`cluster_config.xml`) is available in the code download for this chapter.

Cluster of 2 - 100 Users

The results of this test run are summarized in the following table, with the results of the baseline case on a single instance, for comparison:

	Registered	New	100 users – Single Instance	
			Registered	New
Maximum ART	112.62	105.70	296.15	284.32
Load factor (AART)	24.63	23.50	86.64	86.16
Quality	0.112	0.044	0.056	0.025

We might have expected to see, roughly, a 50% reduction in response time since in reality we are running 50 users on one member of the cluster and the other half on the second member of the cluster. However, the results are better than that. The improvement is over 60% for each script. Admittedly, some of the conditions have changed (the number of threads and the fact that there is a proxy in front of the cluster), so we aren't quite comparing like with like, but in any case we are certainly seeing a nice improvement in performance.

Cluster of 2 - 400 Users

We can now confidently move to the limit case that we established for the single instance test runs. Once again the results are very encouraging, as can be seen in this table:

	Registered	New	400 users – Single Instance	
			Registered	New
Maximum ART	427.56	381.48	3061.49	2040.69
Load factor	71.49	73.91	1035.81	1035.86
Quality	0.243	0.284	0.086	0.090

However, when we look at the quality of the samples we notice that the numbers are on the high side. We checked AART values for each cycle, for the New Customer test script, since it is the one that has actually exceeded the limit:

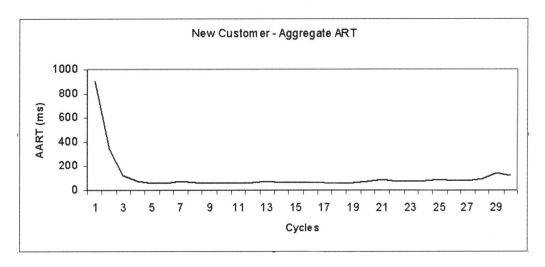

Basically, the AART has stabilized by cycle 5 so this is not the cause of the poor quality value (upon further investigation the slight increase at cycle 29 was caused by a blip in the ART value for request 205 (Create customer). We analyzed the ART behavior of request 215 (the order commit for a new user):

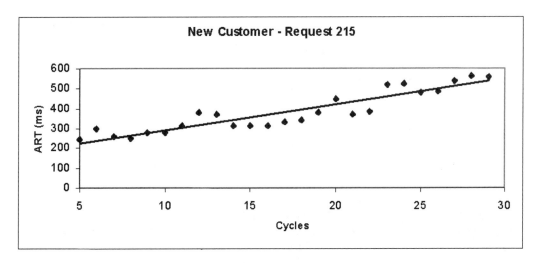

Over the course of the performance test, the observed ART for this request more than doubles. For this test run we have 2 instances of WebLogic, each with a possibility of 14 simultaneous JDBC connections to the database. What we are seeing from the above graph is that the application is quite unstable. Normally we would rerun this test, but since we were not close to our performance limit we decided to press on and check for the same behavior with 600 users.

Cluster of 2 – 600 Users

We were now ready to find out if a cluster of two servers would allow us to meet our performance criteria:

	Registered	New
Maximum ART	3383.80	2989.92
Load factor	1200.68	1529.16
Quality	0.139	0.211

We have clearly exceeded our limit of 3 seconds on the maximum ART for the Registered Customer test script and have basically reached it for the New Customer test script. When we look at the ART profile for the order commit, for the RC test script, we can see that we exceed the 3-second limit from cycle 12 onwards, with the response time showing a continual increase:

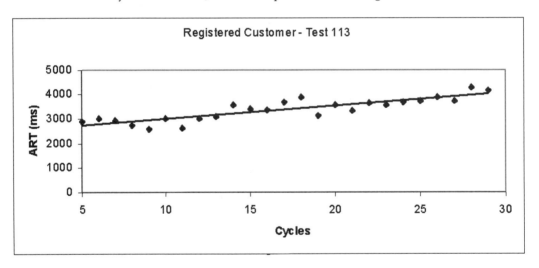

The equivalent request for the New Customer script, as well as the request to create a new customer record, presents a similar pattern. In this case, however, the rise is only by about 25% and the Quality figures are well within our limit.

Once again, the requests that need to access and update the database are limiting the performance of our application. Some of the suggestions made previously would almost certainly improve the situation. However, since we have not implemented these suggestions, we have a situation whereby 28 connections are constantly submitting requests to the database and are putting it under considerable stress, as indicated by the CPU utilization graph for the database server:

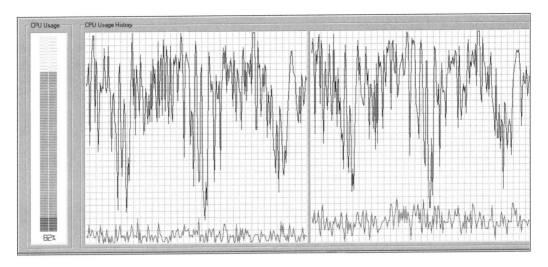

The following screenshot presents the CPU usage of the computer running the iPlanet web server. There is still plenty of capacity:

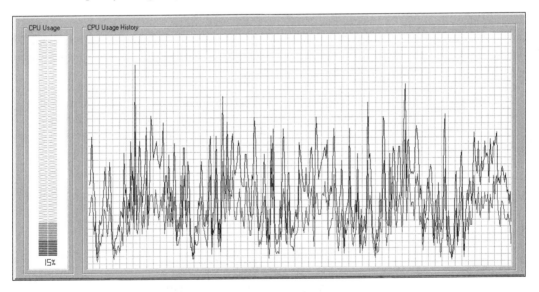

Under the current conditions it is clear that we need to increase the cluster size in order to meet our performance specification – although if we had carried out the performance optimizations suggested previously, we may well have made our target with a cluster of two.

Cluster of 3 – 400 Users

Having a test run with the baseline case would have produced delightful results, but would not really have added anything at this point in time, so we decided to perform our first test run on a cluster of three with 400 users, in order to see how it behaves compared to a cluster of two. We will now potentially have 42 JDBC connections simultaneously submitting requests, so again the issue is how the database will handle this load, given our un-tuned conditions:

	Registered	New
Maximum ART	287.85	310.11
Load factor	49.25	50.73
Quality	0.404	0.218

If we assumed a linear relationship between the number of members of a cluster and the maximum ART (there is no special reason to expect this to be the case, but it gives a reasonable level of expectation) then we might expect the maximum ART to be one-third better than for a cluster of two.

In fact, we see an improvement of 44% for the RC test script and 30% for the NC test script. The quality of the sample for the RC script is pretty bad and, in this case, it is explained by the fact that the ARTs do not stabilize until cycle 9.

A quick review of the order commit charts for the RC test script shows an improvement in response time over the execution of the test run. However, the order commit and the new customer record creation for the NC test script show trend lines with a pretty aggressive increase in the response time. This could explain the reason why we don't see a better than 33% improvement over the result from a cluster of 2.

Cluster of 3 – 600 Users

The numbers of the previous run were good, but let us see how it works with 600 users:

	Registered	New
Maximum ART	1855.52	1359.76
Load factor	345.44	801.97
Quality	0.479	0.623

Judging by these numbers, the answer to 'how big must our cluster be?' is three. However, we will have to examine the results in more detail, especially since the quality indicator is so bad on both test scripts. Let us have a look at the aggregate ART for the RC test script:

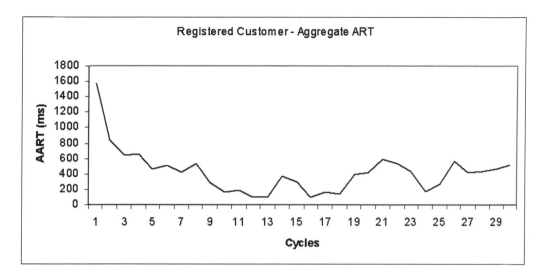

As you can see, the curve is highly irregular and the ART starts to increase again towards the end of the test run. This is the reason for such a bad quality number. Now let's have a look at the aggregate ART for the NC test script, which has an even worse quality indicator:

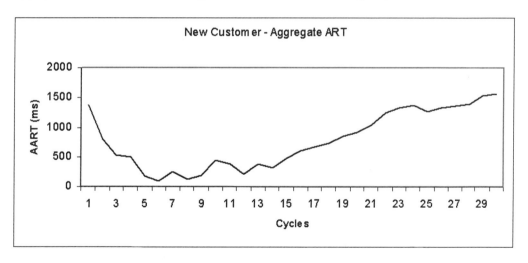

Again, it is clear why we see such a poor quality indicator. The issue here is that even though the averages tell us that we are quite a distance from the 3-second limit, we really need to look at individual response charts of the usual suspects and see if these numbers are sustainable for 1 hour. So first we look at the order commit:

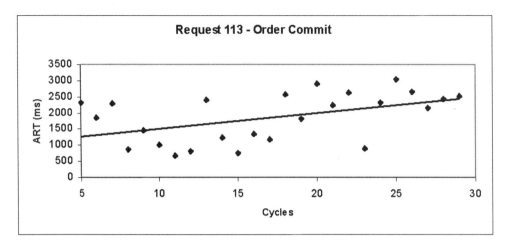

As you can see, we can sustain the response time for 1 hour but probably not for much longer than that. The chart for the order commit for the NC test script is similar, but the maximum value is 2 seconds, so this is less of a concern.

The new customer record creation, however, is pushing the limit towards the end and has a much more aggressive trend as can be seen in the following chart:

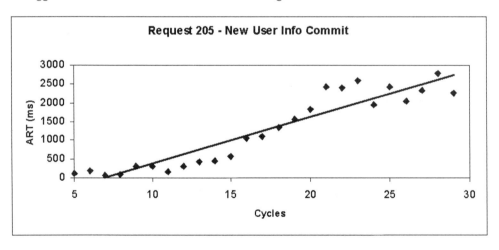

Interestingly enough, we did do various test runs for this case and all of them produced more or less similar results with rather ugly quality numbers. In other words, the behavior was consistent and we could not obtain a test run with a better quality number.

We can conclude that we can handle 600 users with a cluster of 3 WebLogic Servers under the conditions described with a maximum response time of 3 seconds for 1 hour. After analyzing the charts we can also state that we probably could not hold that for more than 1 hour, unless of course some serious work is done optimizing the application and the database.

Conclusion

In this chapter we have seen some of the tests that can be done to better understand your application. The idea is to find the boundaries of the application under the most realistic circumstances of use. We have illustrated the following:

❑ How to use The Grinder and our methodology to performance test your own, unique application.

❑ The importance of selecting the best JVM for your application, in your environment.

❑ How to test the performance of your application on a single instance of WebLogic server, finding the limits of the application and ultimately arriving at a meaningful performance statement. Under our conditions, we found that e-Pizza handle 400 simultaneous users with a maximum response time of 3-seconds.

❑ The importance of investigating the performance of an application over a prolonged period (endurance testing).

❑ Optimizing the number of WebLogic execute threads for your application. Under the conditions in which we ran our tests, we found that the ideal number was 20 threads.

❑ How to analyze your application to find the root cause of any limiting requests (in this case the commit of the pizza order to the database).

❑ How to performance test an application using a cluster of WebLogic Servers. Under our conditions we found that e-Pizza could handle 600 users with a maximum response time of 3 seconds for one hour, on a cluster of three servers.

Finally, once again we have to remind you that this is just an example to illustrate the use of the methodology. It is not meant to be a study of raw performance and it is not a guarantee of performance. The idea is that you run these tests in your own environment.

HTTP and Servlets

The previous chapter of this book concentrated on performance testing a black-box J2EE application. Here, we shift the focus to performance testing while **designing** an application. Design decisions are often based on a set of theoretical assumptions about how certain choices will affect performance. While the theory may well be sound, there is often no real evidence that they hold for a particular, unique application. The goal of this chapter is to investigate the relative performance cost of certain design decisions that will be made while building servlet applications.

While it is far from being a comprehensive investigation of servlet performance, the chapter does tackle the issues that we have found to be most commonly raised, and is largely based on the sort of questions we encounter time and again with regard to servlet performance. Most of the time the sort of questions we are asked relate less to the specifics of the servlet API than they do to general HTTP options and the size of the HTTP response and so on. Thus, in this chapter we investigate:

- ❑ Tuning and JVM options
- ❑ The cost of maintaining an HTTP Log
- ❑ The impact of message size
- ❑ HTTP protocol options
    - ❑ Using persistent connections
    - ❑ Chunked transfer encoding

- ❏ HTTP response compression using Servlet 2.3 Filter functionality
- ❏ Choosing a mechanism for storing session state:
  - ❏ Using the HTTP session object
  - ❏ Using stateful session beans
- ❏ Servlet clustering in a WebLogic Server

A Brief Overview

The Java servlet technology provides web developers with simple methods of extending and enhancing the services of the HTTP server. Servlets accept HTTP requests as input and respond with the HTTP response as output.

A servlet operates inside a **servlet container** (also known as a **servlet engine**). This container takes care of the actual details of connecting to a network, correctly formatting responses, and caching requests. The servlet container is also responsible for handling client requests, passing requests in the form of objects on to a servlet, and returning the servlet response to the client.

Numerous vendors provide servlet containers, including WebLogic, Tomcat and jboss to name but a few. Although the actual implementation of the servlet container will vary from vendor-to-vendor, each container adheres to protocols defined by the Servlet API, which specifies the interface between the container and its servlets. In addition to roles of request handling and protocol translation, the container is also responsible for managing the lifecycle of individual servlet instances. When a servlet is first referenced, either directly at server startup or indirectly through a client request, the container loads into memory. As soon as the servlet has been loaded, the container invokes its init() method, which specifies actions that need to take place at the time of initialization. For each request to the servlet, the container is responsible for calling the appropriate service method, such as doGet() for GET requests and doPost() for POST requests. Finally, when the servlet is removed from the servlet container, the servlet engine calls its destroy() method, which can be used to close resources that were used by the servlet. This life cycle of the servlet is further summarized below:

- ❏ The servlet container creates an instance of the servlet
- ❏ The container calls the servlet's init() method
- ❏ For each request to the servlet, the container invokes the appropriate service method
- ❏ Before the servlet instance is destroyed, the container calls its destroy() method

Designing Servlets for Performance

Due to the dynamic nature of servlet applications and the environment in which they reside, some special considerations have to be taken when designing servlet applications for performance. Before moving on to our actual tests, we will briefly investigate some good servlet design practices that you can hopefully use to develop more scalable and efficient applications. Although the list of topics we cover below is not exhaustive, it represents common issues relevant to most applications.

Using the init() Method for Caching

One of the roles of the servlet container is to ensure that each servlet's `init()` method is called before the servlet is allowed to accept any requests, as discussed above. Although there is nothing that forbids the servlet container from instantiating a new servlet instance for each request, that is rarely the case. Instead, the container stores each servlet instance in memory, which indicates that data initialized in the `init()` method can be shared among all client requests. This makes the `init()` method an ideal candidate for caching frequently used data.

For web applications that generate a mixture of static and dynamic content, this can be useful in reducing the number of `String` objects that are generated for each request. Many people make the mistake of creating a new `String` object for each line of static data, each time a request is made. Clearly, this can be avoided, by declaring global variables with the static content, through the servlet's `init()` method.

For example, consider a simple servlet that generates HTML output through its `doGet()` method. For each request to the servlet, it responds by displaying a static HTML header, followed by some dynamic content, which may be based on specific preferences. Lastly, the servlet appends some static HTML code for the page footer, and responds to the client:

```java
public class MyServlet extends HttpServlet {

    public void doGet(HttpServletRequest req, HttpServletRespnse resp)
        throws ServletException,IOException {

        ServletOutputStream out = resp.getOutputStream();
        out.println("<html>");
        out.println("<head><title>My page</title></head>");
        out.println("<body>");

        // Display dynamic content

        out.print("</body>");
        out.print("</html>");
    }
}
```

The problem with this approach is that, for each request, we generate new `String` objects for the static code we display. Although this may not seem a big problem, imagine what happens when more complex header and footer code is being used, and the number of requests increases. Clearly, reducing unnecessary memory usage and garbage collection can benefit the scalability and performance of the application.

So, instead of instantiating new `String` objects for each request, we might use the servlet's `init()` method to initialize a few variables, which we would share among all requests. This is illustrated in the modified servlet below:

```
public class MyServlet extends HttpServlet {

    private String htmlHeader;
    private String htmlFooter;

    public void init(ServletConfig config) throws ServletException{
        StringBuffer buffer = new StringBuffer();

        // Create the HTML header
        buffer.append("<html>");
        buffer.append("<head><title>My page</title></head>");
        buffer.append("<body>");
        htmlHeader = buffer.toString();

        buffer = new StringBuffer();

        // Create the HTML footer
        buffer.append("</body>");
        buffer.append("</html>");
        htmlFooter = buffer.toString();
    }

    public void doGet(HttpServletRequest req, HttpServletRespnse resp)
        throws ServletException,IOException {

        ServletOutputStream out = response.getOutputStream();
        out.println(htmlHeader);
        // Display dynamic content
        out.println(htmlFooter);
    }
}
```

Choosing a Session Mechanism

When working with servlets, there are various ways of preserving the state of a single session of user requests. Later in this chapter we compare the scalability and performance of two of the most important ones: using the `HttpSession` object and using stateful session beans.

However, regardless of whether we use session beans or the `HttpSession` object to store the actual data, we will most likely use the `HttpSession` interface to associate a server session with a specific client. In doing so, we must consider that a session object created at the server is configured to expire after a given period of time, at which point the servlet engine terminates the object and throws away any data it might be storing. By default, most servlet containers have a parameter configured such that a session object will not expire until 30 minutes have elapsed from the time it was last referenced. For most applications, this time interval is more than enough. If the application stores a large amount of data through the session object, then using a large expiration interval will effectively delay garbage collection because the garbage collector will be unable to remove unused data until the associated session object expires. This can have dramatic effects on system performance as the number of users increases because more and more memory will be required to store stale session objects and their data.

There are a few solutions to this problem. Firstly, we can explicitly terminate a session object by calling the `invalidate()` method of the `HttpSession` interface. This will terminate the session, marking it ready for garbage collection. However, the problem with this approach is that, due to the distributed nature of web applications, there is usually no way of telling when a user has finished using a specific site. For example, on a site that requires user input, it would be really frustrating for the user to spend 15 minutes of filling out forms, just to find that the session has expired and they have to start over. Using the `invalidate()` method, however, might be useful for those sites that require explicit logout. In those cases, the user clearly wishes to leave the site, so the appropriate session object may safely be terminated.

Alternatively, we can reduce the expiration interval for the site. Again, however, users may find their work being lost because of session expiration. it may be necessary to experiment with different timeout intervals (using `setMaxInactiveInterval()` of the `HttpSession` interface): one for general users, say 10 or 15 minutes, and another for users that have explicitly logged on, say 30 minutes.

Managing the Servlet Thread Pool

Since there is usually only a single instance of each servlet running within each container, the servlet engine must account for the case when more than one client requests the servlet at the same time. There are many solutions to this problem. We can synchronize access to the servlet's service methods, thereby ensuring integrity when multiple clients access the servlet simultaneously. This method, however, greatly limits the throughput of the servlet engine, and is therefore not recommended. Another technique is to create a separate execution thread for each request from which to call the servlet's service methods. The balance here is between the increased throughput of the container and the extra cost of creating separate threads for each request. In reality, most servlet containers use a separate thread for each client request, but instead of creating a new thread each time, the container can be configured to use a pool of threads to which incoming requests are dynamically allocated.

When working with a specific servlet container, you should always make sure that a thread pool of the appropriate size is being used. Your servlet engine may create a new thread for every request by default, so you must always make sure to check on the actual threading method used. This default behavior reduces performance because creating and removing threads is expensive, as we mentioned above.

When configuring the thread pool of your servlet engine, you usually specify the minimum and maximum number of threads allocated for the pool, depending on the number of concurrent users for your application. While too few threads in the pool may cause congestion, too many threads will affect your server's performance, by reducing the amount of available memory. For more information about the thread pool, you should consult the documentation of your specific servlet engine.

In the WebLogic Server it is not generally necessary to set a servlet thread pool size. WLS maintains a general pool of threads and it works out how best to use them. However, if you have native I/O disabled, then you can specify the percentage of threads to be dedicated as socket readers. This can be done from the WLS console under the Configuration | Tuning tab.

Closing Resources

Working with network or persistent resources is an integral part of most enterprise servlet applications. For example, the servlet may need to open a database connection or a network socket to a remote system. An important aspect of maintaining a connection to such valuable resources is to ensure that it gets closed after use. Normally, the developer of servlet applications has no prior knowledge of the lifetime of specific servlets, which means that there is no way to directly tell when resource connections should be closed.

Instead, we can use the standard destroy() method of the HttpServlet interface to take actions moments before the servlet gets terminated. The servlet container ensures that before a servlet is destroyed (which usually happens when the container is shut down), its destroy() method is allowed to execute. This makes the destroy() method an ideal candidate for cleaning up resources, closing database connections, and so on.

Disabling Automatic Reloading of Servlets

Finally, a point often overlooked by servlet developers is the necessity of turning off the auto-reload feature of the servlet engine. Most servlet containers have the capability of dynamically loading servlets, which means that changes to the servlet code will not require you to restart the application server. While this feature is very useful at the development stage, as it reduces the time required for server restart, it can have a very negative impact on the system performance in a production environment, placing unnecessary strain on the class loader. When deploying your applications to a production environment, always ensure that the auto-reload feature of the servlet engine is turned off. Further details should be available in the documentation of your specific servlet engine.

Test Servlets and Test Scripts

In order to investigate the behavior of the various HTTP and servlet options, we have written a few simple HTTP test servlets, and a filter class:

❑ **RandomBytesServlet** – this servlet generates responses consisting of random alphabetic characters and is used for the preliminary tests, those assessing the impact of maintaining an HTTP log, the tests investigating different HTTP response sizes, and also those investigating HTTP protocol options. It is mapped to the URL pattern generateRandom and also to the URL pattern generateGZIPRandom (see below).

❑ **GZipServletFilter** – this is a filter class that sits in front of the RandomBytesServlet and which uses the java.util.zip.GZIPOutputStream class (which implements a stream filter for writing compressed data in the GZIP file format) to compress the output from the RBS servlet. In this manner, we assess the cost of using the Servlet 2.3 compression filter. This filter class is mapped to the URL pattern generateGZIPRandom.

❑ **AlterSessionServlet** – this servlet is used to investigate session state management strategies using the HTTP session object, and also in the servlet clustering tests. It is mapped to the URL pattern alterSession.

❑ **SessionServlet** – We use this servlet to test the relative cost of using a HTTP session object versus a stateful session bean for managing session state. Depending on the type parameter, this servlet will store the specified number of random bytes in an HTTP session (type=0) or a stateful EJB (type=1).

In each case, our grinder.properties files (test scripts) will make requests to the appropriate servlet. For example, in the case of RandomBytesServlet:

```
grinder.test0.parameter.url=http://sun1:7001/servlet/generateRandom?size
=32768&setContentLengthHeader=true
```

For each request, in this case, the servlet generates a message of 32KB and sets the content length header parameter on the HTTP message (this will be discussed in more detail when we run the actual tests). Each simulated user will make ten identical requests to the servlet for each complete execution of the test script.

At the start of every test script, we must ourselves define several key parameters. Each test script used in this chapter includes the following information:

```
# HTTP Performance tests

grinder.jvm.arguments=-Xint

# Simulate the number of users from one JVM and run forever
grinder.processes=1
grinder.threads=125
```

```
grinder.cycles=0

# Start/Stop from Grinder Console
grinder.receiveConsoleSignals=true
grinder.grinderAddress=228.1.1.1
grinder.grinderPort=1234

# Agent processes report real-time data to Grinder Console every second
# (the default is every 500 ms)
grinder.reportToConsole=true
grinder.reportToConsole.interval=1000
grinder.consoleAddress=control
grinder.consolePort=6372

# Data logs to the log directory, no debugging logs
grinder.logDirectory=./log
grinder.appendLog=false
grinder.logProcessStreams=false

# Set the initial spread (ramp-up) and think time variation
grinder.thread.initialSleepTime=500
grinder.thread.sleepTimeVariation=0

grinder.plugin.parameter.useCookies=true
grinder.plugin.parameter.logHTML=false

# User the HTTP Plugin with HTTP Client model
grinder.plugin=net.grinder.plugin.http.HttpPlugin
grinder.plugin.parameter.useHTTPClient=true
```

Notice here, in contrast to the `grinder.properties` files seen in Chapter 3, we do not identify each Grinder with a unique `HostID` – every script is the same in this sense. The only parameters we need to alter from script to script are the number of users (threads), the ramp up time and think time and the requests themselves.

> **All of the test servlets used in this chapter are packaged in the `performance3.ear` file, available in the code download for this chapter, where you will also find the `grinder.properties` files that we used, along with all the other required scripts and files.**

Defining Performance Metrics

When testing a complete application we can define our performance metrics rather clearly. In the case of the e-Pizza application that we tested in Chapter 3, we defined a maximum acceptable response time for the end user. Here, we cannot define such rigid metrics – we are performing general research. We have developed a test servlet that will allow us to make comparative judgments on the performance cost of certain aspects of HTTP and servlet programming.

Thus, we must simply define the measurements that are relevant in this context and use our results simply to set a general level of expectation with regard to performance. In this case, we will be analyzing results based on measurements of response time (AART) and of the throughput, or transactional rate (in transactions per second, TPS).

AART

We start by calculating the Average Response Time (ART) for every request in a test script. This is done by calculating the arithmetic mean of every individual response time for every simulated user that runs that test script. The aggregate ART (AART) is then the average (the arithmetic mean) of the ARTs of all the requests that make up the test script.

Throughput: Transactions Per Second (TPS)

This is a measure of the total transactional rate over all of the requests in a test script. In this case, a transaction is a request, so we are in fact measuring Requests per Second (RPS): the number of requests processed over a set period of time (in this case one second). It is important to note that this metric is **not** a "miles per hour" measurement of the speed of the system. It is, in fact, a measurement of **capacity**, as will become clear as we work through the tests. You should note that there is not actually a direct, mathematical relationship between response time and throughput.

Selecting the Sampling Method

For the tests in this chapter we used the fixed time (or snapshot) method of data collection, whereby we continuously take fixed-sized samples of data for a specified time period, regardless of whether or not a particular cycle is completed. In this case, we used five seconds as the sample size (this means that we record our performance metrics every 5 seconds) and collected 120 samples (so the test length was ten minutes). We ignored the first 36 samples (three minutes) in order to take into account the initial test period over which the system stabilizes (you must exclude as many samples as is appropriate in your environment).

One of the issues that we struggled with was choosing the most representative think time to use for these tests. When we were testing a real application in Chapter 3, we could use The Grinder's sniffer proxy to obtain the real think times for our test scripts. Here, we are not testing an application that uses servlets, but exploring the servlet API so we cannot use the real think time, basically because we don't know what it is.

Ultimately, since we could not use a real think time, we decided that the most appropriate course of action was to use **zero think time**. This gives us the most precise results and it could be argued that we will obtain "worse case scenario" performance data, since this puts the system under the maximum stress, for any given number of users.

Having said all this, we did actually perform one initial test that attempted to mimic real-world conditions more closely and thus used a think time of two seconds and a ramp up period of 0.5 seconds.

The Test Environment

The hardware configuration used for the tests in this chapter is presented in the following diagram:

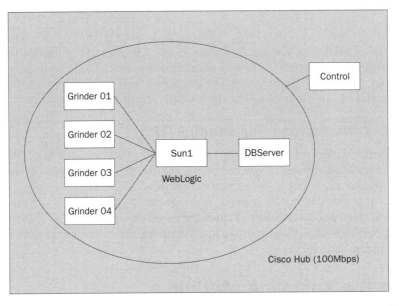

The details of each computer used here (and of those used throughout the book), its operating system and available software, can be found in Appendix B.

Briefly, four Grinder computers (each running on Linux) were available to generate the required workload, each running The Grinder, version 2.8.1. For example, if we needed to generate a load of 500 users, then each Grinder computer would simulate 125 of those users. Each Grinder machine used the Sun JDK 1.3.1 with the –Xint option (interpreted mode only).

We used the "out-of-the-box" configuration for the WebLogic Server 6.1 instance (running on Solaris 2.7) and did not tune any of the parameters.

For tests that required access to the Oracle database, we used the WebLogic OCI type 2 driver, called jdriver (we found that there is a bug in the thin driver which meant that we could not use it for servlet persistence).

The database we used was Oracle 8.1.7.0.0 in the default state (out-of-the-box). We performed no optimizations on the database server or tables.

Setting Up and Running the Tests

This setup is relatively straightforward because the test script is the same for all of The Grinder computers – the only parameter that changes is the number of simulated users. The following instructions describe how to set up the test environment for the single instance tests (which do not require use of the database).

Configuring and Starting WebLogic Server

The first step is to deploy the `performance3.ear` file, provided in the code download for this chapter (and which contains all of the classes needed to run the tests in this chapter), to your WebLogic Server.

For reference purposes, we provide the `config.xml` files for our WebLogic Server machines, sun1 and control. These can be tailored to your setup. For example, if you are not using a WebLogic administrative server in your tests, then the information regarding the control computer can simply be omitted from our file.

In or tests, the control computer housed the WebLogic Server that was the administrative server for all the WebLogic Servers used in our performance tests. Since it was the administrative server, the `config.xml` file contained all the information for the WebLogic Server that hosted the servlets (sun1). The configuration file that we used (`single_config.xml`) is presented here:

```xml
    <?xml version="1.0" encoding="UTF-8" ?>
-   <Domain Name="chapter4">
-   <Server ListenPort="7001" Name="control" NativeIOEnabled="true"
TransactionLogFilePrefix="config/chapter4/logs/">
    <WebServer LogFileName="./config/chapter4/logs/access.log"
LoggingEnabled="true" Name="control" />
    <KernelDebug Name="control" />
    <SSL Name="control" />
    <ServerDebug Name="control" />
    <ServerStart Name="control" />
    <ExecuteQueue Name="default" ThreadCount="15" />
    <Log FileName="config/chapter4/logs/weblogic.log" Name="control" />
    </Server>
    <Security GuestDisabled="false" Name="chapter4"
PasswordPolicy="wl_default_password_policy" Realm="wl_default_realm" />
    <FileRealm Name="wl_default_file_realm" />
    <PasswordPolicy Name="wl_default_password_policy" />
    <Realm FileRealm="wl_default_file_realm" Name="wl_default_realm" />
    <Log FileName="config/chapter4/logs/wl-domain.log" Name="chapter4" />
    <JTA Name="chapter4" />
    <SNMPAgent Name="chapter4" />
    <Cluster Name="c4" />
-   <UnixMachine Name="sun1">
    <NodeManager Name="sun1" />
    </UnixMachine>
```

```
- <Server AcceptBacklog="600" Machine="sun1" Name="sun1">
  <Log FileName="sun1.log" Name="sun1" />
  <WebServer LogFileFormat="common" LogRotationType="size"
LoggingEnabled="true" Name="sun1" />
  <KernelDebug Name="sun1" />
  <SSL Name="sun1" />
  <ServerDebug Name="sun1" />
  <ExecuteQueue Name="default" ThreadCount="15" />
  <ServerStart Name="sun1" />
  </Server>
  <ApplicationManager Name="chapter4" />
- <Application Deployed="true" Name="performance3"
Path=".\config\chapter4\applications\performance3.ear">
  <EJBComponent Name="statelessEJB" URI="statelessEJB.jar" />
  <WebAppComponent Name="servlet" Targets="sun1" URI="servlet.war" />
  </Application>
  </Domain>
```

Next, we go to the computer named sun1 and we start the WebLogic Server with a slightly modified version of the startManagedWebLogic.cmd script that is included in with the product. We called our modified startup script go. For the sake of consistency, our go shell script includes the following lines to delete the log files every time we start it up:

```
rm -f ../../access.log
rm -f ../../sun2.*
```

In order to obtain CPU utilization measurements, we add some lines to start and record the output of the vmstat command just before we start the WebLogic Server:

```
vmstat 5 > $GRINDER_HOME/vmstat.out&
PROCESS=$!
```

vmstat is a Solaris tool that reports various statistics, including process and memory and CPU usage. Every 5 seconds we send vmstat output to the specified vmstat.out file. Every twenty rows or so, the vmstat tool prints the column headers for the data. So, after the execution of the WebLogic Server, we kill the vmstat process and edit the output file to eliminate these recurring header lines:

```
kill $PROCESS

/bin/sed -f $GRINDER_HOME/vmstat.edit < $GRINDER_HOME/vmstat.out >
$GRINDER_HOME/vmstat1.dat
```

The instructions for the stream editor, sed, in the file vmstat.edit are as follows:

```
/proc/ d
/ r / d
```

This will delete all the lines that have the word `proc` and all the lines that have the letter `r` surrounded by blank spaces, which achieves our objective of removing the header lines. The `vmstat` data, stripped of recurring headers, is saved in the file `vmstat1.dat`.

When operating in this manner, you cannot stop the WebLogic process with a control-C as this will not kill and edit the output of the `vmstat` process. The way we handle this is by stopping the process from the WebLogic console by left-clicking on the name of the server as can be seen in the following screenshot:

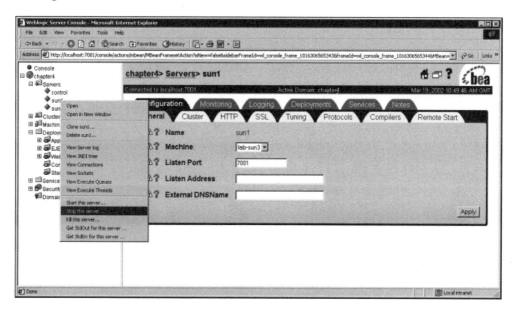

Setting Up The Grinder

In our lab, we ran The Grinder console on the control computer and had four dedicated Grinder machines.

More detailed instructions for starting The Grinder processes is given in the equivalent section of the previous chapter.

On the control computer start the console of The Grinder with the following commands:

```
set CLASSPATH=C:\grinder-2.8.2\lib\grinder.jar:.
java net.grinder.Console
```

Once the console has started we make sure that we set correctly the fields related to the sample metrics. In this case we set it to a sample interval of 5000 milliseconds on the sliding bar. Then we set it to ignore 36 samples and collect 120 samples.

Then we go to each Grinder computer and start The Grinder process:

```
export CLASSPATH=/home/grinder/shared/grinder-2.8.2/lib/grinder.jar
java -Xint net.grinder.Grinder
```

The Grinder console should look something like this:

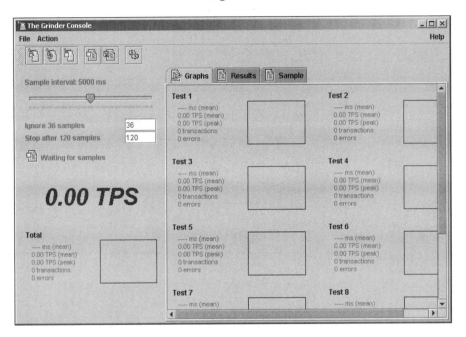

Collecting the Data

Before we start the actual test run by clicking on the start button of the Grinder console, we always verify that all the simulated users required for the test are ready to go. If you are running version 2.8.2 or later, you can do this by looking at the Processes tab in the Grinder console. We also suggest that you make sure that you are connecting to the servlet by first making the request from your browser, on the machine running The Grinder. If you receive the appropriate response, you are set to go.

In this chapter, the Grinder console collects all of the data we need – we no longer use the data_2-0.log file as we did in the previous chapter. If you click on the Results tab on the console, you will see the data that is collected:

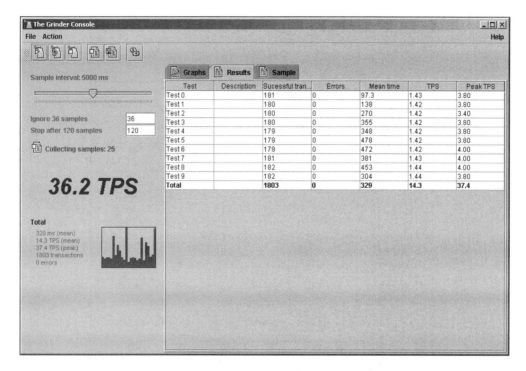

The mean time column is the average response time and the TPS column records the average throughput for each request. When we use the fixed-time method we are calculating a real-time average. Agent processes send over data to the console every second (we set that using the `interval` parameter in the test script). If we set a sample size of 5 seconds, then every 5 seconds the console calculates the ART and TPS over however many times each request has been executed in that period and over however many users. After another 5 seconds, it calculates these metrics again, so we get an accumulative average over the number of samples that we specify. The console then adds together the times for each request to arrive at the total transactional rate.

We stop the test when the Grinder console displays the message Collection stopped in red. Then we click on the save results button of the Grinder console to save the results gathered by the Grinder console into a file. By default this file is named `grinder-console.data` and is saved in the directory from which you are running the console.

Analyzing the Data

We simply import the relevant data collected in the `grinder-console.data` into our Excel spreadsheet:

Microsoft Excel - c4-1-2.xls

File Edit View Insert Format Tools Data Window Help

H1 | =

	A	B	C	D	E	F
1	Chapter 4 - HTTP and Servlets					
2	1. The Basics					
3	*1.2 Response size 32K, think time 0, think time variation 0%*					
4						
5	*ART*	20	40	60	80	100
6	Request 1	116.3	254	411.8	549.4	693.5
7	Request 2	61.79	143.8	219	294.7	373
8	Request 3	58.21	122.8	199.2	273.7	351.9
9	Request 4	59.67	121.1	198.5	277.2	354.1
10	Request 5	59.71	123.1	201.5	277.6	355.5
11	Request 6	60.14	123.7	202.6	277.9	355
12	Request 7	59.64	123.8	201.2	280.3	357.4
13	Request 8	59.86	123.4	201.1	281.4	357.2
14	Request 9	59.45	123.7	201.8	279.4	359.5
15	Request 10	60.32	127	202.9	283.4	359.9
16	Aggregate	65.51	138.64	223.96	307.50	391.70
17	Average 2-10	59.87	125.82	203.09	280.62	358.17
18						
19	Connection cost	*48.52%*	*50.46%*	*50.68%*	*48.92%*	*48.35%*
20						
21	*RPS*	20	40	60	80	100
22	Request 1	19.27	24.07	24.19	24.13	23.82
23	Request 2	19.27	24.06	24.19	24.12	23.83
24	Request 3	19.27	24.06	24.19	24.13	23.81
25	Request 4	19.27	24.06	24.19	24.13	23.83
26	Request 5	19.27	24.06	24.19	24.12	23.82
27	Request 6	19.26	24.06	24.2	24.12	23.82
28	Request 7	19.27	24.06	24.19	24.11	23.82
29	Request 8	19.27	24.06	24.2	24.12	23.81
30	Request 9	19.27	24.06	24.19	24.12	23.81
31	Request 10	19.27	24.05	24.18	24.11	23.81

Summary / Charts / CPU - 100 Users /

Ready

The charts will be automatically generated. In order to obtain CPU usage charts, you need to import the data from the vmstat1.dat file, as follows:

❑ From within Excel, open the data file and specify that it is delimited by spaces.

❑ Select columns U and V, these contain the percentage of CPU utilization for the user processes and the operating system respectively. Copy these two columns into the CPU sheet in the spreadsheet provided. The third column in this sheet calculates the addition of both columns copied over to produce the total CPU usage. We usually start the chart when the actual test run starts and ignore the initial data that presents the CPU usage when the WebLogic Server is starting.

Preliminary Tests

Here, we ran a series of short tests on the application to get familiar with its behavior under various conditions. Specifically, we wanted to:

❑ Establish performance criteria for tests that attempted to emulate a real-world scenario (using think times) and for those that used no think time. From these we would establish a baseline case for our tests.

❑ Optimize the test environment. This included:

  ❑ TCP/IP Tuning.

  ❑ Choosing the best JVM for the application and then defining the optimum heap space. The size of this heap (and the way in which your particular JVM implements garbage collection) is an important factor in determining performance.

  ❑ Determining the optimal number of WLS execute threads.

  ❑ Investigating the effect of using the WebLogic performance pack.

First, let's take a look at the `RandomBytesServlet` test servlet that was used for these tests.

The RandomBytesServlet Test Servlet

To perform our preliminary tests and to investigate the behavior of the various HTTP and servlet engine options, we wrote a simple HTTP test servlet that generates responses consisting of random alphabetic characters (we chose to generate alphabetic characters simply because they make debug traces more readable and are easy to present in this book):

```
package com.wrox.paston.servlet;

import java.io.IOException;
import java.io.OutputStream;
import javax.servlet.ServletException;
import javax.servlet.http.HttpServlet;
import javax.servlet.http.HttpServletRequest;
import javax.servlet.http.HttpServletResponse;

public class RandomBytesServlet extends HttpServlet
{
  private ByteGenerator m_byteGenerator = new ByteGenerator();

  /**
   * See class level javadoc for servlet parameters.
   **/
  public void service(HttpServletRequest request,
          HttpServletResponse response)
  throws ServletException, IOException
  {
```

```
    try {
        // Parse the response parameters.
        int length;

        try {
        length = Integer.parseInt(request.getParameter("length"));
        }
        catch (NumberFormatException e) {
        length = 0;
        }

        int chunkSize;

        try {
        chunkSize =
            Integer.parseInt(request.getParameter("chunkSize"));
        }
        catch (NumberFormatException e) {
        chunkSize = 0;
        }

        if
(Boolean.valueOf(request.getParameter("setContentLengthHeader"))
        .booleanValue()) {
        response.setContentLength(length);
        }

        final boolean random =
        Boolean.valueOf(request.getParameter("random"))
        .booleanValue();

        // Write the response.
        response.setContentType("text/plain");
        final OutputStream out = response.getOutputStream();

        if (chunkSize > 0) {
        for (int i=length; i>0; i -=chunkSize) {

            final int n = i > chunkSize ? chunkSize : i;

            out.write(random ?
                m_byteGenerator.generateRandomBytes(n) :
                m_byteGenerator.generateBytes(n));
            out.flush();
        }
        }
        else {
        out.write(random ?
            m_byteGenerator.generateRandomBytes(length) :
            m_byteGenerator.generateBytes(length));
        }

        // Until case 259386 is resolved.
        out.close();
```

```
        }
    catch (Exception e) {
        log("Exception occurred: " + e);
        throw new ServletException(e);

        // Originally I logged exceptions to the output stream,
        // this doesn't work if the stream itself is hosed.
        // e.printStackTrace(new PrintStream(out, true));
    }
  }
}
```

The servlet can be invoked by making an HTTP request from a HTTP 1.1-enabled web browser, or by using The Grinder (or an alternative HTTP load-generating tool). Let's look at an example of the HTTP interaction that occurs when the servlet is invoked. First, here's the browser request:

```
GET /servlet/generateRandom?length=10 HTTP/1.1
Host: localhost:7001
User-Agent: Mozilla/5.0 (Windows; U; WinNT4.0; en-US; rv:0.9.5+)
Gecko/20011116
Accept: text/xml, application/xml, application/xhtml+xml,
text/html;q=0.9, image/png, image/jpeg, image/gif;q=0.2,
text/plain;q=0.8, text/css, */*;q=0.1
Accept-Language: en-gb, en-us;q=0.50
Accept-Encoding: gzip, deflate, compress;q=0.9
Accept-Charset: utf-8, *
Keep-Alive: 300
Connection: keep-alive
```

You can tell from the headers that the browser made a request to the URL
http://localhost:7001/servlet/generateRandom?length=10. Here's the response from the servlet:

```
HTTP/1.1 200 OK
Date: Sat, 12 Jan 2002 12:31:18 GMT
Server: WebLogic WebLogic Server 6.1 SP2  12/18/2001 11:13:46 #154529
Content-Length: 10
Content-Type: text/plain

NSXCHMRWBG
```

The servlet has generated 10 random alphabetic characters and returned them in the HTTP response body:

Only the first character in the string is chosen using the JDK's random number generator. The remaining characters are generated using a simple, weak pseudo-random algorithm. We found that calling the JDK's random number generator for every character was far too CPU intensive.

If you examine the servlet code, you'll see that there are several parameters that control its behavior:

Parameter	Description
length	Number of bytes to be generated.
random	Default value is false. Set to true to generate every byte using the JDK's random number generator.
setContentLengthHeader	Default value is false. When set to true the servlet will always add a Content-Length header to the response. Setting the content length can influence how efficiently the servlet engine can handle the response stream. Depending on the HTTP version and features used, it might determine whether the servlet engine closes the connection, whether it uses an HTTP 1.1 feature called **chunked transfer**, and whether it has to buffer the entire response before sending. We discuss this in detail below.
chunkSize	Integer value that controls how the servlet writes the response body. If this is set to a non-zero value, n, then the servlet will write *n* bytes to the output stream, flush the output stream, then repeat until length bytes have been written.

You may have noticed that the Content-Length header was present in our response, even though we didn't specify setContentLengthHeader=true. This is because the response was small enough for the WebLogic Server to hold it in an internal buffer, and thus the length could be determined before the response was sent.

From our grinder.properties file (test script) we make requests to RandomBytesServlet as follows:

```
grinder.test0.parameter.url=http://sun1:7001/servlet/generateRandom&size
=32768&setContentLengthHeader=true
grinder.test1.parameter.url=http://sun1:7001/servlet/generateRandom?leng
th=32768&setContentLengthHeader=true
grinder.test2.parameter.url=http://sun1:7001/servlet/generateRandom?leng
th=32768&setContentLengthHeader=true
...
```

You will notice that every request is identical – each simulated user makes ten identical requests to the servlet for each complete execution of the test script.

For each request, the servlet generates a message of 32KB and sets the `Content-Length` header parameter on the HTTP message. Basically, every call to the servlet generates a new 32KB byte array (which is then discarded). We chose the initial message size based on an informal survey: we asked ten people to spend a couple of hours navigating the Internet and saving every page that they accessed (IE saves the initial HTML and then it creates a subdirectory for everything that the initial page requests for download). Based on this, we calculated the average response for HTTP servers on the Internet to be 33.6KB, which we rounded down to 32KB. Of course, this is a rather unscientific technique but nevertheless establishes a reasonable starting point for our tests.

An Initial Test with Think Times

In these tests we wanted to emulate a realistic usage scenario as closely as possible, so we wanted to establish a think time between the execution of each request. Remember that in this case we did not know the real think time, so we chose to use a think time of two seconds between every test with a variation of 20%. We also set a ramp up, or initial spread, of 500 milliseconds. We chose a workload of 500 simultaneous users running the test script as being a good ballpark figure to represent a typical workload for an Internet connected application. Thus, each Grinder machine simulated 125 users and, the `grinder.properties` file for each Grinder defined 10 identical requests to `RandomBytesServlet`.

Thus, in each `grinder.properties` file for this test, we have the following parameters (the full script is provided in the PrelimThinkTime folder of the code download for this chapter):

```
grinder.threads=125
```

```
grinder.thread.initialSleepTime=500
```

```
grinder.thread.sleepTimeVariation=0.20
```

Each individual request in the script is of the following form:

```
grinder.test1.parameter.url=http://sun1:7001/servlet/generateRandom?leng
th=32768&setContentLengthHeader=true
grinder.test1.sleepTime=2000
```

As described previously, the results were collected using the fixed-time sampling method (or snapshot method) using a sample size of five seconds, ignoring the first 36 samples (three minutes), and collecting 120 samples (ten minutes).

We used the "out-of-the-box" configuration for the WebLogic Server 6.1 instance and did not tune any of the parameters. We used the default number of execute threads for the WebLogic Server, 15. The JVM used is Sun's JDK 1.3.1-b24 in HotSpot Server mode, the default on Solaris, with 128MB heap space (this will be set in the WLS startup script provided by BEA).

Each Grinder machine simulated 125 users, and the `grinder.properties` file for each Grinder defined 10 identical requests to the `RandomBytesServlet` servlet. The results for these ten requests (each asking for a 32KB response) are presented in the following table:

Test	ART	TTR
Request 0	373.30	21.60
Request 1	223.10	21.70
Request 2	210.00	21.90
Request 3	201.10	22.03
Request 4	195.00	21.97
Request 5	191.60	21.85
Request 6	190.40	21.76
Request 7	197.10	21.67
Request 8	204.40	21.61
Request 9	207.60	21.60
Totals	219.36	217.69
	(AART)	

As you can see, for this test run the total transactional rate is 218 requests per second, and the AART is 219 milliseconds. However, this AART value is skewed by the fact that the ART for Request 0 – the one that has to establish the HTTP connection – is almost twice as expensive as every other request in the script (we will look at this in more detail in the next section). A common misconception about the meaning of the TPS metric, is to believe that since the response time for Request 0 is almost double that of other requests, then the TPS value for that request will be around half that of other requests. In order to understand why this is not the case, we need to consider how the test works. In order to explain, we will make a few simplifications: we will ignore the initial spread and think time variation. We will round up the response time for Request 0 to 0.4 s and round the response time for every other request to 0.2 s.

We can then describe the process as follows: a worker thread (simulating a user) executes Request 0, sleeps for 2 seconds, executes Request 1, sleeps for 2 seconds, and so on. If you work through this, you will find that after 45 s, Request 0 has been executed 3 times, but it has still only been executed 3 times after 65 s. From these figures, we can get a rough idea for the number of requests per second. In the latter case we get $(3/65 \times 500) = 23$ TPS. Thus, the observed TPS values are pretty much as expected given the simplifications we've made in this analysis. The value will be about the same for all other requests. In this case, the fact that Request 0 takes 400 ms while the others take 200 ms does not affect the overall average for each request. Of course for longer response times ($> 1s$, say) the mathematics will change.

From the WebLogic Server console, we analyzed the behavior of the heap space for this test:

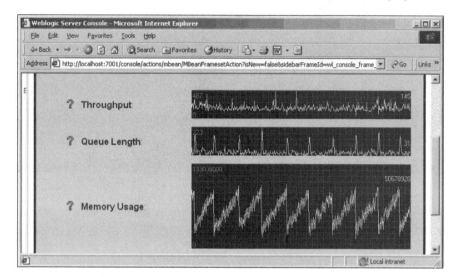

Here we can see that the garbage collection has an impact on the length of the WebLogic Server execute queue. As the garbage collection kicks in, effectively stopping all processing, the queue grows with requests waiting to be processed. The large garbage generation rate is very likely due to the way the `RandomBytesServlet` servlet is written. Every call to the servlet generates a new 32KB byte array, which is then discarded. In our simplistic case, where every request demands a 32KB response, we could have pooled and reused these byte array objects, which would probably have dramatically reduced the amount of garbage generated.

It should be noted that this is speculation. There are probably other causes of garbage in the server than just the 32KB byte array (perhaps the server has some temporary objects allocated) and before you decide to use pooling it is wise to be 100% sure that pooling will reduce garbage collection by a number that you consider significant and worth the coding effort.

We chose not to do so because many application developers take the rational decision not to overcomplicate their servlets by introducing such pooling or by caching static data. As we mentioned at the beginning of this chapter, a natural solution to the problem is to share static data as global variables in the servlet, instead of recreating objects every time through the service methods. A natural place to initialize such static data is in the `init()` method that we discussed earlier. Of course, not all responses can be cached in this fashion. If that were the case, we would hardly need servlets – static files would do just fine! However, by separating common, static content from the dynamic content, we should be able to reduce the number of objects created to some extent.

We can analyze the impact of the garbage collection on the network traffic. The following chart was taken at the end the test run and presents the network usage for this run:

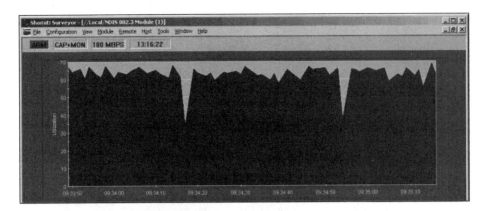

We can clearly see the valleys in the network traffic that, in this case, correspond to the moment the garbage collection happens. It is interesting to note the very large amount of network traffic, in this case using on average a little above 60% of the available 100 Mbps bandwidth.

Finally, we examined the CPU usage of the computer running the WebLogic Server. This chart was constructed using the output of the Solaris `vmstat` command every five seconds:

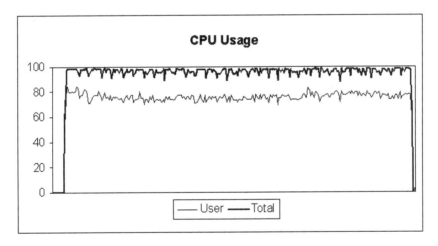

As you can clearly see, the server is very loaded (overloaded) – running at 100% usage for much of this test.

So, this test shows us that we can obtain rather impressive response times of around 200 ms, for a workload of 500 simultaneous users, with throughput values being as expected. However, it also indicated that, under such conditions, the CPU usage on the WLS server is at 100% utilization and a high proportion of the network bandwidth, averaging over 60% of the total 100 Mbps available, is consumed. This sets our general level of expectations of performance in a real world scenario (or at least, under conditions that attempted to emulate realistic usage).

The Baseline Case – No Think Time

As discussed in the earlier section, *Selecting the Sampling Method*, we felt that since we did not know the real think times, a valid approach was to use zero think time between execution of successive requests. After a few exploratory tests we found that, in this stressful environment, we approached 100% CPU usage on the WLS server with 100 concurrent users). Thus, we chose to limit our explorations to 20, 40, 60, 80, 100 simultaneous users.

Each Grinder machine contributed equally to the total user load and in each `grinder.properties` file for this test, we have the following parameters, for the 100 user case (the full script is provided in the **PrelimBaseline** folder of the code download for this chapter):

```
grinder.threads=25
```

```
grinder.thread.initialSleepTime=0
```

```
grinder.thread.sleepTimeVariation=0
```

Then, each individual request (ten in all) in the script is simply of the following form:

```
grinder.test1.parameter.url=http://sun1:7001/servlet/generateRandom?leng
th=32768&setContentLengthHeader=true
```

The data was collected as described in the previous section and the following table summarizes the results obtained for AART and ATPS:

Number of Users	20	40	60	80	100
AART /ms	65.51	138.64	223.96	307.50	391.70
TPS	192.69	240.60	241.91	241.21	238.18

Let's consider the response times first. The following chart presents the ART values for the selected number of users:

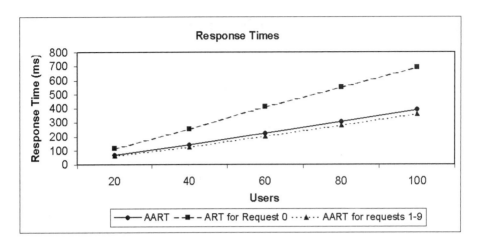

The chart has three lines. The top one is the ART for the first request in the test script. It is the most expensive one because the request has first to establish the HTTP connection with the server. The second line is the aggregate ART for all the 10 requests that make up the test script. The third line, the cheaper one, is an average ART of all the requests in the test script except for the first one. We can calculate the cost of the HTTP connection simply by subtracting the values of the **Average 1-9** line from those of **Request 0** line.

Now let's have a look at the ART results for each individual request:

Number of Users	20	40	60	80	100
Request 0	*116.30*	*254.00*	*411.80*	*549.40*	*693.50*
Request 1	61.79	143.80	219.00	294.70	373.00
Request 2	58.21	122.80	199.20	273.70	351.90
Request 3	59.67	121.10	198.50	277.20	354.10
Request 4	59.71	123.10	201.50	277.60	355.50
Request 5	60.14	123.70	202.60	277.90	355.00
Request 6	59.64	123.80	201.20	280.30	357.40
Request 7	59.86	123.40	201.10	281.40	357.20
Request 8	59.45	123.70	201.80	279.40	359.50
Request 9	60.32	127.00	202.90	283.40	359.90

For this particular set of requests, the cost of the HTTP connection is approximately 49%, meaning that 49% of the ART for the first test is spent establishing the HTTP connection.

Now let's consider the observed TPS values. We can see that the throughput for these test runs stabilizes at about 240 TPS:

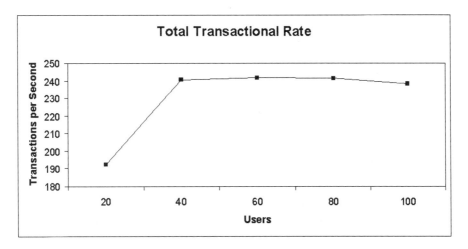

This shows us that throughput (TPS) is really a measure of capacity. The servlet engine was able to handle about 190 transactions per second with 20 users, but when the number of users increased it also increased the throughput. However, the throughput is limited to about 240 TPS under the conditions of the test. Recall the supermarket analogy from Chapter 1, whereby shoppers are analogous to requests and the supermarket staff restocking the shelves are analogous to the components of your system working to cope with the demand. If you tell ten people that they will get for free everything they can put in their shopping trolley in 15 minutes, that does not mean that everything in the shopping trolleys at the end of that time was all there was available in the supermarket. However, as you increase the number of shoppers, you will get to a point where you have enough shoppers to empty the supermarket in that time. At this point, we have reached the maximum capacity of the system. As you increase the number of shoppers beyond that point, crowding in the aisles will mean reduced shopper mobility (longer "response times") and the throughput stabilizes. However, if you continue increasing the number of shoppers, then eventually the throughput will start to drop as well.

Test Environment Optimizations

Now that we had an idea of the behavior of the HTTP server functionality of the WebLogic Server, as well as the servlet engine, we moved on to tune our environment.

TCP/IP Tuning

So far we had been using the WebLogic Server out of the box, running with no optimizations. The documentation for the WebLogic Server (http://edocs.bea.com/wls/platforms/sun/index.html)offers some guidelines for tuning Solaris. These suggestions are rather generic and mainly pertain to setting buffers for the TCP/IP stack. We applied these suggestions and performed some test runs to gauge their impact.

The comparative results between the "tuned" and "untuned" test runs were inconclusive. When tuned, the cost of an HTTP connection improved by 7%, but the AART only improved a negligible 3%. On the other hand, the throughput in the untuned state was about 6% better.

Based on this we conclude that the tuning suggestions do not have any significant performance impact on our tests. This does not diminish the importance of properly tuning the TCP/IP stack. As a matter of fact, it reinforces the notion that you cannot generalize when it comes to tuning. We strongly suggest that whatever tuning you do to the operating system, JVM and application server has to be done for your particular application, and under the conditions it will be used in the real world. TCP/IP tuning is particularly important when handling large numbers of HTTP clients.

JVMs and Heap Space

So far we had been using the HotSpot Server option of JDK 1.3.1-b24 with a heap space of 128MB. We moved on to compare this with the performance obtained using the HotSpot Client option, with the same heap space. We used just two data points: 20 and 100 connections. The results can be seen in the following bar chart:

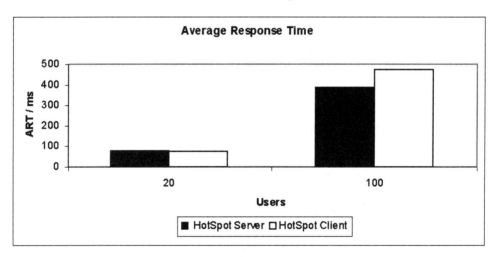

Although at the low load of 20 connections the difference is negligible, there is a big difference at 100 connections. The difference is about 22% in favor of the HotSpot Server option. Let's take a look from the perspective of the transactional rate (throughput):

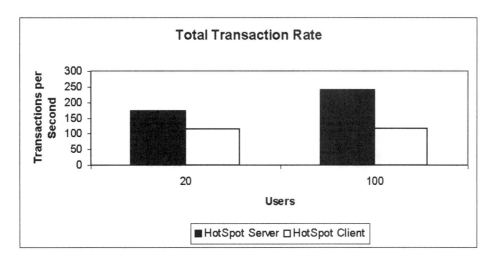

In this case the difference is even bigger. With 20 connections the Server option is approximately 34% better, but this figure rises to over 100% with a load of 100 connections. It seems pretty obvious that the better JVM for this set of tests is the HotSpot Server option, JDK 1.3.1-b24.

Next, we determined the optimum JVM heap size for our test scenario. We investigated performance with heap sizes of 32MB and 64MB, and compared the results with those obtained for 128MB:

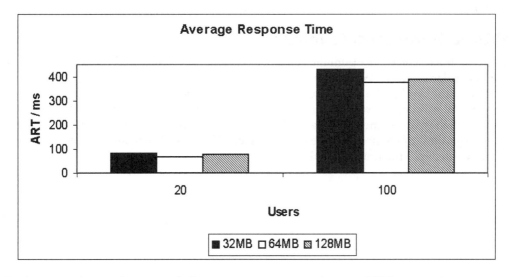

In this case, the results were a little surprising: it seems that a 64MB heap space is more appropriate. The improvement over 128MB is about 20% for 20 connections, falling to around 3% for 100 connections. Let's look at the transactional rates for these test runs:

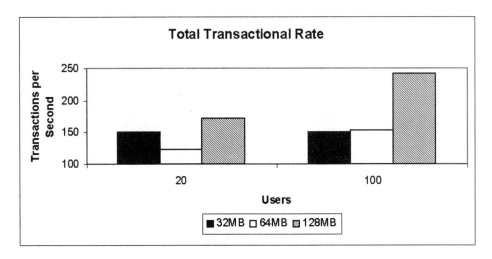

Again, the results are very interesting. The transactional rate for 32MB is flat at a little above 150. The best transactional rate is obtained with a heap of 128MB, whereas the one obtained with a heap of 64MB is poor, although it improves as the load increases. This put us at odds on selecting the heap size. We finally decided to use 64MB because in general our priority is to achieve the best response times. We speculate that by increasing the heap size you increase the throughput, since garbage collection can be deferred longer and the time to garbage collect increases with the number of live objects but also increases with the size of the heap. Thus the pauses due to garbage collection might be prohibitively long in the 128MB case, resulting in very bad response times for a few transactions.

WebLogic Server Execute Threads

Here, we investigated the optimum number of execute threads in the WebLogic Server, for our particular example. We performed test runs with 10, 20, and 50 execute threads and compared the results with those previously obtained using the default value of 15. Our expectation was that 'more is better' for both the ART and the throughput (TPS). To our surprise the response times for 20 and 100 connections were pretty much the same (within 3.5%) regardless of the number of execute threads. However, the picture was quite different when we analyzed the transactional rates:

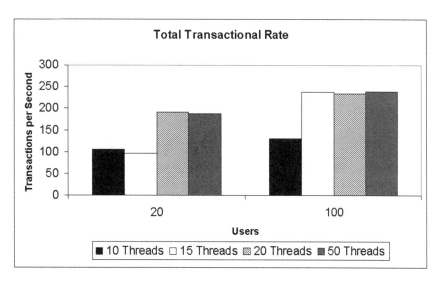

This chart clearly indicates that the best transactional rates are obtained using either 20 threads or 50 threads – the differences between the two are negligible (a very small 1.75% in the worst case).

We chose to use 20 threads for the rest of our test runs. The main reason for this is that, all things being equal, we prefer to use fewer execute threads in order to minimize the context switches on the operating system. Every time the operating system has to execute a thread, it has to perform a context switch. In the long term, a large number of context switches could have a negative effect on the execution of an application (a fuller discussion on this topic appears in Chapter 3).

WebLogic Performance Pack

The native I/O, as the performance pack is also known, is turned on by default. When using WebLogic performance pack, you bypass the socket methods offered by the JRE by creating a pool of sockets directly at the operating system level. In general this feature increases performance when sockets are heavily used by an application. We wanted to have an idea of how much a difference it makes, since these tests are heavy on I/O.

The average response time for 20 users was better by as much as 50% when using the performance pack. This difference diminished to around 17% when the load was increased to 100 users. When looking at the transactional rate the situation is quite similar:

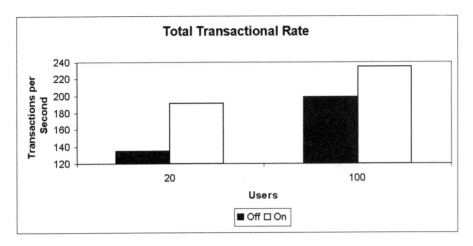

As you can see, the total transactional rate is a lot better with the native I/O turned on. With 20 users the difference is in the order of 42% and with 100 users the difference is smaller, but still a healthy and significant 18%.

We were now ready to move on to the formal performance tests.

The Test Plan

As discussed in the introduction to this chapter, we could not realistically provide a comprehensive investigation of servlet-related performance issues – and doubtless we have omitted some key areas. The test plan was limited to those issues that, in our experience, are raised repeatedly by servlet developers. Therefore, we:

❑ Investigated the performance cost of maintaining a HTTP Log

❑ Determined the effect of the size of the HTTP response

❑ Investigated HTTP protocol options, including the use of persistent connections and of chunked transfer encoding

❑ Assessed the costs and benefits of using the Servlet 2.3 Filters to compress the HTTP response

❑ Performance validated session state management strategies on WLS (HTTP session object versus stateful session beans)

The Cost of Maintaining a HTTP Log

For many web applications, it is important to maintain a log of all incoming client requests. This is especially true for applications whose business model relies on the number of users that access a given web site, for example, in relation to advertisement or commerce. Information logged in such a manner can be analyzed and grouped according to various criteria. For example, it can be useful to know the number of unique clients that access a given site each day, or the types of browsers that are used for that access.

Care must be taken, however, when writing logs on web site activity to the file system. For sites with considerable traffic, perhaps more than a few thousand requests each day, log files are very fast to grow in size, and this can have an impact on the performance of the system if no care is taken to reduce the file size. What happens when a log file exceeds a given size, say a few hundred MBs? Do large files hinder the file writing process? And if so, what can be done to reduce the size of our log files?

Thus, we were interested in ascertaining the actual cost of maintaining an HTTP log in the typical `access.log` file. A typical entry that our test servlet generated in the log file, following the common log format, looks as follows:

```
10.5.1.91 - - [17/Mar/2002:12:03:45 -0500] "GET
/servlet/generateRandom?length=32768&setContentLengthHeader=true
HTTP/1.1" 200 16
```

We performed test runs for 20 and 100 users, using zero think time and generating a response size of 32KB. We collected 120 samples (ignoring the first 36) and the sample size was again 5 seconds.

We expected that the need to keep a log for all the HTTP operations would have quite a significant impact on performance, especially for the 100-user case, which would generate a sizeable log file. The AART results (in milliseconds) were as follows:

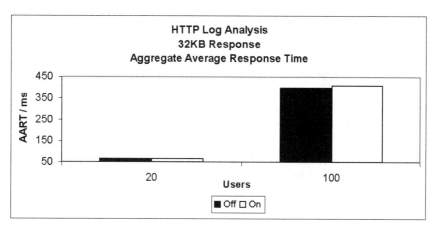

The 100-user test run created a 30MB log file over the course of the 13-minute test but, as you can see, the performance impact of maintaining this HTTP log is negligible. We were surprised by this result but, nevertheless, recognized the possibility of it being somewhat deceptive. Real applications end up with log files that measure in the order of hundreds of megabytes in a single day of operations, so we were keen to validate our results in similar conditions. In order to achieve this, we basically needed to increase the number of entries in the log file. We felt that the easiest way to do this would be to increase the number of users, reduce the message size and increase the sample time.

Thus, in these tests we had 500 users request a response of 16 bytes and changed the test length from 13 minutes to 2 hours. With logging enabled, the test run generated a log file of 709MB over the 2-hour period. The following chart compares the observed AART values, with and without logging:

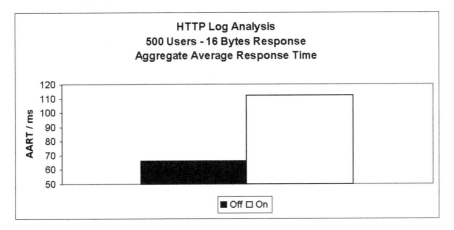

These results indicate an improvement of about 40% in the AART when logging was disabled. Interestingly enough, the total transactional rate is only 7% higher with logging disabled, although this could be due to the fact that we are at maximum capacity anyway.

We do not always have to log everything that happens in the HTTP server. We have the following options available:

❑ Reduce the amount of information being logged. In addition to the common log format, most HTTP servers, including WebLogic, support the extended log file format, version 1.0 (as defined by the W3C, http://www.w3.org/TR). The extended log format allows us to specify the type and order of information recorded about each HTTP communication. We could for example, turn off logging for any HTTP operation except the requests for all the JSP and HTML pages.

❑ Use a log rotating mechanism. Most HTTP servers offer the functionality of rotating the log file based on either the size of the file or a specified length of elapsed time. When one of these two criteria is met, the current access log file is closed and a new access log file is started. This will avoid having the log file grow indefinitely.

Given the differences we have seen in this set of test runs, we strongly encourage you to research this point in more detail as it can have a big impact on the performance of your application.

The Effect of the Response Size

Another area we wanted to explore was the impact of the size of the response generated by the test servlet. Up to now, our tests had used a 32KB response size so we conducted a series of test runs requesting the servlet to generate responses of 8KB, 16KB, 64KB, and 128KB. Although these numbers are not a direct scientific measure of all the pages being served on the Internet, they do cover a very broad range of common sites. Of course, we must keep in mind that in many cases, the servlet only serves the markup language in question – not the images, files, etc. Although it may be rare to see HTML files that are more than a few kilobytes in size, we must be sure to count for all cases. It is not uncommon for applications to use servlets to dynamically display images, stylesheets, streaming video content, and so on – which is the reason why we chose to cover such a broad range of different content sizes.

We performed 25 test runs, generating the above message sizes with 20, 40, 80, and 100 users. We used zero think time, collected 120 samples (ignoring the first 36) and used a sample size of 5 seconds.

Our expectation was that the bigger the size of the response, the slower the response time and the lower the transactional rate would be. What we didn't know was exactly how much of an impact the response size would have. The following chart shows the AARTs of the test runs for the selected response sizes:

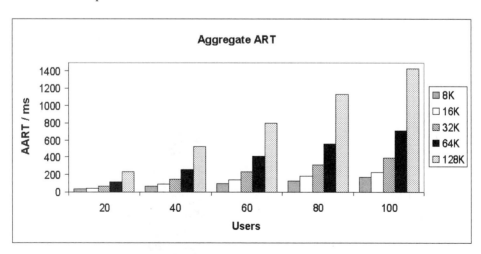

As we move from a message size of 8K to 16K, we see a relatively small degradation in performance, even for the 100-user case. However, as we increase the message sizes from 32K to 64K to 128K, the AART approximately doubles each time, for loads of 60 users and above.

Let's take a look at the results for the total transactional rate:

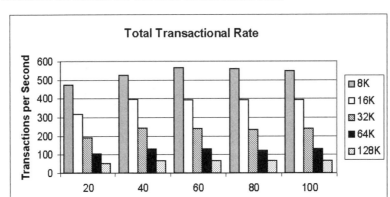

Notice how for loads of 40 users and above, the plots look virtually identical – this is because we have reached capacity throughput at a load of 40 users. In terms of the variation in TPS with increasing message size, we see basically the same trend (in reverse) as observed for AART: as we successively double the size of the response we roughly halve the observed TPS. Here, the trend is clearly observable from 16KB upwards.

At this point we have enough arguments to support the intuitive notion that a smaller response is more efficient – particularly for response sizes of less than 32KB. However, there is another interesting data point we can use to consolidate (or invalidate) this conclusion. As before, we can analyze the proportion of the total response time (AART) that is spent establishing the HTTP connection:

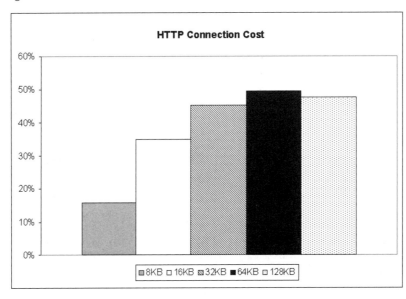

We can conclude that, for message sizes up to 32KB, the exact choice of message size will have a big impact on performance. Above, we can see that the ideal size of the response is 8KB. One of the main reasons that we obtain far better performance with an 8KB response will be explained in detail in the following section.

However, before we leave this issue behind us, we should mention that aside from increasing the transaction rate of the application, there is another advantage to reducing the size of our response. By reducing the response *size*, we also reduce the response *time* of the client, as there is less data that needs to be transferred over the network. Thus, by processing less data for each client response, we increase system performance by **two factors**: less data has to be transferred to the client and the server can handle more requests. Together, this makes the reduction of response size an issue well worth pursuing.

Different HTTP Protocol Options

The challenge for HTTP 1.0 and 1.1 is how the servlet marks the end of the response stream so that the browser knows the size of the message it is receiving, thus handling it more efficiently. It is important to note that in both versions of HTTP the response may be split into several physical IP packets. Handling IP packets is not a function of the servlet, WLS, or even the JVM. It is a function of the network stack, thus the importance of correctly tuning the parameters associated to it.

In the original implementation of HTTP, each request created a new socket connection to the server. The request was sent and the response was read from that connection and then the connection was closed and the browser marked the end of the response from this close process. This was a simple but very slow process and is the main reason why the World Wide Web was so much more painful when it started back in the mid 1990s. In response to this situation the concept of Keep-Alive emerged, the basic idea being that a connection between the browser and the server was kept open for subsequent requests within the same page (thus providing faster download for embedded objects such as images), in order to avoid the pain of re-establishing it every time.

HTTP 1.0 introduced the ability to stipulate "Connection: Keep-Alive" in request and response headers. Otherwise, the default behavior is to close the connection each time. HTTP 1.1 introduced an official specification for how Keep-Alive should operate. If the browser supports Keep-Alive then the default behavior is to attempt to keep the connection alive (unless you explicitly close it in a header).

The HttpServlet, HttpServletRequest, and HtppServletResponse classes implement Keep-Alive automatically but the actual Keep-Alive behavior that occurs depends on two factors: setting content length, and size of output. This leads to the following three possible scenarios:

❑   If the content length header is specified in the response, this determines the end of the response stream and the servlet engine will use Keep-Alive.

❑   If the content length is not explicitly set by the servlet and the servlet does not flush the response, and the response length is less then a certain size (in the case of the WebLogic Server this number is 12KB), than the servlet engine figures out the content length by itself and sets the content length header. The behavior is the same as in the previous case, but we expect the performance to be lower because the server has to buffer the response to calculate the length.

The final scenario will vary according to the version of HTTP:

❑   For HTTP 1.0, if the conditions presented in the previous bullets are not met, then the connection is closed after every request.

❑   For HTTP 1.1, if the content length is not set, or the servlet flushes the response at any time or the content length exceeds 12KB, the WebLogic Server will use an HTTP 1.1 feature called **chunked transfer encoding**, which splits the response into chunks delimited by lengths. In this situation, we have chunks of data being sent one after another via a connection that is not broken after each separate chunk is sent.

To verify the second scenario we ran a series of tests, using HTTP 1.1, with 100 simultaneous users. We used different sized responses, with and without setting the content length header (CLH). The results can be seen in the following histogram:

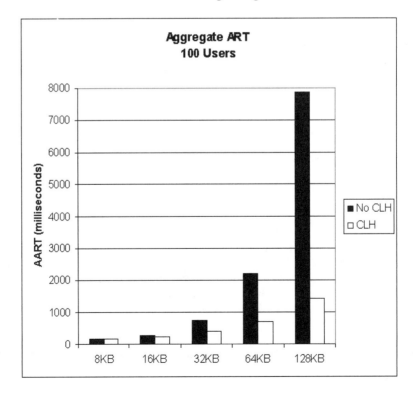

As predicted, for a response size that is smaller than 12KB, the observed AART is the same both with and without setting the CLH. However, for responses above 12KB, the response time increases roughly exponentially as we double the size of the response. The main reason for this differential is the cost of manipulating the data stream without knowing the size of it. When there is a CLH the servlet engine can directly copy the characters to the stream that is sent back to the client. When there is no CLH, the servlet engine has to copy the characters to a buffer until the end of the response, and then it can start sending the characters to the client.

For the third scenario, again using HTTP 1.1, we were interested in understanding the costs of using different size chunks (there is actually no default chunk size – the chunks are dynamically created as the information comes through). For this set of tests we used a 32KB size response and forced a flush using the chunkSize parameter of the test servlet. In the following histogram you can see the resulting AARTs:

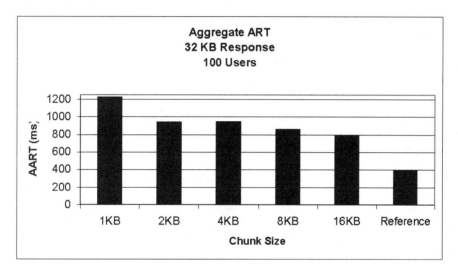

The Reference column shows the comparable performance when the CLH is set. A 16KB chunk size seems to be the most effective, but we still see a factor of two decrease in performance over the reference. It is interesting to note that using a 1KB chunk size is substantially more expensive than the others. The other sizes all exhibit AARTs of around 900 milliseconds.

Based on this particular example we dare generalize that, using the WebLogic Server, better performance can be achieved by having many calls to servlets that generate responses that are smaller than 12KB in size, rather than making fewer calls that generate larger responses. The importance of setting the content length header is obvious given the observed performance improvement.

Using the Servlet Compression Filter

One of the features available in version 2.3 of the Servlet API is filtering (see http://java.sun.com/products/servlet/index.html for details). Filters are not servlets – they do not create a response. A filter class processes requests and responses before they reach and after they leave a servlet. Given the results of our tests with different sizes, we decided to investigate use of this feature to compress HTTP responses, since we thought that this might improve the performance of applications that generate large HTTP responses.

For these tests we developed GZIPServletFilter, which is configured to act on RandomBytesServlet.

GZIPServletFilter

The full GZIPServletFilter class is available with the code download for this chapter. Briefly, the filter implements javax.Servlet.Filter, as do all filter classes:

```
import java.util.zip.GZIPOutputStream;
import javax.servlet.Filter;
import javax.servlet.FilterChain;
```

We use the GZIPOutputStream class to compress the output from the servlet. The filter implements the three methods of javax.Servlet.Filter. The setFilterConfig and getFilterConfig methods set and return the filter's configuration object:

```
public class GZipServletFilter implements Filter
{
    private FilterConfig m_filterConfig;

    public void setFilterConfig(FilterConfig filterConfig)
    {
        m_filterConfig = filterConfig;
    }

    public FilterConfig getFilterConfig()
    {
        return m_filterConfig;
    }
```

The doFilter method does the actual filtering. It receives the current request and response objects, as well as the FilterChain containing the filters that still must be processed:

```
    public void doFilter(ServletRequest request,
                ServletResponse response,
                FilterChain filterChain)
        throws IOException, ServletException
    {
        final HttpServletResponse httpResponse =
(HttpServletResponse)response;
```

```
        httpResponse.setHeader("Content-Encoding", "gzip");

        filterChain.doFilter(request, new
    MyResponseWrapper(httpResponse));
    }

    private void log(String s)
    {
      m_filterConfig.getServletContext().log(s);
    }


    /** Just implements the subset of HttpServletResponse that the
     * ResponseLengthServlet uses. **/
    private class MyResponseWrapper extends HttpServletResponseWrapper
    {
      private final GZIPOutputStream m_zipStream;

      public MyResponseWrapper(HttpServletResponse response)
          throws IOException
      {
          super(response);

          m_zipStream = new GZIPOutputStream(response.getOutputStream());
      }

      public ServletOutputStream getOutputStream() throws IOException
      {
          return new ServletOutputStream() {
                public void write(int b) throws IOException
                {
                  m_zipStream.write(b);
                }

                public void write(byte[] buffer, int offset, int length)
                  throws IOException
                {
                  m_zipStream.write(buffer, offset, length);
                }

                public void close() throws IOException
                {
                  m_zipStream.close();
                }
          };
      }
    }
  }
}
```

Running the Tests

Our objective was to find out how much we could improve the performance by using this feature. For this we used the same test script as before, but calling the new servlet:

```
grinder.test0.parameter.url=http://sun1:7001/servlet/generateGZIPRandom?
length=32768
```

The size of the response from the RandomBytesServlet was 32KB. However, note that we do **not** set the CLH, since we do not know the size of the **compressed** response that will leave the filter. We performed test runs using zero think time. We collected 120 samples (ignoring the first 36) and the sample size was again 5 seconds.

We started our tests with 20 users and we almost immediately ran out of memory on the JVM, indicating that the compression process is quite memory-intensive. The original response is copied to memory and then the compression algorithms are applied. The algorithm itself uses quite a bit of memory to create and handle intermediate tables.

We increased the heap size from 64MB to 256MB and we still ran out of memory with 20 users. We gradually reduced the number of users to 8, at which point we could perform a test run where we did not run out of memory. The following table compares the response times for 8-user test runs, both with and without using compression:

	Compressed Response	No Compression	Difference
Request 0	52.48	40.33	23%
Request 1	41.79	26.51	37%
Request 2	41.67	26.29	37%
Request 3	42.33	27.06	36%
Request 4	42.05	27.01	36%
Request 5	42.77	26.27	39%
Request 6	43.07	26.71	38%
Request 7	41.79	26.30	37%
Request 8	42.81	27.02	37%
Request 9	41.86	26.78	36%
Aggregate ART	43.26	28.03	35%

In fact we see that the no compression case gives about 35% better performance (and we consume an awful lot less heap space).

However, before we get carried away, we must remember that the compression filter was specifically designed to reduce the bandwidth used on **slow network connections** – for example, when sending digital information to PDAs or a Bank communicating with its branches over a 64KB telephone line. Thus a more realistic test would use a modem, as opposed to a 100 Mbps hub.

Thus, our next test configuration used an Intel Pentium III laptop with a 56KB modem as a client, executing exactly the same test script. The test runs are based on eight users running the test script over a 46,600 connection via an ISP, which also uses VPN. The response times (in milliseconds) are as follows:

	Compressed	Standard	Difference
Request 0	1990	11900	x 6
Request 1	1260	9180	x 7
Request 2	870	14800	x 17
Request 3	877	7850	x 9
Request 4	1040	8150	x 8
Request 5	1050	11300	x 11
Request 6	1450	8390	x 6
Request 7	928	11900	x 13
Request 8	1050	13000	x 12
Request 9	1040	7750	x 7
AART	11555	104220	x 9

Here, we see the compression filters really come into their own – the response times are an average of nine times faster when we compress the responses. Looking in more detail, we can see that the compressed message is 124 bytes (from the original size of 32 KB), which obviously makes a significant difference on a modem-based communication.

These tests do not measure the time a client would need to uncompress the response, which is highly dependent on the compute power of the client. This would add a little more time before the client could actually display the response. In a couple of informal tests we measured this time of decompression to be around 10 to 20 milliseconds for the laptop we used on the modem tests.

We can conclude that using compression does make a very big difference when using slow connections, but on the other hand, it is very expensive in terms of memory usage in the JVM. The lesson here is to only use functionality for the purpose for which it was designed. Compression might be good, for example, in intranet applications, where there are constraints on the number of connections being made and the type of hardware being used (in other words, there is a limited number of employees working at the company, and hardware information is readily at hand). On the other hand, compression might not be such a good idea for general web applications, where both the number of users as well as the hardware they use is generally unknown. For such applications, filtered compression might easily bring down the server as the number of users increases, and not all clients will be able to benefit from the compression. In your own applications, you should take into account the exact scenario, when determining the relative advantage of using compression filters.

Managing Session State

The ability to share state between successive requests from a single user is an important aspect of many web applications. A series of requests to a certain domain from the same user-agent (that is, browser or handheld device) is commonly identified as a **session**. For HTTP servlet applications, a natural way of managing the state of a session is to use methods of the `HttpSession` object, which associates with a unique user-agent through the use of cookies, URL-rewriting or any other session-tracking mechanism. The actual mechanism used, however, is generally transparent to the application developer, as well as to the user.

Although the `HttpSession` object is usually the best way of keeping track of users, it may not be the ideal way of actually storing the session state. For EJB applications, there is the alternative of using stateful session beans for storing the session data, as we will see later. In some cases, a mixture of the two methods may well be the best approach. For example, it might be appropriate to separate business logic from presentation logic by storing business-related information in a session bean and navigation and presentation state in an `HttpSession` object.

In either case, no matter what method you choose to maintain the state of your sessions, there are performance considerations that must be investigated. For example, what is the impact of storing massive amounts of session data for a large number of users, on server performance? What actions can be undertaken to reduce the effect of session state managements on server resources, such as memory? Also, which one of the two methods we mentioned above, `HttpSession` and session beans, will scale better in the long term?

We investigated these issues in more detail by performing a series of measurements on the performance of applications storing session state.

HTTP Session Objects

Probably the most common way of maintaining temporary information for an end user during an HTTP connection is by storing it in an HTTP session object. Intuitively we know that the size of the HTTP session object and the way it is manipulated will have an impact on performance. By manipulation, we mean how the session object is updated, which can basically be done in two different ways:

❑ By storing a single object in the HTTP session object and completely updating it every time.

❑ By storing many smaller objects in the HTTP session object and updating each object as required.

Our objective was to explore the costs of manipulating the HTTP session object as described above. We did this based on two sizes of session data: 2KB and 5KB. Based on an informal survey we found that the average amount of data stored through a session object to be about 2KB and chose that as a reasonable starting point. We investigated the 5KB case in order to provide a more complete picture.

Of course, we expect there to be a performance penalty for using a larger session object. However, we were also interested in gauging the performance impact of different manipulation techniques for the same size object. There are basically two programming styles when it comes to updating the session object. The first one uses many small objects in the session object. Every time a change happens only the necessary small objects have to be updated. The second style treats the session object as one single monolithic object and any small change implies updating the whole session object every time.

An analogy here would be a `Customer` object that stored the name, shipping address, phone number, and billing information. Using the former approach implies that if we update a small piece of information in the `Customer` object, such as the phone number, we must update all the other information in the object. Using the latter approach implies that the phone number may be stored in a discrete "subobject" and only that will be updated. Instinctively, one would expect the latter approach to be more efficient, but it has been a matter of some debate in the programming community.

AlterSessionServlet

To achieve the above objectives we wrote another servlet, `AlterSessionServlet`, which allowed us explore those particular issues.

For each HTTP request made to the `AlterSessionServlet`, a specific number of randomly generated bytes are stored in the HTTP session associated with the request. The exact number, and the method used to store the bytes, varies according to the parameters supplied with the request, as we describe below. Each session contains a hashmap of objects. Each object is a byte array of random bytes. Each request can either add new objects, or replace existing objects. The request specifies the size of the new arrays.

```
public class AlterSessionServlet extends HttpServlet
{
    private ByteGenerator m_byteGenerator = new ByteGenerator();

    private String m_uniquePrefix;
    private int m_nextUniqueNumber = 0;
```

The generateUniqueKey() method is a utility method that returns a unique string, used in keys into our HTTP session. It needs to be unique for different servlets because many servlets can belong to one web application, and hence share one HTTP session. It needs to be unique across servers because HTTP sessions can fail over to new servers. It does not need to be unique across web applications because WLS will ensure that requests are routed appropriately to the appropriate web application for the HTTP session:

```
    private synchronized String generateUniqueKey()
    {
    return m_uniquePrefix + m_nextUniqueNumber++;
    }
```

The init() method is called when the servlet is deployed:

```
    public void init(ServletConfig servletConfig)
      throws ServletException
    {
    super.init(servletConfig);

    // Use JMX to get server information to ensure that keys are
    // unique across servers. Another web application might
    // generate a match, but the key is unique for the scope of
    // HTTP sessions.
    try {
```

We calculate a string that is unique across all deployments of this server for use by generateUniqueKey. This involves three steps. Step 1 is to get a string that is unique for this server and servlet:

```
        final String uniqueServerID =
            new LocalServerInformation().getJVMID() +
            servletConfig.getServletName();
```

Step 2 is to hash it to create a shorter, unique byte array. The other reason to hash is to restrict the characters that are used – important when using cookie replication:

```
                // Calculate an MD5 hash.
                final ByteArrayOutputStream byteArrayOutputStream =
                  new ByteArrayOutputStream();

                new BufferedWriter(new
          OutputStreamWriter(byteArrayOutputStream).
                  write(uniqueServerID);

                final byte[] messageDigest =
                  MessageDigest.getInstance("MD5").digest(
                    byteArrayOutputStream.toByteArray());
```

Step 3 is to convert the byte array to a string we can use to prefix unique IDs:

```
                m_uniquePrefix = byteArrayToHexString(messageDigest) + "-";
            }
        catch (Exception e) {
            throw new ServletException("JMX problem", e);
        }
    }
```

`byteArrayToHexString` is a utility method that converts a byte array to a hexadecimal string:

```
    private static String byteArrayToHexString(byte[] bytes)
    {
      final StringBuffer s = new StringBuffer();

      for (int i=0; i<bytes.length; i++) {
          s.append(Character.forDigit((bytes[i] & 0xF0) >> 4, 16));
          s.append(Character.forDigit(bytes[i] & 0x0F, 16));
      }

      return s.toString();
    }
```

The `service()` method is called for each request:

```
    /**
     * See class level javadoc for servlet parameters.
     **/
    public void service(HttpServletRequest request,
                HttpServletResponse response)
      throws ServletException, IOException
    {
      try {
```

We decode the mode parameter to figure out whether we are adding new objects to the session or changing existing objects:

```
        final String modeString = request.getParameter("mode");
        final boolean add =
          modeString == null ||
!modeString.equalsIgnoreCase("change");

// Decode the number of objects to add/change:
        int number;
        try {
          number = Integer.parseInt(request.getParameter("number"));
        }
        catch (Exception e) {
          number = 10;
        }

// Decode the size of the new objects to create:
        int size;
        try {
          size = Integer.parseInt(request.getParameter("size"));
        }
        catch (Exception e) {
          size = 10;
        }
```

Allow the buffer size to use to send the response to be modified. This is potentially interesting when sending back large cookies:

```
        try {
          final int bufferSize =
              Integer.parseInt(request.getParameter("buffer"));

          response.setBufferSize(bufferSize);
        }
        catch (Exception e) {
        }

        final HttpSession session = request.getSession();

        // We write a trivial response.
        response.setContentType("text/plain");
        final PrintWriter out = response.getWriter();

        if (add) {
```

We're adding number objects:

```
        final String unique = generateUniqueKey() + "-";
```

For each object, generate a new key and insert an array of random bytes into the session:

```
for (int i=0; i<number; i++) {
    session.setAttribute(
      unique + i,
      new String(m_byteGenerator.generateBytes(size)));
}

out.println("Added " + number + " objects of size " + size);
}
else {
```

We are modifying number objects – or rather binning them and replacing them with new ones. There is no servlet API to find the number of attributes (objects) in a HTTP session – we have to guess. If we guess too low, the `ArrayList` has to resize. If we guess too high, the `ArrayList` will waste a little memory.

```
final ArrayList attributeNames = new ArrayList(number * 5);
```

Iterate over all the existing objects and add them to the list:

```
final Enumeration e = session.getAttributeNames();

while (e.hasMoreElements() ) {
    attributeNames.add(e.nextElement());
}
```

We shuffle the list so that we pick random victims:

```
Collections.shuffle(attributeNames);
```

We can't modify more than the total number of objects:

```
final int numberToChange =
    Math.min(attributeNames.size(), number);
```

We replace the old with the new:

```
for (int i=0; i<numberToChange; i++) {
    session.setAttribute(
      (String)attributeNames.get(i),
      new String(m_byteGenerator.generateBytes(size)));
}

out.println("Replaced " + numberToChange +
        " objects with new objects of size " + size);
}
}
```

```
      catch (Exception e) {
          log("Exception occurred: " + e);
          throw new ServletException(e);
      }
   }
}
```

Requests to this `alterSessionServlet` can be made as follows:

```
http://localhost:7001/servlet/alterSession?mode=add&number=1&size=2048
```

The parameters available in this servlet are:

Parameter	Description
mode	When defined as `add` it will create an object in the HTTP session object. The object contains a set of random characters. When defined as `change` the servlet will replace the content of the object with a new set of random characters.
number	The number of objects that will be created or modified.
size	The size in bytes of the object to be created or modified.

Using this information we decided on a set of four tests that would allows us to explore the issues related to updating an HTTP session object:

❑   Using a single 2KB object in the HTTP session object we update the whole object. We will refer to this one as the single object case.

❑   Using four 512 byte objects in the HTTP session object, we update only the relevant 512B object each time. We will refer to this one as the multiple object case.

❑   Using a single 5KB object in the HTTP session object we update the whole object.

❑   Using five 1KB objects in the HTTP session object, we update only one of the objects.

The test scripts we used were similar to the ones used in the previous sections of this chapter. The first test creates the specified object in the HTTP session object and the following nine tests modify the object. The test script for this looks as follows:

```
grinder.test0.parameter.url=http://sun1:7001/servlet/alterSession?mode=a
dd&number=1&size=2048
grinder.test1.parameter.url=http://sun1:7001/servlet/alterSession?mode=c
hange&number=1&size=2048
grinder.test2.parameter.url=http://sun1:7001/servlet/alterSession?mode=c
hange&number=1&size=2048
grinder.test3.parameter.url=http://sun1:7001/servlet/alterSession?mode=c
hange&number=1&size=2048
```

```
grinder.test4.parameter.url=http://sun1:7001/servlet/alterSession?mode=c
hange&number=1&size=2048
grinder.test5.parameter.url=http://sun1:7001/servlet/alterSession?mode=c
hange&number=1&size=2048
grinder.test6.parameter.url=http://sun1:7001/servlet/alterSession?mode=c
hange&number=1&size=2048
grinder.test7.parameter.url=http://sun1:7001/servlet/alterSession?mode=c
hange&number=1&size=2048
grinder.test8.parameter.url=http://sun1:7001/servlet/alterSession?mode=c
hange&number=1&size=2048
grinder.test9.parameter.url=http://sun1:7001/servlet/alterSession?mode=c
hange&number=1&size=2048
```

When using four 512 byte objects to update the session object, the requests look as follows:

```
grinder.test0.parameter.url=http://sun1:7001/servlet/alterSession?mode=a
dd&number=4&size=512
grinder.test1.parameter.url=http://sun1:7001/servlet/alterSession?mode=c
hange&number=1&size=512
....
```

We used the same user loads of 20, 40, 60, 80 and 100 with no think time.

2KB HTTP Session Object

In the first set of tests, we updated the whole 2KB object that was created in the HTTP session object. The average response time results for the selected user loads are as follows:

ART	20	40	60	80	100
Request 1	*121.80*	*216.90*	*310.10*	*414.70*	*509.30*
Request 2	136.70	242.70	352.70	467.90	576.20
Request 3	125.80	232.80	326.30	423.90	543.00
Request 4	126.60	231.00	327.50	433.20	537.80
Request 5	127.60	228.50	329.60	429.00	531.60
Request 6	126.80	228.00	325.70	431.70	538.60
Request 7	127.20	229.40	326.90	427.90	529.50
Request 8	127.60	227.50	326.10	433.90	535.80
Request 9	125.80	228.50	324.80	433.80	534.70
Request 10	127.30	229.00	330.30	426.10	535.50
Aggregate	**127.32**	**229.43**	**328.00**	**432.21**	**537.20**

It is interesting to note that the first request is about 5% cheaper then the average of the next 9 requests. Up to this point, we had seen that the first request was more expensive because of the cost of establishing the HTTP connection. Here, it seems that the cost of establishing the connection, plus the cost of creating the 2KB object in the HTTP session object, is still cheaper than the cost of updating the session object, as we do in the subsequent requests.

You can also see that the second request is slightly more expensive than subsequent requests, when we expected the times to be more or less the same. The reason for this is unclear.

The total transactional rate stabilizes at a load of 60 users, as can be seen in the following chart:

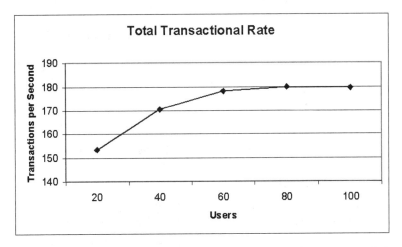

The CPU utilization of the computer running WebLogic was about 50% and the network traffic averaged 7% of the available bandwidth.

The second set of tests created 4 objects of 512 bytes in the HTTP session object. Subsequently, we updated only one of these 4 objects. In this case, we found that the first request was about 20% cheaper than the average of the 9 subsequent requests, suggesting that updating one of four 512 B objects is slightly more expensive than updating a single 2 KB object. In contrast to the results observed for the single object case, in this set of test runs the second request was not found to be more expensive than the 8 subsequent requests.

The following table compares the recorded AART values for the two cases, over the whole range of user loads:

AART	20	40	60	80	100
2KB/2KB	127.32	229.43	328.00	432.21	537.20
2KB/4 x 512B	136.18	242.15	359.29	472.36	581.94
Difference	6.96%	5.54%	9.54%	9.29%	8.33%

The differences are not big, but they can be considered significant (above 5%). Performing the same comparison for the total transactional rates we find an average difference of about 7% in favor of the single object case, which again is not much, but might be considered significant.

These test runs presented similar behavior to the single object case, with regard to CPU utilization and network traffic.

We can conclude that, in this particular case, performance was slightly better when updating the HTTP session object with a single 2KB object, rather than 4 objects of 512 bytes. Of course, this will be highly dependent on the exact size of the object and the pattern of manipulation during the test run. Once again, we strongly encourage you to test your particular case.

5KB HTTP Session Object

In order to obtain a more complete picture of the behavior of the HTTP session object, we repeated the tests using a 5KB object. The results obtained when manipulating a single 5KB object in the HTTP session object can be seen in the following table.

5KB/5KB	20	40	60	80	100
AART	281.10	530.36	736.76	953.48	1163.20
TPS	70.29	74.56	80.74	83.26	85.23

Here, the first request is approximately 16% cheaper then the 9 subsequent requests in the test script (we did not find that the second request was more expensive than the subsequent 8 requests).

For the second set of test runs we used 5 objects of 1KB in size and updated only one of them. The following table compares the recorded AART values for the two cases, over the whole range of user loads:

AART	20	40	60	80	100
5KB/5KB	281.10	530.36	736.76	953.48	1163.20
5KB/1KB	292.09	557.47	749.79	1003.10	1197.60
Difference	3.91%	5.11%	1.77%	5.20%	2.96%

In this case, the performance differences might be considered negligible, since they are around, or below, our 5% limit. However, there is a general suggestion that it is more efficient to manipulate a single object rather than multiple smaller objects. The observed pattern is similar when we analyze the total transactional rate. We cannot make any definite conclusions with only two data points, but the results obtained here suggest that the bigger the HTTP session object size, the smaller the performance difference that is attributable to the exact manner in which the session object is manipulated.

Both of these sets of test runs presented similar CPU usage graphs to those obtained for the 2KB test runs (an average of 50%). The network traffic was also the same, at approximately 7% of total bandwidth.

The Effect of Session Object Size

The following chart compares the aggregate ARTs obtained for the above four tests runs:

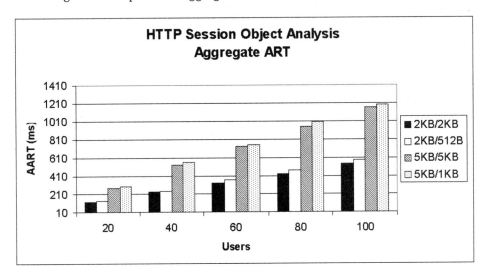

In general, the AARTs for the 5KB tests are approximately 120% higher than those for the 2KB tests. The next chart presents the same comparison for the observer total transactional rates:

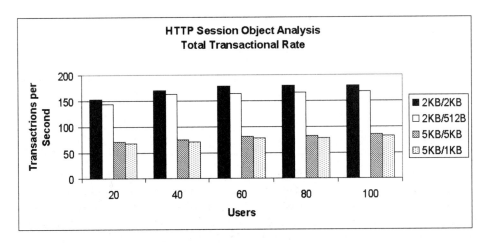

In this case we can see that the transactional rates for the 2 KB case are about double those observed for the 5 KB case – so the trend is very similar to that observed for AART.

We can conclude that the size of the HTTP session object does have an impact on the performance, as measured by response time and by throughput. We also noticed that the first request of our test scripts, which establishes the HTTP connection and creates the object in the HTTP session object, was cheaper than the rest of the requests, which manipulated the object(s) created. Finally we saw that when the object size is relatively small, it is slightly better to handle it as one single object rather than many small ones. This difference seems to become smaller as the object size increases.

HTTP Session Object vs Stateful EJB

One of the big controversies surrounding session handling regards the performance difference of storing session state in an HTTP session object compared with a stateful session bean. It was our expectation that it will be more efficient to store data in an HTTP session object as there is more overhead involved with the infrastructure of session beans in the EJB container. Therefore, we were interested in measuring the performance of each method, in order to either prove or disprove this basic assumption.

Thus, we created a test servlet, SessionServlet, which would allow us to store a specified amount of content in either an HTTP session object or in a stateful session bean, RemoteSessionBean. Overleaf, we briefly describe the code used for the SessionServlet. Both the SessionServlet and the RemoteSessionBean are available for download for this chapter on the Expert-Press web site, packaged in the SessionTest.ear file.

The Session Servlet

The SessionServlet class serves both as a servlet and as a session listener. The servlet's doGet() method is responsible for handling requests and storing data in the associated session, using a specified storage method. The session listener methods are necessary in order to properly remove stateful session beans:

```
package wrox.session;

import javax.naming.*;
import javax.ejb.*;
import java.util.*;
import wrox.session.*;
import javax.rmi.PortableRemoteObject;
import java.io.*;
import javax.servlet.*;
import javax.servlet.http.*;

public class SessionServlet extends HttpServlet
    implements HttpSessionListener {

    /** Session type parameters */
    public final int HTTP_SESSION = 0;
    public final int REMOTE_EJB_SESSION = 1;
```

```
public final int ALLOW_PASSIVATE = 2;

/** Various configuration parameters */
public final String SESSION_TYPE = "type";

// Note that the content size is measured in bytes.
public final String CONTENT_SIZE = "size";
public final int DEFAULT_SIZE = 512;

/** A hash table that stores reference to Handle objects */
private static Hashtable sessions;
private static boolean passivate=false;

/** The home interface */
private static RemoteSessionBeanHome remoteHome;

public final String REMOTE_BEAN_KEY = "RemoteSessionBeanHandle";
private ServletContext sctx;
```

The servlet's init() method is used to initialize a hash table that keeps track of session IDs, in case stateful session beans are used to store the session state. This is necessary in order to properly remove the beans when the sessions expired, as we will discuss further below:

```
public void init() throws ServletException {
    sessions = new Hashtable();
    sctx = getServletContext();
    try {
        Context ctx = new InitialContext();
        ServletConfig sc = getServletConfig();

        // Store the remote session bean home interface.
        Object objref = ctx.lookup("MyRemoteSessionBean");
        remoteHome = (RemoteSessionBeanHome)
            PortableRemoteObject.narrow(objref,
                RemoteSessionBeanHome.class
            );

    } catch (Exception e) {
        throw new ServletException(e.getMessage());
    }
}
```

Most of the work of this servlet takes place in its doGet() method. When the servlet is requested using the argument type=0 it stores data in an HttpSession object, but when run with the argument type=1 it stores the data in a stateful session bean. When using the session bean, we still have to use the HTTP session object to store the bean's handle, in order to associate the bean instance with the client.

```
protected void doGet(
    HttpServletRequest request, HttpServletResponse response)
    throws ServletException, IOException {

    ServletOutputStream out = response.getOutputStream();

    int type = HTTP_SESSION;
    try {
        type = Integer.parseInt(request.getParameter(SESSION_TYPE));
    } catch (NumberFormatException n)  {
    }

    int size = DEFAULT_SIZE;
    try {
        size = Integer.parseInt(request.getParameter(CONTENT_SIZE));
    } catch (NumberFormatException n)  {
    }

    // Create some random content. This is done for each
    // request, since we want to reflect the impact of
    // storing different data for different sessions.
    byte[] data = new byte[size];
    Arrays.fill(data,(byte) 'x');

    // Look up the HttpSession instance.
    HttpSession session = request.getSession();

    // For each request we will store a new, unique
    // attribute, by using the current system time for a key.
    String key = String.valueOf(System.currentTimeMillis());

    // Determine the method of storing session data.
    Handle remoteHandle =null;
    RemoteSessionBean rsb = null;
    switch (type) {

        case HTTP_SESSION:
            session.setAttribute(key,data);
            break;

        case REMOTE_EJB_SESSION:
            remoteHandle = (Handle) session.getAttribute(
                REMOTE_BEAN_KEY);

            // Determine whether we have already initialized a
            // remote Stateful Session Bean for this client.
            // If not, we create a new bean and store its handle
            if (remoteHandle == null) {
                try {
                    rsb = remoteHome.create(session.getId());
                } catch (Exception e) {
                    throw new ServletException(e.getMessage());
                }
                session.setAttribute(REMOTE_BEAN_KEY,
```

```
            rsb.getHandle());
                        sessions.put(session.getId(), rsb.getHandle());
                } else {
                    rsb = (RemoteSessionBean)
remoteHandle.getEJBObject();
                }
                rsb.setAttribute(key,data);
                break;

            case ALLOW_PASSIVATE:
                remoteHandle = (Handle) session.getAttribute(
                    REMOTE_BEAN_KEY);
                rsb = null;

                // Determine whether we have already initialized a
                // remote Stateful Session Bean for this client.
                // If not, we create a new bean and store its handle
                if (remoteHandle == null) {
                    try {
                        rsb = remoteHome.create(session.getId());
                    } catch (Exception e) {
                        throw new ServletException(e.getMessage());
                    }
                    session.setAttribute(REMOTE_BEAN_KEY,
rsb.getHandle());
                        sessions.put(session.getId(), rsb.getHandle());
                } else {
                    rsb = (RemoteSessionBean)
remoteHandle.getEJBObject();
                }
                rsb.setAttribute(key,data);
                passivate=true;
                break;
        }
    }
```

In addition to being a servlet, the SessionServlet additionally extends the
HttpSessionListener interface. The reason we did this was to ensure that all session
beans would be removed from the container when the associated session was invalidated. If
we had not explicitly removed the session beans – by calling the ejbRemove() method –
they would have been passivated by the bean container:

```
public void sessionCreated(HttpSessionEvent event) {}

public synchronized void sessionDestroyed(HttpSessionEvent event) {
    String sessionID = event.getSession().getId();
    Handle handle = null;
    handle = (Handle) sessions.get(sessionID);

    // Remove the bean and the bean handle
    if (handle != null && remoteHome != null) {
        if (!passivate){
```

```
                        try {
                            remoteHome.remove(handle);
                        } catch (Exception e) {
                            getServletContext().log(e.getMessage());
                        }
                    }
                }
            }
```

Running the Tests

Once the `SessionServlet` had been deployed, we set up our measurements using the following test script:

```
grinder.test0.sleepTime=6000
grinder.test0.parameter.url=http://sun2:7001/servlet/SessionServlet?type
=1&size=512
grinder.test1.parameter.url=http://sun2:7001/servlet/SessionServlet?type
=1&size=512
grinder.test2.parameter.url=http://sun2:7001/servlet/SessionServlet?type
=1&size=256
grinder.test3.parameter.url=http://sun2:7001/servlet/SessionServlet?type
=1&size=128
grinder.test4.parameter.url=http://sun2:7001/servlet/SessionServlet?type
=1&size=512
grinder.test5.parameter.url=http://sun2:7001/servlet/SessionServlet?type
=1&size=256
grinder.test6.parameter.url=http://sun2:7001/servlet/SessionServlet?type
=1&size=128
grinder.test7.parameter.url=http://sun2:7001/servlet/SessionServlet?type
=1&size=512
grinder.test8.parameter.url=http://sun2:7001/servlet/SessionServlet?type
=1&size=256
grinder.test9.parameter.url=http://sun2:7001/servlet/SessionServlet?type
=1&size=128
```

The above script stores session data in our stateful session bean. In order to save the data in the HTTP session object, we simply switch to `type=0`. To make sure that the stateful beans were removed at the end of every HTTP session, we set the HTTP session timeouts in the WebLogic Server to 5 seconds and forced the test script to sleep for 6 seconds before starting a new HTTP session. Every request stores a different number of bytes, as you can see in the test script. The total number of bytes stored per session is 3,200.

We ran the tests using 100, 200, 300, 400, and 500 simultaneous users. Once again we were using zero think time between the requests of the test script, so it could be considered that we were running a rather stressful load on the application server. The following chart compares the average response time for request 0 with the AART for all tests in the script, when using the HTTP session object:

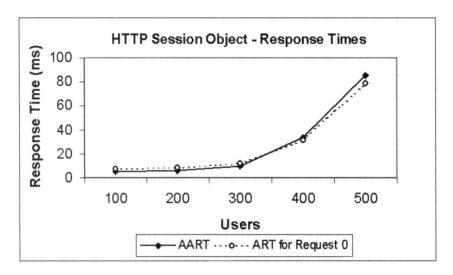

Notice how the first request becomes less expensive than the aggregate value of the response time as the load increases beyond 300 users. This shows that under high loads the manipulation of the HTTP session object is more expensive than the HTTP handshake and the creation of the HTTP session object.

Looking at the chart of the total transactional rate we notice that we have not yet reached the full capacity of the application server as the curve has not stabilized:

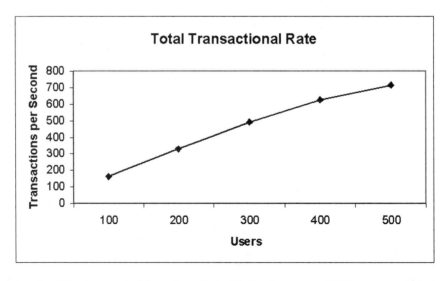

The network utilization varied from less than 1% for the case of 100 users, to less than 4% utilization for 500 users. The CPU usage of the WLS computer running the application varied from an average of 20% for 100 users to 90% for 500 users.

We then repeated the above test, but using the stateful session bean by specifying `type=1` as an argument to the servlet. To our amazement, the results were basically the same:

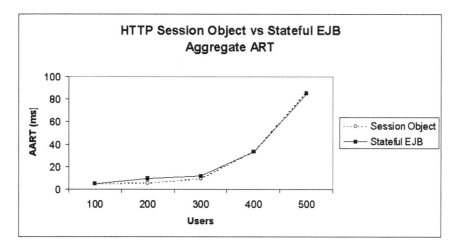

In the case of the transactional rate the biggest difference is of the order of 1%, which is negligible. The network and CPU utilization for this set of tests is basically the same as the ones for the tests using the HTTP session object.

We have to acknowledge the fact that the stateful session bean was not using the security features offered by the EJB container. Nevertheless, it is very interesting to find out that under these conditions, **the comparative costs of storing data in an HTTP session object are roughly the same as storing the same data in a stateful session bean**. To say the very least, this came as some surprise to us.

Once again we strongly encourage you to test your situation taking particular care of the think times you use in the test scripts. These can have a very big impact on the results you obtain.

Using ejbRemove

One of the most common programming mistakes in J2EE is to forget to **explicitly** destroy or remove EJBs once they have been used. This happens most often when calling EJBs from servlets. We mentioned earlier that we took a lot of care in our previous tests to make sure that the EJBs were removed. We did this by implementing a session listener, which made sure that before a session was terminated, all the beans it may have been storing would be terminated. In addition to that, we then made sure that our test script waited until the HTTP session timed out, thus giving the listener some time to remove the EJBs.

From a performance perspective, failing to remove an EJB that should have been removed carries a very high price. Basically what happens is that the EJB will be **passivated** – a very expensive way of removing an EJB from the container since the container first serializes the bean and then it writes it to disk.

One of the tools we use in the lab is Introscope from Wily Technology, Inc. (www.wilytech.com, see Chapter 1), which provides us with a variety of real-time performance information of Java applications running on a J2EE application server. Using a custom probe, we investigated the rate of passivation of the stateful EJB and found that we were averaging 20 passivations per second:

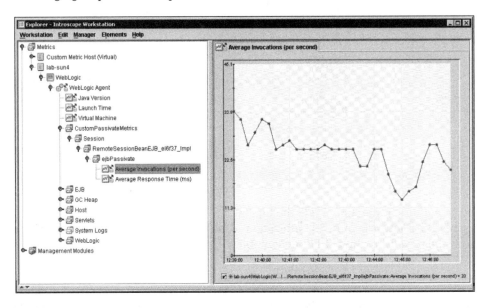

To clearly illustrate the expense of passivation, we modified the servlet we used for the previous tests. We did this by adding a `type=2` test that does not remove the stateful session bean when the HTTP session is terminated. The differences were so big that we had to use a logarithmic scale for the following chart:

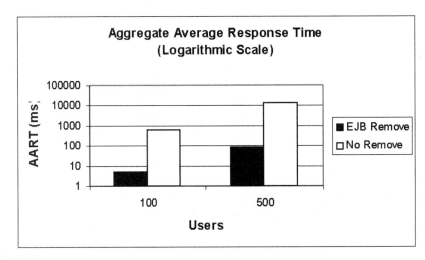

The picture for the transactional rate shows a similar trend:

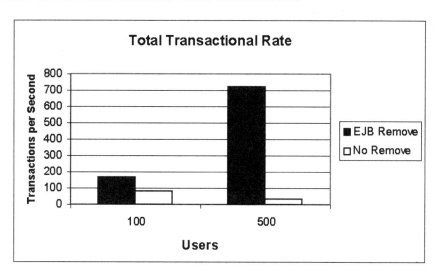

Here you can see that when we are properly removing EJBs, the throughput increases as we increase the user load from 100 to 500. However, when we have EJB passivation, throughput actually decreases, as the number of users increases.

Conclusion

It is amazing to find out that the cost of storing data in an HTTP session object is basically the same as using a stateful session bean, assuming the bean is removed in a proper way at the time the session terminates. However, knowing that the beans must be removed is one thing – actually getting it done in time is another. In fact, it takes a considerable programming effort to ensure that this is done correctly. In our case, we used the session listener mechanism to monitor the session life cycle and then to cut in moments before the beans are passivated. For your own applications, you can use this method, or any other you find more viable. In any case, always make sure to properly test and analyze the system before making any final decisions.

Servlet Clustering

With WebLogic Server we can have two or more instances working together in such a way that the clients think they are dealing with one single monolithic WebLogic Server. By 'working together' we mean that the members of a cluster coordinate their actions to provide scalability and highly available services. The workload can be balanced over the various instances of the server and more servers can be added in a dynamic fashion to increase capacity, leading to high scalability. High availability is based on the ability to send the load of a failed server to another member of the cluster while maintaining knowledge of the state of all the clients of the failed server.

When clustering servlets, the WebLogic Server requires that all the requests go through a web server that acts as a proxy. A special plug-in is provided for various web servers that will round robin the requests from one member of the cluster to the next. You can also use a hardware or software load balancer to achieve the same objective.

Replication

High availability is achieved by replicating the `HttpSession` object. When replication is enabled, the proxy works with the cluster defining primary and secondary instances. Every time there is a call to `session.setAttribute()`, the session object of the primary instance is replicated to the secondary instance of the WebLogic Server. If the primary instance is no longer available, the proxy turns the secondary server into the new primary and selects a new secondary server. When using a load balancer instead of the web server proxy, the inner workings are slightly different but the final result is the same.

Replication is only needed when automatic failover is required, which is not always the case. You can choose to replicate in the memory of the server or, for more reliability, you can persist the HTTP session object to various kinds of persistent data store. This means that the session object has to be copied to the selected data store, implicitly making the operation more expensive. The available data stores are:

- File system.
- Database, using a JDBC driver (jdriver, in this case).
- The HTTP session cookie. This is a very interesting option as the client is the one that carries information rather than the server having to worry about storing it.

So, with these tests, we basically wanted to investigate the relative cost of replication using the different types of persistent data store (and using in-memory replication). As a side issue, we also wanted to continue our investigation of the impact of the various different techniques for manipulating the session object, when working in a cluster. In our single instance tests, we found that it was generally more efficient to update one single monolithic object, rather than handle several smaller objects. We wanted to see whether this behavior held when replication was involved (when the changed portion, or the whole object, has to be replicated to the other instances).

The Test Environment

The configuration used for this set of tests is described in the following figure:

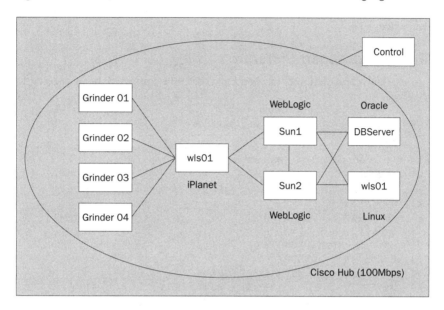

We used a cluster of two members, each running on its own computer. We ran the iPlanet web server on a separate machine, with the WebLogic NSAPI plugin. For the database persistence we used Oracle and for file persistence we used the wls02 computer, running on Linux. Details on the computers and versions of the software used can be found in Appendix B.

For these tests we used `alterSessionServlet` test servlet, which was described earlier in the chapter. The requests in the test scripts (`grinder.properties` file) were of the form:

```
http://localhost:7001/servlet/alterSession?mode=add&number=1&size=2048
```

In this case, we limited our investigations to the 2KB case and thus tested using the following techniques:

❑ Using a single 2KB object in the HTTP session object, updating the whole object (single object case).

❑ Using four 512B objects in the HTTP session object, updating only one of the four objects each time (multiple object case).

These tests were performed with no replication, in-memory replication, and by persisting to various persistent data stores.

Setting Up and Running the Tests

The procedure to follow is actually very similar to that described for the single instance tests. Here we will only detail the new steps that are required in order to use replication, and to run WLS in a cluster.

Setting Up the Database Schema

In order to use JDBC persistence, we need to create the appropriate storage table in the Oracle database:

```
drop TABLE wl_servlet_sessions;

create table wl_servlet_sessions
  ( wl_id VARCHAR2(100) NOT NULL,
    wl_context_path VARCHAR2(100) NOT NULL,
    wl_is_new CHAR(1),
    wl_create_time NUMBER(20),
    wl_is_valid CHAR(1),
    wl_session_values LONG RAW,
    wl_access_time NUMBER(20),
    wl_max_inactive_interval INTEGER,
  PRIMARY KEY (wl_id, wl_context_path) );

COMMIT;

QUIT;
```

On the DBServer computer we must reset the database schema **before the start** of each new test. It is very important that all the test runs happen under the same conditions.

Configuring and Starting WebLogic Server

The steps here are as described previously, except that we use the following cluster_config.xml file on the WLS administrative server:

```
  <?xml version="1.0" encoding="UTF-8" ?>
- <Domain Name="chapter4">
- <Server ListenPort="7001" Name="control" NativeIOEnabled="true"
TransactionLogFilePrefix="config/chapter4/logs/">
  <WebServer LogFileName="./config/chapter4/logs/access.log"
LoggingEnabled="true" Name="control" />
  <KernelDebug Name="control" />
  <SSL Name="control" />
  <ServerDebug Name="control" />
  <ServerStart Name="control" />
  <ExecuteQueue Name="default" ThreadCount="15" />
  <Log FileName="config/chapter4/logs/weblogic.log" Name="control" />
```

```
   </Server>
   <Security GuestDisabled="false" Name="chapter4"
PasswordPolicy="wl_default_password_policy" Realm="wl_default_realm" />
   <FileRealm Name="wl_default_file_realm" />
   <PasswordPolicy Name="wl_default_password_policy" />
   <Realm FileRealm="wl_default_file_realm" Name="wl_default_realm" />
   <Log FileName="config/chapter4/logs/wl-domain.log" Name="chapter4" />
   <JTA Name="chapter4" />
   <SNMPAgent Name="chapter4" />
   <Cluster Name="c4" />
-  <UnixMachine Name="sun1">
   <NodeManager Name="sun1" />
   </UnixMachine>
-  <UnixMachine Name="sun2">
   <NodeManager Name="sun2" />
   </UnixMachine>
-  <Server AcceptBacklog="600" Cluster="c4" Machine="sun1" Name="sun1">
   <SSL Name="sun1" />
   <ServerDebug Name="sun1" />
   <ServerStart Name="sun1" />
   <Log FileName="sun1.log" Name="sun1" />
   <ExecuteQueue Name="default" ThreadCount="15" />
   <WebServer LoggingEnabled="false" Name="sun1" />
   <KernelDebug Name="sun1" />
   </Server>
-  <Server AcceptBacklog="600" Cluster="c4" Machine="sun2" Name="sun2">
   <SSL Name="sun2" />
   <ServerDebug Name="sun2" />
   <ServerStart Name="sun2" />
   <Log FileName="sun2.log" Name="sun2" />
   <ExecuteQueue Name="default" ThreadCount="15" />
   <WebServer LoggingEnabled="false" Name="sun2" />
   <KernelDebug Name="sun2" />
   </Server>
   <JDBCConnectionPool DriverName="weblogic.jdbc.oci.Driver"
Name="PersistentStorePool" Password="{3DES}1F/C/cPv5ShcvyP2GXCtaA=="
Properties="user=weblogic" URL="jdbc:weblogic:oracle:uklab" />
   <ApplicationManager Name="chapter4" />
-  <Application Deployed="true" Name="performance3"
Path=".\config\chapter4\applications\performance3.ear">
   <EJBComponent Name="statelessEJB" URI="statelessEJB.jar" />
   <WebAppComponent Name="servlet" Targets="sun1,sun2" URI="servlet.war"
/>
   </Application>
   </Domain>
```

Selecting the Replication Technique

We can select the type of replication from the WebLogic console. The first step is to select the web application, as shown in the following screenshot:

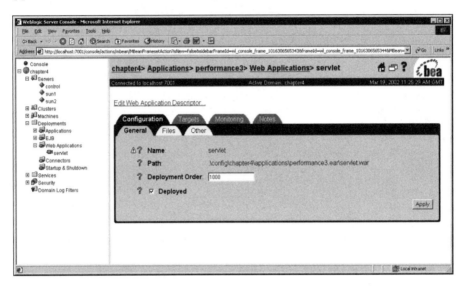

Next you click on **Edit Web Application Descriptor**, which will start another browser with the following content:

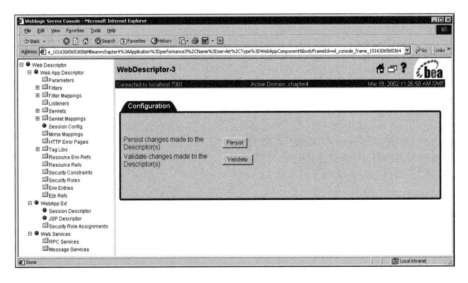

Click on **Session Descriptor** under the **WebApp Ext** node in the list on the left, this will present the following screen:

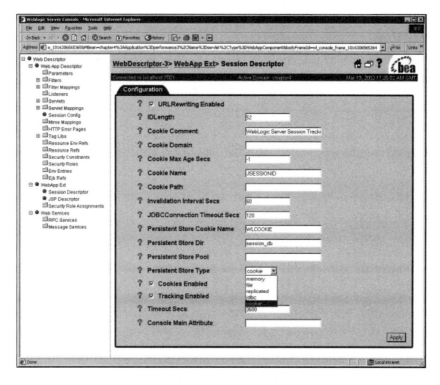

On this screen you can choose the kind of replication you want for the chosen servlet by selecting it from the pull-down menu displayed. Notice that if you select file replication, you will have to provide a directory where the replication will occur. Just define the directory in the entry called **Persistent Store Dir**, which is above the pull-down menu. If you choose to use JDBC replication, you will have to define the name of the JDBC connection pool that will be used. This pool has to be defined beforehand.

Once you have chosen the type of replication, click on the list **Web Descriptor** link. You will be presented with the screen we saw earlier. Click the **Persist** button to persist the changes made to the web descriptor of the test servlet.

Single Object Case

The first test that we intended to perform was with in-memory replication, using connection loads of 20, 40, 60, 80, and 100 users. We started using no think time, as in the previous test runs, but we quickly ran out of memory in the JVM. We increased the heap space to 256MB, but we still ran out of memory. Since we did not observe this behavior for the equivalent single instance tests, we speculate that the cost of running in-memory replication is rather high.

In order to progress with these tests, we introduced a think time of 500 milliseconds to every request in the test script. To minimize the margin of error of the test runs we used no think time variation.

No Replication

In order to set a point of comparison, the first set of test runs used no replication. The following table shows the recorded average response times for each request over the full range of workloads:

ART	20	40	60	80	100
Request 0	*11.56*	*14.39*	*14.15*	*20.67*	*33.79*
Request 1	10.41	12.66	12.79	18.97	31.90
Request 2	10.11	12.43	12.56	19.03	32.11
Request 3	10.83	12.17	12.90	18.25	31.60
Request 4	10.96	12.44	12.63	17.91	31.33
Request 5	10.41	12.30	12.54	18.27	31.80
Request 6	10.61	12.70	12.12	18.30	31.19
Request 7	10.16	12.84	12.06	18.44	31.17
Request 8	10.19	12.75	12.25	18.99	31.55
Request 9	10.06	12.86	12.47	19.03	31.54
Aggregate	10.53	12.55	12.48	18.58	31.58

The aggregate ART is steady up to 60 users, and increases rather significantly for higher loads. We see that, with a cluster of two servers, we have not yet reached capacity throughput with 100 users (in the single instance tests we reached capacity at 40 users):

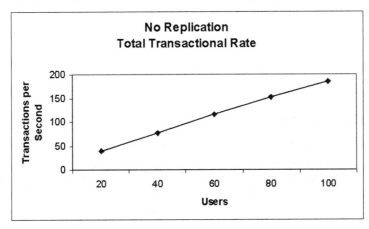

The heap usage presents a clean garbage collection pattern as can be seen in the following screenshot from the console of the WebLogic Server:

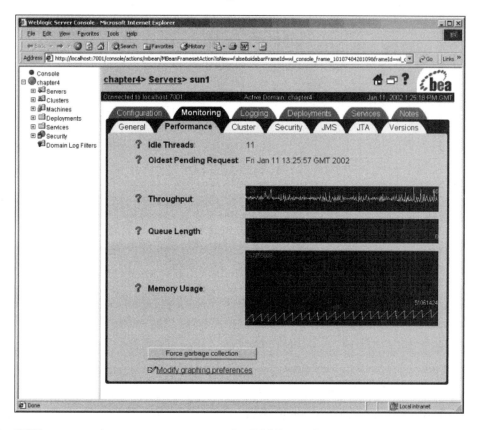

The CPU usage on the computers running the WebLogic Server instances averaged a little under 20%, whereas the CPU usage of the computer running the web server averaged 40%. The network traffic was substantially lower at an average of less than 3% of the 100Mbps bandwidth.

In-Memory Replication

We repeated the above test run, but this time we used in-memory replication. This is the cheapest way to achieve a pretty good level of fault tolerance. From the marketing perspective, it keeps your customers shopping, unless something a little more catastrophic than losing one server (instance) occurs. Of course, if your application handles sensitive transactions and cannot loose a customer session, then you will need to use database replication.

The following graph shows the comparative results for AART:

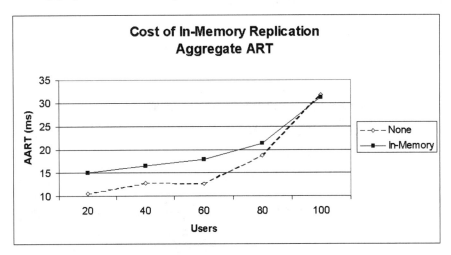

Here we can see that, under these conditions, the response times for loads of 20, 40, and 60 simultaneous users are considerably higher (almost double) when using in-memory replication. However, as the number of users increases to 80 and 100 users, the relative cost of replication starts to diminish. For 100 users, the results suggest that, in terms of pure response time, there is no extra cost involved in using in-memory replication.

A plot of transactional rate versus user load, for in-memory replication, mapped the one obtained for no replication very closely.

We analyzed the CPU usage on the computers running the server and found that usage had increased from about 20% for no replication to about 30% here. The heap space is much higher, as expected:

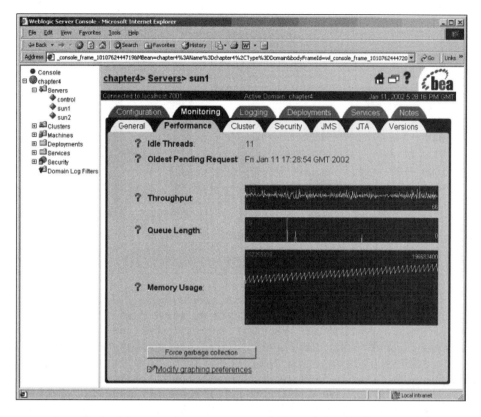

The network traffic had increased to an average of 7% and the CPU usage of the machine running the web server remained very much the same.

As this point we can state that for high user loads the AART cost of in-memory replicating of the HTTP session object is negligible. The TTR cost was negligible over all user loads tested here. Of course, there is a cost involved with using in-memory replication, and that is primarily a much higher usage on the heap space of the JVM, which increases the CPU usage of the machine running the server (there is also a slight increase in network traffic).

Comparing File and Database Persistence

Let us now have a look at the results when performing replication using a persistent store. The following chart presents the Aggregate ART for the test runs, performed as before, using file and JDBC (database) persistence:

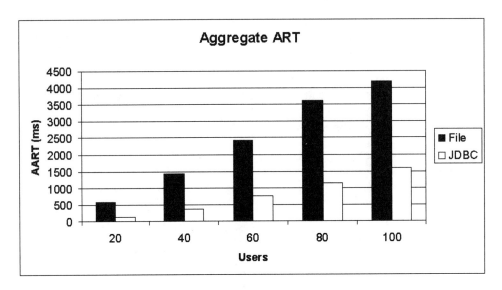

We were expecting the response times to be much higher in these cases (it was difficult to include the no replication and in-memory plots on the above graph since the highest AART, for 100 users, was just over 30 ms). What really surprised us was the fact that file persistence is so much more expensive than database persistence – over 250% more expensive.

We had purposely chosen to do file persistence on a separate machine (running on Red Hat Linux) so that we did not have to burden one of the computers in the cluster with the additional work of handling disk write operations. When we examined the directory that contained the files used for the persistence, we were amazed. The directory occupied about 80MB, there where 240 directories at the higher level, and each one went down 14 levels. At the end of the trail we found a 3KB file that contained the session information.

When using database persistence there is only one table and each session is a record in this table. It is obvious that the database can do a much better job handling one record per HTTP session than the Linux file system handling one file per session.

We took care to delete all of these directories before starting each test run (as well as dropping and recreating the table in the database). Thus, WebLogic Server started faster as it did not have to read the file system or the database to find out which sessions were there.

Let's move on to look at the transactional rates:

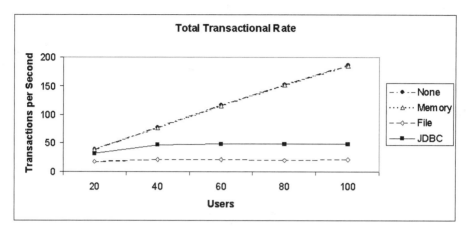

You can see that the TPS values for file and database persistence stabilize at 40 users and above.

The CPU usage charts of the computers that were running WebLogic, when using file persistence, present an interesting pattern:

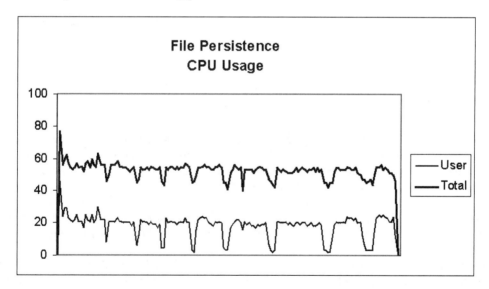

As you can see over half the CPU usage is spent on system operations, most of which are writes to an NFS mounted disk, supposedly cheaper than actual writes on a local disk, since NFS is a stateless protocol. The restriction with this is that the file data store has to be available to all the members of the cluster, so usually they end up being NFS mounted. In contrast, the CPU usage when using database persistence is just below 15%. The heap usage on both cases presented a short see-saw pattern that did not increase over time.

The network traffic for both persistence types was about the same at 5%. This is quite understandable as the actual persistence in both cases was happening over the network on other computers.

The CPU usage of the computer running the web server was about 20% when we used database persistence and about 10% when we used file persistence. The CPU usage of the computer running the database was less than 5%.

Cookie Replication

Finally, using cookie replication we can see that the results are comparable with no replication and in-memory replication, just a little more expensive as we can see in the following comparative chart.

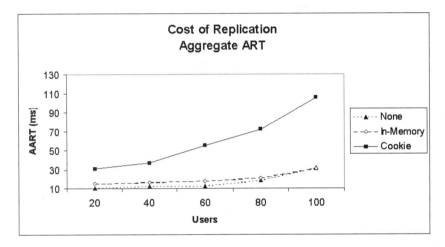

We did observe an interesting thing: the first request is cheaper than the rest, even though it has to establish the HTTP connection. We suspect that this is because it is quite costly to manipulate the cookie – lots of data being sent as cookies to the client so we should expect this to be more and more costly as the user load increases.

When comparing the transactional rates, we also noticed a similar relationship as with the aggregate ART, it is a little slower than no replication and in-memory replication.

From these tests we can clearly conclude that when using a 2KB HTTP session object and persistence is necessary, the better choice is a database. If you are using RAID disks, then file persistence will be more efficient and the picture may change. However, with database persistence you also gain higher reliability. If you are not concerned about security, then using cookie replication is definitely a very interesting option that can highly simplify your application. On the other hand, the WebLogic Server now offers the ability to use secure cookies over an HTTPS connection, so if you really want to use this replication mechanism, this might be an option.

Multiple Objects Case

For these tests, the first request in the test script created 4 objects of 512 bytes each, and the 9 subsequent requests modified one of the four objects. Our first order of interest was to examine if there was any difference in costs between updating a single 2KB object in the HTTP session object and this case. For in-memory replication we found that there was essentially no performance difference, in terms of AART or transactional rates, between either of the update strategies. Analyzing the CPU usage of the computers in the cluster, we found the same behavior as for the single object case. This also applied to the network traffic and the CPU usage of the computer running the web server.

Repeating the tests for file and database persistence, we basically found the same thing: no difference in performance between the multiple object and single object cases. For some user loads, when using file persistence we did notice 4% to 5% improvements in AART in favor of the multiple object case. This could be considered negligible, but if real, may be due to the fact that the file created to persist the HTTP session is smaller than the one created for the single object case.

Using cookie replication, we found the multiple object case to be between 6% and 10% more expensive than the single object case. We suspect this is because there is more cookie manipulation in the multiple object case.

We can conclude then that when using a 2KB HTTP session object, it is basically the same to update the whole object than to update a smaller object of 512 bytes.

Summary

In this chapter we explored the performance of the servlet engine of the WebLogic Server with a specific set of examples:

- **Tuning and JVM options** – you cannot generalize when providing instructions for tuning, specifically in the case of the TCP/IP stack.

- **The cost of maintaining an HTTP Log** – we found that there was a significant performance cost, in terms of response times, for large log sizes (in the region of 30 MB).

- **The impact of message size** – this has a dramatic impact on both TPS and AART. In our system, for loads of 60 users and above we found that as we increased the message sizes from 32K to 64K to 128K, the AART approximately doubled each time. We found that our ideal size of the response was 8KB.

- **HTTP protocol options**

  - **Using persistent connections** – we found that not setting the content length header had a large, detrimental impact on performance.

- ❑ **Chunked transfer encoding** – in our case, we found a 16KB chunk size seems to be the most effective.

❑ **HTTP response compression** using Servlet 2.3 Filter functionality – we found that this was effective in situations for which it was designed (slow network connections). For a 32KB response size, we observed response times that were an average of nine times faster with compression. However, the compression process is quite memory-intensive – we needed to increase the heap size from 64MB to 256MB.

❑ **Choosing a mechanism for storing session state**:

- ❑ **Using the HTTP session object** – we found that, in our case, it was somewhat more efficient to treat the session object as one single monolithic (updating the whole session object every time), rather than use many small objects in the session object (updating only the necessary small objects each time).

- ❑ **Using stateful session beans** – surprisingly, we found that, using WebLogic, stateful beans can be no more expensive, in terms of response times or transactional rates, than using the session object.

❑ **Servlet clustering in a WebLogic Server** – we found that persisting an HTTP session object of 2KB in a file under the Linux operating system was substantially more expensive than persisting it in a database. The cost of persisting a session object in a database was about 50 times more expensive than just keeping it in memory.

We tried to use examples that were generic enough for you to get a decent idea of the behavior of HTTP and servlets in the WebLogic Server. This however is not a substitute for doing performance tests with your specific applications. We strongly encourage you to performance test your application to fully understand its behavior. Hopefully, these examples will help you gain the necessary understanding.

EJB Design Patterns

Although the Enterprise JavaBean (EJB) component model (in version 2.0 at the time of writing) is only one of the whole set of technologies comprising the J2EE platform, it is often seen as fundamental to the platform. The EJB component model offers J2EE developers a great deal of flexibility in their design and implementation choices, and these choices impact overall application performance to (often greatly) varying degrees. For this reason, the EJB layer is often the center of focus, and the center of confusion, when it comes to analyzing J2EE application performance. As a result, a number of EJB design patterns have emerged to address commonly recurring problems, but it is unlikely that any of these patterns represent a "one size fits all" solution.

The overall goal of this chapter is to demonstrate how applying EJB design patterns and design choices can impact performance and scalability, both favorably and (perhaps) unfavorably. As you might expect, the decisions regarding whether or not to apply a particular design pattern, or which patterns to apply, are often driven by weighing many different costs and benefits. Moreover, not all of these costs and benefits are of equal value. The decision criteria change with each design problem at hand.

In some cases, you may decide to intentionally sacrifice a certain degree of performance in the EJB tier in order to gain a larger benefit that the design pattern may offer (looser coupling, coarser granularity, better code reuse, and so on); in other cases, the design pattern's benefit may not justify the performance sacrifice. At the other end of the spectrum, some design patterns are specifically designed to improve performance, scalability, or both, but perhaps at the expense of increased design complexity or some other trade-off. Choosing how and when to apply design patterns can be a delicate balancing act. However, when it comes to choosing and implementing EJB design patterns, J2EE developers frequently apply two guiding principles:

❑ Performance and scalability are always major factors in the cost/benefit analysis of every design decision. This is simply a fact of life for an "enterprise-class" application developer.

❑ You must use performance tests as a tool to determine the true cost or benefit a design pattern for your EJB architecture.

In this study, we selected a few of the more familiar EJB design patterns (from a rapidly growing catalog) to use as examples, implemented in a fictitious ("toy") EJB application representing a catalog of jazz recordings. For each chosen pattern, we'll then design simple test cases that illustrate the impact, positive or negative, of applying the design pattern in that particular case. In doing this, we hope to highlight ways to evaluate an EJB design pattern from the perspective of performance and scalability, as well as the particular performance characteristics of each design pattern (as it is applied in each test case).

Design Patterns

It is tough to find a Java developer these days who isn't actively using design patterns as part of their standard tool set, or that isn't very familiar with their use and application. In fact, design patterns are an implicit part of the Java programming language itself (for example, the Collections framework). A **design pattern** is a reusable solution to a recurring software design problem encountered and solved many times, by many software developers that have come before us. Most software design problems have multiple candidate solutions, but over time and experience, only a few of the solutions emerge as the best choices. Design patterns represent and communicate those "best choices" in a general way that the developer can apply to solve the specific problem at hand.

If you are not already familiar with the general concept of design patterns, a good place to start learning about them is the seminal "Gang of Four" ("GoF") book, *Design Patterns: Elements of Reusable Object-Oriented Software* by Gamma, Helm, Johnson, Vlissides (Addison-Wesley, ISBN 0-201-63361-2).

EJB Design Patterns

Given that good design patterns emerge with time and experience, through the work of many developers solving the same design problem over and over again, one may wonder how design patterns can exist for a technology as recent as EJB and J2EE. There are two sides to this issue. On the one hand, the J2EE platform itself represents the application of numerous design patterns, gleaned from years of experience in the development of distributed systems. For example, the multi-tiered web server/application server/database server architecture (Servlet/JSP, EJB, and database) is an application of the well-trodden Model/View/Controller (MVC) design pattern of Smalltalk. Likewise, the designs of many (perhaps most) of the platform's APIs not only represent applications of classic design patterns, but imply or even force the use of the patterns by anyone using those APIs (for example, the EJB Home interface applies the classic Factory pattern).

On the other hand, many of the design patterns specific to the J2EE platform are still emerging, or still changing as time passes and experience grows. Some patterns have even been "deprecated" within the first 18 months of their publication. One must ask, "By whom?" For an example, see page 201 of *EJB Design Patterns* by Floyd Marinescu (John Wiley & Sons, Inc. ISBN 0-471-20831-0). Other design patterns have been reborn with new names, or new adaptations to changes in an API's specification (this is especially true of EJB design patterns and the arrival of the EJB 2.0 specification). To further complicate the EJB developer's life, most of the current design patterns have multiple variations, ranging from the mundane to the arcane.

The fact is, J2EE and EJB design patterns are in a state of flux, still changing as the J2EE development community discovers new tricks, and as new APIs and specifications emerge. This places EJB developers and architects in a precarious position: is the "design pattern" I choose today really the best choice for my application or for my performance goals? Moreover, for any particular design pattern, which implementation variation is best suited to my application? It is this precarious position that has forced EJB developers and architects to begin testing and performance measurement at the outset, even (and especially) when making the most fundamental design decisions in architecting their enterprise applications. Over time, experience will grow, APIs will stabilize, and many of the design choices we struggle with today will seem obvious. But until then, we test!

EJB Design Pattern Sources

The sources for EJB design patterns continue to grow at an amazing rate. We culled our pattern choices from the following online resources:

❑   The Portland Pattern Repository's EJB Design Patterns page (http://www.c2.com/cgi/wiki?EjbDesignPatterns) is an excellent resource from one of the developer communities at the heart of the design patterns movement.

❑   The Sun Java Center's J2EE Patterns Catalog page (http://developer.java.sun.com/developer/technicalArticles/J2EE/patterns) contains a listing of core J2EE patterns gleaned from the experience of Sun's own consulting organization.

❑   The J2EE Design Patterns page (http://java.sun.com/blueprints/patterns/j2ee_patterns/) is part of Sun's Java Enterprise BluePrints site, and contains another catalog of design patterns used in the J2EE BluePrints reference applications (Java Pet Store Demo).

❑   TheServerSide.com's J2EE Patterns Repository page (http://www.theserverside.com/patterns) is a very active site, containing pattern submissions and discussion from developers actively engaged in J2EE projects.

Of course, there are many more online resources for EJB design patterns; while those listed seem to be the most active, each of them contains links to other useful sites.

Three Fundamental Patterns

There are currently hundreds of J2EE and EJB patterns, some very established and in widespread use, others recently posited and under evaluation by the J2EE development community at-large. In our testing examples, we explore three primary EJB design patterns that seem to be almost universally recognized by EJB developers:

❑ The **Session Facade** pattern appears in most J2EE applications, and is often seen as fundamental to good design in the EJB layer. This pattern allows developers to provide clients and the presentation tier with coarse-grained access to the EJB business logic (via session beans), and significantly reduce network traffic that would otherwise result from direct, fine-grained access to entity beans. See *The Session Facade Pattern in a Nutshell* a little later, for more on details.

❑ The **Value Object** pattern was one of the first patterns to emerge from the EJB development community. Like the Session Facade pattern, the Value Object pattern's primary goals are twofold: to reduce potential network traffic by reducing fine-grained calls to an entity bean's accessors, and provide clients of the entity bean with coarse-grained access to the bean's field values. Some contend that the EJB 2.0 specification has eliminated the need for the remedy that this pattern provides, citing that local interfaces permit direct, fine-grained access to entity beans. However, the pattern is still widely applied and holds "value" for many applications (particularly in remote client access to entity beans and similar situations). For more on this topic, see *EJB Design Patterns* by Floyd Marinescu (John Wiley & Sons, Inc. ISBN 0-471-20831-0). The Value Object pattern is covered in more detail in the *The Value Object Pattern in a Nutshell* section, later in the chapter.

❑ The **Data Access Object** pattern is often used by developers creating BMP entity beans in order to insulate BMP entity beans from vendor-specific code by delegating the data store access. See the section *The Data Access Object Pattern in a Nutshell*, for more on the Data Access Object pattern

As you read through the test result data and analysis contained in the remainder of this chapter, we must extend the following caution. As they say in the automobile commercials: "Your mileage may vary." It would be difficult to establish "benchmark" findings quantifying the performance impact of **any** design pattern, as there are seemingly infinite alternative implementations for a pattern (as well as for any given test design). The pattern implementations found here represent only a very small sampling of alternatives, intended to serve as subjects for our testing examples. We encourage you to download the example code, make alterations, and experiment to prove things for yourself. You might even try adapting the example code to your own applications.

Why Evaluate EJB Design Patterns and Performance?

If each of these design patterns represents an advantage or remedy of some kind, you may ask why we need to evaluate them? Often, an EJB developer is faced with more than a simple binary choice of whether or not to apply the pattern. By testing, we want to better understand the performance impact accompanying each pattern, and our own implementation of it. For example, there are usually multiple ways to implement a particular design pattern, as well as variations/extensions to the original pattern. Surely we would like to validate that our implementation delivers the performance benefit promised by the pattern. In addition, we'd want to know the magnitude of the performance impact (is it a few milliseconds, or several seconds, that we're losing or gaining?) In each test, we identify the particular questions that we're trying to answer.

Throughout this book we have advocated that performance testing start as early as possible, and that it should certainly be a feature of the design phase. This appears to contradict one of the more common (although not necessarily good) software development strategies: defer performance optimizations for as long as possible. However, it is useful to note a distinction here between "optimization" and fundamental design choices. There are a couple of motivators that encourage this "early performance testing" approach:

❑ The J2EE platform, and EJB component model, are relatively young technologies (consider, for example, the radical changes occurring in the EJB 2.0 specification). As a result, the subtleties and use of these technologies are not yet well understood.

❑ Some newer development methodologies, such as the Extreme Programming (XP) practices, encourage testing from the outset, as a fundamental design and development activity. Incorporating performance testing into these practices is a natural extension. For more on XP, see Kent Beck's *Extreme Programming Explained: Embrace Change* (Addison-Wesley, ISBN 0-201-61641-6).

❑ Automated test tools have evolved to permit performance testing much earlier in the development process, with features that can generate performance test drivers for selected component interfaces. In fact, some IDEs include these kinds of automated test features as part of their basic tool kit.

❑ Another common reason to test EJB design pattern implementation performance early is to establish and understand which pieces of the application's EJB architecture are most sensitive to performance issues. Having this understanding can often make performance problem analysis easier than when performance bottlenecks are uncovered late in the application development cycle. Furthermore, having a ready-made set of performance tests at hand (essentially, these are regression tests) can also aid in performance analysis and debugging, and can often be reused for other purposes (like EJB deployment tuning).

As a result of these motivators, many EJB developers choose to commence performance testing as early as possible, even at the design phase, and continue it throughout the development process (often in addition to the independent performance testing that traditionally occurs at the end of the project).

Better EJB Design Through Testing

As mentioned in the introduction to this chapter, the focus on performance and scalability has made performance testing an implicit part of most EJB developers' and architects' design process.

In order to illustrate this effectively, we adopt a slightly different approach in this chapter to that seen in the rest of the book. We ask you to imagine a scenario where we are in the initial design phases of an EJB application development project. From an EJB design perspective, we will need to make informed choices about which design patterns to apply, and how best to apply them. To help us make these design choices, we will build small "prototype" EJBs representing different design choices, and run performance tests against each one so that we can compare and evaluate them.

Application Scenario

For this development project, imagine that we have been asked to develop the EJB layer for the JazzCat application. JazzCat is to be a web-based J2EE application, enabling music students to search the college's catalog of jazz recordings. We are constrained to build the application on top of an existing database. The JazzCat database schema appears as shown in the following entity relationship diagram (using the common "crow's feet" cardinality notation):

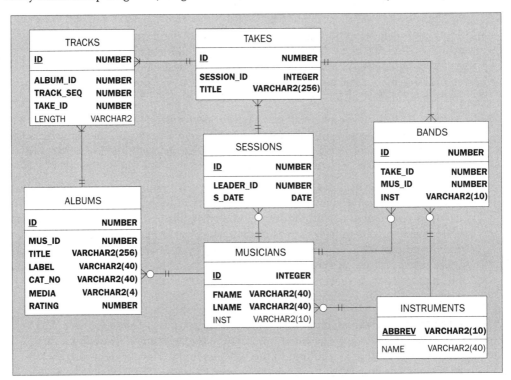

The JazzCat database contains the following tables:

- The INSTRUMENTS table is a list of instrument names and their corresponding abbreviation. In this table, the abbreviation column (ABBREV) is the primary key.

- The MUSICIANS table identifies musicians by name, as well as their primary instrument.

- The SESSIONS table lists the recording sessions led by a particular musician on various dates.

- The TAKES table contains song titles recorded at various recording sessions.

- The BANDS table is essentially a link table, identifying the musicians playing on any given take, as well as the instruments that musicians played on the take.

- The TRACKS table identifies the takes that appear on albums in the catalog. The same take might appear on several different albums.

- The ALBUMS table lists the recordings (CDs, LPs, etc.) currently held in the JazzCat catalog.

To investigate and test EJB design alternatives during this early phase of development, the prototype EJBs we create will be based on this database schema, mapping entity beans to individual tables. In many cases, we will have multiple variants of the same EJB (for example, we may have versions representing BMP, CMP, local interfaces, remote interfaces, and so forth). Although the test beans we develop will not likely represent our final design, or even "good" architecture in many cases, they will serve our purpose of testing a particular design pattern.

In the interest of simplicity, we choose a "bottom-up" approach, deriving EJBs from an existing DB schema. In the real world, when developing new applications from scratch, many developers find a more object-oriented approach is more appropriate. This approach would require a more rigorous OOA/OOD phase, leading to an object model, which is then mapped into a relational schema. Also, it may raise different challenges with respect to performance, and so we encourage you to experiment with the ideas in this chapter, adapting them to your own design methodology.

Test Harness Design

In order to test the prototype EJBs we intend to develop, we need some mechanism for driving method requests to EJB container. Like many performance test tools, The Grinder's default behavior is to issue HTTP requests, simulating browser requests to a web server. Although we have the option of developing a plug-in for The Grinder that can issue method requests directly to the EJB container, we will instead take a more generic approach and build a lightweight dispatcher servlet that will in turn make the method requests to the EJB container on The Grinder's behalf. This mimics real world situations rather well (whereby a web site is the front end to an EJB tier). You may find this approach especially useful if you use one of the commercial load testing tools designed for testing web-based applications, and want to use it to test EJBs and other business logic that resides downstream of the web container. Creating a servlet front-end such as our dispatcher allows you to adapt and apply these test tools to other, non-browser components in your application.

The following sequence diagram illustrates this approach:

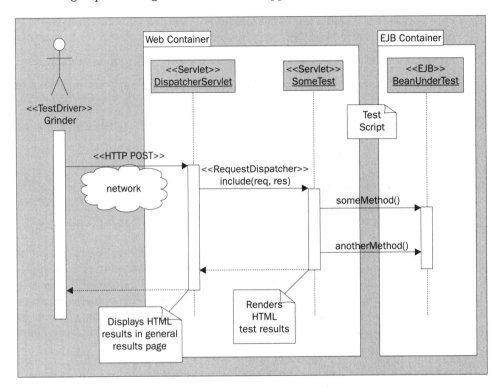

As shown in the diagram, the `DispatcherServlet` handles all HTTP requests from The Grinder and, based on the request, dispatches the request to the appropriate test servlet (via the `RequestDispatcher` interface's `include()` method). Each test servlet represents a discrete test case, and functions as the test script for that test case.

EJB Test Cases

The following table lists the defined EJB test cases we will be running, grouped by design patterns/topics. Included in the table are the test case number, `test_id` (a.k.a. servlet name) to be passed to the `DispatcherServlet`, and a brief synopsis for each test case. For each design pattern, there are always two fundamental tests with names ending in "OnTest" and "OffTest", representing the simplest comparison tests with and without the design pattern applied. Some design patterns also have additional test cases that are designed to illustrate other interesting design issues or alternatives related to the pattern.

A download bundle, called `Jazzcat5.jar`, for all the examples in this chapter is available from the Expert Press web site (http://expert-press.com). We encourage you to download the code and try these tests on your own. The bundle includes source code for the `DispatcherServlet`, test case servlets, all of the JazzCat EJBs, Ant build scripts, and database schema scripts, as well as a deployable EAR configured for WebLogic Server 6.1 SP2. For deployment details, see the README file included in the download bundle.

Also included is a group of test cases (5.4-5.6) designed to compare deployment configuration alternatives. The values chosen for an EJB's deployment descriptor elements can sometimes have a dramatic impact on the system's performance and scalability, and at the same time can be very difficult to choose. The impact of deployment configuration must be well understood from the outset, and monitored/adjusted throughout the development process, so we include these tests even in this early "design" stage of our JazzCat project.

Pattern/Topic	No.	test_id	Synopsis
5.1 Session Facade	5.1.1	FacadeOffTest	Search for Tracks by title without using session facade pattern
	5.1.2	FacadeOnTest	Search for Tracks by title using Session Facade
5.2 Value Object (VO)	5.2.1	VoOffTest	List Albums without using Value Object pattern
	5.2.2	VoOnTest	List Albums using VO
	5.2.3	VoTxTest	List Albums without VO, using UserTransaction
	5.2.4	VoFacadeTest	List Albums via VO assembled in SLSB (container-managed TX)
5.3 Data Access Object (DAO)	5.3.1	DaoOffTest	List Instruments via BMP entity, no DAO
	5.3.2	DaoOnTest	List Instruments via BMP entity using DAO
	5.3.3	DaoBmpTest	Search for Bands by title via BMP entities using DAO
	5.3.4	DaoCmrTest	Search for Bands by title using CMR (instead of DAO)
	5.3.5	DaoSbTest	Search for Bands by title using DAOs directly from a session bean

Table continued on following page

Pattern/Topic	No.	test_id	Synopsis
5.4 Deployment: Transaction Isolation	5.4.1	DdIsoTSTest	Add/find musician entities via CMT, TRANSACTION_SERIALIZABLE
	5.4.2	DdIsoTRCTest	Add/find musician entities via CMT, TRANSACTION_READ_COMMITTED
5.5 Deployment: Access Control	5.5.1	DdSecOffTest	Add/find musician entities without EJB access control
	5.5.2	DdSecOnTest	Add/find musician entities with EJB access control
5.6 Deployment: Entity Cache Size	5.6.1	DdCacheLowTest	Add/find musician entities with lower cache size
	5.6.2	DdCacheHighTest	Add/find musician entities with higher cache size

Running the DispatcherServlet Manually

Although we will be using The Grinder to generate the HTTP requests programmatically, it is useful to see how a Grinder thread invokes the DispatcherServlet to simulate the actions of a single user. In essence, The Grinder represents the load generation engine, and the DispatcherServlet acts as a proxy to an individual test driver. By invoking the DispatcherServlet from a browser, we can visually see the requests/response sequence between The Grinder and any test servlet.

In the real world, this is generally a useful function for developing new performance tests to be added to the test harness, allowing the test developer to validate an individual test script before running it as a load test. It is also useful for debugging regressions that may arise later in the project, allowing the developer to simplify the problem by eliminating the Grinder and running a "single-user" test.

When you access the DispatcherServlet "manually" from a browser, it displays a menu of test cases. To do this, use the URL http://*server.port*/jazzcat/Dispatcher where *server* is the host name (or IP address) of the machine running WebLogic Server and *port* is the port number on which the server is listening for requests.

The following screenshot shows how the `DispatcherServlet`'s menu page appears in a browser:

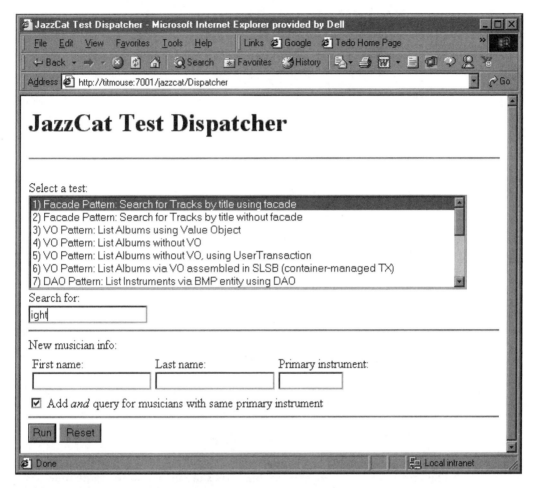

Selecting and running tests is straightforward: select a test in the listbox, and choose the **Run** button at the bottom of the page. Note that some tests require additional parameters, supplied via the input boxes that appear below the menu listbox. In general, test descriptions that indicate a search require that you supply a search string in the "**Search for**" box. Likewise, test descriptions that indicate "**Add/find**" musicians require that you supply a first name, last name, and instrument abbreviation via the three input boxes in the "**New musician info**" section on the page.

For example, if you select test #1 ("**Search for Tracks by title using facade**"), enter the string "ight" in the **Search for** textbox, and choose the **Run** button, the `DispatcherServlet` handles the resulting `POST` request by dispatching the request to the `cFacadeOnTest` servlet, and includes that servlet's HTML output in the result page, as shown in the following code fragment:

```
        String testId = req.getParameter("test_id");

        Test test = null;
        Iterator iter = Test.LIST.iterator();
        while (iter.hasNext()) {
          test = (Test)iter.next();
          if (testId.equals(test.toString())) {
            req.setAttribute("test", test);
            break;
          }
        }

        // Dispatch to appropriate test servlet

        RequestDispatcher rd;
        if (test.toString().startsWith("Dd")) {
          rd = getServletContext().getNamedDispatcher("DeploymentTest");
        } else {
          rd = getServletContext().getNamedDispatcher(test.toString());
        }
        out.println("<H1>JazzCat Test Servlet: " + test + "</H1>");
        out.println("<EM>" + test.LABEL + "</EM>");
        out.println("<HR>");
        rd.include(req, res);   // print test output "inline"
        out.println("<HR>");
        out.println("<A HREF=\"Dispatcher\">Home</A>");
```

In processing the POST request, the DispatcherServlet first extracts the test_id string from the request:

```
        String testId = req.getParameter("test_id");
```

Next, the DispatcherServlet references a Test object, representing a "registered" (known) test identifier (FacadeOnTest).

```
        Test test = null;
```

The Test class is simply a static typesafe enumerator that maps test identifiers (servlet names) to the labels that appear on the DispatcherServlet's menu, and at the same time encapsulates the list of test cases (Test.LIST contains this list of test cases). The idea here is that, when you want to add a new test case to the suite, you simply add another test identifier (servlet name) and corresponding menu label to the Test enumeration.

The DispatcherServlet now uses the test identifier from the POST request (TestId) to locate the corresponding Test object from the list of tests:

```
        Iterator iter = Test.LIST.iterator();
        while (iter.hasNext()) {
          test = (Test)iter.next();
          if (testId.equals(test.toString())) {
    req.setAttribute("test", test);
            break;
          }
        }
```

By adding the Test object as an attribute in the dispatch request, the test case servlet can use the object to display its label (Test.LABEL), or perhaps access other test-specific attributes that might be added to the Test class in the future.

Finally, the DispatcherServlet dispatches the request to the appropriate test case servlet:

```
RequestDispatcher rd;
if (test.toString().startsWith("Dd")) {
  rd = getServletContext().getNamedDispatcher("DeploymentTest");
} else {
  rd = getServletContext().getNamedDispatcher(test.toString());
}
```

Note the alternative dispatch handling of test names beginning with "Dd"; this prefix flags deployment tests, which are always dispatched to a single DeploymentTest servlet (this alternative deployment testing strategy is explained in the next section).

The resulting HTML page appears as follows:

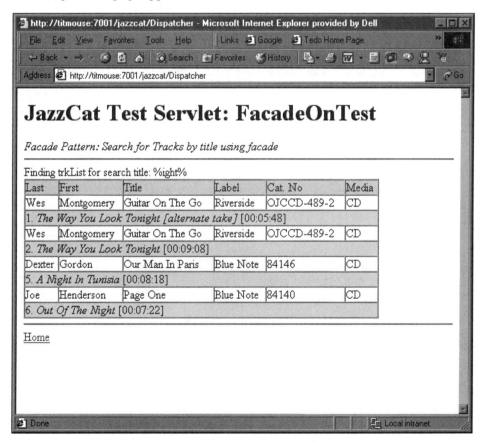

To submit the same form data programmatically, The Grinder must issue a POST request to the same DispatcherServlet URL, with the following parameter string in the body of the request:

```
test_id=FacadeOnTest&search_string=ight
```

where test_id identifies the test case servlet to run (FacadeOnTest), from the list in the previous section, and search_string identifies the substring to use in the track title search ("ight" in this case).

Test Scripts

In our tests, we will be analyzing results based on measurements of response time (AART) and of the throughput, or transactional rate (in transactions per second, TPS). These metrics are defined clearly in Chapter 1. As noted earlier, each request in the grinder.properties files for the tests in this chapter invokes the DispatcherServlet in order to simulate the actions of a user.

> The test scripts for each test case in this chapter can be found in the Grinder.zip file of the code download for this chapter.

The core parameters that are set in grinder.properties take the same values for every test presented:

```
grinder.jvm.arguments=-Xint

# Simulate the number of users from one JVM and run forever
grinder.processes=1
grinder.threads=1
grinder.cycles=0

# Start/Stop from Grinder Console
grinder.receiveConsoleSignals=true
grinder.grinderAddress=228.1.1.1
grinder.grinderPort=1234

# Agent processes report real time data to Grinder Console
grinder.reportToConsole=true
grinder.consoleAddress=control
grinder.consolePort=6372

# Data logs to the log directory, no debugging logs
grinder.logDirectory=log
grinder.appendLog=false
grinder.logProcessStreams=false

# Set the initial spread
```

```
grinder.thread.initialSleepTime=500

# User the HTTP Plugin with HTTP Client model
grinder.plugin=net.grinder.plugin.http.HttpPlugin
grinder.plugin.parameter.useHTTPClient=true
grinder.plugin.parameter.useCookies=true
grinder.plugin.parameter.logHTML=false
```

The requests executed will, of course, vary depending on the test case, but are rather similar in nature since every request calls the dispatcher servlet. For example, following is an extract from the test script for the Facade pattern tests:

```
grinder.test0.parameter.url=http://sun2:7001/jazzcat/Dispatcher
grinder.test0.parameter.header.Content-Type=application/x-www-form-
urlencoded
grinder.test0.description=Search for a track title with an "a"
grinder.test0.parameter.post=search-a.dat

grinder.test1.parameter.url=http://sun2:7001/jazzcat/Dispatcher
grinder.test1.parameter.header.Content-Type=application/x-www-form-
urlencoded
grinder.test1.description=Search for a track title with an "b"
grinder.test1.parameter.post=search-b.dat
...
```

Each request simply calls the dispatcher and the value of the post parameter is the name of the file that contains the data that we wish to post to the URL. In this case the content of the search-a.dat file, for example, is:

```
test_id=FacadeOnTest&search_string=a&fname=&lname=&abbrev=&query=true
```

We are searching for titles starting with a. The request attribute fields fname, lname and abbrev are part of every request to the dispatcher, but are only used when we want to insert a new musician (in the deployment tests).

Please note that we do not specify a think time for any of the requests in the script. So, each request in the script is executed sequentially with zero think time in-between. This will place the application server under the maximum possible stress for any given user load.

Test Configuration

All of our tests run across three machines: one machine hosting the Grinder and its threads, another machine hosting a single application server instance, and a third machine hosting the database server. In this case, the web container and the EJB container run in the same single application server instance on the server machine.

The application server and Grinder configuration details for each test run were as follows (unless specifically stated otherwise):

Grinder Property	Value	Server Environment	
grinder.processes	1	App. Server	WebLogic Server 6.1 (SP2)
grinder.threads	1, 5, 10	JVM	Sun Java HotSpot Server VM (1.3.1-b24)
grinder.thread.initial SleepTime	500ms	JVM Args	-Xms256m -Xmx256m
Sample interval	5000ms	Computer	Dual UltraSPARC II (450 MHz), 512MB
Ignore samples	36	OS	Solaris 2.7
Collect samples	60	Network	100 Mbs

The tests will generally be run for user loads of 1, 5 and 10 users. You must bear in mind that we are using zero think time and initial exploratory tests that we performed indicated that the server was heavily stressed with a load of 10 users, in these extreme conditions (although this does also indicate that use of the EJB container is rather expensive).

*In any event, we are applying a different kind of testing here: the tests presented in this chapter do **not** really represent scalability tests (where tracking performance degradation over an increasing load is the important metric). These "performance" tests are meant to be small, simple, and illustrative, intended to show a technique of comparing design alternatives. We encourage you, the reader, to download the code and use it as a starter for your own experiments.*

For the tests in this chapter, we use the snapshot method of data collection, with five seconds as the sample size (this means that we record our performance metrics every 5 seconds) and collecting 96 samples in total. We ignore the first 36 samples in order to take into account the initial period over which the system stabilizes.

Setting up and Running the Tests

We will only give skeleton details here. For more detailed instructions please refer to the equivalent section in Chapter 4.

On the **DBServer** computer we reset the JazzCat database tables (drop, recreate and repopulate) **before the start** of each new test. It is very important that all the test runs happen under the same conditions. The scripts to drop and create and populate these tables on an Oracle database are provided in the `jazzcat_db.zip` file of the code download for this chapter. Alternatively, you can simply drop and recreate the tables each time and populate them using the Ant build script provided as part of the `jazzcat5.jar` file.

The next step is to deploy the jazzcat5.jar file to your WebLogic server. The only real point to note about the `config.xml` file for WLS (a sample file is provided in the download) is that you will need to configure a `jazzcatDS` DataSource. This is simply involves adding two XML elements to
the `config` file, `<JDBCDataSource/>` and `<JDBCConnectionPool/>`, as shown below:

```
<Domain Name="uklab">

    <!-- Other elements omitted... -->

    <JDBCDataSource JNDIName="jazzcat/jdbc/jazzcatDS" Name="jazzcatDS"
        PoolName="jazzcatPool" Targets=" wls02"/>

    <JDBCConnectionPool CapacityIncrement="2"
        DriverName="oracle.jdbc.driver.OracleDriver" InitialCapacity="2"
        MaxCapacity="10" Name="jazzcatPool" Properties="user=tedo"
        Targets=" wls02" URL=" jdbc:oracle:thin:@DBSERVER:1521:UKLAB "/>

    <!-- Other elements omitted... -->

</Domain>
```

The `URL`, `Properties`, `Targets` and `DriverName` attributes will need to be set appropriately for your environment.

Testing the Session Facade Pattern

Suppose that we need to provide JazzCat users with a means to search the catalog for albums containing a particular song title. We can start to model this functionality with a few entities representing the data that a web client might need to assemble to provide this listing: `Album` (the thing we're searching for), `Take` (holds the song title), `Track` (identifies occurrences of `Takes` on `Albums`), and `Musician` (identifies the artist name for an `Album`). Using these entities, a web component could perform the simple title search (maybe via a finder method on the `Take` bean), fetching the necessary data from the entities to produce a result listing.

The Session Facade Pattern in a Nutshell

Before proceeding any further with the model, we might realize that, from design perspective, a web client making calls to the entities' accessor methods would create a fine-grained coupling between the web tier and the "business objects" in our application:

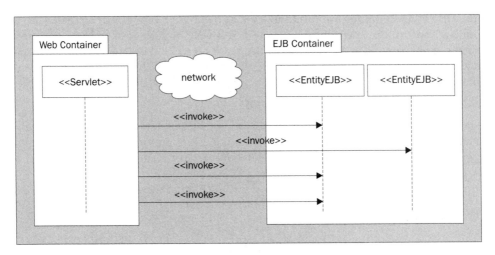

It would be nice if we could insulate web components from the details of our data model. Also, from a performance perspective, web components making multiple, potentially remote method calls to these four entities could prove costly. But how costly? Is it a few milliseconds? A few seconds?

It is these two problems, the expense of remote method calls, and fine-grained coupling between tiers, that the Session Facade pattern is intended to help remedy. The pattern's approach is to use a Session Bean to encapsulate the accessor logic that the web component needs to execute. The following sequence diagram illustrates this strategy:

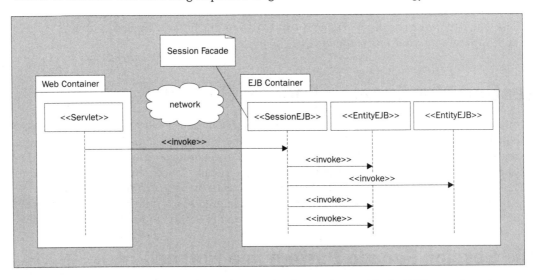

As you can see in the diagram, the web container's coupling with the EJB container is now greatly simplified, and the expense of multiple fine-grained remote calls on entity accessors is now reduced to a single coarse-grained remote invocation.

You can find a more formal description of the Session Facade pattern, including variations, nuances, and related patterns, on the following web pages:

http://developer.java.sun.com/developer/restricted/patterns/SessionFacade.html

http://java.sun.com/blueprints/patterns/j2ee_patterns/session_facade/index.html

Because the Session Facade bean resides in the same EJB container as the entities we wish to access, or at least in the same tier, we should expect better performance as a result of applying the pattern. However, a couple of questions remain:

❑ What is the magnitude of the performance benefit?

❑ What if the web container and the EJB container both reside on the same server, and in the same application server instance (essentially eliminating the trip across the network "cloud"), as in the case of our deployment? Will this remove the bottleneck?

❑ Is the performance boost enough to justify creating and maintaining an additional EJB component for our simple application?

To get a feel for the performance cost of making the "remote" method calls (or the magnitude of the performance boost we can realize by implementing the design pattern), we can design and run a couple of simple test cases representing the album search functionality, and then compare their results.

Test Case 5.1.1: FacadeOffTest

As its name suggests, the `FacadeOffTest` prototypes a track search without using the Session Facade pattern, and instead calls each entity bean accessor directly from a servlet in the web tier. The following sequence diagram illustrates this simple prototype:

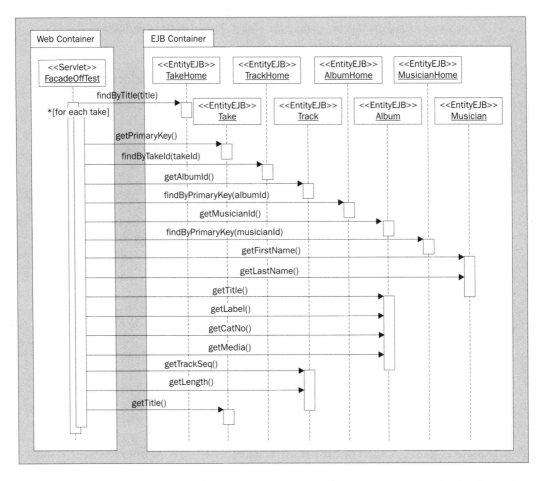

As you can see, this album search implementation involves quite a few method calls to the EJB tier, and this sequence of calls is multiplied by the number of iterations required to process each Take entity found in the initial search (findByTitle(title)).

Test Results Summary

For our purposes, the results of this baseline test aren't particularly interesting by themselves – we are more interested in how they compare to the alternative design (where we will apply the Session Facade pattern).

The following graph shows the baseline response time results for FacadeOffTest, measured at increasing user loads of 1, 5, and 10 users:

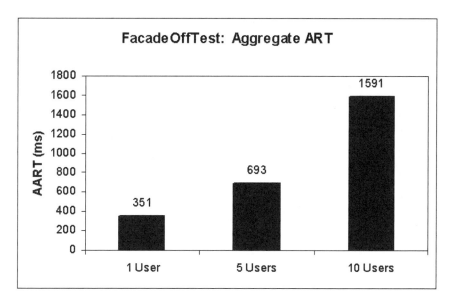

The following graph shows the transactional throughput for `FacadeOffTest` measured at increasing user loads:

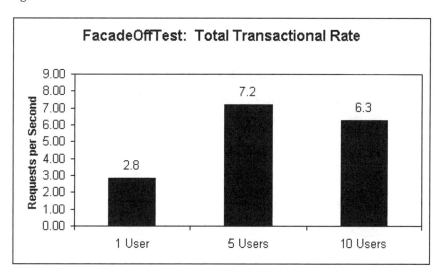

It would appear that the transactional rate (throughput) for 10 users is slightly less than that observed for 5 users. What seems certain is that we reach a throughput capacity of around 7 RPS with a load of 5 users. According to our supermarket analogy from Chapter 1, this is the point where we have enough shoppers to empty the supermarket. When we to increase the number of "shoppers" beyond this point, we eventually see the transactional rate start to deteriorate ("crowding in the aisles"). The following graph shows the CPU utilization for `FacadeOffTest` at a load of 10 users:

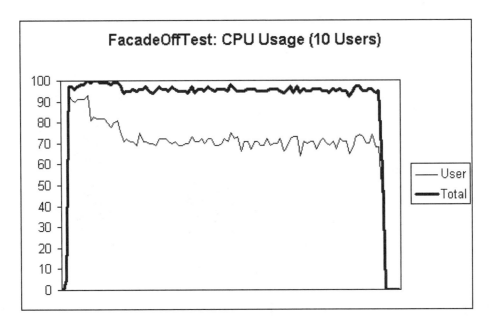

As you can see, the CPU usage was close to 100% for the 10-user run. Now that we have acquired some baseline data, the next step is to create and run a corresponding test case (FacadeOnTest) that applies the Session Facade design pattern, and compare the results.

Test Case 5.1.2: FacadeOnTest

The FacadeOnTest again prototypes an album search, this time making use of the Session Facade pattern by calling entity accessors from a stateless session bean. The following sequence diagram illustrates this:

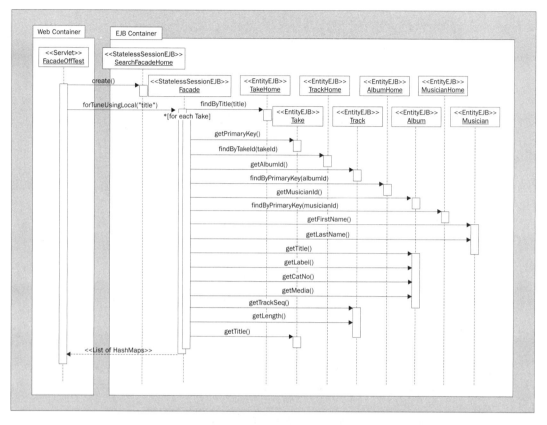

As the diagram shows, all of the entity bean method invocations that were made directly from the `FacadeOffTest` servlet in the last test are now all made from a stateless session bean named `SearchFacade`. All of the entity method calls are encapsulated in a single session bean method:

```
public Collection forTuneUsingLocal(String searchTitle)
```

The method's implementation is almost line-for-line identical to the sequence of entity bean method invocations found in `FacadeOffTest`. This is important, as we want to keep the comparison as fair as we can. In addition to the fact that `FacadeOnTest` implements the Session Facade pattern, there are a couple of interesting points about this revised test case.

Local or Remote Interfaces?

As its name implies, `forTuneUsingLocal` makes its accessor method invocations on the **local** interfaces of the four entity beans.

```
public Collection forTuneUsingLocal(String searchTitle) {

    TakeLocal take;
```

```
    TakeLocalHome takeHome;

    TrackLocal track;
    TrackLocalHome trackHome;

    AlbumLocal album;
    AlbumLocalHome albumHome;

    MusicianLocal musician;
    MusicianLocalHome musicianHome;

       try {
          Context ctx = new InitialContext();

          takeHome = (TakeLocalHome)ctx.lookup
          ("java:comp/env/ejb/TakeLocalHome");

          trackHome = (TrackLocalHome)ctx.lookup
          ("java:comp/env/ejb/TrackLocalHome");

          albumHome = (AlbumLocalHome)ctx.lookup
          ("java:comp/env/ejb/AlbumLocalHome");

          musicianHome = (MusicianLocalHome)ctx.lookup
          ("java:comp/env/ejb/MusicianLocalHome");

          // etc.
```

This is a very natural "EJB 2.0" thing to do, taking advantage of the fact that the SearchFacade bean is co-located in the same JVM as the entity beans it accesses.

For an explanation of local and remote interfaces, EJB 2.0 features, and other EJB topics, see Professional EJB *(Wrox Press, ISBN 1-861005-08-3),*

In fact, the SearchFacade bean's component interface happens to contain another method, forTune, that is almost identical to forTuneUsingLocal, except that forTune invokes the remote interfaces of the entities.

```
    public Collection forTune(String searchTitle) {

       Take take;
       TakeHome takeHome;

       Track track;
       TrackHome trackHome;

       Album album;
       AlbumHome albumHome;

       Musician musician;
       MusicianHome musicianHome;

       try {
          Context ctx = new InitialContext();
```

```
    takeHome = (TakeHome)
      ctx.lookup("java:comp/env/ejb/TakeHome");
    trackHome = (TrackHome)
      ctx.lookup("java:comp/env/ejb/TrackHome");
    albumHome = (AlbumHome)
      ctx.lookup("java:comp/env/ejb/AlbumHome");
    musicianHome = (MusicianHome)
      ctx.lookup("java:comp/env/ejb/MusicianHome");

    // etc.
```

However, when deploying an EJB container smart enough to recognize that `SearchFacade` and the entity beans are co-located, it is unlikely that we would see any measurable performance difference between the two methods. Practically all application servers have this optimization, including WebLogic Server. Nevertheless, you may wish to download the code and test this on your own server.

Using the Data Transfer HashMap Pattern

Another interesting feature of `FacadeOnTest`'s implementation is that it makes use of another useful design pattern, the **Data Transfer HashMap**, a pattern often found within Session Facade implementations. Because `FacadeOnTest` is requesting a list of objects (albums), just as `FacadeOffTest` did, we need some new mechanism to process sets of Album data. This time, however, we are not processing a collection of entity beans; all entity bean access is now taken care of in the Session Facade. We need a lightweight method of transferring arbitrarily complex data objects between the EJB and web tiers.

The Data Transfer HashMap pattern uses a standard `java.util.HashMap` (from the Java Collections framework) to transfer sets of data between the EJB and web tiers. When either the EJB or web component receives a `HashMap`, it accesses the "fields" of the object using the `HashMap`'s keys. The following `FaccadeOnTest` code fragment shows an example of this:

```
Iterator trkList = search.forTuneUsingLocal(searchString).iterator();

while (trkList.hasNext()) {
  HashMap trkInfo = (HashMap)trkList.next();

  out.println("<TR>"
    + "<TD>" + trkInfo.get("fname")   + "</TD>"
    + "<TD>" + trkInfo.get("lname")   + "</TD>"
    + "<TD>" + trkInfo.get("atitle")  + "</TD>"
    + "<TD>" + trkInfo.get("label")   + "</TD>"
    + "<TD>" + trkInfo.get("catno")   + "</TD>"
    + "<TD>" + trkInfo.get("media")   + "</TD>"
    + "</TR>" );
```

In this case, `forTuneUsingLocal` is returning a collection of serializable `HashMap` objects (instead of entity bean references), where each `HashMap` contains the data set (java.lang.String values) for an album found in the search. Using the Data Transfer `HashMap` pattern seems to meet our need, without introducing overhead that would significantly skew the test results.

For more on the Data Transfer HashMap pattern, visit the following URL:

http://www.theserverside.com/patterns/index.jsp

Test Results Summary

As the following response time comparison chart shows, the impact of applying the Session Façade pattern is even more dramatic than we may have first expected:

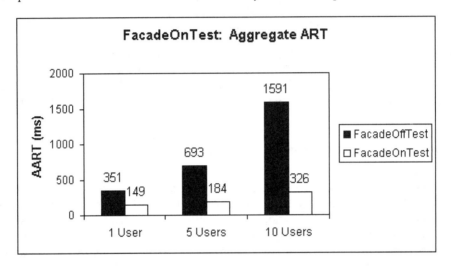

For a load of 1 user, the pattern provides a 57% reduction in response time but for 10 users, the session facade provides an almost 80% reduction. The corresponding impact on the transactional rate is equally dramatic:

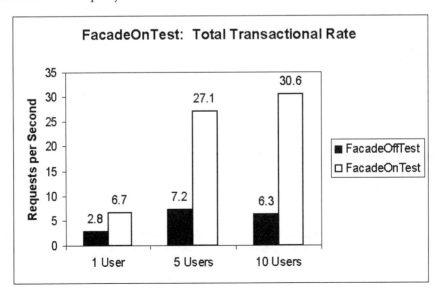

For 10 users, we see an increase in throughput by nearly 386%! The following chart shows that there is little impact on resource utilization :

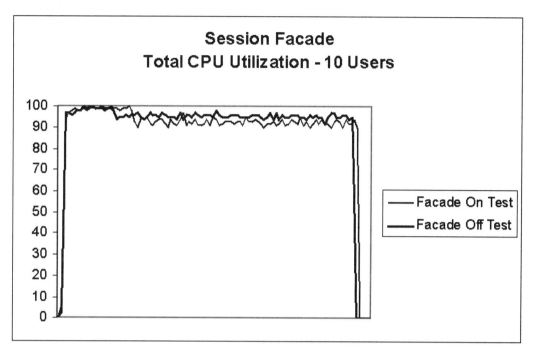

Apparently, use of the VO pattern has a big impact on performance, but as you will see in the test case 5.2.3 this is largely due to the way in which the test was implemented.

One point to note here is that in the "*Using the Data Transfer HashMap Pattern*", we suggested that use of the Data Transfer `HashMap` pattern in `FacadeOnTest` seemed to work without "introducing overhead that would significantly skew the test results". While this is probably true, how can we be certain? In order to prove our hypothesis we could design a test case to measure the overhead introduced by using a Data Transfer `HashMap` with `FacadeOnTest`.

Testing the Value Object Pattern

Another piece of functionality that JazzCat users will likely need is the ability to pick from a list of multiple albums in the catalog. To experiment with this functionality, we could create a test servlet that lists all the albums in our test database, where each row in the listing shows the field values of the album entity: album ID, leader ID, title, label, catalog number, media type, and rating:

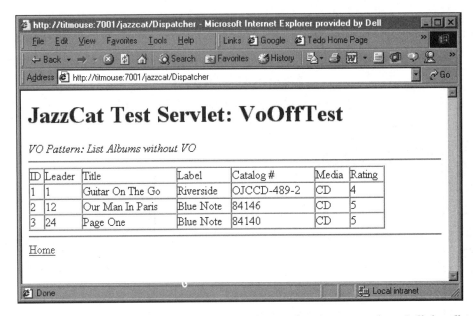

To fetch this album data for display, our test servlet needs to retrieve a list of all the album entities, and then get the individual field values for each entity via the entity's accessor methods.

The Value Object Pattern in a Nutshell

Similar to the problems we encountered with the Session Facade pattern example, such fine-grained, potentially remote entity access across container boundaries might represent a significant performance bottleneck.

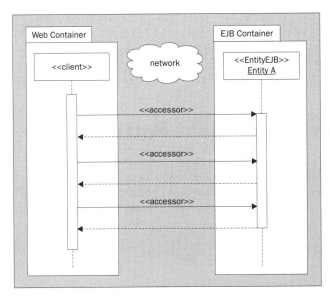

The Value Object design pattern is intended to mitigate the effects of these two problems (fine-grained access and multiple remote calls) by adopting the following strategy:

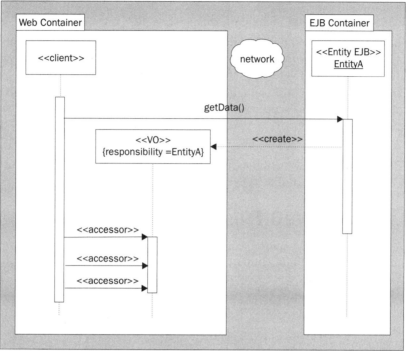

The client (in our case, a servlet) makes a single method call (`getData`) on the entity requesting the entity's data. The entity bean constructs a corresponding Value Object, loads the Value Object with the entity's field values, and returns the object to the requesting client. The client may then access the fields of the local object, where each accessor of the Value Object directly corresponds to an accessor in the entity bean. This strategy seems to lend itself particularly well to read-only situations such as our album listing. (Note that there is also an *Updatable Value Object* variation to the pattern that accommodates client updates using value objects).

For more formal documentation of the Value Object pattern, including variations, nuances, and related patterns, visit the following URLs:

http://developer.java.sun.com/developer/restricted/patterns/ValueObject.html

http://java.sun.com/blueprints/patterns/j2ee_patterns/value_object/index.html

Also note that the Value Object pattern has a number of aliases (such as "Data Transfer Object") and derivative alternatives (including the Data Transfer HashMap pattern we used in the Session Facade example.

273

Having significantly reduced the number of remote calls by applying the Value Object pattern, we should expect better performance as a result of applying the pattern. However, as with the Session Facade example, we like to have answers to the following questions:

❑ What is the magnitude of the performance benefit?

❑ What if the web container and the EJB container both reside on the same server, and in the same application server instance (essentially eliminating the trip across the network "cloud")? Will this negate the bottleneck?

❑ Is the performance boost enough to justify creating and maintaining additional Value Object classes for our simple application? Potentially, when changes occur in an entity bean's interface (in particular, the entity's accessors), a corresponding change must be maintained in its value object.

To answer these questions, we will design and run a couple of initial test cases representing the album list functionality, and then compare their results.

Test Case 5.2.1: VoOffTest

Continuing with our "off/on" naming convention, we first create a `VoOffTest` servlet that fetches a collection of all Album entities, and then gets each Album field using the entity's accessors. The following sequence diagram illustrates this test design:

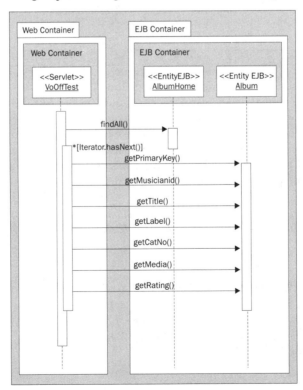

Here, the test sequence is straightforward. The `Album` entity bean's `findAll` finder method returns a collection of `Album` entities, one for each row in the `Albums` table in the database. `VoOffTest` then iterates over the collection, obtaining the field data for each `Album` via the bean's accessor methods.

```
Context ctx = new InitialContext();
AlbumHome home = (AlbumHome)PortableRemoteObject.narrow(
    ctx.lookup("java:comp/env/ejb/AlbumHome"),
    AlbumHome.class );
Album album = null;
Collection albumList = home.findAll();
Iterator albumIterator = albumList.iterator();
while (albumIterator.hasNext()) {
  album = (Album)albumIterator.next();
  // Anti-ACID!!
  out.println("<TR><TD>" + album.getPrimaryKey() + "</TD>"
           + "<TD>" + album.getMusicianId() + "</TD>"
           + "<TD>" + album.getTitle() + "</TD>"
           + "<TD>" + album.getLabel() + "</TD>"
           + "<TD>" + album.getCatNo() + "</TD>"
           + "<TD>" + album.getMedia() + "</TD>"
           + "<TD>" + album.getRating() + "</TD>"
           + "</TR>");
}
out.println("</TABLE>");
```

Test Results Summary

The following baseline results will be interesting to compare with the results we obtained after applying the Value Object pattern (`VoOnTest`):

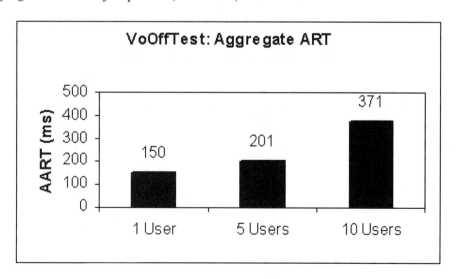

The following graph shows the transactional throughput for VoOffTest measured at increasing user loads:

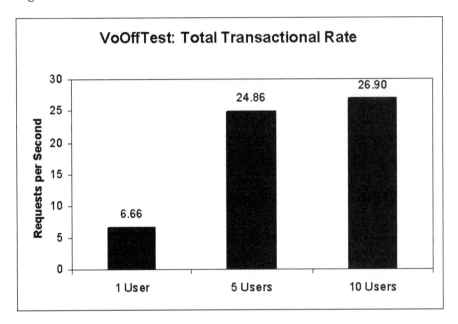

Once again, we see that the throughput effectively stabilizes at a user load of 10 users. The following graph shows the CPU utilization for VoOffTest at the 10-user load:

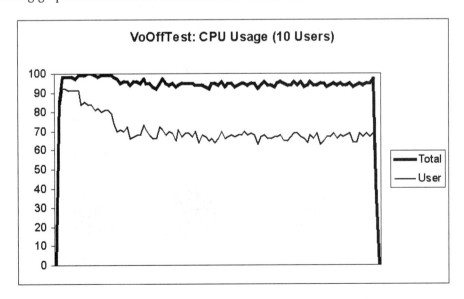

Again, we see that we are close to capacity CPU usage on the WebLogic Server.

Test Case 5.2.2: VoOnTest

We can now create a corresponding test, `VoOnTest`, which applies the Value Object pattern. In order to apply the design pattern, we implement a duplicate of the `Album` entity bean, `Album2`, with exactly the same CMP fields as the original `Album` bean used in the `VoOffTest` servlet. The new `Album2` bean contains an additional method, `getData`, which returns the value object for that entity. We define the corresponding value object, `Album2VO`, with public fields matching those of `Album2`. Because this is a read-only operation, we can get away with publicly exposing the value object's fields rather than implementing accessor methods.

The following sequence diagram illustrates the overall test design:

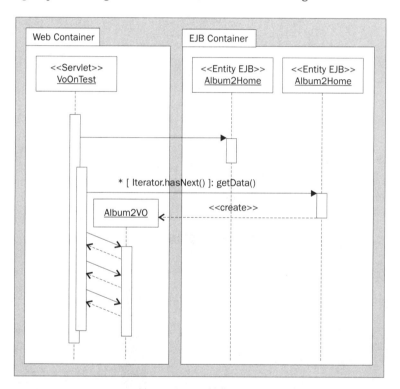

In this revised test case, much of the servlet logic remains the same: obtain a list of entity bean references using the `findAll` method, and iterate over that list to fetch the field values of each `Album2` bean. This time, however, the remote access is limited to a single `getData` method call, which causes the current `Album2` entity to return an `Album2VO` value object, loaded with that entity's attribute values. The revised test servlet even retains much of the same accessor logic found in `VoOffTest`. But in this case, the big difference is that `VoOnTest` accesses the field data of the **local** value object, `Album2VO`, rather than calling the accessors of the remote entity bean.

```
Context ctx = new InitialContext();

Album2Home home = (Album2Home)PortableRemoteObject.narrow(
  ctx.lookup("java:comp/env/ejb/Album2Home"),
  Album2Home.class );

Album2 album = null;
Album2VO vo = null;  // value object
Collection albumList = home.findAll();
Iterator albumIterator = albumList.iterator();
while (albumIterator.hasNext()) {
  album = (Album2)albumIterator.next();
  vo = album.getData();
 // Now these are all local
  out.println("<TR><TD>" + vo.ID + "</TD>"
            + "<TD>" + vo.MUS_ID + "</TD>"
            + "<TD>" + vo.TITLE + "</TD>"
            + "<TD>" + vo.LABEL + "</TD>"
            + "<TD>" + vo.CAT_NO + "</TD>"
            + "<TD>" + vo.MEDIA + "</TD>"
            + "<TD>" + vo.RATING + "</TD>"
            + "</TR>");
}
out.println("</TABLE>");
```

Test Results Summary

The following comparison charts reveal a significant performance improvement resulting from our application of the Value Object pattern:

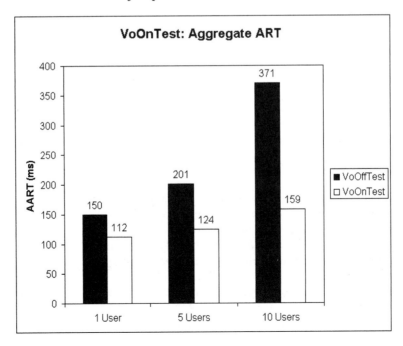

At a 10-user load, we realize a 57% saving in response time. In fact, it seems that the response time savings become greater as the load scales up (25% reduction at 1 user, 38% reduction at 5 users). It is also interesting to note here that our "remote" method calls in these two test cases are not really remote, but only span containers within the same server instance (a result of deploying the test servlets and EJB's as a single application archive, `jazzcat.ear`). We could expect to see an even larger difference if the web container and EJB container were running on different computers or JVMs.

The following chart comparing transactional rates shows a similar increase in performance:

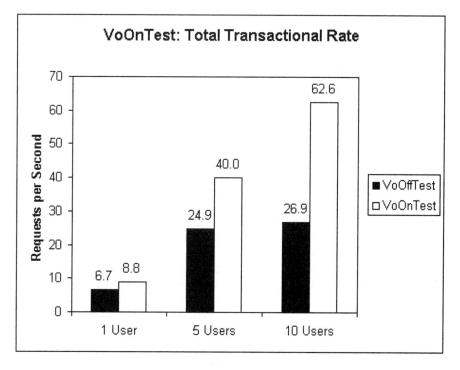

This is a very interesting result. Whereas for the `VoOffTest` we saw the transactional rate stabilizing after 5 users, here we see that use of the pattern has effectively increased our throughput capacity – the throughout continues to increase significantly beyond 5 users.

Finally, even resource utilization seems to have benefited from the change, showing an approximately 20% reduction in CPU usage:

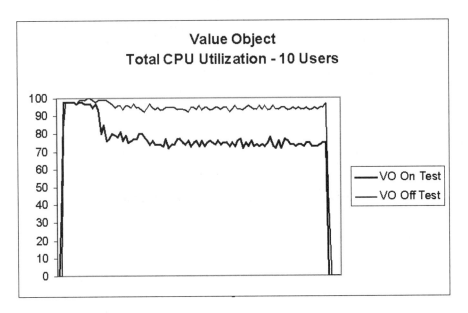

More Interesting Value Object Tests

You may have noticed that in both of our initial tests we ignored transactional considerations and freely violated some of the basic ACID properties. For example, after the VoOnTest servlet fetches the value object for a particular Album entity, and begins to read each field value from the local object, the state of the actual corresponding Album entity that the value object represents might change back on the server side. Likewise, as the servlet traverses the collection of Album entities, the state of any Album in the collection could change after the Album was already "read." While it may be true that this consistency problem is less likely to occur to an Album entity, which we would expect to be a reasonably static entity, it does illustrate a more general concept of how transactional problems like these can occur in entities that are more volatile.

In our initial tests, we ignored transactional considerations in the interest of gathering some basic measurements, because our main focus was on the Value Object pattern. Ignoring transactional considerations is only really acceptable when reading large amounts of data for display-only purposes. In some databases, it is seen as a desirable option because an open transaction may cause locks on the database that keep other clients from accessing the data. This is irrelevant is Oracle because readers never block other readers or writers.

However, having seen a performance benefit in our implementation of the Value Object pattern, it would be interesting to know what kind of overhead might result from adding transactional logic to the test. Actually, we have already been incurring a bit of transactional overhead in the previous test cases. Like most of the CMP entity beans in our application, the Album and Album2 entity bean deployments specify Required for the <trans-attribute> element, and * for the <method-name> element. However, these only resulted in short-lived transactions for each method call, committed before the data is returned to the client.

It would be nice to have answers to the following questions:

❑ What is the performance overhead of using the container's transaction services?

❑ Likewise, what is the performance overhead of adding explicit transaction management to the test client using the `javax.transaction.UserTransaction` object to mark transaction boundaries?

❑ How does explicit transaction management compare with container-managed transactions from a performance perspective?

In the application design phase, this data can help us better establish if or when it's appropriate to use the design pattern. To answer these questions, we will need to design two additional test cases:

❑ `VoTxTest` – list Albums without VO, using explicit transaction management (`UserTransaction`)

❑ `VoFacadeTest` – list Albums via VO assembled in stateless session bean (container-managed transaction)

From a test design perspective, in order to obtain accurate result data comparisons, it is important that the two "transaction" test cases share comparable implementations. To achieve this, we will implement additional versions of the original baseline test, `VoOffTest`, as it contains a sequence of bean accessor method calls that can easily be represented as a transaction, and used as a basis of comparison.

Test Case 5.2.3: VoTxTest

In order to add explicit transaction management to our album listing functionality, we can modify our original non-VO test. We simply wrap the entire set of `Album` beans to remote calls, including the finder and the ensuing iteration, all within a `UserTransaction`, as shown in the following sequence diagram:

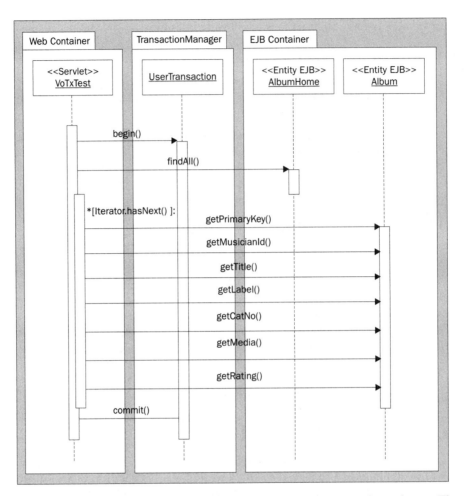

In the diagram, the calls to `begin` and `commit` mark the transaction boundaries. The following excerpt from the new `VoTxTest` servlet shows the necessary code changes:

```
Context ctx = new InitialContext();

UserTransaction utx = (UserTransaction)
    ctx.lookup("java:comp/UserTransaction");

AlbumHome home = (AlbumHome)PortableRemoteObject.narrow(
    ctx.lookup("java:comp/env/ejb/AlbumHome"),
    AlbumHome.class );
Album album = null;
Collection albumList = home.findAll();
Iterator albumIterator = albumList.iterator();

// The following explicit client-side transaction control
// is for test purposes only and not generally recommended
// We need to bypass server optimizations so that we can compare
```

```
            // our own explicit transaction management with that of the
    server.

        utx.begin();

        // Set isolation level to disallow "dirty reads"
        Transaction tx = TxHelper.getTransaction();
        tx.setProperty(TxConstants.ISOLATION_LEVEL,
    new Integer(Connection.TRANSACTION_READ_COMMITTED));

        while (albumIterator.hasNext()) {
          album = (Album)albumIterator.next();
          out.println("<TR><TD>" + album.getPrimaryKey() + "</TD>"
                    + "<TD>" + album.getMusicianId() + "</TD>"
                    + "<TD>" + album.getTitle() + "</TD>"
                    + "<TD>" + album.getLabel() + "</TD>"
                    + "<TD>" + album.getCatNo() + "</TD>"
                    + "<TD>" + album.getMedia() + "</TD>"
                    + "<TD>" + album.getRating() + "</TD>"
                    + "</TR>");
        }

        utx.commit();

        out.println("</TABLE>");
```

Test Results Summary

Comparing the original non-ACID VoOffTest with the new version, VoTxTest, which includes the interposition of the transaction manager, we see some surprising performance results in the following charts:

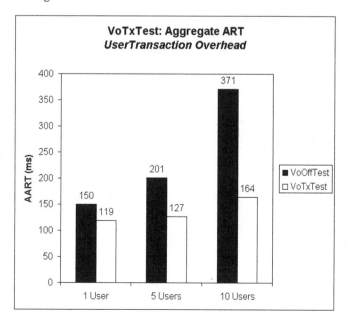

Instead of measuring performance degradation from the "overhead" of explicit transaction management, we instead see a dramatic **improvement** in response time, similar to the improvement obtained after applying the Value Object pattern. The following chart shows a similarly dramatic increase in throughput:

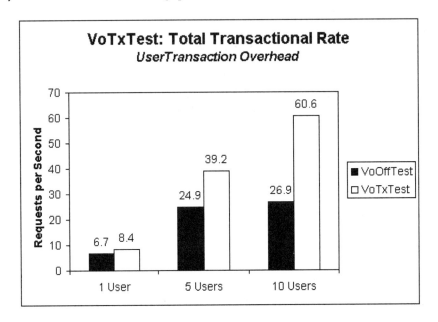

Additionally, we find a significant decrease in CPU utilization:

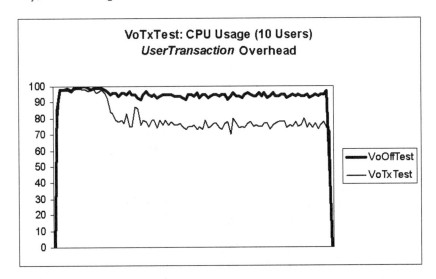

What would explain this phenomenon? One possible explanation is in the deployed transaction attributes of the `Album` bean itself. Examining the EJB deployment descriptor, `ejb-jar.xml`, we see that the `Album` bean's entry in the `<assembly-descriptor>` element is set so that any and all of the bean's methods require a transactional context (the `<method-name>` element's "`*`" wild-card value indicates all methods, and the `<trans-attribute>` element's `Required` keyword value indicates a required transactional context).

```
<!-- ALBUM CMP ENTITY -->
  <container-transaction>
    <method>
      <ejb-name>AlbumBean</ejb-name>
      <method-name>*</method-name>
    </method>
    <trans-attribute>Required</trans-attribute>
  </container-transaction>
```

If the client calls are part of a transaction that is already underway, the `Album` bean methods execute as part of that transaction. However, if there is no transaction underway, the container initiates a **new transactional context with each method call**.

Recall the following sequence from the `VoOffTest` servlet:

```
out.println("<TR><TD>" + album.getPrimaryKey() + "</TD>"
          + "<TD>" + album.getMusicianId() + "</TD>"
          + "<TD>" + album.getTitle() + "</TD>"
          + "<TD>" + album.getLabel() + "</TD>"
          + "<TD>" + album.getCatNo() + "</TD>"
          + "<TD>" + album.getMedia() + "</TD>"
          + "<TD>" + album.getRating() + "</TD>"
          + "</TR>");
}
```

With the `Required` transaction attribute setting in effect, and no existing transaction already underway, these seven discrete method calls result in seven discrete transactions, one for each method call. This is all compounded by the iteration over each `Album` entity in the collection returned by the finder (`findAll`, also triggering an additional transaction).

But the real penalty occurs in the life-cycle events that bracket each transaction, and most specifically data synchronization with a persistent store. In other words, the ejbLoad and ejbStore calls – or the subsequent lazy database I/O – are where we pay the price for the multiple transactions triggered by `VoOffTest`. Also note that actual results are highly dependent on the commit option that we're using.

It is also interesting to note how this new `VoTxTest` compares with `VoOnTest`, in which we implemented the Value Object pattern. In terms, of AART performance, they are virtually identical:

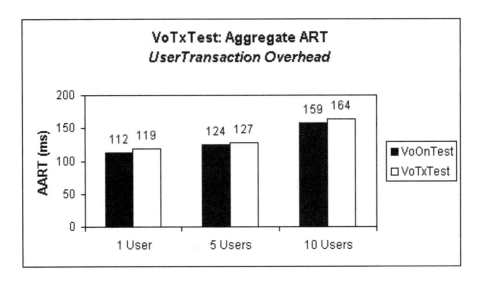

The observation holds for the throughput:

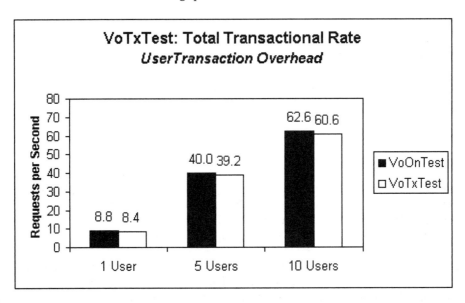

When we check the CPU usage, we see that they are very similar in each case, with the usage being slightly lower for the VoOnTest case:

286

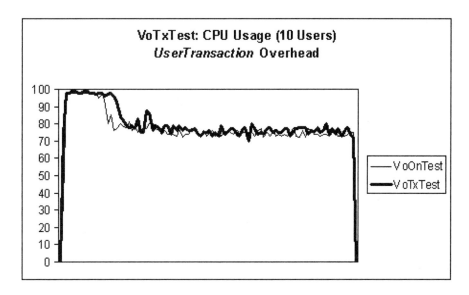

These results seem more in line with our original expectations, but one has to ask how they are comparable, as VoOnTest implements the pattern, and VoTxTest does not. Here, too, the interesting comparison lies in the deployment of the Album2 bean. Recall that, in creating the Album2 bean to replace the original Album bean, we added a getData method in order to replace the multiple accessor method calls with a single call to fetch the value object. While that change eliminated the multiple method calls, it also eliminated the corresponding transactions associated with each call. The Album2 bean's deployed transaction attributes are identical to the original Album bean:

```
<!-- ALBUM2 CMP ENTITY -->
    <container-transaction>
      <method>
        <ejb-name>Album2Bean</ejb-name>
    <method-name>*</method-name>
      </method>
      <trans-attribute>Required</trans-attribute>
    </container-transaction>
```

Because of the reduced number of calls on the bean's methods, VoOnTest indirectly initiates far fewer new transactions. Of course, we still have multiple remote method calls residing in VoTxTest, while in VoOnTest they are replaced by getData, but that is the interesting thing here.

Originally, we attributed the performance gain seen in the `VoOnTest` results to our having implemented the Value Object pattern, and to the resulting reduction in the number of remote method calls. But the new `VoTxTest` results suggest something else. `VoTxTest` contains the same number of remote method calls as the baseline `VoOffTest` (neither test case implements the VO pattern), and yet now, comparing `VoTxTest` results with `VoOnTest`, we see no dramatic difference in performance due to applying the pattern (`VoOnTest`). We can now reassess our analysis, and attribute the performance gain to the reduction in new transactions, rather than the reduction in method calls. By wrapping the remote method calls within a transaction, we actually reduced the number of new transactions that the container would otherwise have initiated. This also expains the results observed for the Value Object test.

Perhaps the bigger lesson to be learned here is in the danger of making premature conclusions based on preliminary test result analysis. This is especially easy to do when the preliminary test results appear as "good news."

Test Case 5.2.4: VoFacadeTest

We must now design a new test that corresponds to `VoTxTest`, one that will allow us to compare the performance of explicitly managed transactions with that of container-managed transactions. In our design, we can apply the following strategy: Take the finder method call and sequence of accessor method calls in `VoTxTest`, and relocate them in a stateless session bean method named `getAlbumList`. This is essentially another example of the Session Facade pattern (hence the test name `VoFacadeTest`). By doing this, we can then use the transaction attributes of the stateless session bean to force a container-initiated transaction to occur (corresponding to the `UserTransaction` we explicitly initiated in `VoTxTest`). At the same time, we avoid triggering multiple new transactions that would otherwise result from calling the Album bean methods without a client transaction context underway. As result, the number of method calls, and the number of transactions initiated by the stateless session bean, should be roughly equivalent to the number initiated by `VoTxTest`.

There will be one minor difference: because the session bean is now interposed between the test servlet and the `Album` bean, we need a way to transfer the resulting `Album` data from the session bean back to the test servlet for display. For this purpose, we can use our `Album2VO` value object, as this seems to be a fairly lightweight mechanism that should have little impact on the test results.

The following sequence diagram illustrates this test design:

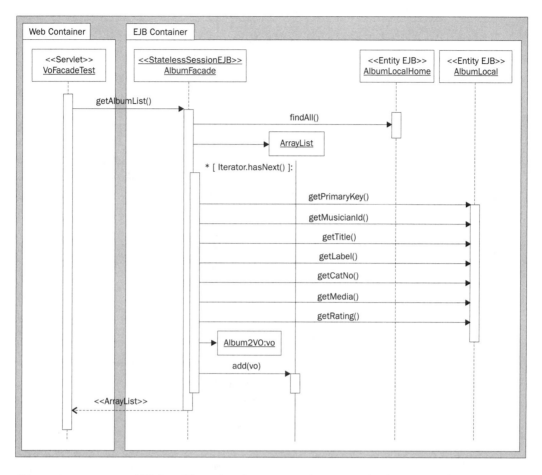

Just as in our original Value Object implementation's test servlet (VoOnTest), VoFacadeTest will need to unpack the list of Album2VO objects returned by getAlbumList.

Test Results Summary

The following result charts, comparing the performance of explicit transaction management in VoTxTest with the performance of container-managed transaction (CMT) services in VoFacadeTest, suggest that we sacrifice a significant amount of performance by attempting to manage transactions from the client using a javax.transaction.UserTransaction. In the best case (10 concurrent users), use of the CMT services yielded a 21% reduction in response time:

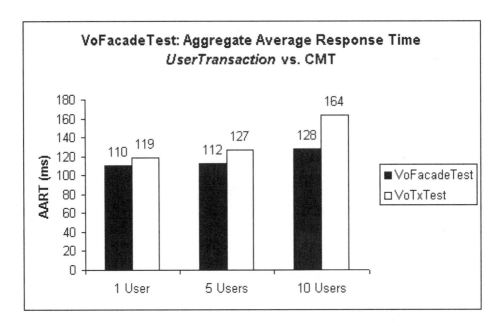

Likewise, the throughput increased by nearly 28%:

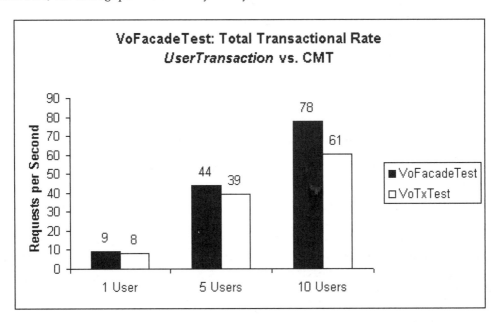

As shown in the following chart, the decrease in CPU utilization was also sizable:

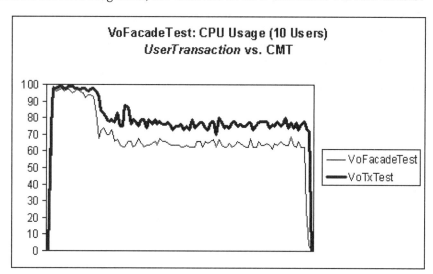

How can we account for the performance difference? One likely contributor is the container's superior resource management (something our `VoTxTest` servlet doesn't even attempt). This is evidenced by comparing the CPU utilization against the response time and throughput results. In the CMT test results (`VoFacade`), the server is working less hard and at the same time delivering better performance. Also, our using explicit transaction management in `VoTxTest` requires the servlet to fetch a `UserTransaction` reference from the JNDI tree:

```
UserTransaction utx = (UserTransaction)
    ctx.lookup("java:comp/UserTransaction");
```

JNDI access can sometimes represent a significant contributor to performance degradation. By comparison, the EJB container likely has its transaction resources lined up in advance. This brings up another interesting point: EJB server vendors are only required to support the JTA's `javax.transaction.UserTransaction interface`. The EJB container may not even use the JTS for its transaction service, and instead implement its own proprietary transaction service for better performance. This is often cited as one of the principal advantages of declarative services, and these test results seem to confirm this.

Test Design Issue: Data Marshalling?

In looking at our `VoFacadeTest` design, we may be suspicious of the different ways in which the data is returned to the client servlet in our tests. In `VoTxTest`, the data returned to the test servlet is the individual EJB field values, which are all simple types (primitives and `String` objects). In `VoFacadeTest`, the session bean used to trigger a single container transaction returns value objects (`Album2VO`) to the test servlet, which are wrapped up in an `ArrayList` and sent back through a remote interface. Both tests access the EJBs through remote interfaces. But, unlike `VoTxTest`, the Value Object data returned in `VoFacadeTest` is being marshalled, which can be horribly slow by comparison.

While this is a potentially valid concern, **it does not apply to here**. As we described earlier in discussing our `FacadeOnTest` results, many vendors implement optimization strategies to recognize components that are co-located in the same server instance (or same EAR file). This is the case with WebLogic Server, where the vendor-specific `<enable-call-by-reference>` deployment element enables EJB method calls from within the same server to pass arguments by reference (even when using an EJB's remote interface). This is the default behavior for WebLogic Server (`<enable-call-by-reference>` is `true`), so we cannot attribute any performance differences to data marshalling.

However, the current test design limits how we deploy our test components. If we were to choose to deploy the test servlets (like `VoFacadeTest`) on a different server instance in the EJB components, it is likely we would trigger the additional expense of data marshalling between tiers.

Thus, we are currently faced with two variables in comparing the test cases:

❑ Overhead introduced by using the `AlbumFacade` stateless session bean, along with the use of `Album2VO` value objects as a data transfer mechanism between tiers, and

❑ Overhead introduced by invoking the EJB container's transaction management services.

By minimizing the differences between test case designs, we could eliminate the first possibility with more certainty, and perhaps obtain a more reliable measurement. To make the test cases more comparable, we might do the following:

1. Modify `AlbumFacade` by adding a `getAlbumListCMT` method, identical to the original `getAlbumList` implementation.

2. Modify the `AlbumFacade` deployment configuration to guarantee that the container always applies transaction management to `getAlbumList`, and never applies transaction management to `getAlbumListCMT`. The following lines from the `<assembly-descriptor>` stanza of `ejb-jar.xml` would accomplish this:

```
<!-- ALBUM FACADE STATELESS SESSION -->
  <container-transaction>
    <method>
      <ejb-name>AlbumFacadeBean</ejb-name>
      <method-name>getAlbumList</method-name>
    </method>
    <trans-attribute>RequiresNew</trans-attribute>
  </container-transaction>
  <container-transaction>
    <method>
      <ejb-name>AlbumFacadeBean</ejb-name>
      <method-name>getAlbumListCMT</method-name>
    </method>
    <trans-attribute>Never</trans-attribute>
  </container-transaction>
```

3. Create a new `VoFacadeCMTTest` that is identical to `VoFacadeTest`
    implementation, but instead calls `getAlbumListCMT`.

After doing this, we could redeploy and run the two tests, and then compare the performance
of `VoFacadeTest` against that of `VoFacadeCMTTest` with more confidence, isolating the
impact of adding container transaction management.

Considering the potential expense of object serialization and data marshalling,
`VoFacadeTest` illustrates a test design principal we introduced earlier in the chapter: care
must be taken to ensure that the two tests being compared are indeed comparable. By
introducing a second variable into the test (namely, the use of a seemingly innocuous value
object), we risk skewing test results by triggering a different kind of server overhead (data
marshalling) than that which we intended to measure (transactions).

If you are interested in performing further tests, then you might consider designing a new
`VoFacadeCMTTest` test case as described, to correct the problem we encountered in
comparing `VoTxTest` with `VoFacadeTest`. Or, you could design a test case to directly
compare using the Data Transfer HashMap with `VoOnTest`, where the `Album` entity bean
returns a `HashMap` instead of a `Value Object` (Album2VO).

Testing the Data Access Object Pattern

In thinking about preliminary design options for the JazzCat application, we might want to
evaluate alternatives for accessing the persistence tier. For example, we may want to
implement bean-managed persistence (BMP) in our entity bean layer, to give us more
flexibility in integrating data from a variety of sources as the application grows. One obvious
trade-off here is that adopting a BMP strategy requires a lot more coding, but it may be worth
the effort if we foresee a future need to obtain data from data sources that would be difficult or
impossible to map to our entity beans using container-provided tools. Furthermore, by
including vendor-specific SQL within our bean implementation, we also limit the portability
of our components.

Perhaps the biggest performance risk of adopting a BMP strategy is posed by what is
popularly known as the "**n+1 problem**". It can be explained in the following way:

> For a BMP entity, the finder method will return only primary keys. Each entity instance
> that needs to access its state will require a subsequent database access. An EJB container
> can get around this problem for CMP beans by "eagerly loading" their state, so that there
> is only one database access. In fact, ideally it should be possible to configure the eager
> loading of related state data, too. Consider a BMP finder that returns 20 customer
> entities. Suppose each customer has 20 orders, and each order has 20 line items.

Assuming that all this data is used in the transaction, that the relationships are loaded via finders, and that each BMP bean manages its state, the original finder will result in 1 + 20 + 20 + 20*20 + 20*20 + 20*20*20 SQL SELECT queries (finder query + customer states + orders + order states + line items + line item states). In this circumstance, is quite likely that the customer entity will be written as a coarse-grained object to manage the state of the orders and line items, reducing the total number of database SELECT statements back down to 1 + 20*3 (finder query + customer states + order states + line items states).

In theory, a finder for a CMP entity can be configured to load all this data using only three SQL SELECT statements: one for the customers, one for the orders, and one for the line items. Support for this "eager-loading" behavior will vary between EJB containers or third party tools, but eventually this will be a ubiquitous capability. Note that this is using fine-grained CMP entities. Coarse-grained CMP entities buy you nothing here, and you lose the (EJB 2.0) standards-based support for relationships (and portability for your object-relational mapping).

To begin experimenting with BMP designs and avoid writing a lot of code, we'll choose to model the simplest table in our schema: INSTRUMENTS. The corresponding Instrument bean needs only two String fields: abbrev and name. We can put this EJB to use by implementing a simple piece of functionality that we will surely need in the JazzCat application, obtaining a list of all instruments. The test servlet that simulates this functionality would produce output like the following:

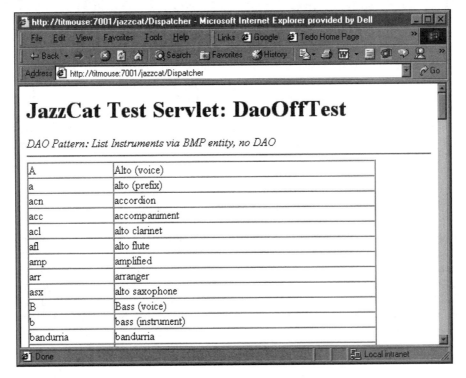

Perhaps we know there is a general, long-range goal to integrate instrument data from a music publisher's old IMS system, and also a near-term plan to include instrument data from another college's jazz catalog data, which is expressed in XML. To maximize flexibility in integrating data from a variety of sources, we will need to figure out a way to avoid coding separate versions of our BMP Instrument bean for each new data source.

The Data Access Object Pattern in a Nutshell

The Data Access Object design pattern is often used to insulate BMP entity bean design from the specific requirements of the underlying data source they access for their persistence. The most common example of this is vendor-specific SQL statements that appear in the entity bean's implementation code, depicted in the following sequence diagram:

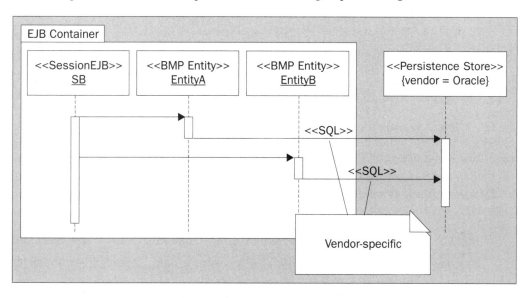

This use of vendor-specific SQL severely limits the portability of a BMP bean. The same holds true for any data access code in the BMP bean that is directly affected by changes in the underlying data store. The Data Access Object pattern insulates the BMP bean by introducing an object that proxies data access requests from the BMP entity. When changes occur in the underlying data store, only the data access objects are affected. The following sequence diagram illustrates this strategy:

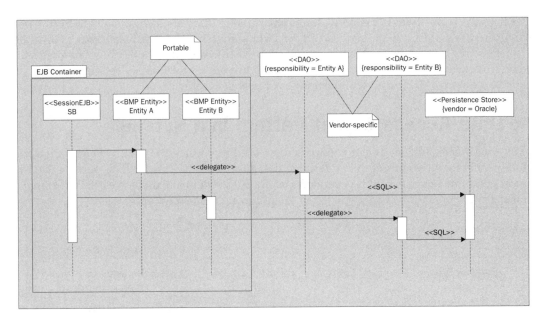

The DAO objects contain the vendor-specific data access code, and mirror the data access methods in their corresponding BMP entity. When the BMP entity needs to perform a data access function, it delegates the task to its corresponding data access object.

> *For a more formal documentation of the Data Access Object pattern, including variations, nuances, and related patterns, visit the following URLs:*
>
> http://developer.java.sun.com/developer/restricted/patterns/DataAccessObject.html
>
> http://java.sun.com/blueprints/patterns/j2ee_patterns/data_access_object/index.html

The Data Access Object pattern represents a design choice intended to maximize flexibility and portability. One obvious trade-off is increased complexity and code management. From a performance perspective, we'd like to know the following:

❑ What is the impact of the increased indirection in accessing the data store?

❑ What is the impact of the increased number of object instances?

To answer these questions, we will design and run a couple of initial test cases representing the instrument list functionality with and without the Data Access Object pattern applied, and then compare the results.

Test Case 5.3.1: DaoOffTest

The following sequence diagram illustrates the baseline `DaoOffTest` implementation:

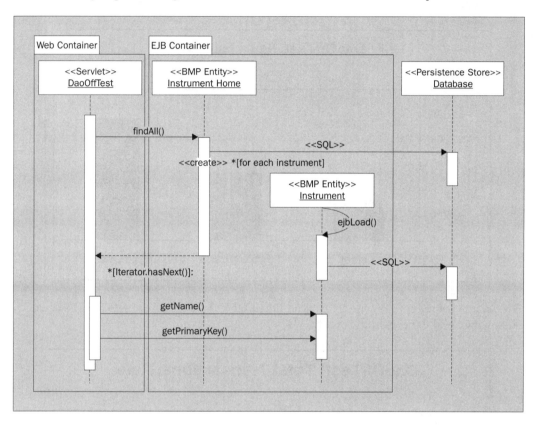

As you can see, this test is extremely simple: obtain a collection of all `Instrument` beans, and for each bean the name and abbreviation (primary key). In the diagram, the `create` and `ejbLoad` details shown within the home and component interfaces of the BMP bean are included to represent data access implementation code that the developer has to write for a BMP bean (code that is generated by the container for CMP beans).

Test Results Summary

The following are baseline results that we will later compare with our Data Access Object implementation.

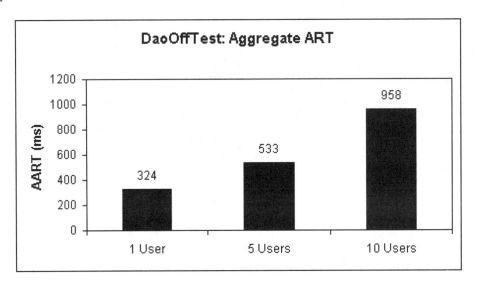

We see the response times rise by 64% and then 80% as we step from 1 to 5 to 10 users. Following are the throughput results:

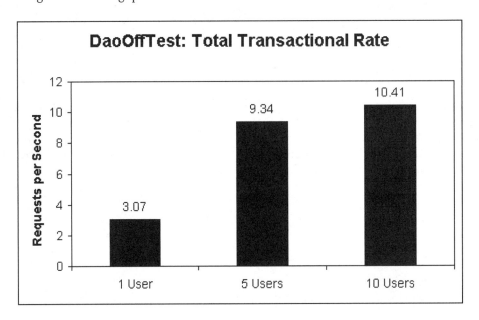

We see that throughput is at capacity (or close to capacity) with a load of 5 users. Finally, we present the CPU usage chart for the WebLogic server, and again note that we are close to maximum usage capacity:

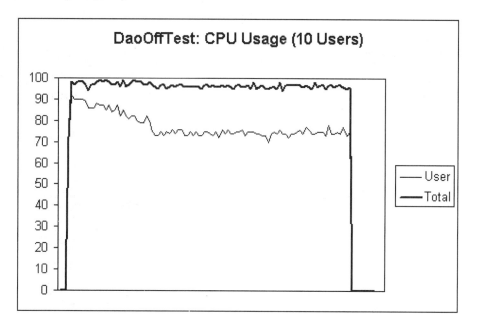

Test Case 5.3.2: DaoOnTest

The following sequence diagram shows the same instrument list operation, this time including the use of a data access object, InstrumentDAO.

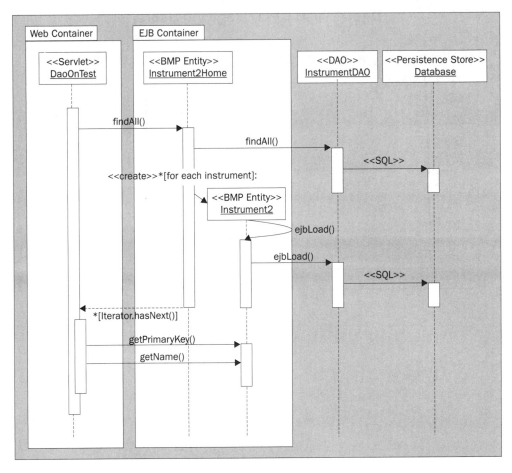

As the diagram shows, when using a data access object, any methods within the BMP entity bean's implementation that would normally interact directly with the underlying data store, now delegate those tasks to the corresponding method in the data access object. Consider, for example, the ejbLoad container callback method, which the container calls to load the entity bean's state whenever the container deems it necessary (for example, on activating a passivated bean). The implementation of ejbLoad appears in the Instrument2EJB implementation class as follows:

```
public void ejbLoad() {
  try {
    dao.load( (String)ctx.getPrimaryKey() );
    isModified = false;
  } catch (JazzcatDAOException je) {
     throw new EJBException(je);
  }
}
```

Instead of accessing the database directly, as is normally done in a BMP entity bean, `ejbLoad` invokes the corresponding `load` method in the `InstrumentDAO` data access object instance (`dao`). It is the data access object's load method that issues the SQL statements via JDBC calls. This is shown in the following source excerpt from `InstrumentDAO`:

```
public void load(String pk) throws JazzcatDAOException {
  try {
    String sqlStmt = "SELECT abbrev, name FROM Instruments "
                   + "WHERE abbrev = ? ";
    conn = ds.getConnection();
    PreparedStatement stmt = conn.prepareStatement(sqlStmt);
    stmt.setString(1, pk);
    ResultSet rs = stmt.executeQuery();

    if (rs.next()) {
       this.name = rs.getString("name");
    this.abbrev = pk;
    stmt.close();
    // etc...
```

Test Results Summary

A comparison of the results between `DaoOffTest` and `DaoOnTest` shows only negligible differences in AART performance:

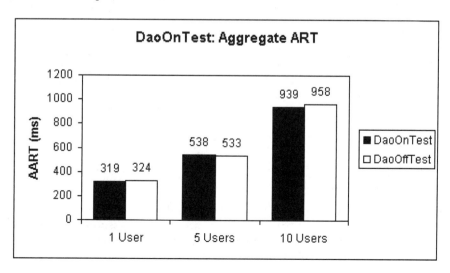

The throughput performance is also essentially the same in both cases:

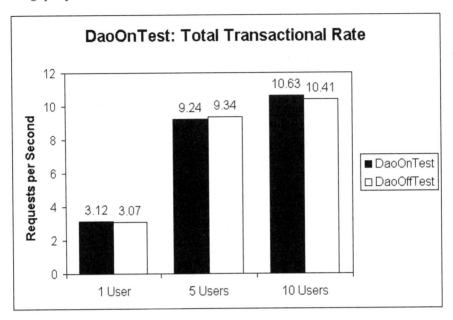

And finally, we see no alteration in CPU usage:

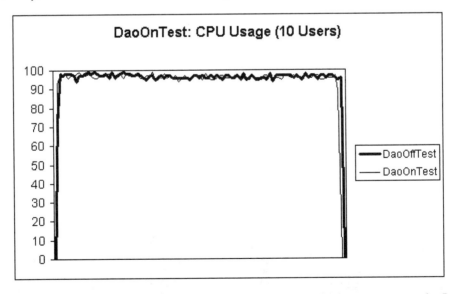

Using the Data Access Object pattern introduces a level of indirection in our code. In essence, by comparing DaoOffTest and DaoOnTest, we are merely measuring the performance impact of that indirection. The results show that this kind of indirection in EJBs is essentially free, given the relative overhead of the J2EE stack.

More Interesting Data Access Object Tests

Although our initial testing of the Data Access Object pattern did not show any significant performance impact from introducing the pattern, the test scenario itself was extremely simple. We now would like to probe a little deeper, and investigate the impact of managing relationships between beans. Specifically, we would like to find answers to the following questions:

❑ How does the performance of bean-managed relationships (implemented using BMP entity beans and DAOs) compare with similar functionality provided by the container (CMP entity beans using EJB 2.0 Container-Managed Relationships)?

❑ How does the performance of bean-managed relationship implementation of a session bean directly accessing DAOs compare with the other two relationship management implementations?

To answer these questions, we need to build a few more test cases:

❑ DaoBmpTest – Search for Bands by title via BMP entities using DAO

❑ DaoCmrTest – Search for Bands by title using CMR (instead of DAO)

❑ DaoSbTest – Search for Bands by title using DAOs directly from a session bean

These three new test cases all implement the same piece of functionality in the JazzCat application: given a song title to search for, the test servlet displays a list of takes matching the title, along with the band members playing on each particular take of that title. For example, typing "Geno" in the Dispatcher's search box and clicking the Run button should produce the following band listing of a single take:

Test Case 5.3.3: DaoBmpTest

For the baseline test case, implement a number of bean-managed relationships using BMP entity beans and data access objects. These will serve as a basis of comparison for the other two tests (CMR, and session bean/DAO). Referring again to the underlying database schema, we can see there are a number of relationships required to produce this listing:

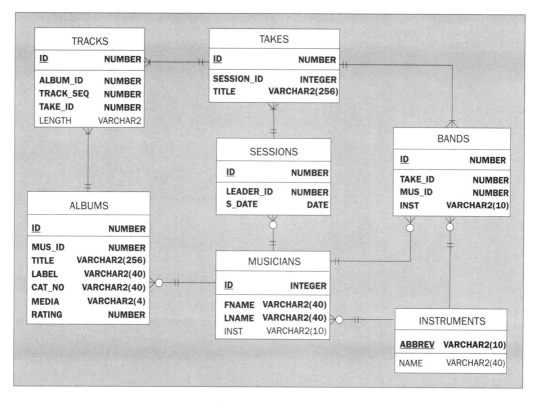

For example, there is a one-to-many relationship between Takes and Bands (a Take has many Band members). And there is a many-to-one relationship between Bands and Musicians (several different bands can have the same musician as a member). A number of other relationships and navigations exist.

> *If you are curious about the details of this EJB implementation and the various relationships between beans, we encourage you to download the source code and explore it on your own. Here, we will instead concentrate on the overall test design and result comparisons to avoid the risk of getting sidetracked by EJB implementation and development details.*

In implementing this test case, we build the required BMP entity beans and a corresponding data access object for each bean. Note that the data access object maintains the relationships. This is because the data access object contains the SQL statements that select the rows identifying related entities. This point will be useful later on, when we create a test case that bypasses the entity beans altogether and instead performs the search using a stateless session bean and the same data access objects. With this collection of BMP entity beans and data access objects, we can create a DaoBmpTest test servlet that triggers the search and displays the resulting list. The following sequence diagram shows the various BMP entity beans and DAOs involved in the test:

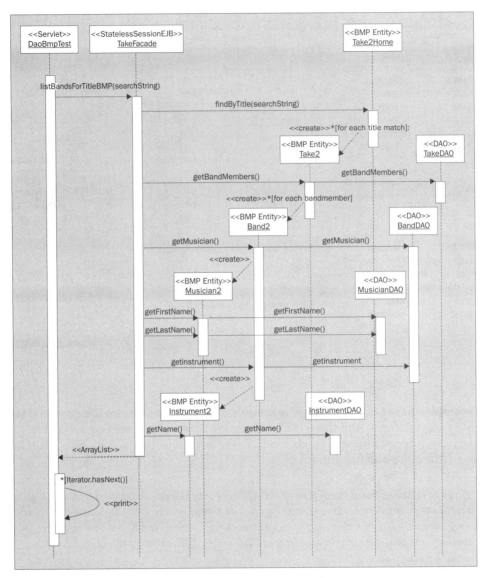

Note the use, again, of the Session Facade pattern (TakeFacade). This time, however, we are using the stateless session bean for slightly different purpose. We want implementation of all three tests to be comparable. As we know the last of the three tests will involve using a stateless session bean to directly manipulate data access objects, we use the stateless session bean as a facade for all three tests, so that we may keep the logic between each test servlet and EJB container nearly identical. Thus the TakeFacade bean serves as a single point of access to all three servlets, and contains three matching methods, one for each test case: listBandsForTitleBMP (called by DaoBmpTest), listBandsForTitleCMR (called by DaoCmrTest), and listBandsForTitleDAO (called by DaoSbTest).

As you can see in the diagram, this test case involves quite a few more object interactions than our two initial DAO test cases did. As a result, we should feel more confident that tests are not too simplistic to yield meaningful results.

Test Results Summary

As with our previous baseline results, the following result data will be most interesting when compared with the alternative designs that follow:

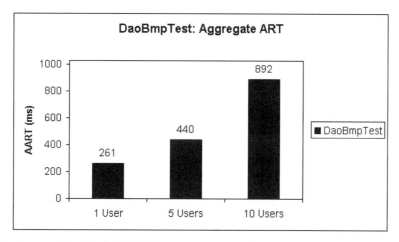

The trends observed for both AART and transactional rate mimic those seen for the DaoOff and DaoOn tests.

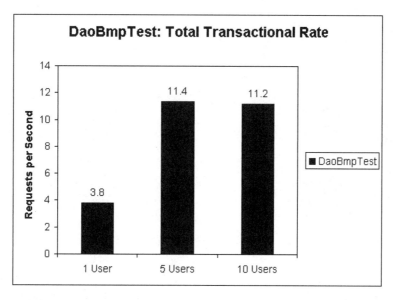

Again, the total CPU usage was close to 100%.

Test Case 5.3.4: DaoCmrTest

We can now move on to implement a new test that corresponds to the baseline `DaoBmpTest`, but replaces the BMP entity beans and data access objects with matching CMP entity beans and container-managed relationships declared in the deployment descriptor. The following sequence diagram shows the similarity between tests. Although there are no longer any data access objects, the bean relationships and multiplicities remain the same.

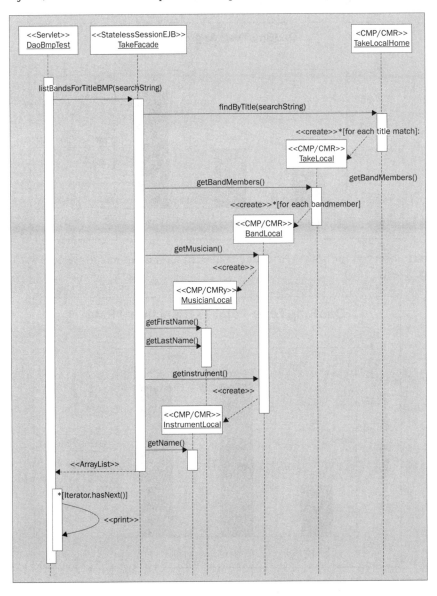

Test Results Summary

The following charts show that, compared with the bean-managed relationships implemented using BMP entity beans and data access objects, the declared container-managed relationship implementation yielded generally better performance on all three counts (response time, throughput, and CPU utilization).

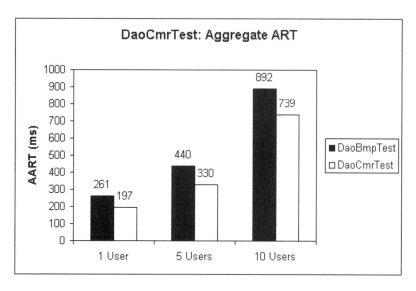

The average response time data shows that the CMR implementation (DaoCmrTest) produced a 17% saving in response time. As you might expect, the response time improvement shows up conversely as an increase in throughput:

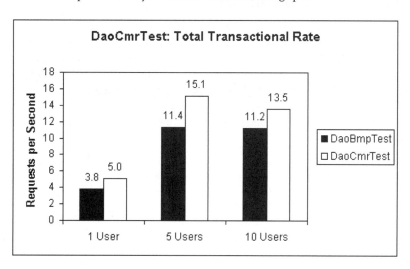

The CPU usage shows little change from that observed in the bmp tests:

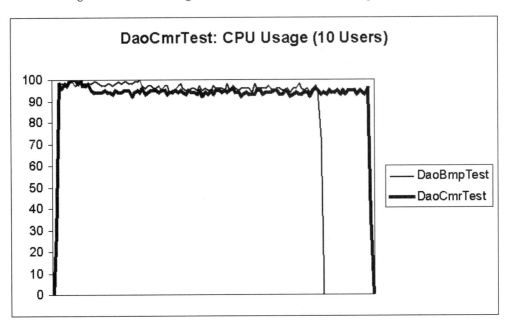

We can see in these results that, even without tuning or paying much attention to deployment configuration, by using CMP/CMR the EJB container can apply "eager-loading" from the database and other strategies that yield a significant performance benefit.

Test Case 5.3.5: DaoSbTest

In the last of our three "relationship" DAO comparison tests, `DaoSbTest`, we evaluate a third related design alternative, in which we eliminate the entity beans from the design altogether, but continue to use the data access objects directly from a stateless session bean. Comparing the results of this test with the previous two tests will allow us to verify whether or not the entity bean layer itself represents any kind of data access performance bottleneck.

The sequence diagram for this test case shows that its implementation closely follows that of the other two tests.

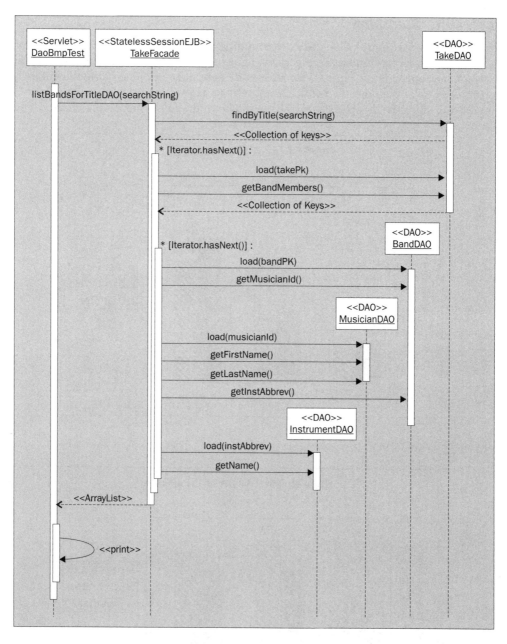

In a general sense, the data access objects act as surrogate entity beans. Note the calls to the load method for each DAO – this is roughly equivalent to the findByPrimaryKey method found in each of the corresponding entity beans, and serves as the mechanism by which we load state data from the database into the DAO.

Test Results Summary

When compared with the other two corresponding tests, `DaoSbTest` yields some surprising results. Given the direct database access via lightweight data access objects, and a stateless session bean replacing the entity bean layer, we might have predicted a significant increase in performance over the other two entity bean designs. However, the test result data for `DaoSbTest` suggests the opposite is true, as shown in the following AART chart:

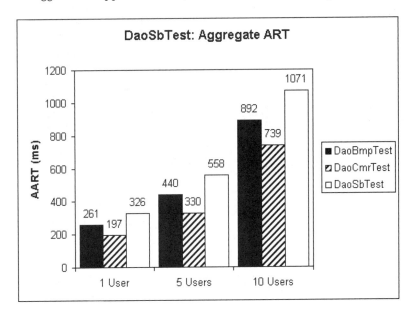

And again in the throughput chart:

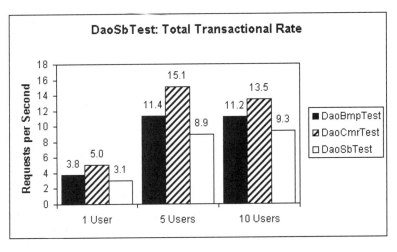

The `DaoSbTest` showed a drop in CPU usage of around 10 % compared to the Bmp and Cmr tests (from 75% to 65%).

To explain these results, we must refer back to our implementation of `DaoSbTest`. Looking at our sequence diagram for this test case, we see that both `findByTitle` and `getBandMembers` methods return a collection of primary keys. In having the DAOs return primary keys to locate data this way, rather than eagerly loading all the data (as the container is most likely doing), we trigger the "n + 1" problem described earlier in the chapter. Essentially, the DAOs are forcing many more trips to the database than necessary.

This DAO design problem occurs because, in coding the DAO classes, we simply copied the data access code from the corresponding BMP entity beans that already existed. This was done to try to ensure a fair comparison between the BMP entity beans and their DAO counterparts, by having the two objects accomplish their data access in the same way. However, while the EJB specification demands that BMP entity bean finders return primary keys, DAOs are under no such obligations.

There are a couple of interesting further tests that the interested reader could run here. For a start, we could re-implement a new set of DAO classes that avoid the "n+1" problem encountered in `DaoSbTest`. Also, we could design a test that uses a session bean to issue the JDBC SQL calls currently located in the data access objects, bypassing the DAO and entity layers completely. Compare the performance of this design with a corresponding test that uses a Session Facade and entity beans as the data access mechanism

EJB Deployment Configuration Testing Strategy

In EJB deployment testing, we are trying to measure the effect on system performance that results from a change to a particular element value in the EJB deployment descriptor. One simple strategy to measure the effect of change is by comparing two EJB deployments that differ only in the value of the same deployment parameter. In most cases, when we compare two alternative parameter values, the more we can isolate the change to a single parameter, the more confidence we can have in our results analysis. If other, additional parameters changed between the two deployments being tested and compared, it would be difficult to determine precisely which parameter change caused the change in system performance.

Therefore, in EJB deployment configuration testing, it is important that all other deployment settings are identical for any two test results being compared. Likewise, it is critical that we execute the exact same test script when comparing any two alternatives for the same deployment parameter, in order to eliminate the possibility that the difference between test scripts contributed to the difference in system performance. To address these constraints, we can adopt a slightly different strategy for comparing deployment alternatives.

First, we'll reuse the same set of EJB classes for each test by deploying the chosen EJB (in our case, the MusicianBean) multiple times in the prototype enterprise application, assigning a different JNDI name for each deployment. In this way, we have different "flavors" of a single bean concurrently deployed in the application. Each deployment represents a specific deployment configuration for the MusicianBean, each being a single EJB deployment descriptor element variation. Doing this helps guarantee a more accurate comparison by ensuring identical bean implementations between the two test cases. More importantly, it saves us a lot of time, as we don't have to code separate beans for each deployment test. It also conveniently confines all of our test case definition work to editing the deployment descriptor.

We should note here that, by adopting this "simultaneous deployment" testing strategy, we risk sacrificing some accuracy in our measurements, as it is possible to tax the EJB container with the "extra" EJBs deployed (whereas, in the real world, we intend to only deploy a single version of bean). However, as we are most interested in the change between two otherwise static deployments, the impact on result accuracy should not be significant provided we don't take this technique to extremes. In addition, this risk is easily controlled, as the underlying objects are identical and only the JNDI names differ. For example, in any given test run we can set the cache size and other parameter values to limit the number of potential instances of the "extra" EJB objects. In this case, to maintain fair result comparisons, it would be important to apply identical limits for any two test runs being compared.

As an example, the following excerpt from ejb-jar.xml shows two such deployment variations of the MusicianBean, (MusicianDdIsoTSBean. and MusicianDdIsoTRCBean), each representing a different transaction isolation level (TRANSACTION_SERIALIZABLE and TRANSACTION_READ_COMMITTED, respectively):

```xml
<!--
    NOTE: The following deployments are all variants of the same
        MusicianBean for the deployment tests
-->

<!-- MUSICIAN (DD_ISO_TS) CMP ENTITY -->
    <entity>
      <description>
      Musician CMP Entity (TRANSACTION_SERIALIZABLE isolation level)
      </description>
      <display-name>MusicianDdIsoTSBean</display-name>
      <ejb-name>MusicianDdIsoTSBean</ejb-name>
      <home>jazzcat.ejb.cmp.MusicianHome</home>
      <remote>jazzcat.ejb.cmp.Musician</remote>
      <local-home>jazzcat.ejb.cmp.MusicianLocalHome</local-home>
      <local>jazzcat.ejb.cmp.MusicianLocal</local>
      <ejb-class>jazzcat.ejb.cmp.MusicianEJB</ejb-class>
      <persistence-type>Container</persistence-type>
      <prim-key-class>java.lang.Integer</prim-key-class>
```

```
    <reentrant>False</reentrant>
    <cmp-version>2.x</cmp-version>

    <abstract-schema-name>MusicianDdIsoTSSchema</abstract-schema-name>
    <cmp-field>
      <field-name>id</field-name>
    </cmp-field>
    <cmp-field>
      <field-name>firstName</field-name>
    </cmp-field>
    <cmp-field>
      <field-name>lastName</field-name>
    </cmp-field>
    <cmp-field>
      <field-name>instrument</field-name>
    </cmp-field>

    <primkey-field>id</primkey-field>

    <ejb-ref>
      <ejb-ref-name>ejb/IdGeneratorHome</ejb-ref-name>
      <ejb-ref-type>Session</ejb-ref-type>
<home>jazzcat.ejb.stateless.IdGeneratorHome</home>
<remote>jazzcat.ejb.stateless.IdGenerator</remote>
<ejb-link>IdGeneratorBean</ejb-link>
    </ejb-ref>

    <query>
      <query-method>
        <method-name>findAll</method-name>
        <method-params></method-params>
      </query-method>
      <ejb-ql>
     SELECT OBJECT(m) FROM MusicianDdIsoTSSchema AS m
      </ejb-ql>
    </query>

    <query>
      <query-method>
        <method-name>findByInstrument</method-name>
        <method-params>
       <method-param>java.lang.String</method-param>
    </method-params>
      </query-method>
      <ejb-ql>
     SELECT OBJECT(m) FROM MusicianDdIsoTSSchema AS m
     WHERE instrument = ?1
      </ejb-ql>
    </query>

  </entity>

<!-- MUSICIAN (DD_ISO_TRC) CMP ENTITY -->
    <entity>
```

```
        <description>
    Musician CMP Entity (TRANSACTION_READ_COMMITTED isolation level)
        </description>
        <display-name>MusicianDdIsoTRCBean</display-name>
        <ejb-name>MusicianDdIsoTRCBean</ejb-name>
        <home>jazzcat.ejb.cmp.MusicianHome</home>
        <remote>jazzcat.ejb.cmp.Musician</remote>
        <local-home>jazzcat.ejb.cmp.MusicianLocalHome</local-home>
        <local>jazzcat.ejb.cmp.MusicianLocal</local>
        <ejb-class>jazzcat.ejb.cmp.MusicianEJB</ejb-class>
        <persistence-type>Container</persistence-type>
        <prim-key-class>java.lang.Integer</prim-key-class>
        <reentrant>False</reentrant>
        <cmp-version>2.x</cmp-version>

        <abstract-schema-name>MusicianDdIsoTRCSchema</abstract-schema-
name>
        <cmp-field>
          <field-name>id</field-name>
        </cmp-field>
        <cmp-field>
          <field-name>firstName</field-name>
        </cmp-field>
        <cmp-field>
          <field-name>lastName</field-name>
        </cmp-field>
        <cmp-field>
          <field-name>instrument</field-name>
        </cmp-field>

        <primkey-field>id</primkey-field>

        <ejb-ref>
          <ejb-ref-name>ejb/IdGeneratorHome</ejb-ref-name>
          <ejb-ref-type>Session</ejb-ref-type>
        <home>jazzcat.ejb.stateless.IdGeneratorHome</home>
        <remote>jazzcat.ejb.stateless.IdGenerator</remote>
        <ejb-link>IdGeneratorBean</ejb-link>
        </ejb-ref>

        <query>
          <query-method>
            <method-name>findAll</method-name>
            <method-params></method-params>
          </query-method>
          <ejb-ql>
         SELECT OBJECT(m) FROM MusicianDdIsoTRCSchema AS m
          </ejb-ql>
        </query>
```

```
        <query>
          <query-method>
            <method-name>findByInstrument</method-name>
            <method-params>
           <method-param>java.lang.String</method-param>
            </method-params>
          </query-method>
          <ejb-ql>
        SELECT OBJECT(m) FROM MusicianDdIsoTRCSchema AS m
        WHERE instrument = ?1
          </ejb-ql>
        </query>

      </entity>

  <!-- etc. -->
```

The important point to note here is that both deployments identify the same underlying EJB classes and interfaces:

```
        <home>jazzcat.ejb.cmp.MusicianHome</home>
        <remote>jazzcat.ejb.cmp.Musician</remote>
        <local-home>jazzcat.ejb.cmp.MusicianLocalHome</local-home>
        <local>jazzcat.ejb.cmp.MusicianLocal</local>
        <ejb-class>jazzcat.ejb.cmp.MusicianEJB</ejb-class>
```

We now have two identical EJB deployments for use in deployment comparison tests.

Secondly, instead of creating a separate test case servlet for each deployment test case, we will instead reuse a single servlet, named `DeploymentTest`, for all of the deployment tests. In this deployment testing approach, each EJB *deployment* represents a discrete test case, instead of the test driver. Here too, running the same servlet logic against each deployment variation also helps guarantee accurate comparisons. In this case, the `DispatcherServlet`'s `test_id` parameter identifies the unique *JNDI name assigned to the EJB deployment*, instead of a unique test case servlet. Thus, for a test named **DdCacheLow**Test, there is a corresponding EJB deployed with the JNDI name `MusicianDdCacheLowHome`. Likewise, for a test named **DdCacheHigh**Test there is a `MusicianDdCacheHighHome` EJB deployed.

The following sequence diagram illustrates this strategy:

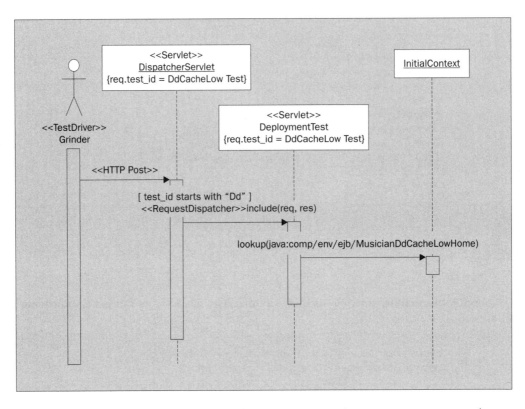

When the test executes, the DispatcherServlet parses the test_id parameter (set to DdCacheLowTest in the diagram). If the parameter value starts with "Dd" (signaling a deployment configuration test), the DispatcherServlet dispatches the HttpRequest object (containing the selected test_id parameter) to the DeploymentTest servlet. The DeploymentTest servlet also parses the test_id parameter, this time to form the JNDI name string for use in the context lookup for the EJB home interface (for example, java:comp/env/ejb/MusicianDdCacheLowHome).

> *Because EJB deployment options can vary by application server vendor, this test strategy is particularly handy when experimenting with vendor-specific deployment features.*

Testing EJB Deployment Alternatives

As noted in the previous section, our example test suite includes a set of test cases designed to measure the performance of a few EJB deployment alternatives. Often, the deployment configuration of an application's EJBs is inherently part of the EJB design, and so must be considered from a performance perspective when evaluating the merits of a particular design implementation.

There is another advantage to performance testing EJB deployment alternatives. EJB developers taking advantage of the "declarative services" model offered by the J2EE platform are often left with an interesting question: if we simply declare the configuration of low-level services like transaction management and access control in the EJB deployment descriptor, and thereby defer the implementation of those services to the EJB container, what impact does the container's implementation of those services have on the overall performance of the EJB layer?

In the deployment configuration tests that follow, we look at two such "declarative services": transaction isolation and access control. As mentioned earlier, we will adopt a variation of our test strategy here by deploying multiple versions of the same EJB, each with a different deployment configuration. Thus we will be rerunning the exact same servlet test script, `DeploymentTest`, against the exact same bean implementation, `jazzcat.ejb.cmp.MusicianEJB`, in every deployment test case. The only thing that differs between each Musician EJB deployment is the value for a chosen deployment configuration parameter in the deployment descriptor, and the EJB's JNDI name.

For JNDI names, we use the following naming convention: `MusicianXxxBean`, where *Xxx* is the test case identifier, representing some unique deployment configuration. All deployment test identifiers share a "Dd" prefix, indicating they are "deployment descriptor" tests. Thus, our JazzCat EAR contains the following six additional EJB deployments:

`<ejb-name>`	**JNDI Name**	**Deployment Element**
`MusicianDdIsoTSBean`	`MusicianDdIsoTSHome`	`<isolation-level>`
`MusicianDdIsoTRCBean`	`MusicianDdIsoTRCHome`	
`MusicianDdSecOffBean`	`MusicianDdSecOffHome`	`<method-permission>`
`MusicianDdSecOnBean`	`MusicianDdSecOnHome`	
`MusicianDdCacheLowBean`	`MusicianDdCacheLowHome`	`<max-beans-in-cache>`
`MusicianDdCacheHighBean`	`MusicianDdCacheHighHome`	

The impact of cache settings on performance has already been covered in Chapter 4 in the Session object versus Stateful bean tests (by not using `ejbRemove`, we were quickly filling the cache and thus starting bean passivation). Therefore, here, we'll limit our investigations here to transaction isolation and security. However, we include the `DdCacheLow` and `DdCacheHigh` tests in the code download so that the more curious readers can download and run these tests on their own.

The DeploymentTest Script

The `DeploymentTest` servlet test script (`DeploymentTest.java`) is shared by all deployment configuration tests, and performs a simple function: add a new `Musician` entity to the `Musicians` table in the database. This requires input values for the new musician's first name, last name, and primary instrument (abbreviation). The `DispatcherServlet` contains corresponding input boxes to collect these required strings:

New musician info:

First name: Last name: Primary instrument:

☑ Add *and* query for musicians with same primary instrument

When the form data is submitted, these three values are included as fname, lname, and abbrev parameters in the resulting HTTP POST request that is dispatched to the `DeploymentTest` servlet. The `DeploymentTest` servlet fetches these parameters from the request as shown in the following code fragment:

```
String fname  = req.getParameter("fname");
isEmptyParam = isEmpty(fname);
String lname  = req.getParameter("lname");
isEmptyParam = isEmpty(lname);
String abbrev = req.getParameter("abbrev");
isEmptyParam = isEmpty(abbrev);
```

Subsequently, the `DeploymentTest` servlet uses these values in an EJB create call to add the new musician:

```
Context ctx = new InitialContext();
MusicianHome home = (MusicianHome)PortableRemoteObject.narrow(
 ctx.lookup("java:comp/env/ejb/Musician" + testName + "Home"),
 MusicianHome.class );

// Create musician
home.create(fname, lname, abbrev);
```

Because the `DeploymentTest` servlet is potentially shared among many test cases, it would be nice to add a little flexibility to the script so that we can trigger some kind of access contention among executing Grinder threads. This might prove useful in deployment tests involving transaction services, like our transaction isolation tests. To accomplish this, we add an option to trigger a query (via an EJB finder) after adding a new musician. The query is for a list of musicians with the same primary instrument. The desired effect is that, while some client threads are adding new musicians, other threads might attempt to access that same data. Although arbitrary, the data access contention that does occur should more likely be at stricter transaction isolation levels.

To implement this functionality in `DispatcherServlet`, we add a checkbox that determines whether the query occurs after the musician is created:

☑ Add *and* query for musicians with same primary instrument

This results in another request parameter, `query`, in the form data dispatched to the `DeploymentTest` servlet, serving as a flag variable:

```
String query = req.getParameter("query");
```

If the checkbox is enabled, the `DeploymentTest` servlet executes the following code:

```
if (query != null && query.equals("true")) {
    // List musicians with same primary instrument
    out.println("Musicians playing: " + abbrev);
    out.println("<TABLE WIDTH=\"500\" BORDER=\"1\" CELLSPACING=\"0\"
            "
            + "CELLPADDING=\"0\"> ");

    Iterator musIter = (home.findByInstrument(abbrev)).iterator();
    while (musIter.hasNext()) {
      Musician mus = (Musician)musIter.next();
      out.println("<TR>");
      out.println("<TD>" + mus.asString() + "</TD>");
      out.println("</TR>");
    } // next musician

    out.println("</TABLE>");
} else {
    out.println("Added musician: " + fname + " " + lname
            + " [" + abbrev + "]");
}
```

Transaction Isolation and EJB Performance

For EJB developers, transaction isolation must always be considered from two perspectives: application design and performance. As the "I" in the "ACID" transactional properties, transaction isolation is implicit to EJB application design, determining the safeguards applied in concurrent access to an EJB's underlying data. However, those safeguards are likely to come at a price in application performance. In comparing the performance impact of any two transactions' isolation levels for an EJB's underlying data, we would expect to see performance degrade as transaction isolation increases. The reasoning is that higher isolation results in more locks on data, and thus more clients are forced to wait for data access until the lock is released. In the next two sections, we compare the difference in EJB performance between applying two different transaction isolation levels: TRANSACTION_SERIALIZABLE and TRANSACTION_READ_COMMITTED.

TRANSACTION_SERIALIZABLE represents the most restrictive transaction isolation level, specifying the safest strategy for concurrent transactions trying to access the same data. With this isolation level, each transaction has exclusive read/write access to the data, locking out other transactions until it commits.

TRANSACTION_READ_COMMITTED is a substantially more permissive transaction isolation strategy, only requiring that data read by a transaction be restricted to committed data. Data being changed within a different transaction cannot be read until the other transaction commits. This prevents the classic "dirty read" problem, but still permits "non-repeatable reads" and "phantom reads" to occur. This is the most commonly used isolation level in database applications.

> *For a full explanation of isolation levels, transactions, and EJBs, see* Professional EJB
> *(Wrox Press, ISBN 1-861005-08-3).*

To compare the performance impact of these two isolation levels, we will deploy two identical EJBs, one for each transaction isolation level setting and test them using the same test script (the DeploymentTest servlet).

The implementation and behavior of transaction isolation control will generally vary between application server vendors. In the case of WebLogic Server, we declare an EJB's transaction isolation in the vendor-specific weblogic-ejb-jar.xml deployment descriptor.

The following is an excerpt from weblogic-ejb-jar.xml:

```xml
<transaction-isolation>
  <isolation-level>TRANSACTION_SERIALIZABLE</isolation-level>
  <method>
    <description>
      All MusicianDdIsoTSBean methods are TRANSACTION_SERIALIZABLE
    </description>
    <ejb-name>MusicianDdIsoTSBean</ejb-name>
    <method-name>*</method-name>
  </method>
</transaction-isolation>

<transaction-isolation>
  <isolation-level>TRANSACTION_READ_COMMITTED</isolation-level>
  <method>
    <description>
      All MusicianDdIsoTRCBean methods are TRANSACTION_READ_COMMITTED
    </description>
    <ejb-name>MusicianDdIsoTRCBean</ejb-name>
    <method-name>*</method-name>
  </method>
</transaction-isolation>

<!-- etc. -->
```

Test Case 5.4.1: DdIsoTSTest

The implementation and behavior of transaction isolation control will generally vary between application server vendors. In the case of WebLogic Server, we declare an EJB's transaction isolation in the vendor-specific weblogic-ejb-jar.xml deployment descriptor, using the <transaction-isolation> element. Our first test case, DdIsoTSTest, requires that we configure a version of the Musician entity (MusicianDdIsoTSBean) with its transaction isolation levels set to TRANSACTION_SERIALIZABLE. The following lines from weblogic-ejb-jar.xml show this deployment declaration:

```
<transaction-isolation>
  <isolation-level>TRANSACTION_SERIALIZABLE</isolation-level>
  <method>
    <description>
      All MusicianDdIsoTSBean methods are TRANSACTION_SERIALIZABLE
    </description>
    <ejb-name>MusicianDdIsoTSBean</ejb-name>
    <method-name>*</method-name>
  </method>
</transaction-isolation>
```

WebLogic Server allows transaction isolation control at the method level, and with <method-name> set to "*", we have specified that TRANSACTION_SERIALIZABLE is applied to all of the bean's methods.

Test Results Summary

The following graphs show the results of running the DdIsoTSTest both with and without the optional query. Here, we are executing SQL INSERT statements rather than SELECT queries and, in our initial tests, we found that we could now scale up the test thread load beyond 10 users. Therefore these tests were carried out with user loads of 10, 20, 30, and 40 concurrent users. First, the results for AART performance:

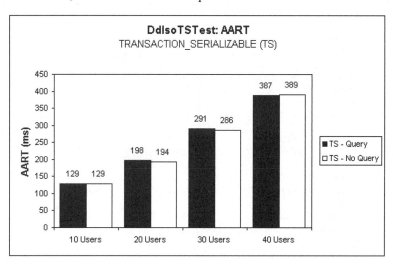

323

As you can see, the results are virtually identical in each case. Next, we present the throughput performance:

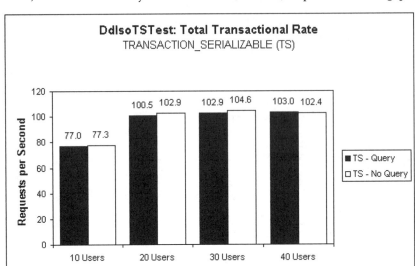

Once again, and as expected, the results are very similar. The CPU usage chart for 40 users was found to be close to 100%.

Test Case 5.4.2: DdIsoTRCTest

In order to test the alternative transaction isolation level, TRANSACTION_READ_COMMITTED, we simply need to configure the corresponding EJB deployment, MusicianDdIsoTRCBean, as shown in the following lines from weblogic-ejb-jar.xml:

```
<transaction-isolation>
  <isolation-level>TRANSACTION_SERIALIZABLE</isolation-level>
  <method>
    <description>
      All MusicianDdIsoTSBean methods are TRANSACTION_SERIALIZABLE
    </description>
    <ejb-name>MusicianDdIsoTSBean</ejb-name>
    <method-name>*</method-name>
  </method>
</transaction-isolation>

<transaction-isolation>
  <isolation-level>TRANSACTION_READ_COMMITTED</isolation-level>
  <method>
    <description>
      All MusicianDdIsoTRCBean methods are TRANSACTION_READ_COMMITTED
    </description>
    <ejb-name>MusicianDdIsoTRCBean</ejb-name>
    <method-name>*</method-name>
  </method>
</transaction-isolation>
```

As a result, we have isolated the difference between the two EJBs to a single parameter for comparison, that being the value of the `<isolation-level>` deployment descriptor element.

Test Results Summary

The following graphs compare the initial `DdIsoTSTest` results with those of `DdIsoTRCTest`. As you can see, the graphs show surprisingly little difference in performance despite the change in transaction isolation level:

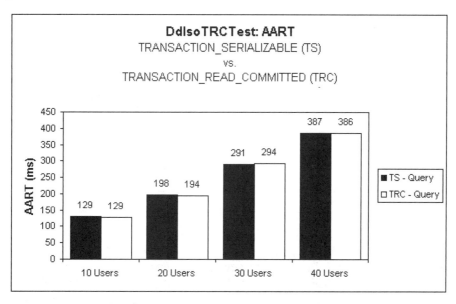

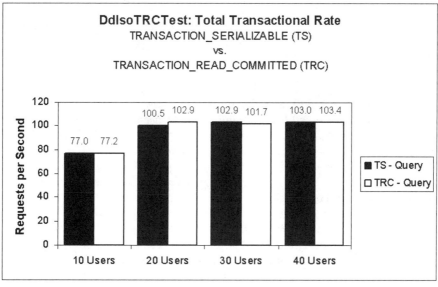

Once again, CPU usage for 40 users approached 100%:

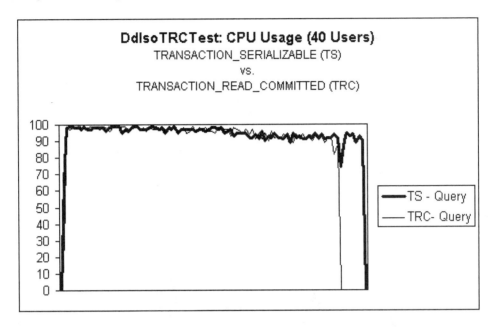

The CPU usage graph shows that, even with a relatively small load, the server is being sufficiently taxed. This is due to the fact that we are using zero think time. The server does not have much time to "catch its breath" between client requests. More importantly, it allows us to eliminate one possible suspicion about why there's so little difference between test results: too few threads. If we are confident that our server machine is of adequate power, then we can be confident that increasing the load will probably not produce differences between the two test results. The application server is being adequately loaded, so if performance differences between the two test cases were going to manifest themselves at all, they should show up under the current user loads.

So why did the change in EJB transaction isolation levels fail to produce conspicuous differences in the test results? One explanation lies in how the EJB container implements this service. In many (perhaps most) EJB containers, the transaction isolation level setting is simply passed on to the underlying database management system (DBMS). How the underlying DBMS implements its locking strategy, and how it handles transaction isolation in general, will generally determine the performance impact of the EJB's transaction isolation deployment configuration. In the case of this particular test run, we used an Oracle system as the underlying database. For Oracle, the difference between TRANSACTION_SERIALIZABLE and TRANSACTION_READ_COMMITTED is in how the database makes "snapshots" of the data on which the application works. For TRANSACTION_READ_COMMITTED, each new statement can use a new snapshot. For TRANSACTION_SERIALIZABLE, the view of the data is consistent between statements. In neither case (without a FOR UPDATE clause) does Oracle issue read locks.

Therefore, because no read locks are occurring, there is no measurable difference in performance between the two isolation levels in our example application. With a different underlying DBMS system, and thus a different locking strategy, our results might have been entirely different. These test results once again demonstrate the need to test our assumptions about performance.

Access Control and EJB Performance

Another container service that could potentially impact an EJB's performance is access control. Here too, the EJB developer's concerns are twofold: application design and performance. Control over client access to the business logic encapsulated in different EJBs is implicit to a J2EE application's design. However, the developer must also wonder if this container-provided service comes at a cost to application performance, and what that cost might be.

Unlike transaction isolation, the way in which the developer declares access control for an EJB is defined by the EJB component model: we grant or restrict access to EJB methods for defined security roles in the deployment descriptor's <assembly-descriptor> element.

> *For a full explanation of role-based EJB access control, see* Professional EJB *(Wrox Press, ISBN 1-861005-08-3).*

The EJB specification does not, however, stipulate how this EJB access control service is to be implemented by the EJB container, nor does it specify how the underlying security system's authentication mechanism is bound to the EJB access control role names. Many server vendors offer a variety of mechanisms for configuring one or more underlying security services for use with EJB access control. This vendor-specific implementation aspect is another motivation for using testing to examine the performance cost of a particular vendor's implementation of this EJB container service.

To measure the suspected performance impact of invoking the access-checking mechanism on our EJB method invocations, we can again use our "simultaneous-dual-deployment" testing strategy: Deploy two identical EJBs, one declaring unchecked access to the EJB's methods (MusicianDdSecOffBean), and one restricting method access to a particular role (MusicianDdSecOnBean). We can then test both using the same test script (the DeploymentTest servlet) and measure any performance difference.

Test Case 5.5.1: DdSecOffTest

Our first test case, DdSecOffTest, must establish a result baseline for comparison by measuring performance with no access control checking occurring. We do this very simply, by declaring unchecked access to the MusicianDdSecOffBean's methods in the deployment descriptor. The following <assembly-descriptor> lines from ejb-jar.xml accomplish this, making use of the newer EJB 2.0 <unchecked/> element tag:

```
<method-permission>
  <unchecked/>
  <method>
    <ejb-name>MusicianDdSecOffBean</ejb-name>
    <method-name>*</method-name>
  </method>
</method-permission>
```

With `<method-name>` set to "`*`", we have specified that access attempts for all of `MusicianDdSecOffBean`'s methods are to go unchecked.

Test Results Summary

The following graphs show our initial baseline results.

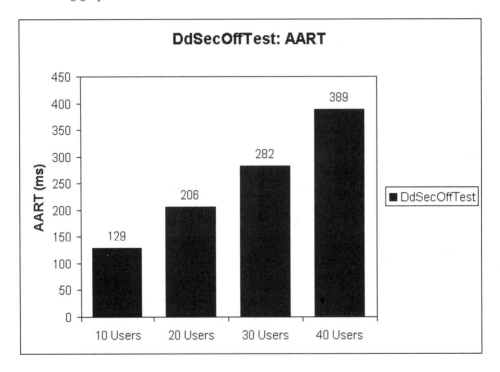

The jump in response time from 10 to 20 users is around 60%. After that, the AART increases by around 37% each time. The throughput results were as follows:

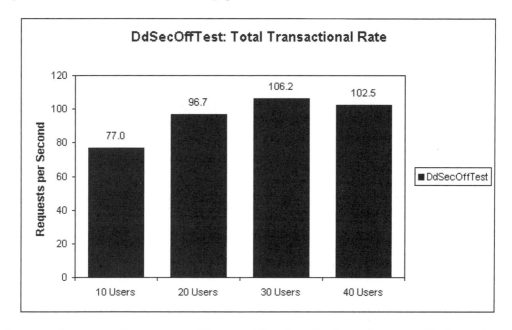

It seems that we reach capacity at 30 users. After that, the throughput is stable (or perhaps falls slightly). The CPU usage average around 55%:

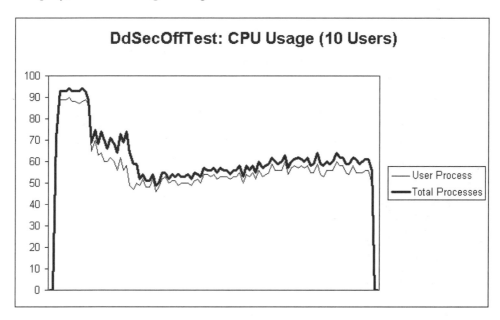

Test Case 5.5.2: DdSecOnTest

Having baseline results in hand, we can now proceed to configure a second test, DdSecOnTest, that invokes the container's role-based EJB access control checking service. However, this implies that you must first have a security role defined. Let's imagine that we wish to restrict the "add musician" function to only those clients having the Librarian role. This means the client's security identity (java.security.Principal) must appear in some kind of logical access control list named "Librarian". As suggested earlier, tying the underlying security system's authentication to the EJB access control mechanism is vendor-specific. In the case of WebLogic Server, this name mapping is declared in the weblogic-ejb-jar.xml deployment descriptor:

```
<security-role-assignment>
  <role-name>Librarian</role-name>
  <principal-name>system</principal-name>
  <principal-name>guest</principal-name>
</security-role-assignment>
```

These lines define a new security role named "Librarian" and included to the default WebLogic Server login identities, system and guest, as members in the Librarian access control list.

Having defined the Librarian role, we can now declare the role in ejb-jar.xml and configure the MusicianDdSecOnBean EJB to restrict access. The following deployment descriptor lines highlight the necessary changes to the <assembly-descriptor> element:

```
<assembly-descriptor>

  <security-role>
    <description>User allowed to create/update/delete</description>
    <role-name>Librarian</role-name>
  </security-role>

  <method-permission>
    <role-name>Librarian</role-name>
    <method>
      <ejb-name>MusicianDdSecOnBean</ejb-name>
      <method-name>*</method-name>
    </method>
  </method-permission>

  <method-permission>
    <unchecked/>
    <method>
      <ejb-name>MusicianDdSecOffBean</ejb-name>
      <method-name>*</method-name>
    </method>
  </method-permission>

  <!-- etc. -->
```

In this case, `<role-name>` element declares its EJB container should perform method access checking for the Librarian role, and `<method-name>` set to `"*"` specifies that the access checking will occur on all MusicianDdSecOnBean methods.

Lastly, we make use of one more and newer (J2EE 1.3) deployment declaration. We need to have a convenient and portable way of ensuring that DdSecOnTest always runs with the Librarian role, even if the current user is not system or guest. This would eliminate the hassle of configuring new security identities and updating the security role assignments when the test and EJBs are deployed into new environments. To insulate the test from these security environment changes, we can modify the web application deployment descriptor and configure the `<ejb-ref>` element for MusicianDdSecOnHome so that any test servlets referencing that EJB, do so using the Librarian role. We can accomplish this using the J2EE 1.3 `<run-as>` element, as shown in the following excerpt from web.xml:

```
<!-- MUSICIAN (DD_SEC_ON) CMP ENTITY -->
  <ejb-ref>
    <ejb-ref-name>ejb/MusicianDdSecOnHome</ejb-ref-name>
    <ejb-ref-type>Entity</ejb-ref-type>
    <home>jazzcat.ejb.cmp.MusicianHome</home>
    <remote>jazzcat.ejb.cmp.Musician</remote>
    <ejb-link>MusicianDdSecOnBean</ejb-link>
    <run-as>Librarian</run-as>
  </ejb-ref>
```

With the web application EJB reference for MusicianDdSecOnHome configured in this way, web-tier access to the MusicianDdSecOnBean always occurs using the Librarian role, regardless of the underlying security principle.

Now we can run DdSecOnTest, invoking EJB access control, and compare the results with those of the previous test.

Test Results Summary

The following result graphs compare our new test DdSecOnTest results with the baseline we established with DdSecOffTest..

The following chart shows the AART performance:

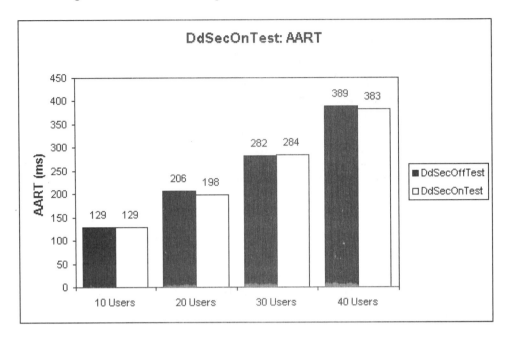

And following are the throughput results:

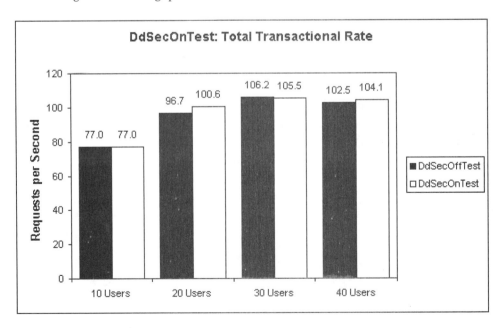

The CPU usage was around 55%. These results seem to suggest that the EJB container's access-checking mechanism, as implemented by this particular vendor, introduces little or no impact on the EJB's performance. However, it is our use of the `<run-as>Librarian</run-as>` element in the web application's deployment descriptor (`web.xml`) that misleadingly makes us draw this incorrect conclusion. Using `<run-as>` in this way bypasses interaction with the underlying authentication system, as the role identity is already pre-established in the deployment descriptor. Because the access control check is not doing any authentication, it's easy to see why it doesn't take any time. We'd get different results with a test that needed to access an LDAP server for authentication (for example).

Thus, this test establishes that the access control checking mechanism by itself introduces little or no meaningful performance overhead. If using `<run-as>` in this way is truly part of our application design, then this results data is sufficient. On the other hand, if our application design requires using the client identity to establish the role identity, this test is easily modified. To measure the additional overhead of the authentication system check, we would simply remove the `<run-as>` element from the web application's deployment descriptor, causing the server to match the client's principal identity with the `<principal-name>` elements defined in the `<security-role-assignment>` stanza of `weblogic-ejb-jar.xml`.

Again, there are further tests that the interested reader might like to pursue:

- ❑ Run `DdIsoTSTest` and `DdIsoTRCTest` using an underlying database system other than Oracle. Compare the results you obtain with those appearing in this chapter. You will probably need to research your own database system's locking mechanism to analyze the results.

- ❑ Oracle permits two transaction isolation settings: `TRANSACTION_SERIALIZABLE` and `TRANSACTION_READ_COMMITTED`. If your own underlying DBMS permits other settings like `TRANSACTION_READ_UNCOMMITTED` and `TRANSACTION_REPEATABLE_READ`, try deriving new test cases from `DdIsoTSTest` and `DdIsoTRCTest` to measure the impact of these alternative isolation levels.

- ❑ Modify `DdSecOnTest` to make use of the authentication system, by removing (or commenting out) the `<run-as>` element in `web.xml`. Redeploy the jazzcat application YEAR, and rerun the test (along with `DdSecOffTest`). Your own WebLogic Server configuration may require you to also alter the `<security-role-assignment>` stanza's `<principal-name>` elements to include the principal name you want to use in running the test. When you rerun the `DdSecOnTest`, you'll need to run The Grinder while logged in as a user that has been configured in WebLogic Server as one of the `<principal-name>` identities.

Summary

The overall goal of this chapter was to demonstrate the importance of testing specific EJB designs and design pattern **implementations**, and the importance of doing so early, as well as to illustrate some alternative EJB performance testing approaches and potential hazards. Along the way, we discovered some interesting points:

- EJB design patterns represent a rapidly growing catalog that is still in flux. This warrants early performance testing of EJB design alternatives.

- Creating a simple yet flexible browser-based test harness (for example, the Dispatcher servlet) can extend the usefulness of your existing web-based test tools.

- Although deployment testing is often considered an end-game activity in EJB development, it is critical to EJB performance and thus it is important to tackle it as early as you can (even during the design phase).

- It's frequently worth pursuing variant test cases that extend or elaborate on your initial EJB design tests, as these extended tests often yield results that force reconsideration of initial analysis. For example, it was only in the extended tests of the Value Object pattern that we learned the real reasons behind the improved performance (fewer transactions) that we initially attributed to the pattern's reduction of multiple remote method calls.

- It's sometimes difficult to design tests that guarantee fair comparisons between test cases. Great care must be taken to ensure that the implementation of two design alternatives is truly comparable. Even greater care must be taken in analyzing results.

JMS Point-to-Point Messaging

Here we begin our performance analysis of some typical JMS architectures. This chapter focuses on the point-to-point (PTP) messaging model and the following chapter covers the publish-and-subscribe model. Our personal experience has been that every messaging application is truly unique. Of course, they all have in common the fact that they need to send and receive messages of various types and sizes, but most real-world point-to-point messaging applications are too specific and too complex to make suitable examples for a general investigation of performance. With this in mind, we decided to focus on common point-to-point architectures:

- ❑ Classic **fan-out** architecture – this involves one message producer, one message queuing system and many consumers receiving messages from that queue.

- ❑ **Multiple Queues** architecture – this is used for handling cases where the messages must be processed in a strict sequential order and is defined by the fact hat there is only one consumer per message queuing system.

In order to perform these tests, we wrote two custom plug-ins for The Grinder that can send and receive messages from a JMS queue, hosted on WebLogic server (the JMS version was 1.0.2). Our key performance metric here is **throughput** (Messages Per Second, MPS). One of the most important performance issues in any messaging system is the size of the message and so we investigated the impact of two different message sizes (1KB and 16KB). In addition, we looked specifically at two features of the JMS API and how their implementation might affect throughput performance:

❑ **Acknowledgement** – the mode in which a consumer acknowledges a message to the server that handles the queue.

❑ **Persistence** – messages can be placed in a data store to increase the reliability of the system.

On the face of it, this sounds rather straightforward but, as you will see, we are in fact dealing with a rather complex set of interdependencies (and, of course, there are many other potential issues to investigate on top of these). As much as any other chapter in the book, this one clearly illustrates the point that we cannot generalize performance results – we must obtain performance data for our own applications. All we can do here is demonstrate clearly how to obtain the data for your JMS application and to present the results for our own specific environment, in order to set a general level of expectation.

An Overview of JMS Point-to-Point Messaging

In order to maintain a focus on architecture and performance issues, we assume basic knowledge of the fundamentals of the Java Message Service (JMS) API. For a detailed discussion of the API, we would refer you to the online sources such as http://java.sun.com/products/jms/, or to other reference sources such as the book, *Professional JMS Programming* (Wrox Press, 1861004931).

The main goals of the JMS model were to provide a standard, unified interface to enterprise messaging systems – often called Message-Oriented Middleware (MOM). Essentially what we have is a standard, Java-based interface to the JMS Service Provider layer implemented by a specific MOM vendor. Remember, the JMS specification is vendor-neutral – it defines the interface but does not dictate how it is implemented. The specific vendor may provide facilities and services not explicitly defined in the specification. Here, we will be using WebLogic JMS, which is a fully-featured messaging system (for further details, see http://e-docs.bea.com/wls/docs61/jms/intro.html).

A JMS Session provides the context for producing and consuming messages. A Session creates `MessageProducer` and `MessageConsumer` objects, which transmit and receive messages (in this chapter we just use the terminology message producer and message consumer).

The central MOM concept is that of a **destination** (a **queue** or a **topic**). Message producers send messages to the MOM, which then routes these messages to the appropriate message consumers. The **Point-to-Point** (PTP) architecture is based on a model whereby a message producer (sometimes called a queue sender) sends messages to a specific **queue**, and the message consumer (sometimes called a queue receiver) receives the messages from that same queue. Each individual message is only delivered to one consumer and the message producer defines which consumer will receive the message. If multiple receivers are listening to messages on the queue, the messaging server determines which one will receive the next message based on the routing information available in the message header. If no receivers are listening to the queue, the messages remain in the queue until a receiver attaches to the queue.

JMS PTP Architectures

In this chapter, rather than trying to analyze all possible uses of the JMS PTP model, we will concentrate on a couple of problems that we feel are the most representative of PTP messaging.

The most common use of message queues involves two applications (or separate components of the same application) needing to exchange messages (such as data, notifications, and so on) whereby this exchange can be carried out time-independently and loosely coupled, meaning that neither application has to know about the other, or whether it is even up and running. All the application needs to know is how to send and receive messages and be assured that sent messages would be processed within some timeframe. Message queues are also extensively used to continue processing over unreliable links and, in fact, are increasingly preferred to the more traditional mainframe style batch processing.

As well as single point-to-point messaging, two common messaging design patterns in use today are **fan-out parallelism** and **fan-in parallelism**. In both cases, the order in which the processing happens is irrelevant, meaning the messages can be processed in any order. The **fan-out** architecture is presented in the following diagram:

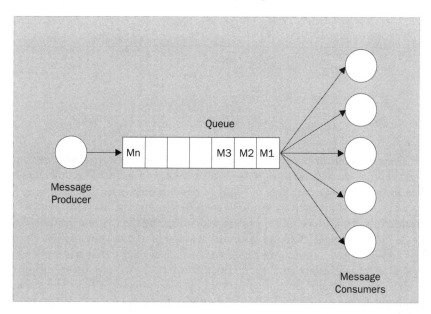

This design pattern has one producer per queue. The producer places the messages in a queue and at the other end one or more consumers pick up the messages and process them (remember that in the PTP model there is only a single potential receiver of each individual message). Upon completion of processing, the consumer goes back to the queue to pick up another message. This has now become the classic model when moving batch processing style applications off the mainframe and onto distributed systems.

This kind of architecture is typically used for processing credit card transactions. At the end of the day a merchant will send a file with all the transactions to a processing center. There, all the files are collected and handled by a single batch process, which places every credit card transaction on a queue as a message. Multiple consumers will then pick up messages from the queue and process them accordingly. This way they can achieve large scalability by processing in parallel as many transactions they can in the allocated period of time available, usually a window of a few hours every night.

In the **fan-in** architecture, we have multiple producers feeding into a single queuing system, as illustrated in the following figure:

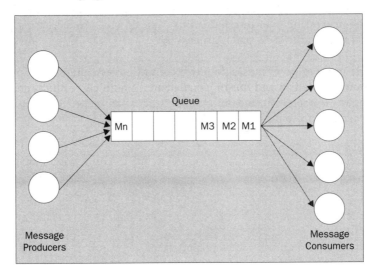

This is the classic model for branch-based companies with centralized processing and distribution facilities such as retail outlets, retail banks, and so on. The objective here is to collate data from possibly thousands of Point-of-Service terminals. For example, first from a branch network controller, then from the branch network controllers to regional distribution centers, and finally from there to the central processing facility. At each point, we have requirements for guaranteed delivery without message loss (persistence). Another example of this kind of architecture is found on lottery systems. Every store that has a lottery till will dial up a central location and place in a queue the information of every lottery ticket sold. At the other end there are multiple consumers picking up these messages from the queue and processing them. As we get closer to the Draw night, more consumers are added to handle the increased load of lottery tickets purchased.

These architectures work well when the messages can be processed in any order. When order is important, requiring the messages to be processed in strict sequential order, then the only way to handle it is by having only one consumer per queue. This constraint denies us the faster processing that parallelism offers us, although in some cases it is possible to break down the messages by type and send a message of a specific type to a particular queue. In these cases the architecture will generally be like the one presented in the following figure:

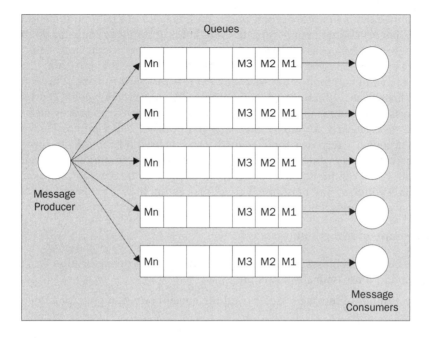

Here, the defining characteristic is that there can be only one consumer for each queue. The producer finds out the type of the message and places it on the corresponding queue. Order is important, so there is only one consumer on the other side of the queue. However, a certain level of parallelism is achieved by separating the messages by types, whereby the message producer in the diagram is not the real producer of the original message but is in effect a pre-processor. This type of architecture is common in large financial institutions.

To set a basic level of expectation regarding performance, we modelled the Fan-out architecture using a single queue, one producer, and multiple consumers. We also modelled the multiple queues architecture used for handling strict sequential order cases, using one producer, multiple queues, and one consumer per queue.

Performance Metrics

Before we discuss our performance metrics when testing JMS applications, we should just clarify the terms synchronous and asynchronous messaging. In an asynchronous messaging system, once the message is delivered to the queue, the producer can immediately continue to process further messages. In a synchronous messaging system, the producer will wait for confirmation that the intended consumer received the message before proceeding. Essentially, RMI and CORBA are for tightly coupled synchronous communications and JMS is designed more for loosely coupled asynchronous communications. Although JMS provides for synchronous messaging, it is actually relatively rare to see it. In this chapter, we focus on asynchronous messaging.

Typically, applications that use asynchronous messages do not fall into the end user interactive category. Some people refer to these kinds of applications as **back-end** or **batch** systems. There are numerous problems that require an asynchronous messaging solution, and just as many applications that cater for them. Most of the time the only thing these applications have in common is the way they express the performance. This is done by measuring **throughput**, which is typically expressed as transactions per second. In this case, a **transaction is a message**, so we measure the number of messages processed per unit of time, for example messages per second, or messages per hour for batch processing. Unlike the "maximum acceptable response time" metric, which is used for interactive applications based on the perceived quality of the application, throughput is based on an actual business requirement, which can be defined as minimum acceptable throughput, for example an overnight time window may exist in which all processing must be successfully completed in order for that company's daily business to resume.

We can measure throughput in two ways:

❑ The number of messages the producer can send to a queue or topic in a specific period of time, typically 1 second.

❑ The number of messages per second the consumer(s) can pick up and process from a queue or topic.

In our study, we did not build and deploy a JMS application, so we could not define a minimum acceptable throughput, as described above. We were simply exploring the behavior of JMS in the PTP architecture under various conditions in order to set a general level of expectation with regard to throughput performance.

> It is important to remember that throughput is a measurement of processing capacity, not speed.

JMS PTP Performance Issues

The list of issues that we could possibly have investigated in this chapter is rather long. There are many features available in the JMS specification that it would have been interesting to explore, such as use of transacted messages and synchronous messages; there are many other messaging issues surrounding guaranteed delivery, use of durable subscribers, and so on. On top of this there are many proprietary features of WebLogic JMS, such as clustering of queues and topics. Things can get rather complex, very quickly. However, in our tests, we aimed for simplicity – we tried to cover the features and issues that will be broadly applicable to virtually any JMS PTP application.

As described in the introduction, we investigated use of two different message sizes (1KB and 16KB), since message size is a key performance issue in any messaging system. As part of our investigation, we looked specifically at how the implementation of two JMS API features, **Acknowledgement** mode and type of **persistence**, might affect performance.

Acknowledgement Modes

When acknowledgement is required, a message will not be deleted from a queue until the message consumer has acknowledged it. Acknowledgement is required if we want **guaranteed** message delivery – if we need to be sure that the consumer picked up the message.

This can hurt the performance of the server handling the queue, but it will also impact the performance of the consumer, as it has to send an acknowledgement back to the server. The acknowledgment modes are the following:

❑ **AUTO_ACKNOWLEDGE**. The consumer acknowledges every message it picks up from the queue. This is the default mode in JMS.

❑ **DUPS_OK_ACKNOWLEDGE**. If the consumer is tolerant of duplicate messages, then this mode allows the JMS Server to deliver the same message more than once. We would expect this to reduce session overhead by minimizing the work required to prevent duplicate messaging in the first place. The situation of duplicate messages mainly occurs when a server recovers after crashing, having missed consumer acknowledgements in the meantime.

❑ **CLIENT_ACKNOWLEDGE**. The client explicitly acknowledges messages by calling the acknowledge() method of a message.

❑ **None**. Messages are not acknowledged by the consumer(s).

WebLogic's implementation of the CLIENT_ACKNOWLEDGE mode is called simply CLIENT (but it works in the same way). However, with the WLS mode the consumer has the ability to acknowledge a group of messages instead of every single message (so the consumer only needs to send one acknowledgment message for every, say, ten messages). The developer decides the number of messages in a group. Under certain circumstances this will improve the performance of the application, but at the expense of reliability.

Persistence

For some applications it is critical that, under any and all circumstances, the consumers receive the messages. It is not very reliable to have the messages living in the memory of the server so it is necessary to persist the messages in an external data store. This way, if the server that hosts the queue fails you can recover the message(s). In the WebLogic Server there are two persistence stores available:

❑ **File message store**. The messages are persisted in a file. The WebLogic Server, using the file system supported by the operating system that hosts the instance of the server, does file management.

❑ **Database message store**. The messages are persisted in a database table. In the particular case of the WebLogic Server, the required tables are generated automatically.

When persisting to a file, WebLogic Server will wait until the write operation has been completed and then continue with the normal processing. This is referred to as a **synchronous write**. The WebLogic Server also offers the possibility of **non-synchronous** writes, whereby the Server will **not** wait for the operating system to confirm the write operation before continuing. This mode can offer substantial performance gains, but again at the cost of reliability. Thus we have three possible modes of persistence, listed in increasing order of reliability:

- File persistence with non-synchronous writes
- File persistence with synchronous writes
- Database persistence (with synchronous writes)

In our tests, we investigated the costs of using each persistence mode.

The Test Configuration

The system architecture used for the tests in this chapter (both for the fan-out and multiple queues test) is summarized in the following figure:

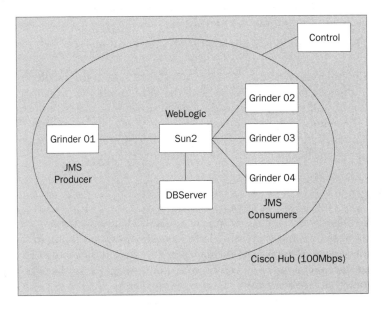

A single Grinder machine generated the producer load and three Grinders were used to generate the consumer load. When database persistence was required, we used an Oracle 8.1.7 database (in its "out-of-the-box" state). Please refer to Appendix B for full details of the test computers used here, and throughout this book.

Sampling Metrics

For the tests in this chapter we used the fixed time (or snapshot) method of data collection, whereby we continuously take fixed-sized samples of data for a specified time period. We used five seconds as the sample size (this means that we record our performance metrics every 5 seconds). We ignored the first 24 samples (two minutes) in order to take into account the initial test period over which the system stabilizes. You must exclude as many samples as is appropriate in your environment. We then collected 60 samples (so the total test time was 7 minutes).

The Grinder Plug-Ins and Test Scripts

In order to explore the JMS PTP architecture, and features of the JMS API as implemented by the WebLogic Server, we used The Grinder and a couple of specially built plug-ins for simulating the producer and the consumers.

> *For details on how to build a plug-in for The Grinder, and on how to create the plug-ins for this chapter in particular, please refer to Chapter 2.*

Using the producer plug-in, `SenderPlugin`, the Grinder continuously generates messages of a specified size and places them in a JMS queue, running on the WebLogic Server. When The Grinder is started, the producer plug-in will establish a JMS connection to the server and open a JMS Session (a JMS connection can have one or more JMS sessions, and each session can receive or send messages, optionally acknowledging them by using any of the methods explained earlier). At this point the Grinder is ready to start sending the messages. As such, the time taken to establish a JMS connection and a JMS session are **not included** in the statistics. Thus, the Grinder producer plug-in executes the following steps:

- ❑ Initialization
- ❑ Establish JMS connection
- ❑ Establish JMS session
- ❑ Grinder timing cycle
- ❑ Create random message payload
- ❑ Send message to queue
- ❑ Await acknowledgement of message received by server, if necessary
- ❑ Write record to the Grinder log file

The consumer side plug-in, `ReceiverPlugin`, simply emulates a consumer picking up messages from the queue (in no specific order). The only operation the plug-in performs after a message has been picked up is to record an entry in the Grinder log. The plug-in allows us to define the number of consumers to be used and the type of acknowledgement that is required.

These plug-ins allow us to obtain our performance metric – the throughput in terms of the number of messages processed per second by the producer and by the consumer. They also allow us to record the average time taken for the producer to place a message in the queue, and for a consumer to pick up a message from the queue – a secondary measurement that we will use occasionally.

Producer Test Script

As described previously, the Grinder running the producer plug-in and test script simply generates messages of a specified size and places them in a JMS queue, running on the WebLogic Server. The test script (grinder.properties file) is rather straightforward:

```
# Producer test script

# Simulate one producer from one JVM and run forever
grinder.processes=1
grinder.threads=1
grinder.cycles=0

# Start/Stop from Grinder Console
grinder.receiveConsoleSignals=true
grinder.grinderAddress=228.1.1.1
grinder.grinderPort=1234

# Agent processes report real-time data to Grinder Console
grinder.reportToConsole=true
grinder.consoleAddress=Control
grinder.consolePort=6372

# Define the plug-in to use and establish the connection
grinder.plugin=com.wrox.paston.jms.queue.grinder.SenderPlugin
grinder.plugin.parameter.serverURL=t3:// sun2:7001
grinder.plugin.parameter.connectionFactoryJNDIName=jms.myConnectionFacto
ry
```

> *T3 is a WLS-only protocol we use for JMS (and internally in the product). It is also known as smart sockets. It is a highly optimized bi-directional, asynchronous protocol.*

Note that we used no think time or ramp up time. Finally, we defined a single request whereby one message of a defined size (in this case, 1KB) will be sent to the JMS queue, MyQueue, running on WLS:

```
grinder.test0.parameter.queueJNDIName=jms.MyQueue
grinder.test0.parameter.messageSize=1024
```

Remember that since we can define a specific queue for each request, then we can also define a different queue for every request.

Consumer Test Script

There were a few more parameters to define in the consumer script, so let's walk through it. First, we define the same parameters as we set for the producer script:

```
# Consumer test script

# Simulate required number of consumers from one JVM and run forever
grinder.processes=1
grinder.threads=25
grinder.cycles=0

# Start/Stop from Grinder Console
grinder.receiveConsoleSignals=true
grinder.grinderAddress=228.1.1.1
grinder.grinderPort=1234

# Agent processes report real-time data to Grinder Console
grinder.reportToConsole=true
grinder.consoleAddress=control
grinder.consolePort=4321

# Note, non-zero sleep times make little sense for the consumer
# Strictly, this line is not required since the default is 0
grinder.thread.sleepTime=0

# Define the Grinder plug-in to use
grinder.plugin=com.wrox.paston.jms.queue.grinder.ReceiverPlugin
grinder.plugin.parameter.serverURL=t3://sun2:8001
grinder.plugin.parameter.connectionFactoryJNDIName=jms.myConnectionFacto
ry
```

When we run the tests, we need to set up two consoles: one for the producer and one for the consumer (we want producer throughput data and consumer throughput data to be presented and saved separately). We want to be able to start and stop the Grinders simultaneously and from either console. We do this by defining the same Grinder address and port in the consoles and the `grinder.properties` files. This way both the producer and the consumers are listening at the same port and both consoles will send the start, reset, and stop signals to the same multicast address (228.1.1.1).

Note, however, that we must specify different console ports for each of the consoles (this is where the Grinders send the real-time information to the consoles). We used `consolePort=6372` for the producer Grinder, and we used `consolePort=4321` for the consumer Grinder.

Next, we define the queue from which the consumer picks up messages. If the parameter queuePerConsumer is set to `false` (the default), then each consumer thread uses the same queue:

```
grinder.plugin.parameter.queueJNDIName=jms.MyQueue
```

However, if we set `queuePerConsumer=true`, which we must do for the multiple queues test, then each consumer thread looks up a unique queue by appending the `grinderID` and process number to the `queueJNDIName`. For example:

```
grinder.plugin.parameter.queuePerConsumer=true
grinder.plugin.parameter.queueJNDIName=jms.queue.paston-0.0
```

Next, we set the `acknowledgeMode` parameter to `CLIENT`, `AUTO`, `NO`, or `DUPS_OK`:

```
grinder.plugin.parameter.acknowledgeMode=NO
```

If `acknowledgeMode=CLIENT`, then the acknowledgeFrequency parameter controls how many messages will be received before an acknowledgement message is sent:

```
# grinder.plugin.parameter.acknowledgeFrequency=50
```

Note that an acknowledgement message is always sent before closing a JMS Session.

That's it – there are no requests to define, since the messages are picked up by the plug-in.

Setting Up and Running the Tests

The following instructions describe how we set up the test environment for the tests in this chapter. You will find that these instructions are somewhat different from other chapters, so we'll go through them in some detail. For a start, we do not deploy an application. The sending and receiving of messages is taken care of by specially built Grinder plug-ins. We have one plug-in for the producer of messages, and one for the consumers of the messages (see Chapter 2 for details of how we built these plug-ins). These set-up instructions are also applicable to the Pub/Sub tests in the next chapter.

The plug-ins (`SenderPlugin` and `ReceiverPlugin`) are packaged in the `performance-client6.jar` file, in the code download for this chapter. This file also includes the `QueueInitialisation.class` that contains code used by both plug-ins.

Setting Up the Persistent Store

The JMS database contains two system tables that are generated automatically by WLS and are used internally by JMS: `<prefix>JMSStore` and `<prefix>JMSState`. The prefix name uniquely identifies JMS tables in the database.

After every test run it is important to erase the file, if you used file persistence, or reset the database. In the latter case, we do this by executing `reset.cmd`, which runs the following statements:

```
drop TABLE jmsjmsstate;
drop TABLE jmsjmsstore;
commit;
```

Configuring and Starting WebLogic Server

The order in which these operations are performed is important, as there are a series of dependencies. For reference purposes, here we provide the `config.xml` files for our WebLogic Server machines, control and Sun2. The control machine is the WLS administrative server and Sun2 hosts the JMS queues. These files can be tailored to your setup. For example, if you are not using an administrative server in your tests, then the information regarding the control computer can simply be omitted from your file.

The `config.xml` file for the administrative server (control) contains all the information for the actual WebLogic Server that hosts the JMS queue. In the case of a single queue (for the fan-out tests), the `SingleQ_config.xml` file that we used is as follows (and is provided in the code download):

```
  <?xml version="1.0" encoding="UTF-8" ?>
- <Domain Name="chapter7">
- <Server Name="control">
  <ExecuteQueue Name="default" ThreadCount="15" />
  <KernelDebug Name="control" />
  <Log FileName="control.log" Name="control" />
  <ServerStart Name="control" />
  <ServerDebug Name="control" />
  <WebServer Name="control" />
  <SSL Name="control" />
  </Server>
  <SNMPAgent Name="chapter7" />
  <ApplicationManager Name="chapter7" />
  <PasswordPolicy Name="wl_default_password_policy" />
  <Realm FileRealm="wl_default_file_realm" Name="wl_default_realm" />
  <Log FileName="chapter7.log" Name="chapter7" />
  <Security Name="chapter7" PasswordPolicy="wl_default_password_policy"
Realm="wl_default_realm" />
  <JTA Name="chapter7" />
  <FileRealm Name="wl_default_file_realm" />
- <UnixMachine Name="sun2">
  <NodeManager Name="sun2" />
  </UnixMachine>
- <Server JMSThreadPoolSize="15" Machine="sun2" Name="sun2"
NativeIOEnabled="true">
  <WebServer Name="sun2" />
  <ExecuteQueue Name="default" ThreadCount="15" />
  <SSL Name="sun2" />
  <KernelDebug Name="sun2" />
  <Log FileName="sun2.log" Name="sun2" />
  <ServerStart Name="sun2" />
  <ServerDebug Name="sun2" />
  </Server>
  <JMSJDBCStore ConnectionPool="JMSPersistencePool"
```

```
   Name="MyJMSJDBCStore" PrefixName="jms" />
     <JMSFileStore Directory="/opt/weblogic" Name="MyJMSFile Store" />
     <JMSConnectionFactory DefaultDeliveryMode="Non-Persistent"
   JNDIName="jms.myConnectionFactory" MessagesMaximum="10" Name="chapter7"
   Targets="sun2" />
   - <JMSServer Name="MyJMSServer" Targets="sun2">
     <JMSQueue JNDIName="jms.myQueue" Name="MyJMSQueue"
   StoreEnabled="default" />
     </JMSServer>
     <JDBCConnectionPool DriverName="oracle.jdbc.driver.OracleDriver"
   Name="JMSPersistencePool" Password="{3DES}1F/C/cPv5ShcvyP2GXCtaA=="
   Properties="user=jms" Targets=""
   URL="jdbc:oracle:thin:@DBSERVER:1521:UKLAB" />
     </Domain>
```

The `MultipleQ_config.xml` file is the same, except that we now define multiple queues, in the following manner:

```
<JMSQueue JNDIName="jms.queue.grinder02.local-0.0" Name="JMSQueue-
1012054103656" StoreEnabled="default" />
   <JMSQueue JNDIName="jms.queue.grinder02.local-0.1" Name="JMSQueue-
1012403546187" StoreEnabled="default" />
. . .
```

Next, we go to the computer named sun2 and we start the WebLogic Server with the same version of the go script that is described in the corresponding section in Chapter 4. The only difference is that when we want to use file persistence with non-synchronous writes, we have to define this in the command file used to start WebLogic. We do this by adding the following line:

```
-Dweblogic.JMSFileStore.SynchronousWritesEnabled=false
```

When operating in this manner, we stop the WebLogic process from the WebLogic console, as described in Chapter 4.

Setting the Type of Persistence

We set the type of persistence required from the WebLogic console. The first step is to indicate that we desire persistence for the JMS connection factory. This is defined from the JMS Services item as seen in this screenshot.

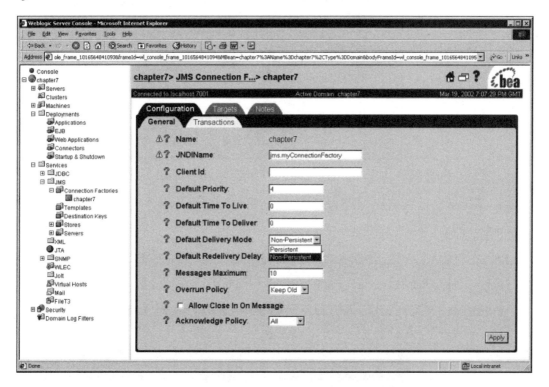

Next you choose the kind of persistence you want to use on the JMS server. In this particular case there are two persistence stores already defined as can be seen in the screenshot.

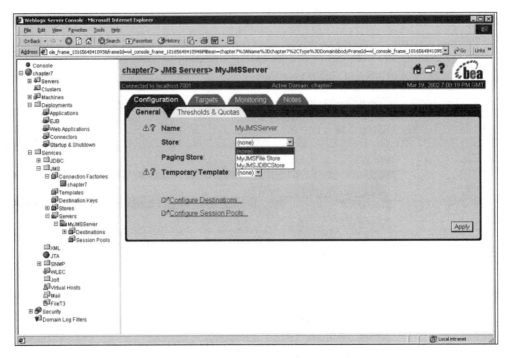

To define a file persistence store, you just have to define the directory in which the file will reside.

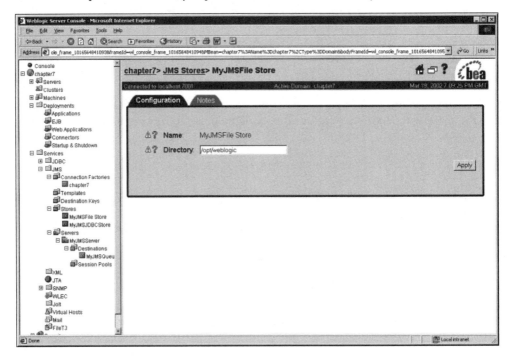

To define a database persistence store, you just define the JDBC connection pool you want to use. There is no need to create any tables in the database as they will be created automatically by WLS.

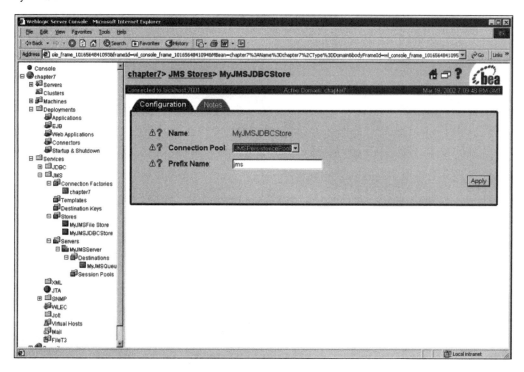

Setting Up The Grinders

For our tests, we used three Grinder computers, each running `ReceiverPlugin`, to simulate message consumers and a single Grinder computer, running `SenderPlugin`, to simulate our message producer. We controlled the consumer Grinders from one console and the producer Grinder from a second console, both of which we ran on our control computer. For example, we might start the producer Grinder console as follows:

```
C:\>cd c:\grinder\grinder-tests\ch07\ProducerConsole

C:\Grinder\grinder-tests\ch07\ProducerConsole>grindersetenv

C:\Grinder\grinder-tests\ch07\ProducerConsole >set JAVA_HOME=C:\jdk1.3

C:\Grinder\grinder-tests\ch07\ProducerConsole >set PATH=.;C:\jdk1.3\bin;

C:\Grinder\grinder-tests\ch07\ProducerConsole >set
CLASSPATH=.;C:\jdk1.3;C:\jdk1.3\lib;c:\Grinder\grinder-2.8
.1\lib\grinder.jar;

C:\Grinder\grinder-tests\ch07\ProducerConsole >java net.grinder.Console
```

We then do the same for the consumer console. The producer console was using port 6372, in our case, and the consumer console automatically trys to use the same port, at which point we receive a message that it "Failed to bind to Console Address". Therefore, we set the consumer console to the port defined in the test script, which was 4321 in our case (select File | Options from the console):

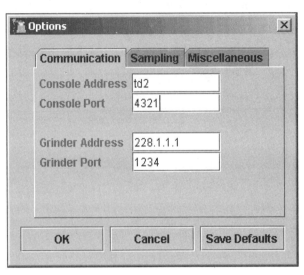

Once the consoles have started, we make sure that we set correctly the fields related to the sample metrics. In this case we set the sample interval of 5000 milliseconds on the sliding bar. Then we set it to ignore 24 samples and collect 60 samples.

In the Producer and Consumer directories of each Grinder computer you must place the appropriate test scripts (`grinder.properties` files).

> The `grinder.properties` files that we used, along with the `performance-client6.jar` file are supplied in the `ch07_TestScripts.zip` file of the code download for this chapter.

Then we go to the grinder01 computer, which will execute the JMS producer test script and start The Grinder process:

```
export CLASSPATH=/home/grinder/shared/grinder-2.8.2/lib/grinder.jar:\
../performance-client.jar:../weblogic.jar
java -Xint net.grinder.Grinder
```

The file `performance-client6.jar` contains the required Grinder plug-ins. Notice that we need to include the `Weblogic.jar` file in the classpath because the plug-ins use WLS classes for JMS access. This file is found in `[WebLogic_Home]/lib` and must be copied over on to the Grinder machines. Alternatively, when running on Windows, we could execute something like:

```
C:\> cd c:\grinder\grinder-tests\ch07\Producer

C:\Grinder\grinder-tests\ch07\Producer>grindersetenv

C:\Grinder\grinder-tests\ch07\Producer >set JAVA_HOME=C:\jdk1.3

C:\Grinder\grinder-tests\ch07\Producer >set PATH=.;C:\jdk1.3\bin;

C:\Grinder\grinder-tests\ch07\Producer >set
CLASSPATH=.;C:\jdk1.3;C:\jdk1.3\lib;c:\Grinder\grinder-
2.8.1\lib\grinder.jar; c:\grinder\grinder-tests\WebLogic.jar

C:\Grinder\grinder-tests\ch07\Producer > java -Xint net.grinder.Grinder
```

In the above example, we will have performed `jar xf performance-client6.jar` directly in the **Producer** directory.

> **Please note that starting The Grinder might take a little longer than expected, since it can take a while to create the JMS connection.**

Next we go to the grinder02 computer (and grinder03 and grinder04, depending on the load we want to generate). Here, we start the Grinder process in the same way we did for the producer, but we use the consumer `grinder.properties` file. Remember to set the number of desired users before you start. Again, it may take some time to establish the JMS connection.

Collecting and Analyzing the Data

As usual, before we start the actual test run by clicking on the start button of the Grinder console, we always verify that all the simulated users required for the test are ready to go. We do this by looking at the **Processes** tab in the Grinder console.

We stop the test when the Grinder console displays the message **Collection stopped** in red. Then we click on the **save results** button of The Grinder console to save the results gathered by the Grinder console into a file. By default this file is named `grinder-console.data` and is saved in the directory from which you are running the console.

As in Chapters 4 and 5, the Grinder consoles collect all of the data we need so we simply import the relevant data collected in the `grinder-console.data` for the consumer and producer consoles, into our Excel spreadsheet. In order to obtain CPU usage charts, we need to import the data from the `vmstat1.dat` file, as described in the corresponding section in Chapter 4.

Fan-out Tests

Our first set of tests used the fan-out architecture, as described in the *JMS PTP Architectures* section. To save you flicking back, we reproduce the appropriate diagram here:

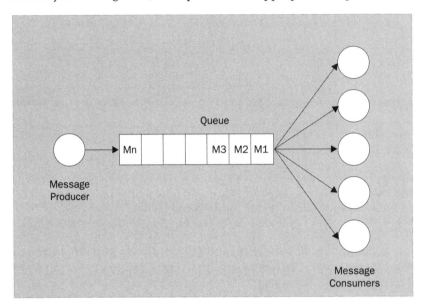

We have one message producer, one queue, and several message consumers. Remember that in the PTP model there is only a single potential receiver of each individual message).

As a result of informal surveys and of discussions with an expert in implementing JMS architectures, we chose a message size of 16KB as being a reasonable message size in PTP systems. For a point of comparison, to investigate the effect of message size, we also performed tests using 1KB messages. For each message size, our plan was to investigate the relative costs of different acknowledgement modes and persistence techniques.

Preliminary Tests

Here, we ran a series of short tests on the application to get familiar with its behavior under various conditions. Basically, we were finding the limits of our system, selecting an appropriate baseline case for comparisons, and then optimizing our test environment.

In real life there are numerous different uses of PTP, and so we wanted to run tests over a wide range of consumer loads – starting with only one and then increasing to 2, 5, 100, 400, 800, 1000, and finally 1500 consumers. Typically, when using this architecture, message consumers will be running in the same JVM so in our initial tests we generated the consumer load on a single Grinder machine. However, for 800 consumers and above, we found that we were reaching the limits of available memory in the computer running the Grinder, and thus were forced to split the load across several Grinder computers.

Thus, the way in which we decided to generate the various consumer loads, as a result of these tests, is described in the following table:

Consumers	JMS Connections	JMS Sessions per Connection
1	1	1
2	1	2
5	1	5
100	1	100
400	1	400
800	2	400
1000	2	500
1500	3	500

In this table, a JMS connection is equivalent to a Grinder process running on its own computer and a JMS Session is equivalent to a Grinder thread.

The Baseline Case (16KB Messages, 100 Consumers)

We started the tests with a message size of 16KB and with 100 consumers. We ran the tests using the **HotSpot Server option of Sun's JDK 1.3.1-b24, with a heap space of 256 MB**. We knew that we would need a rather big heap space, as we would be dealing with a large number of messages that will live temporarily in the WebLogic Server (this value is generally representative of the computers we find in production today).

We used two acknowledge modes: AUTO (an acknowledgement message is sent by the consumer for every message received), and CLIENT with groups of 50 messages (one acknowledgement message is sent by the consumer for every 50 messages received). We used the snapshot (Fixed Time) method with 5-second samples, ignoring the first 2 minutes (24 samples) and collecting 60 samples (5 minutes). The results for producer and consumer performance, in messages per second, are presented in the following table:

Acknowledge Mode	Consumer Throughput (MPS)	Producer Throughput (MPS)
AUTO	177.40	177.30
CLIENT (50 messages)	176.20	176.50

Of course, the consumer throughput we present here is normalized (divided by the number of consumers). This sets a general level of expectation – with 100 consumers, both the producer and each consumer can process around 180 messages per second, in either CLIENT or AUTO mode.

Test Environment Optimizations

Now that we had an idea of the behavior of the system, we moved on to tune our environment. Here we verified that we were using the best JVM, optimized the number of threads in the WebLogic-dedicated JMS thread pool and gauged the effect of using the WebLogic performance pack.

Choosing the JVM

As noted, we ran our initial tests with the HotSpot Server option of Sun Microsystems JDK 1.3.1-b24. For the sake of thoroughness, we compared the observed performance against that obtained using the HotSpot Client option of this JVM.

At the time that these tests were performed, Sun's JDK 1.3.1-b24 was the only JVM that was BEA-certified for use on our chosen server (WebLogic 6.1 with sp2, running on Solaris).

The following table compares the results obtained for the HotSpot Client and Server options, for both consumer and producer throughput (MPS):

Acknowledge Mode	HotSpot Server Option		HotSpot Client Option	
	Producer	**Consumer**	**Producer**	**Consumer**
AUTO	177.30	177.40	174.50	174.50
CLIENT (50)	176.50	176.20	175.90	176.00

As you can see the difference between the two JVMs is negligible (below 2%) in every case. Thus, we had no reason to deviate from our choice of the HotSpot Server option.

Setting the WebLogic JMS Thread Pool

As explained in Chapters 3 and 4, WLS maintains a general pool of execute threads and it works out how best to allocate them. The exception to this rule is JMS. In the case of JMS, WLS maintains a dedicated thread pool, which will not be used by any other tasks running in the Server.

Thus, we needed to determine the optimum number of JMS execute threads for our particular example. The default is 15 threads, so we investigated the behavior at either side of this value, and also explored the possibility of performance enhancement by using a much higher number of threads (50). Once again, we used 100 consumers with a message size of 16 KB. We set the acknowledge mode to AUTO. The throughput results (MPS) are presented in the following table:

Threads	10	15	20	50
Producer	178.10	177.30	177.40	175.20
Consumer	178.10	177.40	177.10	175.20

We can see that, in this case, there is negligible variation in performance with thread pool size, so there is no compelling reason to deviate from the default size of 15 threads for the JMS pool.

Using WebLogic Performance Pack

As described in Chapter 4, when using a performance pack (native I/O), we bypass the socket methods offered by the JRE by creating a pool of sockets directly at the operating system level. In general this feature increases performance when sockets are heavily used by an application. We decided to check out the impact of disabling native I/O in the WebLogic Server (by default it will be enabled, via the `NativeIOEnabled` attribute in your `config.xml` file).

We found that, in general, disabling native I/O led to slightly better throughput for the lower consumer loads, of around 6%. However, we found that behavior was unreliable under high loads (1500 consumers), with throughput dropping to below 1 message per second. Thus our baseline configuration was as follows:

❑   JVM: HotSpot Server option of Sun's JDK 1.3.1-b24, with a heap space of 256 MB

❑   JMS Thread Pool Size: 15

❑   Native I/O: Enabled

The Test Plan

For each message size, 16KB and 1KB, we wanted to investigate the following:

❑   The cost of acknowledgement and the effect of different acknowledgement modes – we focused on the two most common modes, `CLIENT` and `AUTO` (see the earlier *Acknowledgement Modes* section for details).

❑   The cost of persistence and the behavior observed for different persistence modes – we investigated both file and database persistence.

We performed a whole set of tests for 16KB message, and then repeated them for 1KB messages. For each test case, we ran tests for 1, 2, 5, 100, 400, 800, 1000, and 1500 consumers – so 8 tests runs for each case (not including duplicate runs for consistency).

With these tests, we are faced with a complex set of comparisons. On the face of it, the test results for 1KB versus those for 16KB message gives us the effect of message size. However, the performance trends observed for different acknowledge modes and for different types of persistence for 16KB messages is not necessarily going to be the same as those for 1KB messages. Thus we decided to present the results for 16KB and 1KB messages separately, and at the end we draw overall conclusions about the effect of message size, acknowledgement, and persistence.

Tests with 16 KB Messages

We set out to determine:

- Relative performance using different acknowledge modes (no persistence)
- Performance using file persistence, in both AUTO and CLIENT modes
- Performance using database persistence, in both AUTO and CLIENT modes

Investigating Acknowledgment

Here, we wanted to understand the performance cost associated with using Acknowledgment and the relative performance of the different modes (AUTO, CLIENT and DUPS_OK) when we were **not** persisting any messages.

We had certain expectations of the performance of each mode. We expected performance in the AUTO and DUPS_OK modes to be pretty much the same – the reason being that, in each case, the consumer acknowledges every message in the same manner. The big difference is how the developer has to code the logic to receive the message. In one case (AUTO) it requires that the message is received once and only once; in the other case no special logic is needed. This also has an effect on the JMS server, which has to be aware on how to handle situations where more than one acknowledgment is received for the same message.

Our expectations were that, because of the large size of the message, use of the CLIENT mode would actually degrade the performance relative to AUTO mode (or it would be the same, in the best case), for the following reasons:

- The WLS server can only delete a message from the queue once it has received the acknowledgment. Since we are acknowledging in groups of ten, WLS has to keep 10 (or more, depending on the grouping size) messages per consumer before it can delete them from the queue.

- We will possibly push the server memory limits (for the above reason).

- The basic purpose of CLIENT mode is to reduce the cost of acknowledgment. However, we predicted that the cost of acknowledging a 16KB message would be negligible compared to the cost of picking up the message. If this assumption is correct, then there is little to gain from using CLIENT acknowledge mode, in this case.

Test Case 6.1 – No Acknowledge Mode

The following table presents the throughput (MPS) for the producer and the consumers:

Number of Consumers	1	2	5	100	400	800	1000	1500
Producer Performance	204	202	202	197	197	199	199	190
Consumer Performance	205	202	202	197	197	198	200	191

These results suggest that throughput capacity is around 200 MPS. It is interesting to note that the throughput does not change significantly over the whole range of consumer loads – only degrading by a little over 7% from one consumer all the way to 1500 consumers.

We found that the CPU usage on the computer running the server remained pretty much the same for each user load – at about 35%, as can be seen in the following figure:

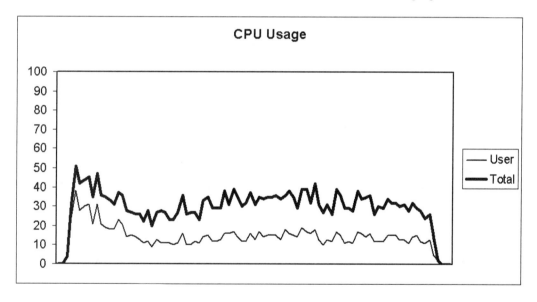

The same applied to network usage, which was always pretty high, with around 55% of the bandwidth of the 100 Mbps network being consumed:

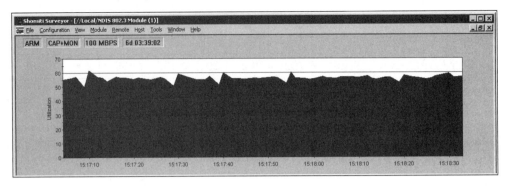

Test Case 6.2 – AUTO Mode

The following table presents the throughput (MPS) for the producer and the consumers:

Number of Consumers	1	2	5	100	400	800	1000	1500
Producer Performance	193	190	188	189	185	186	186	186
Consumer Performance	194	189	188	189	185	187	186	186

Again, the throughput does not change significantly over the whole range of consumer loads – only degrading by a little over 3.5% in this case.

If we compare the results to those with no acknowledgment messages, we can see that the performance cost of acknowledgment, in terms of throughput, is generally around 5-7% over the whole range of consumer loads (with the possible exception of 1500 consumers, where the cost appears to be less). The CPU and network utilization remained the same as observed during the test runs using no acknowledgment.

In addition to our throughput measurements, we can use the Grinder plug-ins that we created for these tests to measure the following:

❑ Time taken for the producer to place a message in the queue

❑ Time taken for a consumer to pick up a message from the queue.

To obtain these measurements, we calculate the arithmetic mean of all the times, over the collection period. This is straightforward in the case of our single producer, as is the case here – our measurement is a straight reflection of the time it takes the producer to place a message. However, our consumer measurement will be a raw mean time, representing the total amount of time required for every consumer to pick up a message. If we divide our measured time by the number of consumers, we will have a normalized time that can be compared with the mean time of the producer. For comparative purposes, we also normalize the producer time, by dividing by the number of consumers:

Mean Time (ms)	1	2	5	100	400	800	1000	1500
Producer	4.83	4.95	4.96	4.96	5.07	5.02	5.03	5.26
Consumer	4.83	5.08	5.23	5.29	5.41	5.36	5.36	5.38

Tongue-in-cheek, we can state that, under the test conditions, it takes approximately 5 milliseconds for a producer to place, and also for a consumer to pick up, a 16KB message in a JMS queue on the WebLogic Server.

However, if we look more closely we can see that, except in the case of one consumer, it seems to take a little more time for the consumers to pick up a message than it does for a producer to deliver it to the queue:

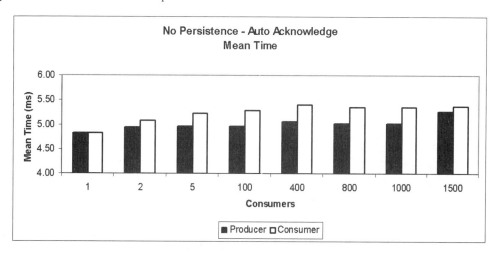

Intuitively, this is the behavior we might expect. In this particular example the consequence is that, for any given number of consumers, the size of the queue will increase over time, and performance could be affected as a result. If you need to investigate this further, we suggest that you run this set of tests over the period of time appropriate for your application.

Next, we performed a similar set of measurements using the DUPS_OK acknowledge mode. We found that, as expected, the results were virtually identical to those obtained for AUTO mode, so we do not present them here.

Test Case 6.3 – CLIENT Mode (10)

In our preliminary tests at the baseline case (100 consumers), we acknowledged in groups of 50 messages so we proceeded with that number. However, we found that when we got to 400 consumers we ran out of memory in the server. Up to that point the CPU and network usage had been the same as for the previous set of tests. Thus, we were suspicious that having to store so many messages in the queue until receiving an acknowledgment used up all the available memory of the JVM. Thus, for these tests only, we configured the CLIENT mode such that the consumers sent one acknowledgment message for every 10 messages received.

In these tests, the CPU usage of the WLS computer was slightly above that seen in AUTO mode (around 40%) but the network usage was approximately the same. The throughput results were as follows:

Throughput (MPS)	1	2	5	100	400	800	1000	1500
Producer	197	191	193	189	184	184	184	183
Consumer	197	191	192	189	183	185	184	184

For comparative purposes we can plot the consumer throughput performance in CLIENT mode side-by-side with that obtained in AUTO mode:

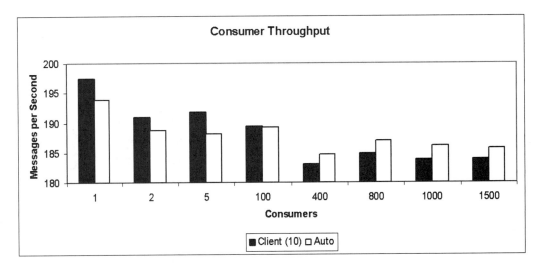

The bar chart seems to indicate a slight performance advantage from using CLIENT acknowledge mode with less than 100 consumers but a performance degradation above that. However, the differences are less than 2%, so they should be considered negligible.

The following chart compares normalized consumer times and producer mean times:

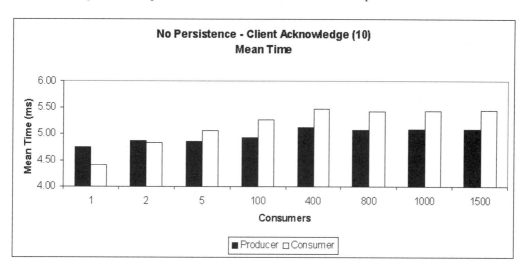

The plot shows that it takes less time for a **single** consumer to pick up a message than for the producer to place it in the queue. The advantage is significant (about 9%). After that, the behavior is as observed in AUTO mode with the consumers lagging behind the producer.

Summary of Results

The following chart presents a comparative view of the throughput of the consumers based on the acknowledgment mode:

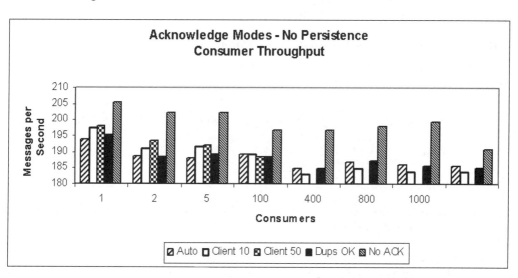

We found that the cost of using acknowledgment was rather small, at around 5-7%. We found that there was no performance gain to be had from using CLIENT mode instead of the default AUTO mode. In fact, we would avoid the use of the CLIENT acknowledge mode here, as we are suspicious that it would run out of memory on a longer run.

Using File Persistence

The intent of these tests was to explore the costs of using file-based persistence. We tested the file data store with both synchronous and non-synchronous writes (see the earlier *Persistence* section for details), and also explored the relative performance of the AUTO and CLIENT acknowledge modes when using file-based persistence. In CLIENT mode we acknowledged groups of 50 messages (here, WLS does not have to retain messages in memory; it is writing them to the file, so the memory problem that we experienced previously should not occur here). We felt that running tests using no acknowledge made little sense when using any kind of persistence.

The file data store resided in a directory on the same WebLogic Server that hosted the queue. No optimizations were performed on the file system. The directory files were deleted after each test run.

We did not really have any detailed expectations regarding the performance, but generally we expected the following:

❑   Throughput would be substantially less in all cases, compared to the no persistence tests.

❑   Non-synchronous writes may perform somewhat better than synchronous writes because, in the former case, the server does not have to wait for a confirmation of the write operation.

Test Case 6.4 – Synchronous Writes In AUTO Mode

The following table presents the throughput (in message per second, MPS) for the consumers and the producer, for each consumer load:

Throughput	1	2	5	100	400	800	1000	1500
Producer	32	57	57	57	56	57	57	56
Consumer	31	57	57	57	56	57	60	57

At the completion of the test, we found that the file created by the server to persist the data was consistently around 500 KB.

For one consumer, we see a throughput of 31 MPS. At two users, we reach the saturation capacity of 57 MPS and the throughput remains very stable at this value for all subsequent loads. We suspect the reason for stability of the throughput is driven by the file system.

As expected, the throughput performance obtained here is substantially slower – over three times slower – than the comparable case using no persistence (test 6.2).

The CPU usage of the server was low (around 20%) and presents a cyclical pattern which smoothes out as we increase the number of consumers. The following chart presents the CPU usage for 1000 consumers. We think that the valleys represent the occurrence of write operations:

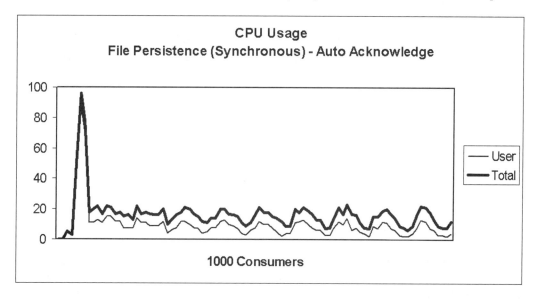

The network usage decreased substantially compared to the no persistence cases, to about 15%:

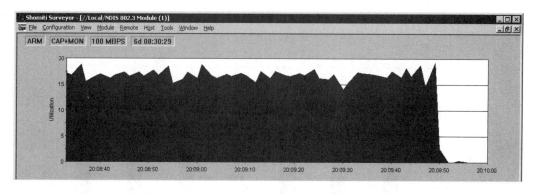

This behavior is to be expected since we are processing less than a third of the number of messages compared to the no persistence cases. This behavior was again consistent across the various consumer loads.

As described in test case 6.2, we measured the mean time taken for the producer to place a message in the queue against that for a consumer to pick up a message:

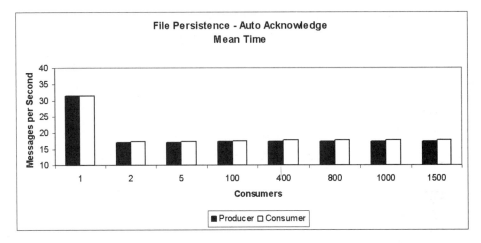

Here, we do not see any difference in the time taken to place a message in the queue to the time taken for the consumer to pick it up.

Test Case 6.5 – Synchronous Writes in CLIENT Mode (50)

We repeated the previous tests using the CLIENT acknowledge mode (groups of 50 messages). Our expectations were that the performance would drop compared to that obtained in AUTO mode. The main reason for this was that the file used for persistence will grow markedly in size, since groups of 50 messages will have to be stored in the file before the acknowledgment is received and the messages can be deleted. The actual size of the observed decrease in throughput will be dependent on how well your operating system handles writes and deletes to the file system. In any event, it was expected that this would make the synchronous write operations slower.

The following chart presents a comparison of the consumer throughput between AUTO and CLIENT acknowledge:

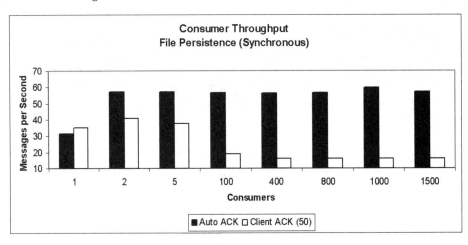

For one consumer, the throughput in CLIENT and AUTO modes is roughly the same. For loads of 2 to 5 consumers, the throughput for CLIENT is down by around 30% on AUTO mode. Above that, the throughput is much slower, over 3 times slower, in CLIENT mode. This can be explained by the size of the file increasing as we increase the number of consumers. The size of the file used to persist the messages ranged from 1MB for 1 consumer to 130MB for 1500 consumers.

The CPU utilization of the WLS hosting the JMS queue tended to show a slight increase over the course of a test, from around 20% at the start to around 30% at the end. The network usage was a mere 4% for 1500 consumers and, conversely, it slightly decreased over time. We suspect that this behavior is related to the increase in size of the file used for persistence – WLS doing more work in the write/delete process and the write operations slowing down.

We can clearly conclude that it is likely to be detrimental to the performance of a JMS application to use the CLIENT acknowledge mode when persisting to a file, although this would need to be verified with tests using different acknowledge group sizes.

Test Case 6.6 – Non-Synchronous Writes in AUTO Mode

Next, we disabled synchronous writes and reran the tests. We were expecting some increase in performance, since the server does not have to wait for a confirmation of the write operation, but the results are quite amazing:

Throughput	1	2	5	100	400	800	1000	1500
Producer	186	182	181	182	177	180	178	177
Consumer	186	182	181	181	177	180	177	177

The performance enhancement very significantly exceeds all expectations – these performance figures are similar to those obtained without the use of persistence. It really was surprising to us to see what a massive difference disabling synchronous writes can make.

At the end of each test we recorded the size of the file used for persisting the messages. It was a 3MB file for one consumer and decreased to 768KB for 1000 consumers. Bear in mind that we observed the file sizes at the end of every test run, once WLS was stopped. This was a manual process that did not happen at exactly the same time every time it was done. As the file used for persistence tends to change size during the execution (as messages are written and deleted) we would expect to obtain a picture of the size at approximately the same moment, but as a manual process this might not have been exactly the same moment for every observation.

We can compare the performance numbers for the consumer with those obtained with no persistence (test case 6.2):

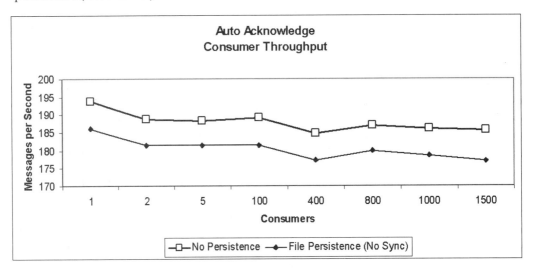

We plotted this as a graph so that you can see how the behavior seen here mirrors that observed using AUTO mode and no persistence (the x-axis is not drawn on a linear scale). The performance cost of using persistence here is only around 4%.

The following chart compares the mean time results obtained here for the producer with those obtained for test case 6.2:

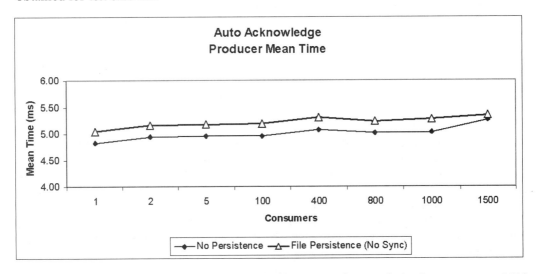

Once again the curves match almost perfectly (there is perhaps a slight discrepancy at 1500 consumers). When we use file persistence, the producer takes about 4.5% longer to place a message than is the case without persistence.

The CPU usage and network usage behavior observed in these tests was very similar to that obtained in the no persistence tests – averaging around 35% and 55% respectively.

Summary of Results

The throughput performance obtained in AUTO mode using non-synchronous writes almost equaled that obtained in AUTO mode with no persistence. Of course, with non-synchronous writes, you are relying heavily on the reliability of your operating system in handling write operations to files. However, if you feel that you can do this, then you might well want to consider this option if your JMS PTP application requires persistence. However, you will want to compare the performance with that obtained using database persistence, for your particular message sizes, before making any firm decision.

In our set-up, we found file persistence **with** synchronous writes, for a message size of 16KB, was over 3 times slower than with no persistence. The behavior here is, of course, highly dependent on the operating system and disks that you use for the tests.

Using CLIENT acknowledge mode is not recommended when using file persistence, be it with or without synchronous writes.

Using Database Persistence

For the database persistence test case, we used Oracle 8.1.7 running on a separate computer. The database tables were deleted after each test run. This form of persistence is also known as JDBC persistence, since a JDBC driver is used to send the messages to the database. The JDBC driver used in this case was the WebLogic Thin Driver (jdriver).

In terms of our expectations, we predicted a performance decrease, compared to no persistence –although we had no idea how much of a decrease. It is important to remember that we were using Oracle "out-of-the-box", without any attempt to optimize the write transactions, tune the database appropriately or investigate other JDBC drivers, such as the OCI driver. Thus, the results presented here are only intended to give you a reasonable feel for the cost of database persistence, when Oracle is used out-of-the-box. Furthermore, using a database gives a much higher level of reliability and opens up a whole raft of associated functionality – the requirements of many applications will dictate the use of a database for persistence for these reasons alone.

Thus, we had no real expectations as to the performance compared to file persistence (obviously with synchronous writes) and do not intend to make close comparisons. Intuitively we would expect a database to perform better than an application server manipulating a file, but then we were writing a lot of 16KB messages to the database and, as discussed, performed no optimizations – so we were not willing to bet on the outcome

Test Case 6.7 – AUTO Mode

The throughput results are interesting:

Throughput	1	2	5	100	400	800	1000	1500
Producer	12	28	28	28	28	28	28	28
Consumer	12	28	28	28	28	28	28	28

For one consumer, we see a throughput of 12 MPS. At two users, we reach the saturation capacity of 28 MPS and the throughput remains very stable at this value for all subsequent loads.

JDBC persistence, in this example, proves to be about two times slower than the equivalent file persistence case (6.4) and about 6.5 times slower than with no persistence at all (6.1). The CPU usage in these tests was minimal, averaging about 10% for all consumer loads. The network usage was also low as can be seen in the following screenshot:

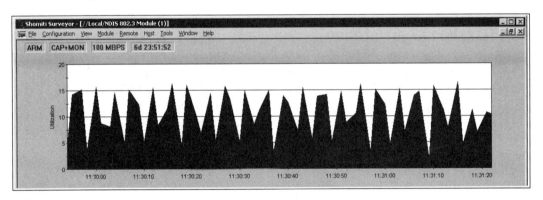

The CPU usage of the computer running the Oracle database was also pretty low, about 15% on only one of the two CPUs available.

Test Case 6.8 – CLIENT Mode (50)

For the last set of tests we used CLIENT acknowledge with groups of 50 messages. As we expected from the results of previous tests, the throughput was lower than obtained using AUTO mode. However, we did observe a quite unusual performance curve:

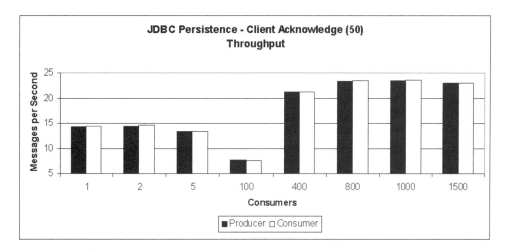

We think that the observed performance increase above 100 consumers may be related to JDBC buffering – it could be the case that with 400 users the default buffer sizes for the JDBC driver were optimal. This can be seen in the screenshots of the network traffic. The following screenshot is for 100 consumers:

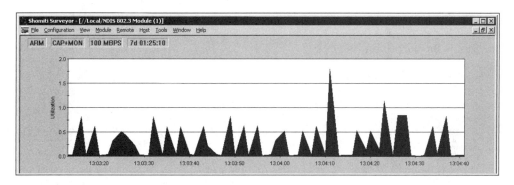

As you can see there is almost no network traffic. Now compare it with the screenshot for 400 consumers:

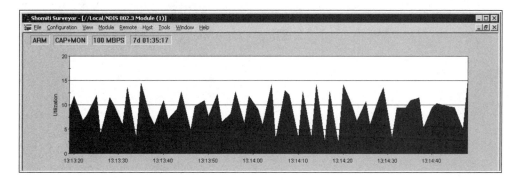

Clearly, the increased consumer load leads to increased traffic, but aside from that we can also see that there are fewer valleys with 400 users. The fact that we have data being more frequently passed over the network implies that the buffers related to the database could be at optimal usage.

SQL Tracing

We were interested in seeing how the writing and deleting of messages to the jmsjmsStore and jmsjmsState tables was performed in the database, so we used the SQL_TRACE and TKPROF tools (see Chapter 3 for details) to gain some insight into the process. Following is an excerpt from a trace file obtained from a no acknowledgment run:

```
INSERT INTO jmsJMSStore (recordHandle,recordState,record)
VALUES
  (:1,:2,:3)
```

call	count	cpu	elapsed	disk	query	current	rows
Parse	1	0.07	0.07	0	0	0	0
Execute	4687	26.92	29.27	0	3	23883	4687
Fetch	0	0.00	0.00	0	0	0	0
total	4688	26.99	29.34	0	3	23883	4687

And here is the corresponding delete:

```
DELETE FROM jmsJMSStore
WHERE
recordHandle = :1 OR recordHandle = :2 OR recordHandle = :3 OR
recordHandle =
    :4 OR recordHandle = :5 OR recordHandle = :6 OR recordHandle = :7 OR
  recordHandle = :8 OR recordHandle = :9 OR recordHandle = :10 OR
  recordHandle = :11 OR recordHandle = :12 OR recordHandle = :13 OR
  recordHandle = :14 OR recordHandle = :15 OR recordHandle = :16 OR
  recordHandle = :17 OR recordHandle = :18 OR recordHandle = :19 OR
  recordHandle = :20
```

call	count	cpu	elapsed	disk	query	current	rows
Parse	1	0.00	0.00	0	0	0	0

Execute	4687	31.43	37.31	2	93749	25801	4687
Fetch	0	0.00	0.00	0	0	0	0
total	4688	31.43	37.31	2	93749	25801	4687

As you can see, each statement is executed 4687 times (the exact numbers are not important) and it takes 27 seconds of CPU time in the case of the insert and 31 seconds in the case of the delete. So Oracle is taking about 0.006 s to execute each statement, which seems reasonable. We do not wish to digress into a detailed discussion of the trace files here – we just wanted to illustrate the sort of information that is available through these tools.

Summary of Results

It has to be stressed here that the file and database persistence results presented here can only set a general level of expectation and will vary depending on your exact configuration (database, applications server, operating system, and so on). For the reasons presented at the start of this section, we are wary of reading too much into comparisons of file and database persistence. However, we saw that, in our case, using JDBC persistence was about 6.5 times slower than no persistence and about 2 times slower than using file persistence.

Tests with 1KB Messages

Although a 16KB message represents a typical message size found on systems that use point-to-point messaging, we wanted to explore the behavior of the JMS implementation using messages of 1KB in size. This gives us another point of reference to investigate the effect of message size. An example of an application that would use a very small message size could be one whereby the message is used as a trigger rather than containing actual content.

Thus, we repeated the same set of test runs as we did with the 16KB message size. In general, our expectations were that we would see better throughput (MPS) performance with the smaller message size. On the other hand, if we were to redefine performance to mean bytes-per-second, then we might expect to find that using the 1KB message size is less efficient due to the higher relative overhead for handling smaller packages (the cost of actually performing the write operation outweighs the time saved by writing only 1KB rather than 16KB. in other words, writing a 1KB message is nowhere near 16 times faster than writing a 1KB message).

The WebLogic Server maintained the same settings as for the runs with 16KB messages. That is, we continued using JDK 1.3.1 HotSpot Server with a 256MB heap space, a JMS thread pool of 15 and native I/O enabled.

Investigating Acknowledgment

We investigated the performance cost associated with using Acknowledgment and the relative performance of the different modes (AUTO, CLIENT and DUPS_OK) when we were **not** persisting any messages.

Once again, we expected performance in the AUTO and DUPS_OK modes to be pretty much the same. With a 1KB message, we expected that CLIENT mode would come into its own more. The cost of acknowledging a 1KB message might be significant compared to the cost of picking up the message. If this assumption is correct, then using CLIENT acknowledge mode should improve performance.

Test Case 6.9 – No Acknowledge Mode

The following table presents the throughput (MPS) for the producer and the consumers:

Throughput	1	2	5	100	400	800	1000	1500
Producer	699	679	675	664	656	665	672	663
Consumer	699	679	673	666	657	665	675	660

As for the persistence case for 16KB messages, the throughput is stable over the whole range of consumer loads – only degrading by a little over 5% from one consumer all the way to 1500 consumers.

Now, we have a feel for the effect of the message size – from a throughput of around 200 MPS for 16KB messages, up to around 670 MPS for 1KB messages, an improvement of over 300%. However, if we quickly convert that to KB per second, we could conclude that using larger message sizes is more efficient.

For these tests, the CPU usage on the computer running the server averaged about 35%. This figure was maintained for all the consumer loads and is similar to the usage pattern observed during the equivalent tests with 16KB messages. The network usage was around 13% for all user loads. This is substantially less than the 55% we observed on the tests with 16KB messages.

Test Case 6.10 – AUTO Mode

The throughput results are presented in the following table:

Throughput	1	2	5	100	400	800	1000	1500
Producer	601	506	503	498	506	484	487	426
Consumer	474	506	504	497	510	484	487	425

From end to end there is a performance degradation of about 40% for the producer and of about 12% for the consumer (but the producer throughput does show a large step-down between 1 and 2 consumers – the degradation from 2 to 1500 consumers is only about 19%).

It is interesting to note that when we have 1 consumer, the producer is able to place messages in the queue a lot faster than the consumer is able to pick them up.

The following chart compares the results for AUTO mode with those for no persistence:

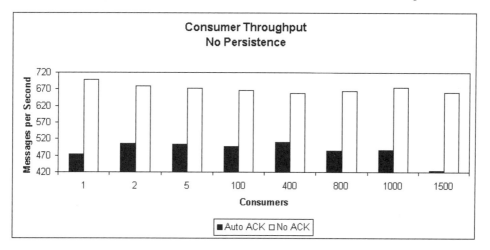

We see that throughput performance in AUTO mode is down over 20% on that obtained using no acknowledgment, proving that relatively high cost of acknowledgment with small messages.

If we look at the following chart of the mean time, we will see that both the producer and the consumers have more or less the same curves, and the consumers lag behind by about 16%.

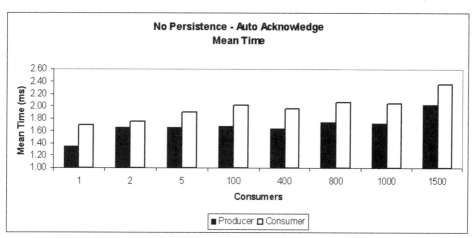

Comparing the absolute value for 1 consumer using AUTO mode against no acknowledge we might dare state that the amount of time dedicated to the acknowledge is an average of 0.75 milliseconds. However, as much as we would like to support this statement, any time below 1 millisecond is suspect as the clocks in the operating system running The Grinder have a resolution of 1 millisecond.

This is again similar to the behavior observed with 16KB messages. Once again we found that DUPS_OK mode gave very similar results to AUTO mode, so we do not present the results here.

Test Case 6.11 – CLIENT Mode (10)

We repeated the previous test run, but using CLIENT mode with groups of 10 messages. The results were as follows:

Throughput	1	2	5	100	400	800	1000	1500
Producer	570	532	525	522	527	534	530	525
Consumer	570	533	525	521	526	536	532	525

The CLIENT acknowledge mode seems to produce an improvement in the overall performance. The following chart presents a comparison of the consumer throughput for AUTO and CLIENT (10) acknowledge modes:

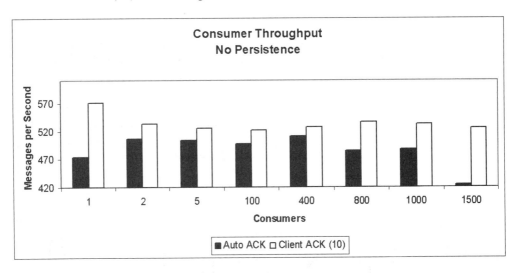

The throughput is consistently higher using the CLIENT acknowledge mode – from a minimum of 3% higher for 400 consumers to a maximum of 20% higher for one consumer. This is quite encouraging.

The CPU usage of the computer running the server, for these tests, was lower than that observed for AUTO mode, about 20% for all the consumer loads. The network traffic was at a similar level to that observed in AUTO mode.

We can clearly conclude that, in this example, using the CLIENT acknowledge mode with groups of 10 messages produces an overall better performance.

Test Case 6.12 – CLIENT Mode (50)

In light of the previous run, we decided to investigate whether increasing the grouping size to 50 would improve performance still further. The results were as follows:

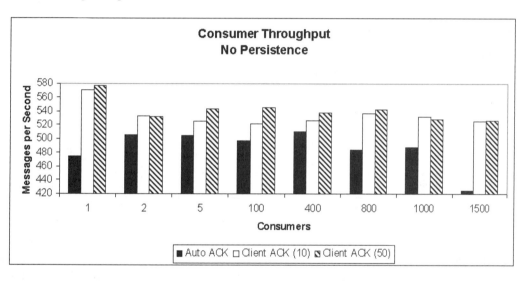

We see an improvement in throughput by as much as 4.6% in the case of 100 consumers over the CLIENT (10) run. The CPU usage remained at about 20%, similar to the CLIENT mode with 10 messages. The same applies to the network traffic, which remained at about 12% throughout.

We performed one more set of tests using a group of 100 messages, and found that we did not increase performance any further. In fact the performance was generally in between that observed for 10 and 50 message groups. We can conclude that, for this example, we can achieve the best performance using CLIENT acknowledge mode with groups of 50 messages. There may well be a sweet spot with even better performance in groups between 40 and 60 messages, but we did not explore this.

Summary of Results

We found that by decreasing the message size from 16KB to 1KB, we increased the throughput, in terms of messages per second, by a factor of about 3. However, if we convert this to bytes per second, we find that using 16KB messages is more efficient by a factor of approximately 5, indicating the relatively high overhead associated with dealing with lots of smaller messages. We found that there was a significant performance gain to be had from using CLIENT mode instead of the default AUTO mode.

Using File Persistence

We performed similar measurements as for the 16KB tests, and again tested the effects of using synchronous and non-synchronous writes, using file persistence. For these tests we didn't really have any firm expectations. On the one hand one might simply expect the smaller message size to lead to better performance, but then there will be many more writes to the file used for persistence, compared to the 16KB case, which could slow things down.

Test Case 6.13 – Synchronous Writes in AUTO Mode

In these tests, the CPU usage presented a similar curve to that one observed for the 16KB message size for all consumer loads, a sinusoidal curve that peaks at 20%. The network traffic was a minimal 1.5%. The size of the file used for persistence was 256KB for all the consumer loads.

The throughput results were as follows:

Throughput	1	2	5	100	400	800	1000	1500
Producer	33	66	66	66	66	66	66	65
Consumer	33	66	66	66	66	66	66	65

In this case file persistence is over seven times slower when compared with no persistence (with 16KB messages, the reduction was by a factor of three). It is very interesting to note that the message size has a big impact on the relative performance – we can speculate that it is more expensive to write many small messages than one bigger one.

To confirm this, let's look at the throughput obtained here compared with the comparable 16KB case:

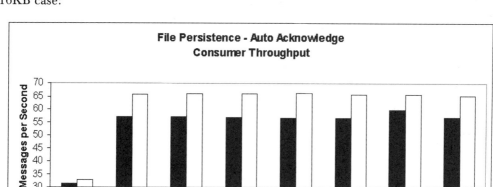

While 16KB versus 1KB comparisons for the no persistence showed an improvement in performance by a factor of 3 for the 1KB case, here we see an improvement of only around 15% for the 1KB case.

Test Case 6.14 – Synchronous Writes in CLIENT Mode (50)

Based on our previous results we expected CLIENT mode to significantly degrade performance (again, the main reason for this being that the file used for persistence will grow markedly in size, since groups of 50 messages will have to be stored in the file before the acknowledgment is received and the messages can be deleted). However, since the messages are much smaller here, we expected the degradation to be less marked. The results were as follows:

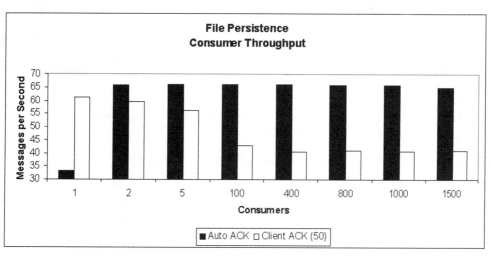

For loads of 2 to 5 consumers, the throughput for CLIENT is down by around 15–20% on AUTO mode (compared to around 30% in the 16KB case). Above that, the throughput is around 60% slower in CLIENT mode (compared to over 3 times slower for 16KB).

Thus the results were as predicted (given the results of 6.5) . It seems to be a recurring theme that we should not be using the CLIENT acknowledge mode when persisting messages in this JMS fan-out architecture.

Test Case 6.15 – Non Synchronous Writes in AUTO Mode

In these tests, the average CPU usage of the computer running the server was 45%, and the network traffic consistently averaged 10% for all the consumer loads.

Again, we see a big improvement in performance over that achieved using synchronous writes – up from around 65 MPS to an average of 400. However, the results are not quite as amazing as those observed for 16KB messages. In that case, by disabling synchronous writes we were able to return almost to the level of performance observed for no persistence (about 4% lower). Here, the performance is still approximately 20% below that observed for no persistence:

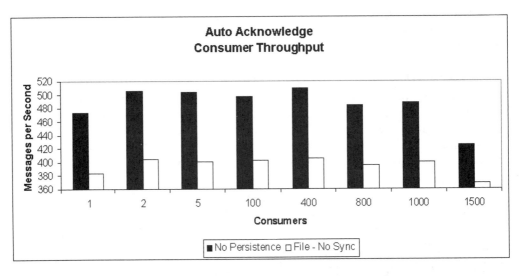

This again would tend to indicate the relatively high overhead involved in writing many small messages to file rather than fewer larger ones.

Test Case 6.16 – Non-Synchronous Writes in CLIENT 50 Mode

By this point we had pretty much accepted that we would not generally see performance gains by using the CLIENT acknowledge mode. However, out of thoroughness we repeated the 6.15 tests using CLIENT mode with groups of 50 messages. Surprisingly, we observed throughput increases of between 5% for 100 consumers, to 20% for 1 consumer. Above 100 consumers, however, the performance degrades relative to the AUTO mode:

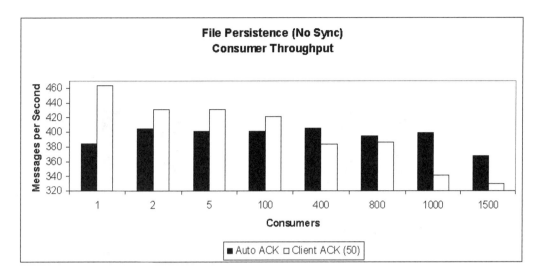

This is encouraging. There must be a sweet spot somewhere between acknowledging 10 and 50 messages where the performance gains are evenly spread over all the consumer loads. We will leave this as an exercise for the reader.

Summary of Results

These tests indicated that there is a relatively high overhead to writing many smaller messages, as opposed to fewer bigger ones. This was apparent in most of the results obtained. For example, file persistence in AUTO mode with synchronous writes was over seven times slower when compared with no persistence (with 16KB messages, the reduction was by a factor of three). Using non-synchronous writes returned the performance level to within approximately 20% of that observed for no persistence.

In general the performance in CLIENT mode was again lower than that in AUTO mode, although with non-synchronous writes, CLIENT mode did seem to offer some advantage for message consumer loads of up to 100.

Using Database Persistence

We investigated the behavior observed using database persistence, using AUTO and CLIENT acknowledge modes. Intuitively, we expected that the database would handle a lot of smaller messages better than it handled fewer bigger messages.

Test Case 6.17 – AUTO Mode

The performance results were actually better than we expected. In fact, the throughput achieved was comparable to that for the equivalent file persistence run (6.13):

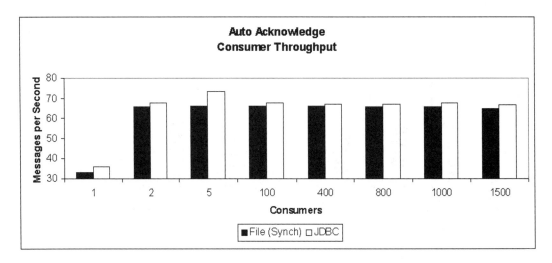

The performance enhancement is not great, but if we had to make a choice we would not hesitate to use JDBC persistence in this case – we get a higher level of reliability for about the same cost. The network traffic is almost nothing, averaging about 2% for all the consumer loads. The CPU of the computer running the database averages about 45% of usage on only one of the two CPUs available.

Test Case 6.18 – CLIENT Mode (50)

Now, we were really interested in checking out the behavior of the database when using CLIENT acknowledge mode. As usual we acknowledged in groups of 50 messages. The results are very interesting and can be seen in the following comparative chart:

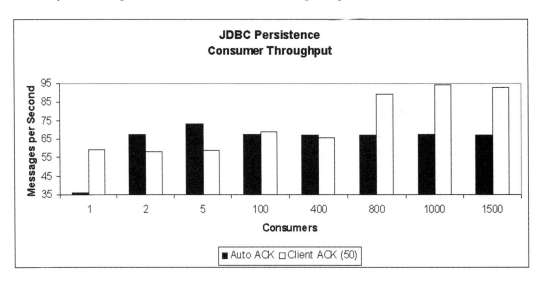

The performance increases as the number of consumers increases and, from 400 consumers onwards, is better than when using AUTO acknowledge mode. It is possible that this behavior is a factor of the settings on the various buffers and caches related to the database.

Summary of Results

The interesting finding here is that JDBC persistence is slightly cheaper than file persistence when handling 1KB messages, whereas for 16KB message file persistence was more efficient. It was also interesting to note that CLIENT acknowledge mode seemed to show better performance than AUTO mode for higher consumer loads (above 400).

Overall Conclusions for JMS Fan-Out

As you have probably gathered, there are many factors to consider when dealing with JMS PTP, and we simply cannot generalize performance results. There are many features and options available in the JMS specification that we have not explored and the many aspects of implementation (of your application server, database, file system, and so on) that we have not touched. The tests performed in this chapter only serve to illustrate the need to obtain performance data for your own, unique application and to do so as early as possible in the development cycle.

With the above provisos, the performance tests that we have performed do set a general expectation level regarding the behavior of JMS PTP under various conditions of acknowledgments and message size. In the following sections, we draw some overall conclusions from our results.

The Effect of Message Size

We found that the throughput in messages per second was about three times higher using 1KB messages than 16KB messages. However, in bytes per second this comes down in favor of 16KB messages. Indeed, our results indicated that there was a high overhead associated with writing many small messages to the file system. In relative terms, our results indicated that persistence to a file store was more effective for 16KB messages, but that database persistence was more effective (as well as being much more reliable) for 1KB messages.

Acknowledgment Modes

When no persistence is required, we found that the different acknowledge modes have a relatively small impact on the performance as can be seen in this chart showing the consumer throughput for 16KB messages:

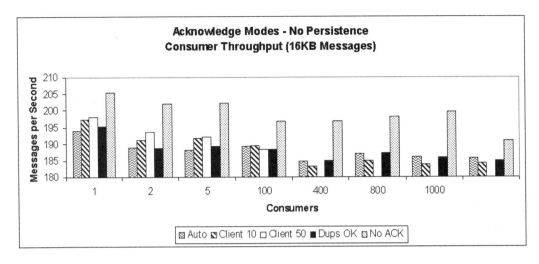

The acknowledge modes have a slightly clearer impact on performance when using 1KB messages:

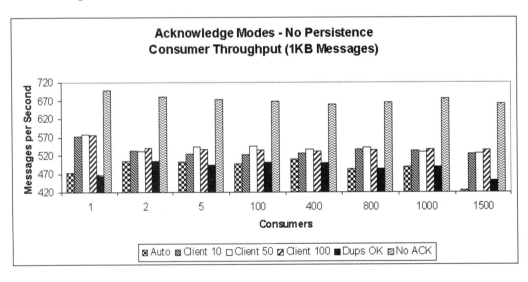

With 1 KB messages, the relative cost of acknowledgement compared to actually picking up the message is more significant, so we do see some performance advantage to sending on acknowledgement message per group pf messages. Of course, while not acknowledging a message or acknowledging in groups is faster, reliability will suffer.

Persistence

In the case of 16KB messages, we found that the price of persisting the messages increases as we increase the reliability level:

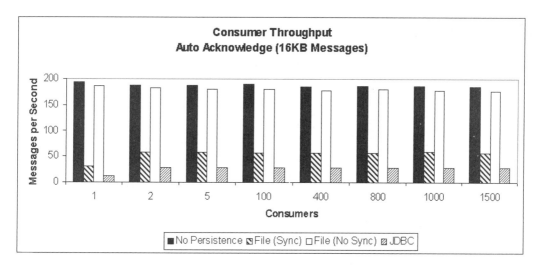

It was interesting to note that using non-synchronous writes gave throughput performance equal to that of the no persistence case.

When we ran the fan-out example with messages of 1KB, the picture was quite different. Varying the persistence modes we found that JDBC persistence was slightly better than file persistence, as illustrated in the following chart:

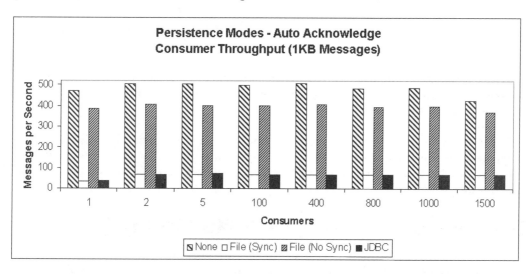

We also saw that CLIENT acknowledge mode did improve the performance in some cases when using persistence. For file persistence the performance improved with small numbers of consumers, while for JDBC persistence the performance improved for higher numbers of consumers.

Multiple Queues

In these tests we explored the performance of multiple queues architecture:

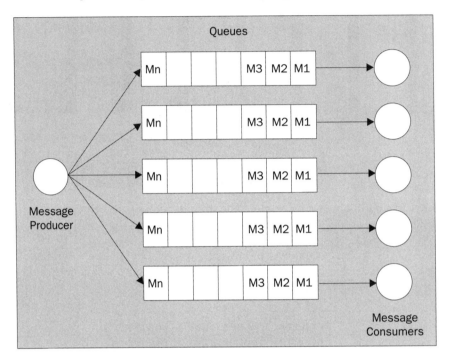

As discussed in the *JMS PTP Architectures* section earlier in this chapter, this particular architecture is used when maintaining the sequential order of the messages is important, thus there is only one consumer for every queue.

From the performance point of view, our interest was in exploring how the multiple-queues model worked when using only one consumer per queue. We conducted various test runs using 2 and 32 queues with two sizes of messages, 16KB and 1KB. A review of the results follows.

Test Case 6.19 – 2 Queues, 16KB Messages

We started our tests by using no persistence and checking the behavior of the various acknowledgment modes. The results are summarized in the following histogram:

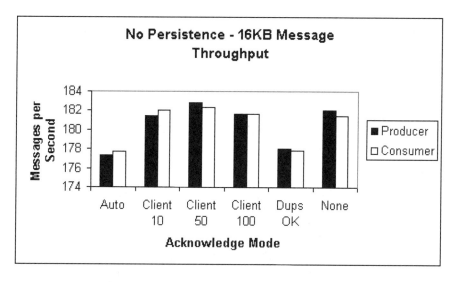

It is interesting to note that use of the CLIENT mode consistently gives rise to a higher throughput than AUTO mode, although the actual differences between the two are not significant (2%).

In the next set of tests we explored the use of the various persistence techniques, using the CLIENT 50 acknowledgment mode in each case:

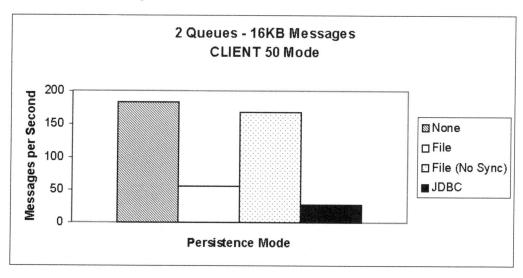

These results are very consistent with those observed for the fan-out tests: the higher the reliability the lower the performance. Putting it in another way, the cost of persisting the messages in a highly reliable data store such as the Oracle database is 7 times more expensive than using no persistence at all.

Test Case 6.20 – 2 Queues, 1KB Messages

To get a more complete picture, we repeated the previous tests using a smaller sized message of 1KB. The first set of tests were based on no persistence, exploring the various acknowledge modes:

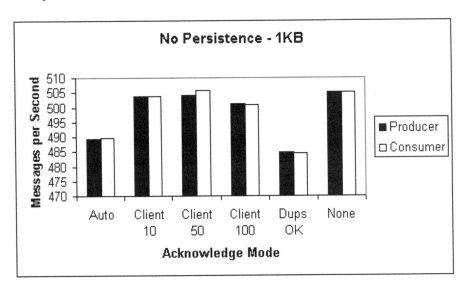

Compared to the 16KB histogram we can see that the relationship between the acknowledge modes is similar. The obvious difference is that the throughput here is about 2.5 times higher than in the 16KB case. Again, this is very consistent with the behavior observed for the fan out tests. The next set of tests investigated the use of persistence. The results were as follows:

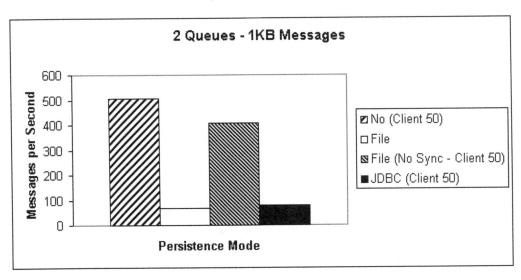

Again, the results mirror those obtained for fan-out. The throughput performance of file persistence with non-synchronous writes, in CLIENT acknowledge mode, is within 25% of that obtained with no persistence. Again, we see that it is better to use database persistence than a file with synchronous writes.

Test Case 6.21 – 32 Queues, 16KB Messages

Now that we have an idea of the performance using just a couple of queues, we reran the previous test cases using 32 queues. The first set of tests deals with the acknowledge modes with no persistence:

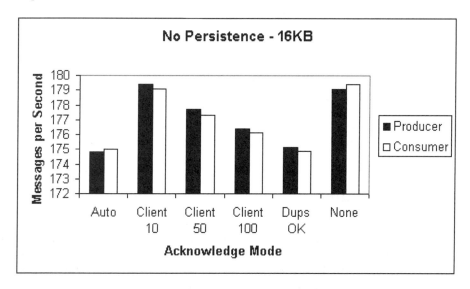

Interestingly enough, for this case the better performance is observed when acknowledging messages in groups of 10, which produces the same performance as no acknowledgment. What is even more interesting is that the test runs done to explore the performance using persistence produced the same results as when using just 2 queues. So we can conclude that for 16KB size messages there is no real difference in performance when using 2 or 32 queues.

Test Case 6.10 – 32 Queues, 1KB Messages

The following histogram displays the throughput results for the various different acknowledgment modes:

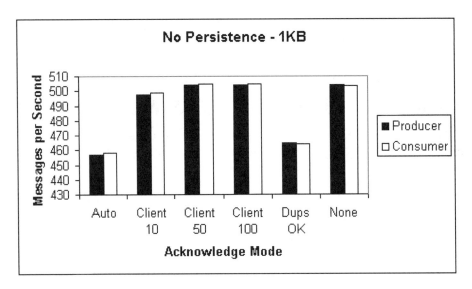

The trend is basically the same as that observed for 2 queues. Not surprisingly, at this point, the results obtained for the different persistence modes were also the same as those observed when using only 2 queues.

Summary of Results

The trends observed for the relative cost of the different acknowledgment modes and types of persistence mirrored those observed for the fan-out tests. From our limited observations, based on only 2 and 32 queues, we speculate that the number of queues has no effect on the observed throughput (MPS). If your application uses this kind of architecture based on multiple queues, we strongly encourage you to explore this in more detail.

Conclusions

In this chapter, there were a virtually limitless number of variables and issues that we could have factored into our performance tests. Instead, we have focused on a couple of basic architectures and have investigated what we consider to be the three most important variables: message size, acknowledgment mode and type of persistence. We have done this to provide you with a guide to what can be tested and how it can be tested. We strongly encourage you to create your own tests, based on your particular case.

JMS Publish/Subscribe Messaging

In the previous chapter we investigated the JMS Point-to-Point (PTP) model, whereby a message producer sends a message to a specific queue and only one consumer can receive each individual message. In the Publish/Subscribe (Pub/Sub) messaging domain, the model is somewhat different. Here, a message producer (called a **publisher**) sends messages to a **topic**, which has been previously set up on the messaging server. In order to see these messages, the message consumer (called a **subscriber**) must subscribe to that particular topic.

This model is extremely useful when a group of applications want to notify each other of a particular occurrence. A publisher publishes an event to a topic, and by subscribing to that topic multiple subscribers can be informed of the event. The Pub/Sub JMS model can be used in many different ways to tackle a wide variety of such situations. In this chapter, we present the results of our performance study of two example applications that we feel are representative of the most common uses of this JMS model:

❑ **A stock ticker** – the most popular example of Pub/Sub messaging. A stock ticker continuously presents all the trades that happen in a stock exchange by providing the name of the company, the number of shares that were traded, and the price of the trade. A subscriber can selectively choose to receive only those messages relating to trades by specific companies.

❑   **An airline seating application** – giving an airline company the ability to assign and guarantee seats to passengers before they board a flight. Here, a JMS publisher continuously generates messages, each one indicating that a seat on a specific flight is now occupied (identified in the message by its flight number). Each airline agent at an airport gate subscribes to the flight they have to dispatch (the messages are subscribed to on the basis of flight number).

Even though they are based on the same architecture they have different reliability requirements and we explored the relative performance in each of these different application scenarios. As in the previous chapter, we used two custom plug-ins for The Grinder that send and receive messages to and from a JMS topic, hosted on WebLogic Server. Our key performance metric is again **throughput** (Messages Per Second, MPS).

An Overview of Pub/Sub Messaging

As described above, the core concept in a Pub/Sub messaging system is the **topic**. Messaging server administrators explicitly create topics so that publishers and subscribers can exchange messages. In the simple example shown below, we have a single topic and six clients (three publishers and three subscribers):

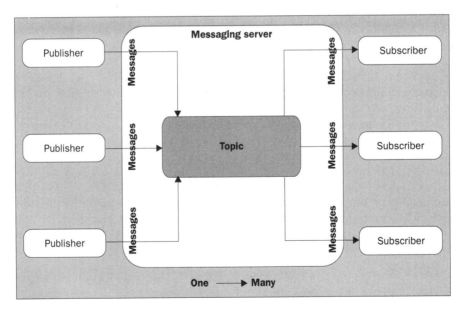

What is particularly interesting with the publish and subscribe model is that more than one consumer can receive the same message, thus making it a one-to-many relationship, in contrast to the one-to-one relation seen in the PTP domain. We can think of the Pub/Sub model in terms of it as a consumer subscribing to an **event**. An event can be anything, typically defined as a value of a property in the message itself. For example, a topic can be "The Weather in London", to which you can subscribe to the event "sunny" (and probably wait a long time before that happens!). In JMS parlance, a publisher sends events to a topic, which are picked up selectively by subscribers by means of something called a message selector. A topic is identified by name, allowing both publishers and subscribers to handle multiple topics simultaneously.

All the subscribers subscribe to certain events in the topic and all the publishers publish messages to the topic. The messaging system takes care of distributing messages from the publisher to the subscriber. The characteristic pattern of interaction is as follows:

❑ During the subscriber's initialization, the subscriber registers an instance of a callback (a message handler invoked by the server) with the topic.

❑ The publishing client arrives at a point in its processing when it needs to send out a message. It creates the message and publishes it to the topic.

❑ The messaging system delivers the message to all its subscribers by invoking the respective callbacks that were registered earlier.

For full details of how JMS messaging works, in the Pub/Sub domain, we would refer you to the online sources such as http://java.sun.com/products/jms/, or to other reference sources such as the book, *Professional JMS Programming* (Wrox Press, 1861004931).

Message Delivery

In some JMS applications, it is vital that a subscriber (or consumer, in PTP terminology) receives every message (as is the case in the Airline Seating example) – we want guaranteed message delivery, under all circumstances. This has certain implications:

❑ The message receiver must acknowledge receipt of the message

❑ We must set the JMS delivery mode to persistent (`DeliveryMode.PERSISTENT`), so that the messaging server will deliver a message even if there are application or network failures. In the default mode (`DeliveryMode.NON_PERSISTENT`), the messaging server will use "At-Most-Once-Delivery" – it will deliver the message to its subscribing client as long as there are no application or network failures.

Such applications might have durable subscribers (which would force the messaging server to attempt to retain all of the messages published on the topic for delivery to those subscribers that are not currently active).

In other situations, guaranteed delivery and durable subscribers do not make sense. In our stock ticker example, if a subscriber was not currently active or if some network or other failure occurred, then by the time that the subscriber was active or the failure had been corrected, the stock trade messages that were produced in the meantime would be out-of-date and the subscriber could simply pick up the most recent messages.

Pub/Sub via Multicast

A message server is required in order to provide the full set of Pub/Sub functionality defined in the JMS specification. The ability to deliver messages after the publisher is no longer available, and the ability to support transactions and durable subscribers all imply that there must be some process other than that of the publisher and subscriber that stores the messages temporarily. A subset of the JMS Pub/Sub functionality, though, can be supported without a server through the use of IP multicast. The advantages to be gained in return for the sacrifice of functionality are performance, efficiency, and simplified administration
Consider what happens when publishing stock prices to 100 subscribers over a single LAN segment via a unicast protocol such as TCP/IP. The Network Interface Card (NIC) of the computer of each subscriber "sees" the same message 100 times, but ignores 99 of them because they are addressed to other hosts. In contrast, multicast provides basic Pub/Sub semantics at the network level.

By definition, multicast packets are sent to a multicast address. Unlike unicast addresses, multicast addresses are not associated with a particular host. Any host can subscribe to a multicast address, and as such a multicast address corresponds to a JMS topic

> *There are definitely some limitations based on the subnets and how the routers are configured. In general multicast cannot jump over a subnet boundary (multicast is restricted to the subnet where it was generated). There are some routers that will allow for this, meaning they will expand multicast messages to other subnets, but you pay dearly for this functionality.*

When using multicast-based Pub/Sub, messages travel directly from publisher to subscriber and they need only be transmitted on the network once, no matter how many subscribers there are. This can make a tremendous difference in performance and scalability.

Raw IP multicast is not a reliable protocol, and in contrast to the unicast world, there is no ubiquitous reliable protocol like TCP that is already embedded in every network operating system.

The current generation of network routers support routing protocols for multicast packets (although this support is not enabled by default). This means that, in theory, multicast network traffic could be routed over wide-area networks. In reality this raises concerns in the areas of security and efficiency. Multicast packets contain a time-to-live (not related to the time-to-live of a JMS message) value; an integer that determines how may routers it is permitted to pass through on its way from publisher to subscriber. A large time-to-live value implies that publishers and subscribers that are intended to interact are spread over a wide area.

When using multicast over such a wide area, it is difficult to guarantee that publishers and subscribers find each other in an efficient manner. It is also more difficult to ensure that only intended parties have access to the messages being sent; remember that anyone can subscribe to a multicast address through a normal socket interface, it does not even require low-level network access. For these reasons, multicast-based messaging is usually only practical in local area networks and with low time-to-live values.

In general, it is probably advantageous to use multicast JMS when possible: in other words, when it is supported by the network and satisfies the system's design requirements. If a Pub/Sub-based system needs to support any of the following features, then a server-based unicast JMS is required:

- ❑ Wide Area Network communications
- ❑ Communication through firewalls
- ❑ Secure communication via SSL
- ❑ Transactions
- ❑ Durable subscribers

In our tests, we investigated the "multicast with no acknowledge" mode. This is a special mode of the WebLogic Server.

Application Architecture

The architectures used for both the stock ticker and the airline applications were identical. In each case, we used the Grinder plug-ins (described in the next section) to implement a rather simple version of each application, using only one topic and a single publisher, as can be seen in the following figure:

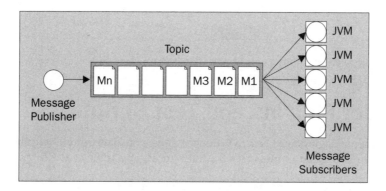

In this diagram a box represents each JVM. The circle within each box represents the single thread simulating the subscriber. This is a big difference between the setup here and that for the point-to-point tests in Chapter 6. Under the Pub/Sub model every consumer usually runs independently on its own JVM, as opposed to the PTP model where typically consumers will run from the same JVM, sharing the same JMS connection. The Pub/Sub model imposes a different kind of stress on the JMS server as every consumer establishes its own JMS connection.

At the time of running the tests, we had four Grinder computers available, so we had one to simulate the publisher and three to simulate the subscribers. Every JVM uses 16MB of heap space and given that our computers had 512MB, we felt that we could only safely simulate about 20 subscribers per machine – much higher and we would start to risk subscribers being swapped out of memory. For these logistical reasons, we limited our tests to a maximum load of 60 subscribers and, consequently, ran test runs using 1, 20, 40, and 60 subscribers. We measure the throughput as the number of messages per second processed by the publisher and by the subscribers.

The hardware set-up was as follows:

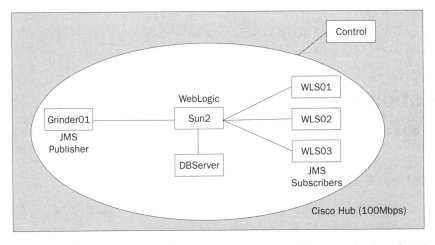

Complete details of the computers and operating systems used here can be found in Appendix B.

The Grinder Plug-ins and Test Scripts

Every Pub/Sub messaging application follows a generic programming template to connect to a topic, publish or subscribe to messages from the topic, and to close the topic connections.

The basic Pub/Sub messaging client program development is as follows:

❏   Get (or create) a topic connection factory object.

❏   Get (or create) a topic.

❑ Use the topic connection factory object to create the `Connection` object.

❑ Use the topic connection object to create the Topic `Session` object.

❑ Decide whether to create a topic publisher or a topic subscriber object. Use the `Topic Session` and `Topic` objects to create the message producers (publishers) and message consumers (subscribers).

❑ Start the connection.

❑ Publish or subscribe to messages.

❑ Close the topic session and connection.

For our performance tests in this chapter we wrote two plug-ins for The Grinder to emulate these processes: one publisher plug-in and one subscriber plug-in.

> **For details on how to build a plug-in for The Grinder, and on how to create the plug-ins for this chapter in particular, please refer to Chapter 2. These plug-ins are packaged in the `performance-client6.jar` file in the code download for this chapter.**

We decided to make them generic enough to easily be used to cover both of our examples. The examples can be modeled on a single topic, and all that really changes is the message selector– the criterion by which a subscriber identifies and selects the desired messages. For example, in a real stock ticker the selector would be a particular company name (or symbol), while on the airline seat assignment it would be a flight number.

Here, we generalize and our message selector is just a number, which we set in the WROX_JMS_MESSAGE_TYPE property of the message. Our message looks like this:

The publisher sets the value of the property, starting with zero and incrementing by one, until it reaches the upper limit defined by the numberOfMessageTypes parameter of the Grinder plug-in. Once it reaches this limit the cycle starts all over again. In the stock ticker example, we simulate 100 different companies, so the message ID # is sequential from 0 to 99. Our subscriber (trader) will only want to subscribe to, say, 25 of those 100 companies. We simulate this by having our subscribers subscribe to a block of 25 contiguous message ID #s (the beginning of the block being randomly selected). It works the same way for the Airline example, except that here we simulate 20 flights, on the gates being dispatched (and the airline agent at a specific gate will only subscribe to the flight that it is dispatching).

The body of the message simply contains a number of random characters (64 in the case of the stock ticker example and 16 in the case of the Airline example).

Publisher Plug-in Parameters

So, the publisher plug-in continuously creates messages and places them in a topic on the JMS server. The full list of parameters available for the publisher plug-in are described in the following table:

Parameter	Description
connectionFactoryJNDIName	The JNDI name of the appropriate JMS connection factory.
topicJNDIName	The JNDI name of the topic to which the message will be published.
sessionPerCycle	Set to true to establish a new JMS session for every execution of the test script. The default value is false.
messageSize	The size of the body of the message in bytes, which is based on randomly selected characters.
numberOfMessageTypes	Defines the number of different message types the publisher will produce. It does so in a round robin fashion, starting from zero up to this number.

Subscriber Plug-in Parameters

The subscriber plug-in simulates our message receivers, picking up only those messages to which they are subscribed. The behavior of the subscriber is defined by the following parameters:

Parameter	Description
connectionFactoryJNDIName	The JNDI name of the appropriate JMS connection factory.
topicJNDIName	The JNDI name of the topic to which the subscriber is subscribed, or the prefix if topicPerConsumer=true

Parameter	Description
topicPerConsumer	When set to `true`, each subscriber thread looks up a unique topic by appending the `grinderID` and process number to the `topicJNDIName`. For example, `jms.topic.grinder01-0.0`. If set to `false`, which is the default, each consumer thread subscribes to the same topic.
sessionPerCycle	When set to `true`, a new JMS session is established for every cycle. The default value is `false`.
sessionLength	If `sessionPerCycle` is set to `true`, then this parameter controls the number of messages that will be received in each JMS session.
acknowledgeMode	Defines the type of message acknowledgment the subscriber should use. Possible values are `AUTO`, `CLIENT`, `NO` for none, `DUPS_OK` for duplicates accepted, and `MULTICAST` for multicast no acknowledge.
acknowledgeFrequency	When the acknowledgment mode is set to `CLIENT`, this parameter defines how many messages will be received before an acknowledgment is sent.
numberOfMessageTypes	The number of message types the publisher creates.
NumberOfMessageTypesPer Subscription	The number of message types to which the consumer will subscribe. The value defines the size of a range of contiguous message types to subscribe. The first number of the range is randomly selected. The value cannot be bigger the `numberOfMessageTypes`.

The value of the `numberOfMessageTypes` parameter should be the same as that for the publisher (if a message receiver is going to subscribe to X contiguous message types, which will be selected randomly, we need to know the total count of message types). The value X is defined by the `NumberOfMessageTypesPerSubscription` parameter.

Note that the `acknowledgemode` applies only to the manner in which the subscriber sends an acknowledgment message, if any, to the JMS server (WebLogic). The server will always acknowledge receipt of the message to the publisher – we did not explore different publisher modes in our study.

The only other thing that the subscriber does (as defined in the plug-in) is to write a line to the Grinder log file for every message it receives.

As you can see, this pair of plug-ins provides a very powerful means of modeling various architectural configurations and different conditions within each configuration.

Publisher Test Script

The following code listing is a quick view of the most important parameters in the `grinder.properties` file for the publisher `plug-in`:

```
# Simulate one publisher from one JVM and run forever
grinder.processes=1
grinder.threads=1
grinder.cycles=0

# Start/Stop from Grinder Console
grinder.receiveConsoleSignals=true
grinder.grinderAddress=228.1.1.1
grinder.grinderPort=1234

# Agent processes report real-time data to Grinder Console
grinder.reportToConsole=true
grinder.consoleAddress=Control
grinder.consolePort=6372

# We are using zero think time (and no initial spread)
grinder.thread.sleepTime=0

# Define the plug-in to use and establish the connection
grinder.plugin=com.wrox.paston.jms.topic.grinder.PublisherPlugin
grinder.plugin.parameter.serverURL=t3://sun2:7001
grinder.plugin.parameter.connectionFactoryJNDIName=jms.myConnectionFacto
ry
```

Finally, there is just a single test to define, whereby a message of a defined size (in this case, 64 bytes) will be sent to the JMS topic, `MyTopic`, running on WLS. We also specify the number of different message types, in this case 100:

```
grinder.test0.parameter.topicJNDIName=jms.myTopic
grinder.test0.parameter.messageSize=64
grinder.test0.parameter.numberOfMessageTypes=100
```

There are no actual requests – the publisher plug-in simply places a message in the corresponding topic, writes an entry to the Grinder log, then starts all over again.

Subscriber Test Script

On the other side of the messaging system, our subscriber plug-in simulates message subscribers. Note that all the consumers share the same grinder.properties, the most important parameters of which are as follows:

```
# Simulate one subscriber from one JVM and run forever
grinder.processes=1
grinder.threads=1
grinder.cycles=0

# Start/Stop from Grinder Console
grinder.receiveConsoleSignals=true
grinder.grinderAddress=228.1.1.1
grinder.grinderPort=1234

# Agent processes report real-time data to Grinder Console
grinder.reportToConsole=true
grinder.consoleAddress=control
grinder.consolePort=4321

# A non-zero sleep time on the subscriber side makes little sense
grinder.thread.sleepTime=0

# Define the Grinder plug-in to use
grinder.plugin=com.wrox.paston.jms.topic.grinder.SubscriberPlugin
grinder.plugin.parameter.serverURL=t3://sun2:7001
grinder.plugin.parameter.connectionFactoryJNDIName=jms.myConnectionFacto
ry

# Define the topic from which the subscriber will pick up messages
grinder.plugin.parameter.topicJNDIName=jms.myTopic

# Set the acknowledgeMode parameter to CLIENT, AUTO, or NO or MULTICAST
grinder.plugin.parameter.acknowledgeMode=CLIENT

# Set how many messages will be received before an
# acknowledgment message is sent (only applies to CLIENT mode)
grinder.plugin.parameter.acknowledgeFrequency=10

# Set the number of different types in total and how many of those will
# be subscribed to
grinder.plugin.parameter.numberOfMessageTypes=100
grinder.plugin.parameter.numberOfMessageTypesPerSubscription=25
```

Once again there are no tests to define – the plug-in constantly picks up the selected messages according to the criteria we defined in the above properties file.

> **In order to set up and run the tests in this chapter, please follow the instructions as set out in the *Setting up and Running the Tests* section of Chapter 6. The config.xml file that we used for WLS is provided in the code download for this chapter.**

The Stock Ticker Application

As discussed earlier, the stock ticker is the most popular example of Pub/Sub messaging. From the JMS perspective we can view a stock ticker application as one that sends an event to a topic, for every trade that occurs in a stock exchange. A consumer receives only the desired events from selected companies by subscribing to the appropriate topic and specifying the company's name.

Using the architecture described previously, we modeled a rather primitive stock ticker application. We had a single publisher continuously publish events (messages) to a single topic. Each message represented a trade by a particular company. In our simulation, there was one trade at a time per company and each company on the exchange traded in an orderly, sequential fashion (this is obviously extremely simplistic, but still effective for our testing purposes). Our message consumers could subscribe to events (trades) of the same companies, so some subscribers received the same messages.

It is very important to note that, because of the transient nature of the information being handled, it does not make sense to insist on guaranteed message delivery. If the message detailing a particular trade were lost for any reason, then by the time the message was recovered from the server it would probably be obsolete anyway (many other stock trades having occurred in the meantime). In this kind of application it makes more sense that the subscriber simply waits for the next message. With this in mind we limited our tests to only two acknowledge modes: NONE and MULTICAST with no acknowledge. Bear in mind, again, that this refers to the subscriber. The publisher acknowledgment mode is always AUTO_ACKNOWLEDGE.

Testing Metrics

In our example, we had a single publisher create 100 different types of messages (the WROX_JMS_MESSAGE_TYPE property stepped sequentially through values 0 to 99). Each message was of size 64 Bytes, which is the average size of this kind of message – here we were allowing for company symbol: 5 characters; date of trade: 8 characters; time of trade: 8 characters; number of shares: 10 characters; price of trade: 10 characters. Thus we were modeling a stock exchange consisting of 100 companies, whereby each company made one trade at a time and always in a sequential fashion.

We used **no think time** at all for the publishing of the messages. The publisher simply delivered a message, wrote a line to the Grinder log file and then delivered the next one. The reason for writing to the log file is that in real life the message producer/publisher normally has to do some kind of operation before publishing the next message. The most generic operation that we proposed as a substitute was to write to a log file (although, in reality, the operation may be more expensive than this and may have an effect on performance).

We ran tests with 1, 20, 40, and 60 subscribers, with every subscriber running on its own JVM and establishing a JMS connection and session before starting the test run. During the test run it just receives the messages to which it is subscribed, which is a block of 25 contiguous messages, the beginning of the block being randomly selected.

In real life a trader is unlikely to subscribe to a block of alphabetically ordered companies. In our model, each subscriber gets the messages to which it is subscribed in one chunk, whereas in reality they would be more spread out over time – and this would have an influence on the performance behavior. Unfortunately, in order to more closely model reality, where subscribers receive messages in a random fashion, the `if` statement would be nearly impossible to handle:

```
if message_type=random_number1 do {}
  else if message_type=random_number2 do {}
...
```

Also, by doing this, the number of subscriptions becomes fixed, rather than being an easily adjustable parameter as it is now. Therefore, for the sake of simplicity, we decided that the message receivers would subscribe to messages in contiguous blocks.

Preliminary Tests

Generally, here, we ran a series of short tests on the application to get familiar with its behavior under various conditions, find the limits of our system, select an appropriate baseline case for comparisons, and then optimize our test environment.

Since, for the logistical reasons described in the *Application Architecture* section, we were actually limited to a maximum subscriber load of 60 users, finding the limit case loses some meaning and we simply set 60 subscribers as our limit case for comparisons.

For the tests, as for all tests in this chapter, we used the fixed time (or snapshot) method of data collection, whereby we continuously take fixed-sized samples of data for a specified time period. We used five seconds as the sample size (this means that we record our performance metrics every 5 seconds). We ignored the first 24 samples (two minutes) in order to take into account the initial test period over which the system stabilizes. You must exclude as many samples as is appropriate in your environment. We then collected 60 samples (or 5 minutes, so the total test time was 7 minutes).

Our initial test environment was somewhat informed by the tests performed in Chapter 6. We chose the HotSpot Server option of Sun's JDK 1.3.1-b24 for the JVMs, each running with a heap space of 16MB. We used the default JMS Thread Pool Size of 15 (although, we were interested to investigate this further here) and had native I/O enabled.

The results for publisher and subscriber throughput performance (no subscriber acknowledgment), in messages per second (MPS) were as follows:

Number of Consumers	1	60
Publisher performance	627.50	195
Subscriber performance	156.4	25.28

The results for 60 consumers were intriguing, so to give ourselves another data point, we performed another test with just one consumer, the results for which are also given above. The throughput of the subscriber has been normalized by dividing the actual throughput number we obtain from the test run by the number of consumers we used. This allows us to compare the results on the same basis, independently of the number of consumers. When analyzing the difference between the observed throughput for the publisher and the subscribers we must account for the effect of the values assigned to the numberOfMessageTypes and numberOfMessageTypesPerSubscription parameters. In this case the values were 100 and 25 respectively. So, each subscriber is only subscribed to 25 of the 100 different message types, and ignores the other 75 types.

Now we are in a position to analyze the results obtained for 60 consumers. The publisher is delivering messages at a rate of just under 200 messages per second (so it creates approximately 2 messages of each type, every second). Your first impression might be that the throughput for a subscriber would be 25% of that of the publisher, since it is only receiving 25% of the messages published. In fact, we do see this behavior for a load of one subscriber, but for all other loads the observed throughput is about half the "expected" value.

The reason for this is that not all the subscriber blocks start at the same message (remember, the start point is randomly selected). Let's illustrate this with a simple example. Assume we have one consumer that is subscribed to a block of messages starting at message number 10 and another consumer, which starts its subscription block at message 50. When message 0 comes through neither consumer picks it up, thus the average consumer throughput is 0 MPS. When message 10 comes through, the throughput of the first consumer is 1 MPS, while the throughput of the second consumer is 0 MPS. The average throughput for both consumers at that moment is 0.5 MPS. This simple example explains the reason why the subscriber performance when there is more than one subscriber is not exactly what we would expect.

This may not be the whole story, because of course there must be some cost associated with opening 60 connections and this may affect subscriber throughput performance – this is something we consider further in the formal tests.

Test Environment Optimizations

We moved on to tune our environment by establishing:

❑   The most appropriate JVM to be used in the tests

❑   The optimum number of execute threads to be used by the application server

Once again, we performed our tests on Weblogic Server, version 6.1, and so needed to establish the optimum environment for this server. You must do the same for your particular application server.

We repeated our tests from the previous chapter, comparing the HotSpot Server and HotSpot Client versions of the Sun JDK 1.3.1-b24 JVM (please refer to the *JVM Options* section in that chapter for full details). As before, we found negligible difference in performance and so selected the HotSpot Server JVM.

The next step was to find the most appropriate number of threads for the JMS pool, which is defined either via the Weblogic console, or by editing the `config.xml` file.

Our expectations were that, for 60 consumers (the maximum load we could generate), the sweet spot was going to be around 60 threads – our gut feeling told us that it would be better to have one thread for every consumer or JMS connection. The following table summarizes the results observed for publisher and subscriber performance (in messages per second) for thread pool sizes of 15, 25, 50, 60, 75, and 150. Again, the message size was 64 Bytes and the test was carried out using no subscriber acknowledgment:

Number of Threads	15	25	50	60	75	150
Publisher performance	195	216	205	215	198	212
Subscriber performance	25.30	22.17	20.93	21.80	25.05	23.98

Confounding our expectations, we see that the number of threads has little significant effect on throughput, for this subscriber load. The best publisher performance is obtained using 25 threads – although, to be fair, the performance is actually very close to that observed for 60 threads. On the subscriber side we can see that the best performance is obtained with 15 threads, with a close second place for 75 threads. The only conclusion we can draw from this is that, for this example, the number of threads does not appear to affect performance in any significant way, and so we'll choose the fewest possible number of threads, 15, which was our original setting.

The following screenshot of the console of WebLogic shows a reasonable pattern for the garbage collector:

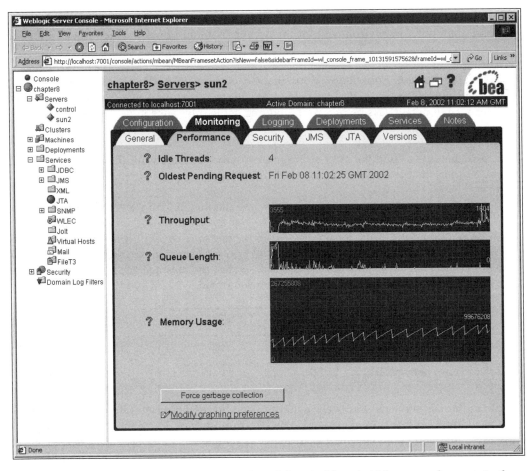

The network usage averaged just below 10% of the total bandwidth, as can be seen in the following figure:

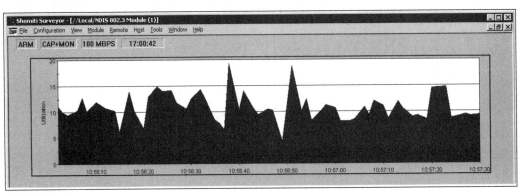

Now that we understood and were happy with our test conditions, we moved on to investigate our stock ticker example.

The Test Plan

As discussed earlier, with the stock ticker application it did not make sense to use acknowledgment or persistence. We simply wanted to test throughput performance with the `acknowledgeMode` parameter in the subscribers' `grinder.properties` file set to `NO` (no acknowledgment) and then with the parameter set to `MULTICAST` (for multicast no acknowledge).

We did not investigate different message sizes in this chapter. Message sizes in the Pub/Sub domain are generally smaller than 128 bytes, so it simply did not make much sense to test with much bigger messages. In any event, this study was more application focused, so it was logical to use the message size that was specifically required for this particular application.

No Acknowledgment Versus Multicast

Using the test parameters set in the previous section and under the conditions established by our preliminary tests, we proceeded to investigate publisher and subscriber performance (MPS) in the no acknowledgment mode, under various subscriber loads:

Subscriber load	1	20	40	60
Publisher	627.50	184.20	189.50	195.10
Subscriber	156.4	25.77	25.50	25.27
Differential	0%	44%	46%	48%

The Differential is the percentage deviation from 1:1 publisher: subscriber throughput (remember that each subscriber is subscribed to only 25% of the messages). There are three interesting points to notice:

- ❏ For the case of one subscriber, the publisher:subscriber performance exhibits a 1:1 relationship (remember that the consumer is subscribed to only 25% of the messages).

- ❏ For other subscriber loads, the throughput is very stable, at around 25 messages/sec.

- ❏ For other subscriber loads, the 1:1 relationship no longer exists. This happens because the consumers are waiting for the events they are subscribed for. If every consumer would be subscribed to exactly the same block of companies we would expect to see a rate of about 47 MPS, but the beginning of the block is randomly selected. This means that many of the consumers will be idle waiting for the first message of their block. This idle time decreases the average of messages received.

411

We repeated the above test run using the multicast no acknowledge mode. As explained previously, we expect this mode to be faster (but it is less reliable). The following chart compares the results of the publisher throughput for multicast no acknowledge (compared with that seen for no acknowledge):

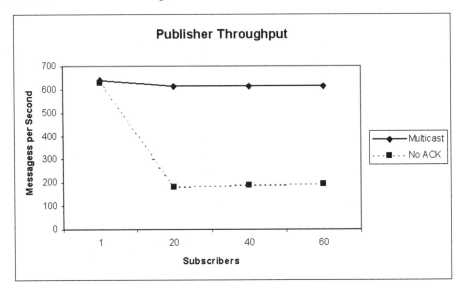

In multicast mode, the throughput is sustained at around 630 MPS over the whole range of subscriber loads – which is over three times faster than for the no acknowledge mode (with the exception of the 1 subscriber case).

The following chart depicts the same comparison for subscriber performance:

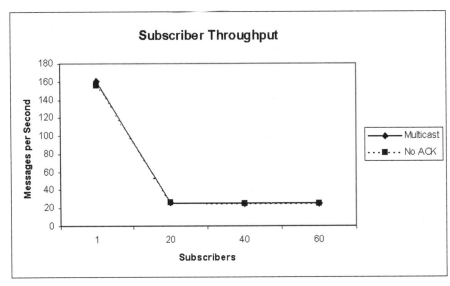

Here we see that the substantially higher publisher throughput in multicast mode does not translate to equivalently higher subscriber throughput. The behavior of subscriber throughput is very similar to that observed with no acknowledge.

We needed to investigate the reasons for this and, first, we had to rule out the possibility that we were losing messages. The following chart shows the network usage for the 60 subscribers case:

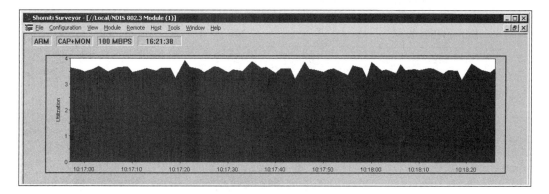

With a paltry 3.5% utilization it is hard to imagine that messages are being lost because of high traffic. This is interesting because the network utilization here is less than half that observed in the no acknowledge mode (and we would expect the utilization to be lower for pub/sub via multicast compared to unicast). We then checked the CPU usage of the computer running the JMS topic (Sun02):

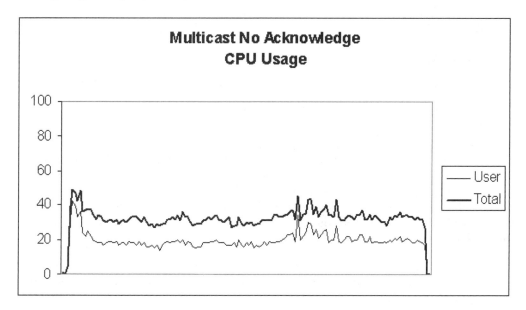

Again, the activity is around half of that observed using the no acknowledgment mode. By limiting our setup to 20 clients per computer, we expected to avoid any swapping, and so ruled this out as an explanation for the observed behavior. We were convinced that these results proved that we were not losing messages.

Our custom Grinder `plug-ins` both provide us with the actual number of messages that are handled during the sample period, so we proceeded to analyze this data. First, we examined the number of messages handled using no acknowledge mode:

Subscriber load	1	20	40	60
Publisher	188462	52322	55535	58708
Subscriber – expected	47116	13081	13884	14677
Subscriber – actual	47006	7744	7699	7603
Differential	0%	41%	45%	48%

These are exactly the results we expect given our previous analysis – a differential of around 40-50% on the subscriber throughput. You may have noticed that a subscriber load of one allows the publisher to generate far more messages. This is because one consumer is a special case whereby the average throughput rate is the same as its individual throughput rate. The moment you have more than one consumer the load pattern changes completely.

We then performed the same analysis for the multicast no acknowledge test runs:

Subscriber load	1	20	40	60
Publisher	193044	185146	184173	185363
Subscriber – expected	48266	46287	46043	46341
Subscriber – actual	48308	7696	7535	7605
Differential	0%	83%	84%	84%

The differential is almost double the expected forty-something percent. After several discussions we concluded that the reason for this problem is simply that the multicast no acknowledge mode is **too fast**. The reason for this is that the consumers were at their maximum throughput with the simple no acknowledgment mode. Using multicast did not increase the processing speed of the consumers – they still could only handle them at the same rate as before. In this case, the consumers are the bottleneck. The messages are not lost; they still are in the topic.

To illustrate this we did a couple of test runs with 60 consumers, but this time we used a think time of 2 milliseconds before publishing every message. We simply added the following line to our publisher test script:

```
grinder.test0.parameter.topicJNDIName=jms.myTopic
grinder.test0.parameter.messageSize=64
grinder.test0.parameter.numberOfMessageTypes=100
grinder.test0.sleepTime=2
```

Following are the throughput results for the publisher and subscriber:

60 Subscribers – 2 ms TT	No ACK	Multicast
Publisher MPS	49.69	49.81
Subscriber MPS	12.46	12.26
Publisher – Messages	14938	14985
Subscriber – Actual messages	3733	3748
Subscriber – Expected messages	3735	3746
Differential	0%	0%

As you can see, now messages are published and consumed at about the same rate. The gating factor is not now the consumer; we have moved it to the publisher by adding the think time. You can see how big an impact even such a small think time has on the results and the interpretation of results. For the no acknowledge mode, the publisher throughput is down to around 25% of that obtained with no think time. This does not really mean the system is performing "worse" – it is still ultimately capable of handling 195 MPS –just that we're measuring it under different conditions. Throughput is not a clear-cut metric, such as speed or response time.

Conclusions

We simulated a primitive stock ticker using the JMS Pub/Sub model and found that using no acknowledgment mode, under the conditions of our tests, we could achieve a subscriber throughput of 25 MPS, sustainable over the whole subscriber load used in these tests (up to 60 subscribers). This was around 40-50% less than the maximum possible subscriber throughput, given that our publisher throughput was 195 MPS and that each subscriber received 25% of the available messages.

This differential was a factor in choosing how to implement this example. Our model had each subscriber receive a block of 25 contiguous message types, the beginning of the block being randomly selected. In order to alleviate the problem of subscribers waiting for messages we should have randomly selected the 25 message types that each subscriber would receive (and this would have been a more realistic model). However, this would have required a very complicated Grinder plug-in code.

Perhaps more than anything else, this example illustrates that Messages Per Second is more a measure of throughput capacity than plain speed. You have to be very careful how you define the throughput for your application and how you interpret the results.

The Airline Seating Example

In this example, we loosely modeled an application that an airline would use to assign passengers to seats before they board a flight. Most airlines will allow you to request a seat assignment at any time, using the central reservation system. However, the responsibility for seat assignment switches to the airport staff approximately four hours before departure time. Our example modeled a subsystem of a full seating assignment application, in that it could be used after responsibility for seating assignment has been transferred to the airport staff.

Normally the airport staff handle seat assignments with a client-side application that updates the seating map of the airplane, and then publishes the new seating assignments. In our simplified example, we did not model this step; instead, we focused on exploring the behavior of JMS when the application published the new seat assignments – in other words, when a message was sent out indicating that a free seat on a specific flight was now occupied.

> *Obviously, there are some complex coding issues to consider here, such as how to handle two different reservations for the same seat at the same time, or the precise definition of when and how a seat is registered as taken, but that was not our focus of our study.*

We modeled this application using the same architecture as that set out in the *Application Architecture* section and so used the same Grinder plug-ins. Since both the Stock Ticker and the Airline Seating examples used the same architecture, we decided not to go through the process of determining the JVM and optimum number of execute threads again (although in strict adherence to the methodology, it is good practice to do so for all cases). Therefore, we used the HotSpot Sever option of the JVM and left the number of JMS threads at the default value of 15, as for the stock ticker tests.

Testing Metrics

We had a single publisher that continuously generated messages, each one indicating an occupied seat on one of the flights that fell within our 4-hour window. In our model, there were 20 flights that fell in this window and so the publisher created 20 different message types. Therefore the WROX_JMS_MESSAGE_TYPE property, representing the flight numbers, incremented sequentially from 0 to 19. The body of the message contained 16 randomly selected characters, which was more than adequate to record the details of the seat that was now occupied. Each subscriber represented an airline agent that subscribed to one particular flight (chosen randomly).

The publisher grinder.properties file was exactly as for the stock ticker example, Once again we used no think time for the publisher. We just needed to make some simple changes to the parameters in the grinder.properties file for our subscribers, to reflect the above conditions:

```
grinder.test0.parameter.messageSize=16
grinder.test0.parameter.numberOfMessageTypes=20
grinder.plugin.parameter.numberOfMessageTypes=20
grinder.plugin.parameter.numberOfMessageTypesPerSubscription=1
```

We ran tests with 1, 20, 40, and 60 subscribers, with every subscriber running on its own JVM and establishing a JMS connection and session before starting the test run.

The Test Plan

In contrast to our stock ticker application, here it was critical that we knew if a seat was taken. Therefore the subscriber had to acknowledge each message and the messages had to be persisted on the server.

First, we investigated throughput performance using the AUTO and CLIENT acknowledgment modes (with no persistence). Briefly, in AUTO mode the subscriber will send an acknowledgment message to the server for every message it receives. In CLIENT mode, the subscriber can acknowledge in groups of messages– for example, sending one acknowledgment message for every 50 messages received.

We then moved on to explore performance when persisting messages to a file on the file system of the computer running WLS. We investigated the costs of using each of the following persistence modes:

- ❑ **File persistence with synchronous writes** – by default WebLogic Server will wait until the write operation has been completed and then continue with the normal processing

- ❑ **File persistence with non-synchronous writes** – here, the server will **not** wait for the operating system to confirm the write operation before continuing (faster, but less reliable).

- ❑ **Database persistence** (with synchronous writes) using Oracle 8.1.7.

Investigating Acknowledgment

Even though our seating example requires guaranteed message delivery, it was useful to investigate the relative performance of the AUTO and CLIENT modes using no persistence (this also gives us a baseline for comparison with the persistence cases).

The basic purpose of CLIENT mode is to reduce the cost of acknowledgment. However, we proved in the previous chapter the cost of acknowledging a big message (16KB) was negligible compared to the cost of actually picking up the message, so there was no performance gain from using CLIENT acknowledge mode. Here, however, the message is so small (16 bytes) that the relative cost of the acknowledgment message is going to be much higher, so we expected the CLIENT mode to really come into its own.

Auto Mode

For our first set of test runs we used the AUTO mode. The following table presents the throughput (messages per second) obtained for the various subscriber loads:

Subscriber load	1	20	40	60
Publisher	643.50	552.70	462.90	335.00
Subscriber	32.21	21.31	21.04	16.57

As before, we normalize the throughput of the subscriber by dividing the transactional rate reported by The Grinder by the number of subscribers. In this example, each subscriber subscribes to only one message out of a possible 20, so the maximum throughput of a subscriber is one twentieth of the throughput of the publisher. In this scenario, with each subscriber receiving only one message, the effect of subscribers waiting for messages to become available should be reduced, so we expected to get closer to this value.

In the following histogram, we have divided the publisher throughput by 20, and compared this with the normalized subscriber throughput:

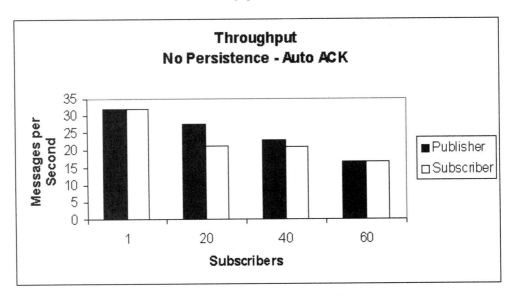

Within very reasonable margins, the publisher and subscriber throughputs are equal.

Client Mode

The next step was to explore the performance using the CLIENT acknowledge mode. The following table presents publisher and subscriber throughput results for acknowledging in groups of 10, 30 and 50 messages, with a subscriber load of 60 in each case:

Message group size	10	30	50	Auto
Publisher	402.70	394.20	394.80	335.00
Subscriber	19.98	19.70	19.70	16.57

Our expectations are met in that the performance for both publisher and subscriber is consistently better than that obtained in AUTO mode. The best performance of all is obtained when sending one acknowledgment message for every ten messages. Somewhat surprisingly, the results for acknowledging in groups of 30 and 50 messages are very similar.

We then moved on to investigate the performance of CLIENT(10) mode across various subscriber loads. Again, we present the publisher throughput (divided by 20) alongside the normalized subscriber throughput:

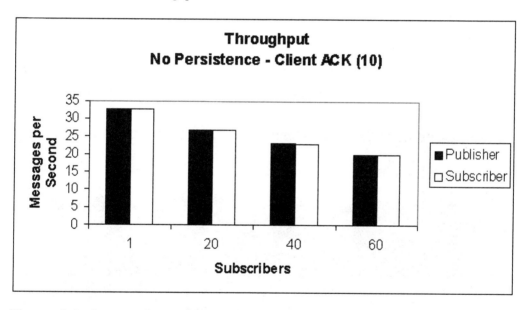

The match is almost perfect, indicating the high efficiency of the CLIENT acknowledge mode in this scenario. We can also see this efficiency when looking at the CPU usage of the computer running the JMS server:

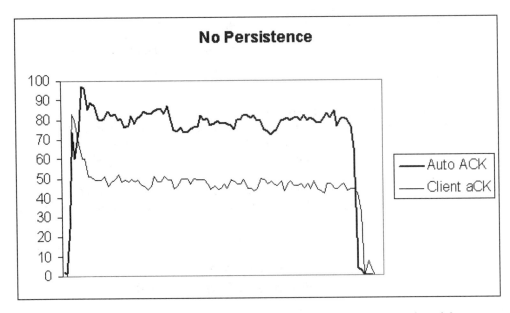

We can see the same effect in the network traffic, where the average is reduced from around 7% to about 5.5% of bandwidth:

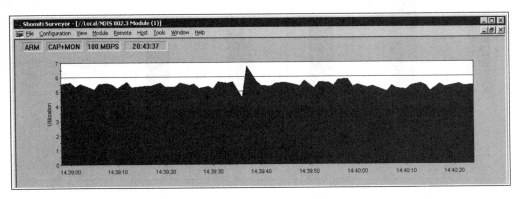

We can conclude that when using such small messages in a Pub/Sub model, and if we have the choice of using no persistence, it is much better to use the CLIENT acknowledge mode, with groups of 10 messages.

File Persistence with Synchronous Writes

When we performed these tests using JMS PTP in the previous chapter, we found that using file persistence with synchronous writes was about three times slower than for the no persistence case with 16KB messages and about seven times slower using 1KB messages. The overhead in actually performing the write is much higher than the time saved by writing only 1KB rather than 16KB. Extrapolating that trend down to 16 byte messages, we clearly expected substantially lower throughput than for the no persistence case.

The following table presents the throughput results using the AUTO mode:

Subscriber load	1	20	40	60
Publisher	38.21	37.61	37.33	37.31
Publisher/20	1.91	1.88	1.87	1.87
Subscriber	1.90	1.88	1.86	1.87

Analysis of these results shows that throughput is at least one order of magnitude down on the no persistence case. This indicates the very high cost of writing many small messages to the file system. Based on the publisher throughput, the subscriber throughput is bang on expectations in each case.

The CPU usage of the computer running the JMS topic is quite low, averaging about 15%. However, the disk usage is high, as we would expect. The following chart presents the number of disk operations per second, based on the output of vmstat every five seconds:

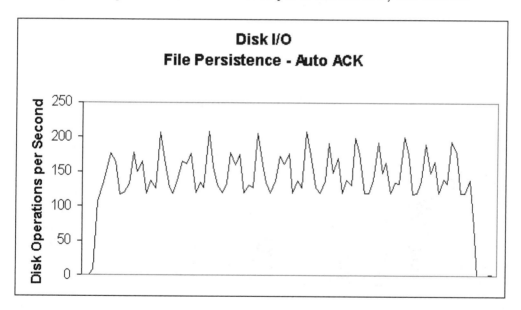

The network traffic was minimal, averaging about 1.5% of the total available bandwidth. The size of the file generated to persist the messages was always 256KB.

We also performed tests using CLIENT acknowledge mode with 10 messages, but the results were exactly the same as those using AUTO mode. This is not inconsistent with the result obtained in the previous chapter for JMS PTP, where we observed that use of CLIENT mode with file persistence was generally to be avoided, but improved with smaller message sizes.

File Persistence with Non-Synchronous Writes

When we performed these tests using JMS PTP, in the previous chapter, we found that throughput performance using file persistence with non-synchronous writes was equal to the no persistence case for 16KB messages and about 20% slower for 1KB messages. So, our general expectations were that non-synchronous writes would be much faster, but more than 20% slower than the no persistence case.

Auto Mode

The following table presents the throughput results using AUTO mode:

Subscriber load	1	20	40	60
Publisher	493.70	378.20	279.90	243.00
Publisher/20	24.69	18.91	14.00	12.15
Subscriber	24.72	18.86	14.00	12.15

As you can see in the following comparison chart, the results are in line with our expectations at about 25% lower throughput than for no persistence:

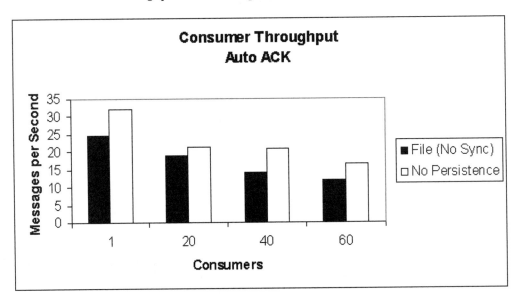

The CPU usage during these tests was a little lower than that observed for no persistence, averaging 75%. However, the disk usage was dramatically lower, as can be seen in the following chart:

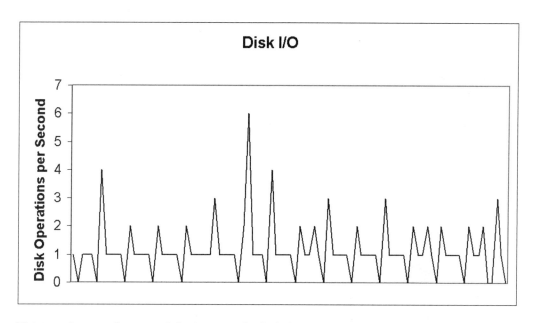

This is a direct reflection of the way in which disk operations work on the computer and operating system (Solaris) that we used. From an average of 150 disk operations per second when synchronizing the write operation, to an average of 1 disk operation per second when leaving it in the write buffers of Solaris. Obviously, using this acknowledge mode will depend on your level of confidence of the reliability of the operating system you are using, considering that non-synchronous writes can fail.

The network traffic was the same as seen for no persistence, averaging about 5.5% of the total available bandwidth. This is what we expect since the write operations are done on the local disk, not over the network.

Client Mode

We repeated the previous test run, but using CLIENT acknowledge mode with groups of 10 messages. Following are the results (the results for AUTO mode and 60 subscribers are shown for comparison):

Subscriber load	1	20	40	60	AUTO (60)
Publisher	496.00	415.60	358.90	313.80	243.00
Publisher /20	24.80	20.78	17.95	15.69	12.15
Subscriber	24.82	23.07	17.94	15.69	12.15

In this case, we see a significant increase in performance over that obtained using AUTO mode. The reason we see this happen for non-sync writes but not for sync writes is because with sync writes we have to go to the actual file and delete the messages that have been acknowledged. With non-sync writes this is very likely to happen in the write buffers of the operating system instead of on disk.

The following chart compares normalized subscriber performance for the two cases:

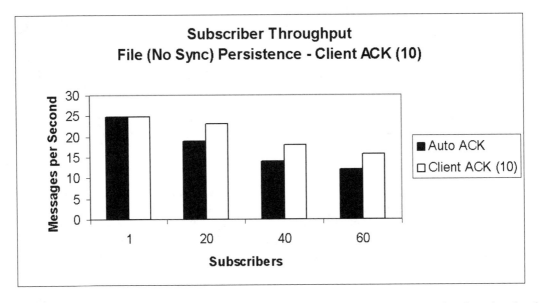

Except for one subscriber, we see a 20-30% increase in performance for each subscriber load.

The CPU usage for these tests diminished significantly from that seen for the AUTO tests, from 75% to an average of 50%, while the disk activity increased to 1.5 operations per second, from an average of 1. The network traffic also diminished, to an average of 4.5%. The size of the file used to persist the messages was again 256KB.

Summary of Results

Use of file persistence with such small message sizes comes at a heavy price in terms of throughput performance, if you need the reliability of using synchronous writes – an order of magnitude down on the no persistence case.

If you are able to use non-synchronous writes, then use of the CLIENT acknowledgment mode is an option you may want to explore, in favor of the default AUTO mode. We suggest that you define the optimum message grouping size for your application

Database Persistence

Many people consider database persistence to be the only persistence to use in terms of reliability. Our experience with JMS PTP showed us that for smaller message sizes (1KB in that case), the use of database persistence leads to comparable or better performance than the use of file persistence (with synchronous writes). As we were now using very small messages, our expectation was that database persistence would give better performance than file persistence. We recognized, however, that the observed behavior is highly dependent on how well the database is tuned and optimized for the way in which you will be using it (heavy insert and delete activity with big or small messages).

Auto Mode

The results for AUTO mode were as follows:

Subscriber load	1	20	40	60
Publisher	47.11	39.88	38.72	38.03
Publisher /20	2.36	1.99	1.94	1.90
Subscriber	2.36	1.89	1.94	1.90

The results do seem to be better than those obtained for file persistence. The following chart compares the publisher throughput for the two:

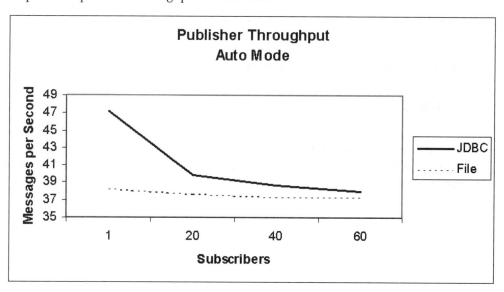

We see better throughput for JDBC persistence, for every data point, but by a decreasing margin as we increase the subscriber load. The following chart makes the same comparison for normalized subscriber throughput:

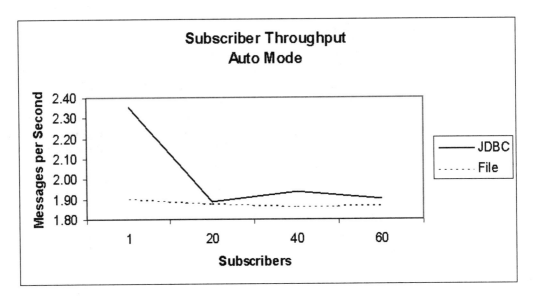

We see a similar trend (although the throughput for the 20 subscriber case may be anomalously low). We can conclude that, in this case, database persistence has the same or better performance than file persistence with synchronous writes.

The CPU usage averaged about 10%, which is also lower than when using file persistence. The network traffic is minimal (at 2%), which is also lower than that observed for file persistence. However, the database server was quite busy, running at about 30% CPU usage

Our tests using database persistence with CLIENT acknowledge mode (acknowledging in groups of 10 messages) produced very similar results to those obtained for AUTO mode.

Conclusions

Although the actual costs are a little different, the basic trends observed for the various combinations of persistent storage types and acknowledge modes met the expectations that were set in the JMS PTP chapter. The following comparative chart presents the throughput performance for the subscriber (the same trends are seen for the subscriber throughput):

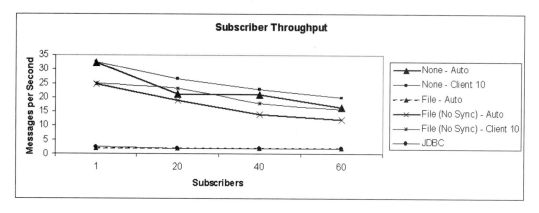

Since we created the example based on the need for persistence and guaranteed message delivery, we can conclude that database persistence is by far the better choice for our airline application. The performance is as good as or better than that observed for file persistence and we get a massive increase in reliability to boot.

Summary

Once again we have proved that throughput is not a straight measurement of speed – it is a measure of capacity. In the Pub/Sub model, publisher and subscriber performances are interrelated and you have to be very careful how you obtain your test data and interpret your results. With zero think time, we found that subscriber performance was our limiting factor. However, with the addition of a small (2 millisecond) think time before the publisher delivers a message to the topic, we find that the limiting factor is now publisher throughput. This merely reinforces what we have been stating all along in this book. No matter how similar your application might look to another one, you cannot extrapolate performance.

The Grinder Reference

This appendix contains reference information about The Grinder performance testing tool that is too detailed to be in Chapter 2. We cover the following:

- ❏ The standard properties that can be set in `grinder.properties`
- ❏ The properties that control the HTTP plug-in
- ❏ How to write more sophisticated string beans for use by the HTTP plug-in
- ❏ A reference to The Grinder console controls
- ❏ How to write a custom plug-in

Standard properties

The table overleaf lists the standard properties that can be set in `grinder.properties` and are interpreted by The Grinder agent and worker processes. The table does not contain any plug-in specific properties. Each of these properties can be used with any plug-in.

Property	Description
grinder.appendLog	Set to true to append to (rather than overwrite) existing log and data files. The default value is false.
grinder.consoleAddress	The IP address or host name to use for communication from the worker processes to the console. Only used if grinder.reportToConsole is not false. If this property is not set, the worker processes attempt to contact the console on their local machines.
grinder.consolePort	The IP port to use for communication from the worker processes to the console. Only used if grinder.reportToConsole is not false. The default value is 6372.
grinder.cycles	The number of cycles of the test script that each thread will perform. 0 means "run forever". The default value is 1.
grinder.grinderAddress	The multicast address to use for communication between the console and The Grinder agent and worker processes. Only used if grinder.receiveConsoleSignals is not false. The default value is 228.1.1.1.
grinder.grinderPort	The multicast port to use for communication from the console to The Grinder agent and worker processes. Only used if grinder.receiveConsoleSignals is not false. The default value is 1234.
grinder.hostID	The name of the host as used in log filenames and logs. The default value is the host name reported by Java.
grinder.jvm	The Java executable that the agent invokes to start the worker processes. The default value is java so you only need to set this if java isn't in your PATH or you want to use an alternative JVM for the worker processes.

Property	Description
grinder.jvm.arguments	Additional command line arguments that the agent process will use when starting the worker processes.
grinder.jvm.classpath	Additional classpath that the agent process uses when starting the worker processes. Anything specified here will be prepended to the classpath used to start the worker processes.
grinder.logDirectory	Directory to write log files to. The directory will be created if it doesn't already exist. The default value is the directory that the agent process was started in.
grinder.logProcessStreams	Set to `false` to disable the logging of output and error streams for Grinder processes. You might want to use this to reduce the overhead of running a client thread. When recording timings with multiple clients it may reduce the measured time. The default value is `true`.
grinder.plug-in	The fully qualified class name of the plug-in to use. Currently each script uses a single plug-in. This is a mandatory parameter; there is no default value.
grinder.plug-in.parameter	Prefix used for parameters interpreted by the plug-in. See "HTTP Plug-in properties" later on for examples.
grinder.processes	The number of worker processes that the agent process should start. The default value is `1`.
grinder.receiveConsoleSignals	Set to `false` if you want the worker processes to start immediately and ignore console signals. The default value is `true`.
grinder.recordTime	Set to `false` to disable reporting of timing information; other statistics are still reported. The default value is `true`.

Table continued on following page

Property	Description
`grinder.reportToConsole`	Set to `false` to disable the reporting of statistics to the console. The default value is `true`.
`grinder.reportToConsole.interval`	The period in milliseconds at which each worker process sends updates to the console. This also controls the frequency at which the data files are flushed. The default value is `500`.
`grinder.test0`	Prefix for Test 0 properties. Test 1 properties have a prefix of `grinder.test1`, and so on. The tests are run in numerical order.
`grinder.test0.description`	Information string used to describe Test 0 in the log files and the console.
`grinder.test0.parameter`	Prefix used for Test 0 parameters interpreted by the plug-in. See "HTTP Plug-in properties" opposite for examples.
`grinder.test0.sleepTime`	The time in milliseconds to wait before performing Test 0. Affected by both `grinder.thread.sleepTimeFactor`, and `grinder.thread.sleepTimeVariation`. The default value is set by `grinder.thread.sleepTime`.
`grinder.thread.initialSleepTime`	The maximum time in milliseconds that each thread waits before starting. Unlike the other sleep times, this is varied according to a flat random distribution. The actual sleep time will be a random value between 0 and the specified value. Affected by `grinder.thread.sleepTimeFactor`, but not `grinder.thread.sleepTimeVariation`. The default value is `0`.
`grinder.thread.sleepTime`	The time in milliseconds to wait between individual tests. Affected by both `grinder.thread.sleepTimeFactor`, and `grinder.thread.sleepTimeVariation`. The default value is `0`.

Property	Description
`grinder.thread.sleepTime Factor`	A factor to apply all the sleep times that have been specified. For example, setting this to 0.1 would cause the worker processes to run the test script ten times as fast. The default value is `1`.
`grinder.thread.sleepTime Variation`	The Grinder varies the specified sleep times according to a normal distribution. This property specifies a fractional range within which nearly all (99.75%) of the times will lie. For example, if the sleep time is specified as 1000 and `grinder.thread.sleepTimeVariation` is set to `0.1`, then 99.75% of the actual sleep times will be between 990 and 1100 milliseconds. The default value is `0.2`.
`grinder.threads`	The number of worker threads that each worker process should use. The default value is `1`.

HTTP Plug-in properties

This section documents the properties that can be set in `grinder.properties` and are interpreted by the HTTP plug-in. These properties are split into two sets: plug-in properties that control the behavior of the plug-in as a whole, and test properties that control individual tests.

Plug-in properties

Each of these properties should be specified with the prefix `grinder.plug-in.parameter`. For example:

```
grinder.plugin.parameter.followRedirects=false
```

Property	Description
`followRedirects`	Set to `true` to follow redirects automatically, so you don't have to have additional URLs in your scripts. The default value is `false`. You should always set this to `false` for TCP Sniffer generated scripts. The TCP Sniffer will record the request for the redirect URL as a separate test.

Property	Description
logHTML	Set to `true` to log response bodies to individual files in the log directory. This is very expensive in disk usage, but can be useful for debugging test scripts. The default value is `false`.
stringBean	Fully qualified class name of a string bean that can provide dynamic strings for test properties. By default, no string bean is used.
useCookies	Set to `false` to disable cookie handling. The default value is `true`.
useCookieVersion String	Set this property to `false` to remove the `$Version` string from cookies. This property is provided to work around problems experienced with The Grinder cookie handling a JRun 2.3.3 server. The property is used only when `grinder.plugin.parameter.useHTTPClient` is `false` (when `useHTTPClient` is `true` the `HTTPClient` cookie handling is used instead). The default value is `true`.
useHTTPClient	Set this property to `false` to use an older, alternative HTTP plug-in implementation that uses the `java.net.HttpURLConnection` instead of the implementation that uses the `HTTPClient` library. The default value is `false`.

Test properties

Each of these properties is set for individual tests and should be specified with the prefix `grinder.testX.paremeter`, where X is the number of the test. For example:

```
grinder.test5.parameter.url=http://java.sun.com/
```

All of these properties can be varied using a string bean, see Chapter 2 for details.

Property	Description
basicAuthenticationPassword basicAuthenticationRealm basicAuthenticationUser	Used together, these specify an HTTP basic authentication header that will be sent with the request. If you specify one of these values, you must specify all three.

Property	Description
header.X	Add an X: HTTP header to the request with the specified value. X can be an arbitrary string.
Ok	Assert that the returned response contains the specified string. An error will be recorded if the response does not contain the string.
post	Specify that the test should make the request using the HTTP POST method. The value of the property is the name of a file containing the POST data to send. By default, the HTTP GET method is used.
url	The URL to call. The HTTP GET method is used unless the grinder.testX.parameter.post property is specified. This is a mandatory property; there is no default value.

The Console Controls

This section provides detailed documentation on the console controls.

File Menu

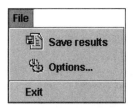

Menu option	Purpose
Save results	Saves the currently captured results to a comma separated value file. It is best to stop statistics collection before saving the results.
Options	Opens the console options dialog.
Exit	Exits the console. You probably want to select "Stop Processes" from the Action menu before doing this.

Action Menu

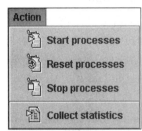 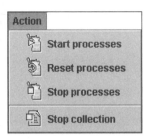

Menu option	Purpose
Start processes	Send a "start" message to all worker processes listening on the Grinder Port.
Reset processes	Send a "reset" message to all worker processes listening on the Grinder Port. Upon receiving this command, the worker processes exit and their parent processes reread grinder.properties and start new worker processes.
Stop processes	Send a "stop" message to all worker processes listening on the Grinder Port. Upon receiving this command, the worker processes and their parent agent processes exit.
Collect statistics	Re-arm the console to start statistics collection when reports are received from worker processes.
Stop collection	Manually stop statistics collection.

Help menu

Menu option	Purpose
About The Grinder	Opens the About dialog.

Options Dialog

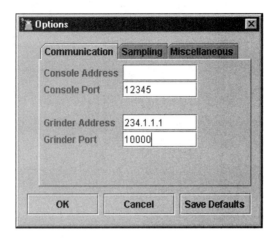

Control	Purpose
Console Address	The IP address or host name of a local network interface that the console should use to listen for reports from worker processes.
	Valid range 1.1.1.1 to 223 255.255.255.
Console Port	The TCP port that the console should listen on.
	Valid range 0 to 65535.
Grinder Address	The IP multicast address the console should use to send commands to the worker processes.
	Valid range 224.0.0.0 to 239.255.255.255.
Grinder Port	The multicast port that the worker processes are listening on.
	Valid range 0 to 65535.
OK	Confirm the changes made and close the dialog.
Cancel	Discard the changes made and close the dialog.
Save Defaults	Confirm the changes made, close the dialog, and save the current values as defaults.

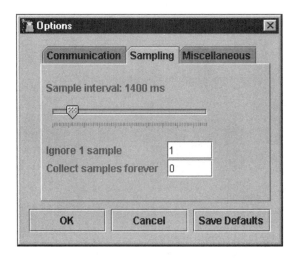

Control	Purpose
Sample interval	The size of the sample interval.
	Valid range 100 milliseconds to 10 seconds.
Ignore samples	The number of initial samples to ignore.
	Valid range 1 to 999 999.
Collect samples	The number of samples to collect.
	Valid range 1 to 999 999.

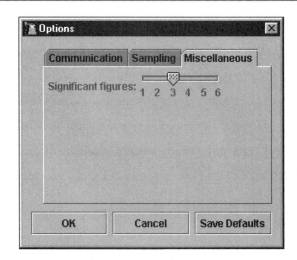

Control	Purpose
Significant figures	The number of significant figures to display floating point values to. Valid range 1 to 6.

Hardware and Software

The following is a listing of the computers and software used for the tests in this book. The tests were carried out in a clean (the only network traffic was that generated by the tests), high-speed Ethernet environment (Cisco Hub 400, 100 Mbps).

Hardware

Computer Name	Type	CPU	Memory	Disks	OS
Sun1, Sun2	Sun Microsystems Ultra 60	2 x Ultra SPARC II 450MHz	512 MB	1 x 9 GB IPI	Solaris 2.7
WLS01–03	Compaq ML350	1 x Pentium III 600EB (600MHz)	512 MB	1 x 9 GB	Dual Boot: NT Server 4.0 sp 5 and Red Hat Linux 7.1
WLS04	(as above)	(as above)	(as above)	(as above)	Dual Boot: NT Server 4.0 sp 5 and Windows 2000 Advanced Server

Table continued on following page

Computer Name	Type	CPU	Memory	Disks	OS
WLS05, WLS06	(as above)	(as above)	(as above)	(as above)	NT Server 4.0 sp 5
DBServer	Compaq DL380	2 x Pentium III 900 MHz	512 MB	4 x 9 GB RAID 5	NT Server 4.0 sp 5
Grinder01-04	Compaq Deskpro EN	1 x Pentium III 800 MHz	256 MB	1 x 9 GB	SuSE Linux 7.0
Control	Compaq Deskpro EN	1 x Pentium III 800 MHz	256 MB	1 x 9 GB	Windows 2000 Advanced Server

Software

J2EE Application Server	WebLogic 6.1 service pack 2 (http://www.bea.com)
Database	Oracle 8.1.7.0.0 Enterprise Edition (http://www.oracle.com)
HTTP Server	iPlanet Enterprise 4.1 service pack 9 (http://www.iplanet.com)
Network Monitor	Shomiti Surveyor 3.0 (http://www.shomiti.com)
Java Virtual Machines	Sun Microsystems 1.3.1 for Solaris and Linux (http://javasoft.sun.com)
	Sun Microsystems 1.3.0 for NT (http://javasoft.sun.com)
	Sun Microsystems 1.2.2 for NT (http://javasoft.sun.com)
	IBM 1.3 for NT (http://www.ibm.com)
	JRockit for NT (http://www.jrockit.com)
Java Compiler	Jikes 1.15 (http://alphaworks.ibm.com)
Java Performance Monitor	Introscope 3.0 (http://www.wilytech.com)

Comparing ECperf and the Testing Methodology

In this appendix, we briefly compare the capabilities, strength and weaknesses of ECperf and our testing methodology. For full details on ECperf, please refer to http://java.sun.com/j2ee/ecperf/ and http://ecperf.theserverside.com/ecperf/.

ECperf will be repackaged as SPECjAppServer2001, and administered by SPEC. Expansion of the number of J2EE API's defined in the workload is slated for upcoming releases of SPECjAppServer2001. Official SPECjAppServer2001 results will be posted on the www.spec.org site.

ECperf is an Enterprise JavaBeans (EJB) benchmark from JavaSoft. It stresses the ability of EJB containers to handle the complexities of memory management, connection pooling, passivation, activation, caching, and so on. ECperf, like any performance testing methodology, articulates the following steps:

- ❏ Define Testing Objectives
- ❏ Understand the Environment
- ❏ Specify the Test Plan (identify which J2EE API's to test)
- ❏ Define the Test Workload (characterize application and user scenarios)

- Setup the Test environment (controller and virtual users)
- Run Tests
- Analyze Test Results (determine location of the bottleneck,)

ECperf does a great job of all these steps and, based on its specific test **workload** and application scenario, the user can forecast how the system will respond to realistic loads before it goes into production.

Its performance objectives and workloads are measurable and repeatable and help to identify the limits of the application server's capabilities and to establish a baseline for the resources that will be consumed at different thresholds of use.

Unfortunately, no single benchmark can represent the performance of a system for all types of applications. The interplay between unique user configurations, applications, operating systems and workloads, make pinpointing performance problems of systems very challenging. The ECperf Benchmark application is complementary to the "open testing methodology and framework" presented in this book. Each framework has strengths and weaknesses that should be considered when developing your own performance testing strategy.

The greatest strength of the methodology presented in this book is that it will allow the user to define each step of the methodology. The Grinder test environment gives the ultimate flexibility to help the users define their specific application and workload conditions on different hardware and software systems. The results can be analyzed in order to give a thorough understanding of how an application will perform or to explore various design issue. They will also help to pinpoint areas of the system that will be limiting in terms of performance.

ECperf does not have the flexibility of the methodology presented in this book. It is based on a specific EJB application and is reasonably complex to set up. However, it is very useful when evaluating application servers and when identifying key performance indicators/parameters/options in the application server, operating system, or database server.

Definition and Architecture

	Testing Methodology / Grinder	ECperf Benchmark
Definition	Grinder composed of agent processes, worker processes, console, user recording, scripting language and plug-ins. The methodology provides a flexible framework for measuring the performance of any J2EE application.	ECperf, composed of the Specification and the Kit, was prototyped and built in conjunction with Java 2 Platform, Enterprise Edition server vendors It is being developed under the Java Community Process. The audience is both the J2EE user and server vendor.
Architecture	Multiple client drivers with varied transactions.	Single client driver with varied transactions.
Language	Java	Java

Process

	Testing Methodology / Grinder	ECperf Benchmark
Define testing objectives	Designed to measure performance and scalability of any J2EE application.	Designed to measure performance and scalability of EJB/J2EE application systems.
Specify the Test Plan	Operating System. A set or subset of: EJB Server & Container, JMS Container, HTTP Server / Container, Java Virtual Machine, Database Server, JDBC Driver.	Operating System EJB Server & Container, Java Virtual Machine, Database Server, JDBC Driver.

Table continued on following page

447

	Testing Methodology / Grinder	ECperf Benchmark
Define the Test Workload (characterize application and user scenarios)	Allows any application characterization and user scenarios via test scripts (grinder.properties files), creation via a TCP/IP recorder or individually crafted.	User Behavior based on real-world business problems such as manufacturing, supply chain management. Workload specifically defined by the benchmark.
Setup the Test environment (controller and virtual users)	A single **agent process** runs on each test client machine *virtual user). Grinder agent processes create worker processes. The Grinder console (Controller) coordinates processes and collates statistics.	ECperf Reference Beans, the Driver (controller) and load programs (virtual users).
Run Tests	Detailed test description defined by the **user**.	Detailed test description defined by the benchmark.
Analyze Test Results	Real time analysis via Grinder Console as well as post analysis reports via log files.	Detailed pass/fail criteria defined by the benchmark specification.

Strengths and Weaknesses

	Testing Methodology / Grinder	ECperf Benchmark
Strengths	HTTP and HTTP(S) load generation. Totally open source.	Deriving application server, operating system, and database server specific tuning parameters.
	Very easy to setup and get started with.	Very well defined pass/fail criteria, very repeatable.
	Extensible. Can benchmark any application with existing plug-ins. If existing plug-in doesn't exist, it can be created. Very scalable via distribution of load between JVMs.	Limited in scalability because of inability to distribute load effectively.
Weaknesses	There are no formal results published for comparative analysis.	EJB specific Difficult to setup for particular application server vendors Showcased hardware configurations are expensive Partially open source, driver source not available.
	No specifically defined pass/fail criteria built in.	Does not allow for re-factoring of design of the EJB or SQL. Not extensible. Cannot measure HTTP (web applications) or JMS applications.

A Guide to the Index

The index covers the main text but not the Appendices. Unmodified headings identify the main treatments of topics. An asterisk (*) indicates variant endings; a tilde (~), repeated beginnings and acronyms have been preferred to their expansions as main entries, on the grounds that they are generally easier to recall.

B

back-end applications
defining performance for, 5
throughput as performance metric for, 13
back-end systems *see* **asynchronous messaging systems.**
baseline case
as part of preliminary testing, 30
establishing, e-Pizza, 124
cluster-based stress test, 156
endurance test, 140
JVM selection, 125, 128, 130
preliminary tests, 124
single instance stress tests, 131
FaçadeOffTest test, 264
JMS PTP & Pub/Sub testing, 357, 407
NO think time test, HTTP servlets, 189
batch systems, *see* asynchronous messaging systems & back-end applications.
beginCycle/end~() methods, StringBean, 56
beginCycle/end~() methods, ThreadCallbacks
JMS queue sender plug-in example, 69, 70
plug-in adding per-cycle behavior, 64
benchmarking
definition & comparison with performance testing, 6
Bickford, Peter
maximum acceptable response times, 23
bind variables, SQL tuning, 147
e-Pizza application, 147
BMP (Bean-Managed Persistence) strategy, 293
bottlenecks, 7
branch-base companies
suitablity of JMS PTP fan-in parallelism for, 340
buffering effects, 373, 385

C

cache settings
testing EJB deployment alternatives, 319
caching
can make test data unrealistic, 16
init(), using, 167
example, 168
prepared statement caching, 149
capacity
interactive application performance & capacity planning, 4
throughput as measure of, 5
chunkSize parameter, HttpServlet, 184
HTTP protocol options analysis, servlets, 203
Classic option, Sun JDK 1.3, 91
selecting, e-Pizza, 130
CLH (content length header), HTTP
HTTP protocol options analysis, servlets, 202

CLIENT_ACKNOWLEDGE mode, JMS, 343
1kB messages, results, 378
10 message-groups, running, 378
50 message-groups, running, 379, 382
16kB messages, results, 363
baseline test results, 357
file-based persistence, 368, 381
airline seating application, 421, 423
performance effects, 387
performance risk from, 369, 371, 382
JDBC persistence, 372, 384
airline seating application, 426
performance effects, 387
memory problems from using, 366
NO persistence
airline seating application, 418
clock accuracy, 378
clustering HTTP servlets, 227
configuring test environment, 229
AlterSessionServlet example, using, 229
configuration, diagram, 229
multiple objects case, testing, 241
replicating HttpSession object, 228
in-memory replication, 235
in-memory/cookie/NO replication tests, 234, 235, 240
replication technique, setting up, 232
setting up & running tests, 230
database schema, setting up, 230
replication technique, setting up, 232
WebLogic Server, configuring/running, 230
single object case, testing, 233
cookie replication, 240
file & database persistence, comparing, 237
in-memory replication, 235
NO replication, 234
clusters, WebLogic Server, 154
e-Pizza stress tests using, 154
CMP (container-managed persistence)
CMP entity EJBs, e-Pizza using, 153
CMT (container-managed transactions)
isolating effects of, 293
performance effects, 289
compression filters, *see* filters, HTTP servlets.
config.xml file, WebLogic Server, 349, 405
connections, HTTP
response size effects analysis, servlets, 200
console, The Grinder, 36, 40
functionality, 40
diagram, 40
TPS, calculating, 41
recording model, 51
running processes, example, 48
starting, 46
Console Address blank field, 48
e-Pizza, 115
servlets, HTTP, 177
TCP/IP, setting, 45
Linux & Windows, 45
test script, 46
consumer loading
generating loads for JMS PTP testing, 357
consumers *see* subscribers.
Content-Length header, HTTP
setting, setContentLengthHeader(), 184

Notes

Notes

Notes

Notes

Notes

Notes

Notes

EXPERT

Expert writes books for you. Any suggestions, or ideas about how you want information given in your ideal book will be studied by our team. Your comments are always valued at Expert.

Free phone in USA 800-873 9769
Fax (312) 893 8001

UK Tel.: (0121) 687 4100   Fax: (0121) 687 4101

Registration Code: | 4000D2HJPJNIJB01 |

J2EE Performance Testing – Registration Card

Name _____

Address _____

_____

_____

City _____ State/Region _____

Country _____ Postcode/Zip _____

E-Mail _____

Occupation _____

How did you hear about this book?

☐ Book review (name) _____

☐ Advertisement (name) _____

☐ Recommendation _____

☐ Catalog _____

☐ Other _____

Where did you buy this book?

☐ Bookstore (name) _____ City _____

☐ Computer store (name) _____

☐ Mail order _____

☐ Other _____

What influenced you in the purchase of this book?

☐ Cover Design   ☐ Contents   ☐ Other (please specify):

How did you rate the overall content of this book?

☐ Excellent   ☐ Good   ☐ Average   ☐ Poor

What did you find most useful about this book? _____

_____

What did you find least useful about this book? _____

_____

Please add any additional comments. _____

_____

What other subjects will you buy a computer book on soon?

_____

What is the best computer book you have used this year?

Note: This information will only be used to keep you updated about new Expert titles and will not be used for any other purpose or passed to any other third party.

Check here if you DO NOT want to receive support for this book ■

EXPERT

Note: If you post the bounce back card below in the UK, please send it to:

Expert, Arden House, 1102 Warwick Road,
Acocks Green, Birmingham B27 6HB. UK.

Computer Book Publishers

BUSINESS REPLY MAIL
FIRST CLASS MAIL   PERMIT#64   CHICAGO, IL

POSTAGE WILL BE PAID BY ADDRESSEE

Expert
29 S. LA SALLE ST.,
SUITE 520
CHICAGO IL 60603-USA

NO POSTAGE
NECESSARY
IF MAILED
IN THE
UNITED STATES